The Soul's Secret
Unveiled in the Book of Revelation

Kristina Kaine

The Soul's Secret Unveiled in the Book of Revelation
First Published as a weekly Newsletter between April 2007 and April 2010
Second Edition published as Kindle ebook in December 2012 in two volumes.
This Edition published at Create Space in March 2013 in one volume.

This book is written from the insight of the author, if similar information is found in other books this is co-incidental. Quotes by other authors are referenced.

Copyright © 2013 by Kristina Kaine. All rights reserved. This book contains material protected under International and Federal Copyright Laws and Treaties. Any unauthorized reprint or use of this material is prohibited. No part of this book may be reproduced or transmitted in any form or by any means, electronic or mechanical, including photocopying, recording, or by any information storage and retrieval system without express written permission from the author / publisher.
kristina@esotericconnection.com

Published by
I AM Press
Cover designed by Adriana Koulias
Cover artwork by Joldos Dan Emanuel
ISBN: 0-9874617-3-5
ISBN-13: 978-0-9874617-3-5

DEDICATION

This book is dedicated to you.

May you discover your soul's secret, your hidden jewel.

Kristina Kaine is one of the most profound thinkers of our age. She has digested the thinking of great initiates like Rudolf Steiner and reworked their insights into marvelous revelations to us. I strongly recommend her book to anyone who is the least bit curious about how we Human Beings relate to the Cosmos and how we can better get along in this world today.

                Andrew Flaxman
http://www.spiritualsciencebiblestudies

CONTENTS

	Acknowledgments	i
	Prelude	ii
1	Chapter One	1
2	Chapter Two	21
3	Chapter Three	52
4	Chapter Four	82
5	Chapter Five	88
6	Chapter Six	95
7	Chapter Seven	137
8	Chapter Eight	147
9	Chapter Nine	164
10	Chapter Ten	179
11	Chapter Eleven	187
12	Chapter Twelve	208
13	Chapter Thirteen	224
14	Chapter Fourteen	246
15	Chapter Fifteen	272
16	Chapter Sixteen	289
17	Chapter Seventeen	307
18	Chapter Eighteen	319
19	Chapter Nineteen	333
20	Chapter Twenty	348
21	Chapter Twentyone	357
22	Chapter Twentytwo	365
	Afterword	374
	Addenda	376
	Reviews	381
	Resources	384

The Book of Revelation is one of the most deliberated documents of all time. There are hundreds, probably thousands of attempts to understand this ineffable writing. The best, by far, are those who are able to appreciate the mythic dimensions and are able to steer away from using the work as a blunt moral club-stick or neatly digitally dividing it all into 'good' versus 'evil', and those who try to use the text as a literal prediction of the demise of the world. I find, for example, the reading by D.H. Lawrence cuts through the preachy overlay and gets to the embodied nature of the imagery. And, right up there I find Kristina Kaine's extensive and detailed reading of St. John to be close, intimate, and in a true sense, written out of what Rudolf Steiner has called the 'new mythic consciousness.'

This reading of the work of St. John is mythic in the defining sense of myth as 'that which has never happened but is always happening'. That is the quality pervading this reflection by Kristina Kaine. And, it is a reading for this time, the time in which the truth here revealed is the truth of our being that is as close to us as the spiritual "I" each of us unfolds as. Kristina Kaine has found the key and the key is her and the key is anyone who does not accept her reading as 'gospel', but her reading as a way of entering the work to find out for ourselves.

Robert Sardello, Ph.D.
Director, The School of Spiritual Psychology

ACKNOWLEDGMENTS

Thank you to all those who encourage me to write. Thank you to all those who read what I write. Thank you to all those who have proof read what I write.

PRELUDE

The human race is going through an incredible awakening. Like Snow White, we have been asleep for hundreds of years. Now our prince has come to give us the kiss of life.

You might be asking what the story of Snow White and the Book of Revelation has in common. If you looked into it you might be surprised. Who is the prince? Wait and see.

What has it meant to have been asleep? We all know that when we are asleep we are unaware of our surroundings and if we awaken from a very deep sleep we sometimes do not know where we are or what we are supposed to be doing. This lack of awareness is the problem we face today. If we are not fully aware of who we are, where we are (in terms of the cosmos) and what our purpose is how can we possibly be content, let alone happy?

The pursuit of happiness has taken us to extremes causing damage to the planet as well as to our minds and bodies. The extreme abuse, of ourselves and others, in every facet of human life is atrocious. How are we to live with these extremes? Or do we ignore them to stay sane? If you keep these things in mind and read quickly through The Revelation to John it is not difficult to think that John saw into the present 21st Century.

So it doesn't take much to realise that something has to change if we are not to fall further and further into decadence. But this won't be achieved merely by demanding that something be done by someone else, governments etc. What has to change relies on each individual, it relies on each person discovering his or her own soul's secret.

The Book of Revelation, or "The Revelation to John" as it should be called, describes how the human mind is changing, and not just in terms of becoming smarter. At the same time there is something within us that resists change. We are comfortable when things remain the same. We don't always have the energy necessary to embrace change. Could it be that the extreme situations that we are facing today, for example in the financial system, in the weather and the wars everywhere, are trying to wake us up?

There is another aspect to this as well. In the face of change we can experience a loss of control, which naturally enough is followed by efforts to regain control. This lack of control is also directly tied to the level of awareness we have about our own character and makeup. Keep this thought in mind as we continue to explore the notion of the soul's secret.

As we wonder about the nature of human consciousness we may rightly ask if it changes at all. We may think that the ancient Egyptians who built the pyramids had the same consciousness that we have today, or we may even think that they were more advanced than we are. The key to understanding this lies in the word 'different'. Keen observation shows that human beings are continually evolving by awakening unused potential and learning how to use it. This can mean discarding some kinds of awareness to develop new ways of being aware.

The writings of philosophers down the ages speak clearly about this once you know what you are looking for. One crucial clue for this observation is that we are beings with body, soul and spirit. Furthermore, we are spiritual beings who use our physical bodies as vehicles to express ourselves in this earthly environment. In broad terms, we can call this spiritual component the Real Self or true identity. We can refer to it as our Higher Self. And yes, this is the Prince.

The leading thought we have to grasp is that physical life is the mirrored reflection of our Real Self. This thought can be a bit unnerving because it challenges our ideas about reality. This is why it helpful to remember the Prince who is getting ready to kiss us. Not only that, but he is going to marry us, we will become one with him. This Prince is in fact our I AM which we are striving to connect up with. (See the Addenda for a more detailed explanation about this.) The term I AM is used in this book to refer to the highest that we can achieve. In our daily life the term 'I' which only we can say to mean ourselves is used. In my book, "I Connecting: The Soul's Quest" (Kindle edition "I AM The Mystery") I put it this way:

"Our 'I', this 'self', experiences life through our soul and our body. The 'I' is the artist, the soul his work of art and the body is the canvas. Similarly, the 'I' is the gardener, the garden is our soul and the soil is our body."

So, if we think of our Real Self, our highest I AM experience, as the source of all our inspiration we come a bit closer to understanding the dynamics. It is only when we can experience the truth of this that we realise that human development is a work in progress. Both artists and gardeners have varying degrees of success. And the Prince isn't always there.

As spiritual beings we had to learn how to use our physical vehicle, and this meant losing conscious awareness of our spirit. Why would this be you ask? Well, if life was more satisfactory when we were aware of our Real Self why would we want to lose consciousness of that? So when we perfected that stage in our development, when we became fully aware of our physical being and perfected our use of it, then - and this is where we are now – we have to re-connect with our spirit. A better way of putting this would be to say that we are in a process of spiritualising our physical being. For we don't discard it like we do an old car but rather we recycle the parts and put them to a different and higher use. The turnkey is the freedom we have to do this - or not! Again from my book -

"This picture of the evolving soul reveals that there was a time when our soul was not directly controlled by us. Then the soul belonged to the tribe under the direction of the tribal elder. By all indications the soul began to 'internalise', and our inner life began to arise, around the time of the ancient Egyptians. At this time we can see the development of a sophisticated culture, a culture that clearly distinguished the human being from animals.

At the time of Buddha the focus was deeply on the individual and the external world was seen as an illusion. Today, scientists say that the only reality is the external world of matter. They also say that mind is the body because they cannot prove otherwise in their laboratory. At the same time, these scientists say that they cannot explain the deepest human wonder which is love.

If we start from the premise of accepting that we do have a soul and a spirit, rather than denying it, we discover that we can logically explain some of the things scientists cannot replicate by 'mechanical' means. Mapping out the evolution of consciousness reveals the place and purpose of the soul and spirit in the lives of human beings. Page 23-24

….

It is interesting to consider that when humanity didn't have full use of the soul and didn't have an awareness of his personal 'I', the role of the Pharaoh and the King was important. The diminishing role of royalty (especially since WWI) all over the world is testimony to the development of the highest soul level, as well as the awareness of the human spirit through the strengthening of the sense of self. Perhaps the death of British Princess Diana in 1997 or the murder in 2001 of the Nepalese king and queen by their son, or the rejection of the authoritarian Nepalese king in 2006 has a message to tell. These are the kinds of things that we should think deeply about; they may be the signposts of changing consciousness."

Page 27 "I Connecting: The Soul's Quest" by Kristina Kaine

When considering human consciousness it is important to contemplate the advent of Jesus the Christ, not necessarily from a so-called religious point of view for this being has been misrepresented and misunderstood over the last two thousand years. A good starting point is: Why this being? and why then? My simple response is that the answer is directly tied to the way our consciousness has evolved. It is linked to our own ability to personally connect with our own 'I', our Prince, the result of which changes our consciousness. Pre-Golgotha, this was only possible for a few high initiates; post-Golgotha, it is possible for any human being to freely decide to express the power and purity of their 'I' to the extent that they are able. The Revelation to John reveals how this might happen. In fact, careful contemplation of this Revelation is the catalyst for us to connect with our 'I'.

Today we are at a turning point; we are drowning in illusion. As a society we continually try to identify the enemy outside ourselves, when all the while the enemy is within. We grope in the dark when we should turn on the light of our own consciousness. Then we will see that we are often defeated by our own thinking, feeling and actions, and that these activities have become so automatic that we often cannot control them. We habitually respond to life's situations instead of meeting them in new ways. At the same time, all that meets us from outside reinforces this; the media, politicians, so-called celebrities, corporate leaders, etc..

Where are our heroes people ask? We need to look up to something or someone and aspire to something higher. Each time we think we have found one they fall off their pedestal in one way or another. This is not the path to the future for the hero is now within us, our Prince poised to kiss. We need to raise this hero up and place it on a pedestal within us – the very shape of the letter 'I' suggests this. Then we can be heroes to one another but now by example.

I ask that you don't simply accept what my words but test them in your daily life. If my ideas withstand this test, then we can assume that they carry some truth, if they don't then it is a sign to strive harder to bring spiritual truth to life in our lives. As Garfield famously said, "It's not the having but the getting."

One of the primary ways to explore sacred writings like The Revelation is to try to discover what the words really mean according to original intent. This can be difficult when human consciousness has changed so much since The Revelation was written. At the very end of his June 1908 lectures on The Apocalypse of St John, Rudolf Steiner suggested that one needs to penetrate into the spirit of the writing which the translators did not seem able to do. The very first words, "The revelation of Jesus Christ, which God gave him to show to his servants what must soon take place;" should really say, "The revelation of Jesus Christ, which God gave him to show to his servants I will briefly describe what will take place;"

The same is true of my Reflections on The Revelation. For often I see more detail than I am able to write. Sometimes I don't have the words; sometimes it would take too many words to include a lengthy precursory background; and sometimes it is simply better to leave a space for the reader's own ideas and understanding. In this way the work lives; it can grow and change according to the consciousness of the reader. Come with me now to find your Prince and discover the Soul's Secret.

Kristina Kaine November 2012

PS: These Reflections were written weekly, each Reflection contains between 800 and 900 words, hence the bible texts are sometimes repeated.

If some of the terminology is unfamiliar please refer to the Addenda at the end.

CHAPTER ONE

The revelation of Jesus Christ, which God gave him to show to his servants what must soon take place; and he made it known by sending his angel to his servant John, who bore witness to the word of God and to the testimony of Jesus Christ, even to all that he saw. Blessed is he who reads aloud the words of the prophecy, and blessed are those who hear, and who keep what is written therein; for the time is near.
Rev 1:1-3

We can read and contemplate the Bible in many ways. We should certainly take notice of the literal meaning of its stories. This becomes a most difficult task when we read the Revelation to John. The imagery is shocking, mystifying and bizarre, especially when we place it outside ourselves. It more closely resembles our dream life rather than our waking life.

If we place this Revelation within us and use it to chart the development of our consciousness, it will speak to us quite differently. If we accept the idea that our consciousness evolves, that we haven't always been able to think the way that we do today, we then realise that we tread a path towards becoming increasingly conscious. What does it mean to be conscious? In essence it means that we know ourselves fully and completely. We become aware of why we think, feel and act the way we do. Becoming aware of ourselves in this way changes us. Our understanding of ourselves grows and as a result we can be more forgiving of ourselves. As a consequence we are less harsh in our judgment of others. To be conscious therefore means to see clearly and to understand what makes us tick and what makes the world tick. When we begin to do this we start to experience tremendous freedom.

We might ask why we can't see ourselves clearly already. Simply because we are not strong enough! We do not have sufficient control of our will to be able to know ourselves fully. Just think about how we react when we are criticised or our ideas are opposed. It is through the mastery of our will that we can face ourselves with understanding. This path of mastery is revealed in the Revelation to John.

If we compare St John's Gospel with his Revelation, we can see that in his Gospel, St John carefully maps out the ways in which human beings connect up with the highest expression of their 'I' which we can call the I AM. The I AM is that fourth member of our being (see explanation of terms in the Addenda for a description of the four members of the human being) which is the essential tool for us to become fully conscious. St John, in his Gospel, also shows us how we, as human beings, receive the Christ impulse into our physical body as Jesus did. Then, through the crucifixion of the physical body, St John shows how we can be reborn – resurrected – into a different level of awareness.

St John, through his Revelation, shows us in detail what happens to our consciousness as we awaken and integrate this Christ Impulse that has been slumbering deeply within us since the Mystery of Golgotha. He shows us how our consciousness is transformed by this Christ Impulse. Step by step, through the chapters, he shows us how we move from living our lives as if we were just a physical body to learning how to use our total being; body, soul and spirit. If we think that we are just a physical body then we see ourselves as a car without an engine or a driver. In fact, far too many people are like remote controlled cars and they don't even know who has the remote!

The Revelation of Jesus Christ to John (the beloved) is the revealing of these two principles within the human being. The Jesus principle, which is the I AM, and the Christ principle which is that cosmic force that makes human beings gods. John specifically records this fact in his Gospel.

The Jews answered him, "It is not for a good work that we stone you but for blasphemy; because you, being a man, make yourself God." Jesus answered them, "Is it not written in your law, 'I said, you are gods'? Jn 10:33-34

This Revelation could only be given to John the beloved. Only in the presence of the immense love that passed between Jesus the Christed One and his beloved companion John could such a Revelation be unravelled. When two people love each other deeply, respectfully and without self-interest, this love cannot be contained within their beings. It flows out from them and changes, not just the immediate environment but also the cosmos; the universe in which dwell the angels and all manner of spiritual beings. Only when we are able to express and receive this depth of love, this intensity of love are we able to begin to grasp the Revelation of Jesus Christ to John.

The Revelation begins in this way:

The revelation of Jesus Christ, which God gave him to show to his servants what must soon take place; and he made it known by sending his angel to his servant John, who bore witness to the word of God and to the testimony of Jesus Christ, even to all that he saw. Rev 1:1-2

It is always helpful to ask questions when we read Bible passages. If we accept that not a single word is used without purpose then an immediate question arises here. If John was the beloved disciple why didn't Jesus Christ speak directly to him? John records direct conversations between the resurrected Jesus Christ and his disciples at the end of his Gospel. Why, now, does Jesus Christ need an intermediary, an angel? If we say that this is because Jesus Christ had returned to his Father then why did the information have to come from God, *theos*? After all, isn't God part of the same trinity with Christ? Furthermore, why the chain of command; from God to Jesus Christ, to the angel, to John, and then to us? If we are gods then why can't God speak directly to us?

It is very important to examine each word and ask ourselves the question: why this word and not that word? The very first word of this book of the Bible is *apokalupsis* which in the Greek is rendered a revelation, not the revelation. This suggests that it is one of other possible revelations, not the one and only. Could it be that God (presumably the Father) was waiting to see if Jesus could actually manage to assume the Christ Spirit, the Christ Impulse, and then actually pull off the resurrection? After all, it was touch and go there for awhile. The sweating of blood in the Garden of Gethsemane tells us that Jesus almost didn't make it to the cross. He was given extra strength by an angel to get him through it, as Luke says; "Then an angel from heaven appeared to him and gave him strength." Lk 22:43

This would support the idea that a Revelation, an unveiling, only takes place when we successfully connect with our I AM and awaken the Christ Impulse within us. Then, like water spilling down a fountain, this Revelation flows, profoundly touching everything it comes into contact with. It sweeps through each being; from the fountainhead to Jesus Christ, to the angel, to John and then to us, as if to say: this is big; you all have a role to play.

There are a few other noteworthy ideas in these first two verses. Why is John talking about seeing the word instead of hearing it? The clue to understanding this can be found in the word 'witness', *marturia*. This word is used twice in verse two; once translated as witness, once translated as testimony. *Marturia* doesn't mean to witness something at a distance but rather to enter into a living experience, as if it were happening in the moment to us. It doesn't involve describing a past event; it involves continually re-experiencing it in the present, at will. So it is neither seen nor heard with our external ears and eyes but it is a personal inner experience revealed to us through our inner sight and echoing within our being. Then we know, firsthand, about this Revelation.

We know from experience that any account from a witness about an event is always subject to interpretation. It is rare that a person is conscious enough to remember an event in all its detail. John is saying that his account is not sufficient either –

Blessed is he who reads aloud the words of the prophecy, and blessed are those who hear, and who keep what is written therein; for the time is near. Rev 1:3

This Revelation, this unveiling, can be called a prophecy, a speaking forth, because John is trying to guide us towards what we can know. He is giving us clues about how to know ourselves in more detail. Furthermore, he is saying that the time is near, it is pressing.

We do live in crucial times, there is a sense of urgency to get on with it ... but we don't know what 'it' is. We are swamped with philosophies and theories of psychology all claiming to reveal to us who we really are. They may shine some light here and there, but they cannot give us an immediate experience of our I AM or Christ. The reason for this is because we are each so individual. The only way we can come to self-knowledge is through our own striving, our own action. 'Hear' and 'keep' John says.

Is he saying that we must sit and read aloud this Revelation recorded in the Bible? Or are we being encouraged to attune ourselves to our I AM which knows all things for it is our Real Self and has experienced every single life that we have lived on this earth, and every sojourn between lives. John is telling us that we must urgently find ways of reading and hearing our I AM. We no longer need prophets, for the time is here already when we can connect with our essence, our I AM. He is also saying that we are not alone in this task. Blessed, *makarios*, indicates that the Christ Impulse will awaken in us as a result of our work, and assist us to use John's mysterious words for self-revelation.

Greeting to the Seven Churches

Now John greets his audience. Such greetings can be found at the beginning of many of the books in the New Testament. These greetings are easily overlooked. However, they should not be ignored because they provide the key to what follows. In fact, we could say that this book, Revelation, is summed up in these four verses. Furthermore, if we accept that the whole Bible is the story of the evolution of consciousness, we could even say that the whole Bible is condensed in this greeting.

John to the seven churches that are in Asia: Grace to you and peace from him who is and who was and who is to come, and from the seven spirits who are before his throne, and from Jesus Christ the faithful witness, the first-born of the dead, and the ruler of kings on earth. To him who loves us and has freed us from our sins by his blood and made us a kingdom, priests to his God and Father, to him be glory and dominion for ever and ever. Amen. Rev 1:4-6

The first thing we notice is that John is greeting seven churches. The word 'church' in koine or common Greek is the word 'ekklesia' which literally means 'out of a calling'. These seven churches could relate to seven areas of our consciousness which respond 'out of a calling'. Who is calling? Christ and the spiritual worlds are calling. In Ephesians 1, which seems to echo something of the four verses we are considering, we read that the church is Christ's body.

... according to the working of his [God's] great might which he accomplished in Christ when he raised him from the dead and made him sit at his right hand in the heavenly places, far above all rule and authority and power and dominion, and above every name that is named, not only in this age but also in that which is to come; and he has put all things under his feet and has made him the head over all things for the church, which is his body, the fulness of him who fills all in all. Eph 1:20-23

If the ekklesia, the church, is Christ's body, and we become part of this ekklesia, then we become part of Christ's body and share his consciousness. It is an astounding thing to consider because then we can begin to wonder how to best respond to life if we share such a consciousness and body.

If we follow this idea through, we realise that we must overcome the tendency to think of Christ as a being confined to a form like human beings are. He did that once and through the resurrection changed his form forever. Through our imagination we can see him as a force or a power. It doesn't matter how we mould this image, as long as we create some image. Paul saw him as a blinding light; others have said the same down the centuries. John sees him as a Lamb in The Revelation.

If we are to understand this Revelation then we must work on our understanding of the transformation that will take place within us. As our consciousness responds to this calling we actually become part of the Christ power, the Christ Impulse. We become Christ-ened. This is the possibility that lies before us. If we do the work, all that Christ achieved for us during his earthly sojourn in the body of Jesus is at our disposal. But we must do the work.

John tells us that this work takes place in Asia and has, at its core, grace and peace. We could take the reference to Asia to mean the east, the place where the sun rises and the new day dawns. This is a new work we are involved in. Never before in the evolution of the human being have we had to do such a work ourselves, individually. Furthermore, whether we do the work or not is entirely our own choice.

Being "freed from our sins" means that we have time on our hands, we have been given leave of certain duties associated with our karma and it is our choice how we use this spare time. Revelation is the story of the possibilities at our disposal as we claim this freedom; what will happen if we use it in the right way or the wrong way. Only we can know about our own ekklesia with Christ, it is not for others to judge if we are right or wrong. Henry Thoreau, the 19th Century philosopher said, "The greater part of what my neighbours call good I believe in my soul to be bad …." These 'neighbours' are often closed to anything but their own ideas which they go to lengths to promote. This is not freedom. Freedom at its core is to be free from opinions and more.

In his greeting John is urging us to see the freedom that already exists, now. His words, "who is and who was and who is to come" alert us to the fact that we are participating in an event that straddles the past, present and future. In other words, we enter into the eternal now where the boundaries of space and time are without limits. It is through our I AM that we can stand in it. This is true freedom.

John also tells us that we have a prototype to follow, the firstborn, the *prototokos*. Now we must be re-born, not only that, but self-born through the power of the ekklesia that is at our disposal.

… and from Jesus Christ the faithful witness, the first-born of the dead, and the ruler of kings on earth. To him who loves us and has freed us from our sins by his blood and made us a kingdom, priests to his God and Father, to him be glory and dominion for ever and ever. Amen. Rev 1:5-6

In his greeting John tells us that through the deed on Golgotha we have been made a kingdom, *basileia*; the place where the ruler rules. We have also been made priests, *hiereis*; the ones who offer sacrifice.

To shed some light on this strange statement it is helpful to picture the evolutionary journey of the human being. Simply put, it is about the human spirit drawing matter to itself to fashion an earthly form. The consequence of which was to become 'dead' to its spiritual home; occupying the physical earth with no knowledge of its spiritual heritage. After thousands of years the God Christ took the same journey and assumed a physical form in the man (albeit a high and complex initiate) Jesus. He then became a faithful witness to the earthly human experience – he experienced it firsthand. Then he showed us how to overcome death and in so doing he became the prototype for the personal resurrection we must now execute though our own effort. This is more about being self-born than re-born. This is the virgin birth of our spiritual being which has been dead to us for ages. A strange tale indeed and it leaves us wondering what its purpose could be. It seems so simple but at the same time so complex.

If we say that our spiritual being is our I AM and we are separated from it, then the purpose of our existence is to be reunited with it. We may wonder why this just doesn't happen as a matter of course, why does it have to be so dramatic. Couldn't God just do it for us? He probably could, but we would be lesser beings for it. We must do this ourselves, consciously, and we can only do it while we occupy this physical body. When this happens we become priests. However, if the priest is the one who sacrifices, and Jesus Christ has already made that blood-sacrifice, freeing us from our sins, what kind of sacrifice is there left for us to do?

The clue lies in the word 'kingdom'. He made us a kingdom. So we are now a kingdom and this kingdom must be ruled. Yet, if we are honest, our kingdom is often unruly. We are swamped by our emotions, our thoughts take their own habitual course, and our willpower can be weak. This is why we need to be a priest – a priest to ourselves, within our own being. Within our being we offer the sacrifice of our animal tendencies that arise in our lower nature. In this way we make way for our higher nature, our I AM, to influence our emotions, thoughts and behaviour.

John is telling us that a new priesthood is emerging, one which does not need a church or an altar. No longer do we need an external authority telling us what to think and feel and how to behave. We must now assume that responsibility for ourselves. We must make it our business to understand the new spiritual code of ethics and live by it. However, as Henry Thoreau said, what seems to be good could be bad. Discovering what really is good and what is bad is the work of making ourselves priests; I AM-priests.

It is surprisingly common today to hear people say that they have an innate sense of being a priest. Perhaps this is a past life memory, or longing, or perhaps it is the experience of the Christ Impulse in their being. Now, it is not so much about having a sense of being a priest but of how we are functioning as a priest. This new priest first presides within themselves. These are the ones who have an innate sense of awe and reverence for their own being and for every other human being they encounter. They express love and forgiveness for themselves and others, creating a sense of community that does not depend on membership of an external church. Furthermore, it can straddle belief systems. Those who are functioning as this new priest are an example for others to experience the kingdom and the priest within themselves.

As this new priest, we belong to the inner church, the ekklesia - the body of Christ - and John is encouraging us to take very seriously this task of making ourselves a priest. He gives us the blessing of grace and peace which he knows we are going to need as we take on the task of following in Christ's footsteps. Through our striving we become alive to our spiritual being, allowing it to rule in the kingdom of our earthly being. With John we can then give thanks, saying "to him be glory and dominion for ever and ever. Amen."

John to the seven churches that are in Asia: Grace to you and peace from him who is and who was and who is to come, and from the seven spirits who are before his throne, Rev 1:4

Before we continue on we should take a moment to consider the many spiritual beings mentioned in these first six verses of this Revelation of Jesus Christ to John. Our modern intellect has difficulty straddling the concept of beings that are not visible. Although, consider that for some people, God, Jesus Christ and the Devil are perfectly acceptable spiritual beings, and, for some others, angels exist. For the most part we don't really have adequate images of the different spiritual beings or powers that are an integral and essential part of life in the universe. As we travel through this Revelation we will meet many of these beings and come to understand something of their role in our existence.

Ed Smith, in his wonderful reference book, "The Burning Bush" lists them. He explains them in this way, "Between Trinity and Humanity were the Hierarchies ... The Hierarchies are ninefold, being in three ranks of three. The highest rank comprises, in descending order, and using their names as reflected in scripture, the Seraphim, Cherubim and Thrones; the second rank [though variously ordered by different Christian authorities] comprises the Dominions, Powers and Authorities; and the third rank the Principalities, Archangels and Angels. [Rudolf] Steiner gave each of these a name in keeping with its character in the creative process. The Greek terminology corresponded with the English terms, but it is noteworthy that the Hebrew term for "Authorities," or for the "Exousiai" in Greek, was "Elohim," the plural term used for God in Gen 1." www.bibleandanthroposophy.com Overview page 2

It is these Elohim that John is referring to when he says "and from the seven spirits who are before his throne". Many of the spiritual beings in the Bible are broadly considered to be God. However, understanding that God can have different expressions gives us a much clearer picture of the spiritual company we keep. We start to see how we are affected by the actions and functions of these beings who we could say stand above us (just as we stand above plants and animals) yet exist in our environment - but in a different dimension. We could also say that these beings have a greater or different experience of the universe than we do.

We should not take lightly the different ways these beings are referred to, for here we find the clues to their roles e.g. dominions, powers and authorities. Then, for instance, we can ask why John refers to the "him who is and who was and who is to come" instead of simply saying God? Or indeed, does he mean God? In verse 8 we read:

"I am [ego eimi] the Alpha and the Omega," says the Lord God, who is and who was and who is to come, the Almighty. Rev 1:8

Ego eimi, the I AM, was in the beginning, was first (alpha) and is to come, that is, last (omega). This is not God, this is our own eternal being, our I AM. To fully understand all the implications of this we need knowledge of reincarnation and karma. It is this I AM that holds all our incarnations together like a string of pearls. The first pearl and the last pearl are all on the one string. In our present state of consciousness we can only see one pearl, the life we are living now. Although, we are at a stage in our evolution that it is becoming more and more common for people to experience memories from other lives in other countries and at other times in history. It is surprisingly easy to test the validity of reincarnation and karma if we decide to do it. This then gives us greater insight into some of the events in our lives. One of the most common experiences is déjà vu, that feeling of having experienced something before but we cannot place it.

So in just these six verses many spiritual beings are mentioned: Jesus Christ, God, the angel, him who is and who was and who is to come, the seven spirits who are before his throne, the ruler (*arche*) of the kings, the Father, the dominions and perhaps there are some others hidden in the words, for example the logos, the word, is also spoken of as a spiritual being. If we don't have any ideas about the functions of these spiritual beings how can we possibly make sense of The Revelation?

As we become more aware of our I AM, and as we become more conscious in our thinking process, and more aware of the mysteries of the universe, we don't feel so alone. We experience the company of the spiritual beings who are very keen for us to wake up to the reality of our being and theirs. This is what in fact has happened to John which is why he is able to describe The Revelation. He is showing us the way, sketching a map to guide us through the realms of consciousness, and assisting us to recognise the spiritual powers that we will encounter. Initially, it is through grace and peace and gratitude that we will navigate this strange landscape. Later on, there will be tribulation which will require patient endurance as he explains in verse nine. Above all, we must never forget that the whole point of the journey is to connect up with our I AM and consciously experience the Christ Impulse in our being. In this knowledge lies great comfort and assurance.

Behold, he is coming with the clouds, and every eye will see him, every one who pierced him; and all tribes of the earth will wail on account of him. Even so. Amen. "I am the Alpha and the Omega," says the Lord God, who is and who was and who is to come, the Almighty. I John, your brother, who share with you in Jesus the tribulation and the kingdom and the patient endurance, was on the island called Patmos on account of the word of God and the testimony of Jesus. Rev 1:7-9

"Behold", says John. He is calling our attention – probably urgently – to the need to sharpen our sense of sight. He is calling us to action. Look at the clouds; clouds which usually obscure things but which can also reveal what is hidden by them. John relates his own experience to us so that we know what to expect. John the beloved, the human prototype, is explaining what we are likely to see and experience as we become more conscious. What kind of seeing is it when clouds are associated with our ability to see rather than clouding our vision? If clouds obscure what we normally see and they can also reveal to us what lies unseen within all living things then we can assume that they represent a spiritual force which we must discover.

Think of a piece of fruit freshly picked, it is plump and full of vitality. Place it in a bowl and over time watch how it shrivels. It shrivels because something in it is depleted. It is the life-force, the etheric force, that gradually leaves and eventually the fruit will decay. We also have such a life-force in our own body. As long as our life-force is connected with our body we live; if it disconnects, we die.

The earth too has this life sustaining force keeping it alive and preventing it from decay and death. We can look to the plant kingdom to discover its secret. Indeed, the deterioration or destruction of the plant kingdom in some areas of the earth means that the earth's life-force has been interfered with leaving that part of the earth desolate. The water crisis experienced in many places on the globe which is also connected with clouds and climate change, could also be linked to this.

John is urging us to be observant, to see and pierce - *ekkenteo*, Greek for 'to prick out' - the surface to reveal the life-force at work in us and in this earth. Since Golgotha we can find Christ in this life-force. As Christ appeared on earth in the physical body of Jesus, he now appears in the life-force of this earth – this is the secret of the resurrection. When Christ walked the earth in Jesus' body only a few people saw him, and only one soldier pierced him. Now that he is free of his physical body everyone, everywhere can see him. The sight that makes this possible is the sight we receive through our I AM. This sight is resurrected, no longer the ancient psychic vision, now the clear thinking vision that we can only experience when we are connected with our I AM.

John is pointing to this resurrected vision when he says "all the tribes will wail over him" - *koptontai ep auton* speaks of mourning. It was the deep grief of mourning that Mary experienced at the empty tomb that led her to see the life-force of Christ which still retained the shape of his physical body after the physical body had disappeared. John in his Gospel tells it this way:

Jesus said to her, "Woman, why are you weeping? Whom do you seek?" Supposing him to be the gardener, she said to him, "Sir, if you have carried him away, tell me where you have laid him, and I will take him away." Jn 20:15

Then John, reminding us again of our I AM - "I am [is] the Alpha and the Omega," - emphasises that we are not alone on this journey. "I John, your brother, who share with you in Jesus" - *sunkoinonos* means more than share; it means a co-sharer, a companion, someone to really communicate with. We are part of a brotherhood with John, companions who support each other through this difficult stage of human development.

John spells out why we need companions when he says, "the tribulation and the kingdom and the patient endurance". The word used for tribulation in Greek is *thlipsis* which means 'a pressing'. He has chosen this word because he knows that the I AM presses in on us as it tries to make the connection that is necessary before the Christ Impulse can become active within us. The agony of the crucifixion is a graphic picture of how we are nailed to the consciousness of this earth. If we can bear patiently this pressing down on us by our I AM, and if we can rule within our own kingdom, then John's experience becomes our experience. With John we will experience the logos, the word of God, and the *marturia* (testimony), which means that we experience Jesus as if we were him.

The Revelation Being

I was in the Spirit on the Lord's day, and I heard behind me a loud voice like a trumpet saying, "Write what you see in a book and send it to the seven churches, to Ephesus and to Smyrna and to Per'gamum and to Thyati'ra and to Sardis and to Philadelphia and to La-odice'a." Then I turned to see the voice that was speaking to me, and on turning I saw seven golden lampstands, and in the midst of the lampstands one like a son of man, clothed with a long robe and with a golden girdle round his breast; his head and his hair were white as white wool, white as snow; his eyes were like a flame of fire, his feet were like burnished bronze, refined as in a furnace, and his voice was like the sound of many waters; in his right hand he held seven stars, from his mouth issued a sharp two-edged sword, and his face was like the sun shining in full strength. When I saw him, I fell at his feet as though dead. Rev 1:10-17

Where exactly was John when he says that he was "in the spirit"? The Greek word for spirit is pneuma which means wind or breath; the wind or breath is unseen but we can certainly feel them. Has John transported himself to some lofty place? Or has he been meditating and entered into a different state of consciousness? Or has he actually become conscious of his own spiritual being? We can only be conscious of our spiritual being by fine-tuning our faculties of thinking, feeling and willing. They become purified and accentuated and not, as some people think, subdued by a technique that can actually make us unconscious. John is telling us what happens when we experience this super-sharp consciousness when we activate our spiritual being.

One of the most important things that we can do each day is to become aware of how conscious we are. We are threefold beings of body, soul and spirit, each facet of which is in various stages of connecting up with our I AM. Mostly we experience life through our body; our strongest experiences are those of hunger and thirst, warmth and coldness, comfort and discomfort.

To a certain extent we are conscious of the activity of our soul; at this level thinking is our most conscious activity, then, in a dreamy way we experience our feelings, and to a lesser extent we are aware of our will. At this point in our evolution we are only now starting to become aware of the activity of our spirit and this happens as our will awakens. Since John is the forerunner, he is trying to explain to us what we are going to experience as we become more conscious of the spiritual activities of our being.

It is in our soul that we feel, think and will prior to expressing these in our body through our speech or behaviour. Much of what we express is automatic. We only become conscious of what takes place in our soul when our I AM, our Higher Self, is able to press into us. Our I AM is like a shaft of light shining into the darkness of our unconsciousness, revealing all that goes on there.

Over time, as we become more conscious of what is at work in our soul, we also begin to use our spirit more consciously. The first experience of our spirit is Imagination. This is spiritual Imagination which is the ability to use our thinking to create pictures, living images of what we are thinking. For instance, instead of thinking of a rose we can see the rose bush producing the bud and then the bud opening into a full bloom in a time-lapsed sequence. If we exert ourselves we can even experience its fragrance.

This is the process John is describing to us in verses 10-17; this is the Imagination of the fully developed, fully conscious human being. This is the human being who has developed the ability to hold the powerful forces of his I AM as it presses into his being. John now describes the detail of this Imagination to assist us to prepare for this experience in our own being. A feeling of deep gratitude rises up within us when we are able to imagine John's courage as he went through these experiences alone (on an island) and record them for our guidance. Then we can use our Imagination to place him at our side, as our companion, as we awaken our consciousness to the reality of our own being. John, in his Gospel, recorded Jesus speaking of this experience of spirit:

When the Spirit of truth comes, he will guide you into all the truth; for he will not speak on his own authority, but whatever he hears he will speak, and he will declare to you the things that are to come. Jn 16:13

Jesus' words here are heralding what will happen when we become conscious of our spiritual being. In Revelation 1:10 John is the first human to experience these "things that are to come." He says,

I was in the Spirit on the Lord's day, and I heard behind me a loud voice like a trumpet saying ... Rev 1:10

The Lord, the *Kyrios*, of our being is our I AM. Day is when the light shines. So John is saying that he was experiencing the I AM's day when the light of his I AM shone into the darkness of his being. Then he became conscious of a being speaking loudly. John is not hearing and seeing anything physically standing behind him. To see, *blepo*, is about inner perception and reveals that John is experiencing these things with his spiritual faculties.

There are three spiritual faculties; Imagination, Inspiration and Intuition. These facilities of perception develop as our I AM has a more direct influence in our being. When our I AM is the Lord, the *Kyrios*, of our soul forces - feeling, thinking and will - we then refine them into spiritual faculties. In Imagination we use our thinking to create living images. Inspiration means that we can perceive spiritually, we inspire, breathe in or take in, through inner hearing, things that normally come to us from outside in our ordinary consciousness. The third spiritual faculty, Intuition, means we enter into things spiritually; we experience things from the inside instead of the normal way of experiencing the surface of things. At this point our I AM becomes aware of itself connected to our being on this earth as an 'I'-being. This is our goal, and each of the churches reveals how it takes place in our being till we can stand in Chapter 12 and give birth to the Christ child.

And a great portent appeared in heaven, a woman clothed with the sun, with the moon under her feet, and on her head a crown of twelve stars; she was with child and she cried out in her pangs of birth, in anguish for delivery. Rev 12:1-2

In Revelation 1:12-17 John places this most unusual and vivid Imagination of the Revelation Being before us and tells us very clearly that this is our I AM. He uses similes to describe the qualities that will develop in our consciousness as we connect with our I AM to give it expression in our lives. If we give life to these similes in our mind we prepare ourselves for the changes we will experience as we grow in spiritual stature.

Then I turned to see the voice that was speaking to me, and on turning I saw seven golden lampstands, and in the midst of the lampstands one like a son of man, Rev1:12-13

The son of man is our own offspring; our own creation born from our ability to achieve balance between our lower self and our

Higher Self through the indwelling Christ. John continues, [this being is]

clothed with a long robe and with a golden girdle round his breast; his head and his hair were white as white wool, white as snow; his eyes were like a flame of fire, his feet were like burnished bronze, refined as in a furnace, and his voice was like the sound of many waters; in his right hand he held seven stars, from his mouth issued a sharp two-edged sword, and his face was like the sun shining in full strength. Rev 1:13-16

As we attune ourselves to inner development, the first thing that we experience is an inner voice. John said that he heard the voice or sound, *phoné*, behind him but he needed also to see it - *blepo*, to perceive it. This meant that he had to turn. There are many Greek words for 'turn'. This one is *epistrepho* and it speaks about conversion. Our attention is converted from one view to another. When we experience our Higher Self echoing in our being we cannot continue to live our lives as we did before. This is a life-changing experience and our consciousness will never be the same.

What can happen is that we try to turn back to our old consciousness, particularly when we have to engage in our contemporary life. The letters to the churches explain the consequences of this.

When John turned the first thing he saw was seven golden lampstands. But where are the lamps? These lampstands, *luchnia*, are for holding small hand-held oil lamps. Lamps such as these were carried by the ten virgins who went to meet the bridegroom (see Mt 25) and they symbolise the fire of the Holy Spirit that we must carry in our being to prepare for the presence of Christ. John only saw the stands because the lamps are now within him and burning perpetually. We can find a reference to this in Solomon's collection of Proverbs:

The spirit of man is the lamp of the LORD, searching all his innermost parts. Pr 20:27

The presence of this being indicates that we have developed the ability to work with our spirit - which means that our faculties of Imagination, Inspiration and Intuition are, to an extent, available to us, - and then the bridegroom, who is Christ, lights up our being revealing all our ideas and motives.

John's description can be understood in the following way. We are clothed in the robe of justice and dignity warmed by the gold shining from our breast. The white head and hair represents our thinking which is pure, balanced and wise – white being a combination of all the colours of the rainbow. Our eyes no longer devour the light, they produce light and perceive with burning precision and enthusiasm. From them comes an illumination that can assist others to see.

Our burnished bronze feet allow us to stand in the refining fire of this earth, the proving ground of our spiritual identity. Our will is forged with fiery purity. This goodwill can be heard in the sound that flows from us like water; that life-giving substance without which we could not dwell on this earth. It flows never-endingly because we use it wisely.

When we can hold the stars in our hand we occupy the whole cosmos. We no longer see the cosmos as separate from us influencing us from outside our being. Then we know that every word from our mouth cuts away all illusion. In the precision of our words stands truth. Our face reveals to all that the sun is within us. It shines without reserve and warms everyone who sees it.

If this image lives within us, if we work with it to give it specific meaning in our own lives, we will be well prepared for what lies ahead. The world urgently needs more people who have a connection with their Higher Self, their I AM. These are people who are strong enough to express the future human being in raw truth as Christ did at Golgotha. Courageous people who can stand in the face of misunderstanding because the being John describes here that we will be misunderstood. These are the fearless people who know that they are in good company because of the work of John who wrote what he saw in the book, and sent it to the seven churches.

When I saw him, I fell at his feet as though dead. But he laid his right hand upon me, saying, "Fear not, I am the first and the last, and the living one; I died, and behold I am alive for evermore, and I have the keys of Death and Hades. Now write what you see, what is and what is to take place hereafter. As for the mystery of the seven stars which you saw

in my right hand, and the seven golden lampstands, the seven stars are the angels of the seven churches and the seven lampstands are the seven churches. Rev 1:17-20

While this being is the Imagination of our own being when our I AM is able to fully influence our consciousness, it is also the Imagination of the human being in whom the Christ Spirit lives. When we have achieved this state of being, Christ can speak through us as if we were him. So John has turned from his every day vision to his spiritual vision to see this Imagination and after he has seen it, and remembered the detail of it, he fell down.

Did he physically fall down? Or did this image cause all that he had been before to cease, to fall away from him? There is an echo here of the raising of Lazarus described by St John in chapter 11 of his Gospel. Many esoteric writers say that when Lazarus was resurrected he was given a new name, John. This John, they say, is the beloved disciple and writer of this Revelation. He would also have been in the upper room and experienced the fear when the resurrected Christ Jesus appeared out of nowhere. Through fear comes the assurance of a new way of being. Then we can hear the words, "[The] I AM is the living one".

There are several words for 'life' or 'living' in the Greek, this one is *zoe*. Zoe is that life-force associated with the resurrection. This is the Life Spirit associated with our spiritual Intuition. It is I AM-infused life-force. This means that the life-force, the etheric, that keeps our body alive is raised up and spiritualised so that it becomes a living force no longer bonded to the physical. "I died, and behold I am alive for evermore" means that our life-force previously bound to our physical body has now been raised and gives life to our spiritual body as well – while we still occupy our physical body!

This places great demands on our mind for now we must be able to look into all our experiences with equanimity. This is one meaning of having the "keys of Death and Hades". With our resurrected consciousness we can enter into the underworld of our old consciousness, that place where our old consciousness had no life. When we have the vision of the Christed I AM we can no longer oscillate between the old and the new consciousness. With our new consciousness we must learn how to live fully in this modern world. Often this will be like living in hell. We will see how the values, as well as standards of behaviour, of those who do not strive to connect with their I AM are deteriorating. We see this happening already in the world today, and it is escalating.

"What is, and what is to take place" refers to this panorama of consciousness which we must navigate. Those who can use their higher consciousness do not become the keepers of those who do not. Only by example can they unlock the door for those who come behind them. The power of equanimity always strikes a deep cord in those who observe it. When one person acts out of forgiveness a gate is unlocked. One of the most potent stories about this was recounted by Bill Cody who was found working in a Nazi concentration camp in the 1940s.

' "We lived in the Jewish section of Warsaw," he began slowly, the first words I had heard him speak about himself, "my wife, our two daughters, and our three little boys. When the Germans reached our street they lined everyone against a wall and opened up with machine guns. I begged to be allowed to die with my family, but because I spoke German they put me in a work group."

'He paused, perhaps seeing again his wife and five children. "I had to decide right then," he continued, "whether to let myself hate the soldiers who had done this. It was an easy decision, really. I was a lawyer. In my practice I had seen too often what hate could do to people's minds and bodies. Hate had just killed the six people who mattered most to me in the world. I decided then that I would spend the rest of my life – whether it was a few days or many years – loving every person I came in contact with." ' George G. Ritchie, Elizabeth Sherill, Return from Tomorrow.

Bill Cody was able to straddle two consciousnesses at once; his resurrected consciousness took the lead. Imagine what would have happened if he had moved into the Hades of his other consciousness. By being able to relate the details of his experience he was obviously not denying it either. This is our goal too, to have such a mobile will, combined with a depth of courage, that we can make higher choices, not blindly but by using our spiritualised thinking. When we do we will feel that right hand upon us and hear the words, "Fear not."

CHAPTER TWO

Messages to the Seven Churches

Ephesus

"To the angel of the church in Ephesus write: 'The words of him who holds the seven stars in his right hand, who walks among the seven golden lampstands, "'I know your works, your toil and your patient endurance, and how you cannot bear evil men but have tested those who call themselves apostles but are not, and found them to be false; I know you are enduring patiently and bearing up for my name's sake, and you have not grown weary. But I have this against you, that you have abandoned the love you had at first. Remember then from what you have fallen, repent and do the works you did at first. If not, I will come to you and remove your lampstand from its place, unless you repent. Yet this you have, you hate the works of the Nicola'itans, which I also hate. He who has an ear, let him hear what the Spirit says to the churches. To him who conquers I will grant to eat of the tree of life, which is in the paradise of God.' Rev 2:1-7

John now relays seven messages to us. He is directed to write these letters to the angel of each church. Angels are beings one stage higher than human beings, as animals are beings one stage lower than humans. As we care for our animals, so angels watch over us. The Greek word *angelos* means messenger. So angels are intermediaries who help and guide the evolution of human consciousness. Rudolf Steiner wrote a beautiful prayer to our angel which describes their role.

> You, my heavenly friend, my angel,
> You who have led me to the earth
> and will lead me through the gate of death
> into the spiritual home of the human soul;
> You, who have known the path for thousands of years;
> Never cease to enlighten me, to strengthen me, to advise me,
> that I may emerge from the consuming fire of destiny
> a stronger vessel,
> and learn ever more to fill myself
> with a sense for the goals of the spiritual world.

By Rudolf Steiner

If we assign angels a role within our being we could place them in that area where our spiritual Imagination is expressed; the first region of our spiritual being. Rudolf Steiner refers to it as Spirit Self or Manas. This is the region just above our soul which starts to awaken when we are able to engage with our I AM. At the end of the last chapter John told us "the seven stars are the angels"; as stars connect us with the cosmos so angels connect our spirit to our soul and body.

John also told us that "the seven lampstands are the seven churches." The lampstands, *luchnia*, symbolise the fire of the Holy Spirit, given at Pentecost, which we must keep burning within our being to prepare for the presence of Christ. John only saw the stands because the lamps are now within him burning perpetually. Some translations of the Bible say that these are candlesticks. A lamp differs from a candle; the candle light consumes the candle and it disappears, the oil in the lamp can be perpetually replenished.

The words written about the seven churches are metaphors for our developing consciousness. There are many things in life that occur in sevens; seven colours of the rainbow, seven musical notes, seven days in the week etc. Each seven years we human beings enter into different life phases. We can also compare our spiritual development to the seven stages of a plant's growth; seed, roots, leaf, bud, flower, fruit and seed. This is cycle is repeated throughout our life according to our "works". By contemplating these phases of growth and comparing them to the words written to each church a pattern emerges. It helps to be mindful that a new seed is produced out of destruction. Each of the messages speaks of an up-building process followed by something destructive. This is as it should be, and through our individual effort we can produce the seed for the next cycle, the next church.

The first stage in this development that John writes to us about is the Ephesus stage. Ephesus was an important centre in Asia Minor and was famous for the great temple of Diana or Artemis. It was also a busy commercial centre. The name Ephesus essentially means desire. At the core of our being are two important forces that keep us alive; drives and desires. Our drives keep us alive because they are a trigger for us to eat and drink, to regulate our temperature and keep comfortable. These drives develop into desires pressing us to act so that we satisfy our hunger and thirst and keep warm and safe.

Because we are not simply physical beings, because we are spiritual beings developing our consciousness in a physical body, all our bodily functions have spiritual counterparts. So while the activity in our being arises from desire; the desire to eat, to be warm, to love, to create; we also have desires to spiritually progress. We do not become aware of these desires until we connect with our I AM – remember that it is our I AM that is telling John what to write.

In fact, the dissatisfaction, anxiety and depression experienced by increasingly more people today has its root cause in the pressing down on us of our I AM. No amount of medication and counselling will alleviate these problems. The only possible remedy is for each of us to allow our I AM to take its rightful place in our being. Then, when enough of us "have an ear to hear what the spirit says to the churches" this will set up a living force which will take on a life of its own. When philosophies such as Marxism became a reality in people's consciousness it was because of the numbers of people who supported them. As one writer said of Marxism, "These thoughts spread out and became a force which urgently demanded realisation." Unless we have thoughts about the I AM, thoughts based on real knowledge and a real experience of our I AM, these thoughts cannot spread out and The Revelation to John explains the consequences.

"To the angel of the church in Ephesus write: 'The words of him who holds the seven stars in his right hand, who walks among the seven golden lampstands, "'I know your works, your toil and your patient endurance, and how you cannot bear evil men but have tested those who call themselves apostles but are not, and found them to be false; I know you are enduring patiently and bearing up for my name's sake, and you have not grown weary. Rev 2:1-3

The message to each church comes from a different aspect of the I AM archetype. The introductory words spoken to Ephesus are, "The words of him who holds the seven stars in his right hand, who walks among the seven golden lampstands". The words spoken to Smyrna are, "The words of the first and the last, who died and came to life." The words spoken to Pergamum are, "The words of him who has the sharp two-edged sword" and so on. As we contemplate each message we should give due consideration to why each message is coloured in these particular ways.

This image of the one who expresses the words to Ephesus gives a sense of the wide universe – holding seven stars in one hand. These stars, we already know, are the angels of the churches. The lampstands are the churches. This is a powerful and commanding being that holds these angels and walks, figuratively speaking, among the combined energy of all seven churches. We get a real sense of the hidden forces of the 'seed' phase of consciousness. The survival of each seed that falls into the earth is dependent on the cosmic elements – the sun, the moon, the seasons and the weather.

By comparing the messages to each of the seven churches as stages in the growth of a plant, the message to Ephesus gives a deep impression of a seed. Imagine the patience within the seed's sheath as its forces wait for the right conditions to set down roots and push up shoots. This image of patience stands in contrast to the urgency behind modern culture demanding to have things instantly. It isn't just in agriculture that seeds are forced to flower sooner and to flower out of season. In our consciousness we are conditioned to expect what we want, when we want it, with as little effort as possible.

The development of our spiritual consciousness must be a nurturing process. We cannot expect to have deep insight into the meaning of things instantly. We cannot fully understand spiritual ideas without patience. We must allow the seed within us to slowly swell with unseen forces of regeneration. The regeneration is required to give freedom to our earthbound ideas. This also means that we must allow our ideas to gestate. The right nourishment for our ideas produces roots and shoots that are strong and healthy.

The I AM, preparing itself to receive the Christ Impulse, is the source of nourishment that we need. When our ideas are fertilized in this way they echo with truth. When we hear this echo we are then able to identify the false apostles, the false teachers. These are the ones who want to impose their philosophies on us, convincing us that they know the secret.

We must resist these promises because they actually distract us from the generative power of the seed within us. This is our seed, which we have produced from a past blossoming and which only we can nurture. We must not seek instant gratification for our Ephesian desires, but by purifying them this seed will produce a better blossom than the last and hence a better seed for future plants.

Each day can be seed-creating. Do we take each day seriously enough? Do we fully consider how today's events will colour tomorrow? Do we patiently work on our consciousness today so that tomorrow we will have a clearer vision of who we are and a deeper understanding of our purpose? Or do we perform our morning meditation and for the rest of the day respond to life's situations instinctively? These instincts arise from our karma, they are the fruits of the past, and if we do not toil and have patient endurance they will side-track us. By stressing patience John is advising us to think twice before we act and also to think before we think.

Each morning as we greet the day we could ask, "How will

today change me?" What "works", what "toil / labour" can I undertake today that will create a different future? How can we release the right forces from the seed so that our consciousness can meet the future as it approaches us with such intensity? It is only through patience with ourselves and with others as well as endurance that we can raise our consciousness to that level where our I AM and Christ can use us.

We also must be alert for the weariness that can overtake us. These are the moments when another person's philosophies give us instant gratification. This could be theories about the changing climate blamed for warming the globe, or particular foods causing cancer, or puerile books like "The Secret"; very seductive and very deadly for the growth of our consciousness. Is "taking a personal stand against climate change", and "reducing our carbon footprint" really the answer? The only answer is to put every effort into becoming fully conscious, of knowing that we are beings of body, soul and spirit. Then, responding to that ancient call, "Man, know yourself," we will transform this earth completely.

But I have this against you, that you have abandoned the love you had at first. Remember then from what you have fallen, repent and do the works you did at first. If not, I will come to you and remove your lampstand from its place, unless you repent. Yet this you have, you hate the works of the Nicola'itans, which I also hate. He who has an ear, let him hear what the Spirit says to the churches. To him who conquers I will grant to eat of the tree of life, which is in the paradise of God.' Rev 2:4-7

The message to each church has a constructive phase and a destructive phase just like the life of a plant. Verses 4-7 speak about what can be rescued from the dying phase to create a new seed for the future.

When we first experience the call to develop our spiritual being, or to embark on a new stage of growth, we are filled with an intense love for the task. There are four words for love in Greek and this one is agape. It is divine love, Christed love, and it quickens us motivating us to do the necessary "works". We become like a plant intent on flowering. However once we bloom we often want to preserve the flower and lose site of the purpose of the flower which is to produce the seed for the next stage of growth. John's words, "Remember then from what you have fallen" could be addressed to the seed – remember that you have fallen from the flower and you must continue your "works" to produce flower after flower. One flowering is not enough and a seed is of no use unless it produces a new plant. So it is with the growth of our consciousness. It is not the flowering that is the point of it; it is the continual growth, the continual striving, the "works". That is the point.

Many problems within us, and within the world, are connected to this principle. We give greater value to the end result rather than the creative process of producing the result. We don't always see that the result of each work is simply a stepping stone to the next phase; as the bloom must produce the seed for the next phase in the life of a species of plant. Everywhere we look in the world we can see past creations dragged into the present instead of the "works" for a new creation. Think of the implications when plants are genetically modified not to produce seeds! Impotent plants! How far removed is this from the tree of life from which we aspire to eat?

The tree of life contains a life-force which nourishes our spiritual development. We could say that the tree of knowledge in the Garden of Eden is our lower self. When we ate of this tree, we left the spiritual worlds and became earthly beings. Now, through our own "works", we can conquer this part of being, and then we rule in our own kingdom.

The tree of life is then our Higher Self, the most beautiful bloom of all. Our "works" create the seed for this bloom. Through our repeated earthly incarnations and initiations, through producing seed after seed, bloom after bloom, we will eat - we will merge with our inner being - this tree of life, our Christed Higher Self.

However, this would all be placed in jeopardy if we lose our lampstand? The lampstand is the sign that the lamp is within us lighting up our inner being. When this happens we will see our inner motives and thoughts in all their reality. It takes great courage to look at the reality of our inner being. This can certainly dampen the love we had at first. It is like entering into a new romance, once the glow subsides the flaws in the character of our lover can cool down our emotions.

So, within us, we must face the flaws in our lower self, accepting them, repenting – changing the way we think and feel about them – and keep our focus on the "works". This means that we must brave the criticism that we will hear from our Higher Self (and from others). It will also mean that we treat ourselves gently, as we treat others gently; avoiding actions that cause discomfort to ourselves, and to others. Certainly we must forgive our lower self as we would also be forgiving of others, regardless of what they do. This is agape for self and for others. This is the way to be a priest to ourselves and an example to others.

The Bible does not give a clear indication about who the Nicola'itans are, but the name Nicolaus means 'conqueror of people'. If the Nicola'itans are those who try to conquer others then they would be those who impose their will on others. It is so easy to decide what others should do. It is second nature to apply our ideas, our standards and values - in other words, all our experiences from the past - to the behaviour of others. This means that we are using the forces of past seeds instead of the forces of the present seed as it silently works to produce a new, hopefully better, bloom. So for these reasons we must hate the works of the Nicola'itans knowing that the first rule of spiritual development is never to impose our will on another person. We must strive to allow each person to do what they 'will' do. Our task is to purify our own will so that our lower and higher selves become aligned.

At the same time we must be watchful that the budding purified will forces in our own being are not imposed upon by our unconscious, pre-conditioned will. This is a key reason that we work to become as conscious as possible. Otherwise our unconscious will can manipulate the freewill we develop through our "works", especially the freewill that is developed though the forces of agape in our being. Let us not abandon our first love, but keep our eye trained on the prize, "to eat of the tree of life, which is in the paradise of God."

Smyrna

"And to the angel of the church in Smyrna write: 'The words of the first and the last, who died and came to life. "'I know your tribulation and your poverty (but you are rich) and the slander of those who say that they are Jews and are

not, but are a synagogue of Satan. Do not fear what you are about to suffer. Behold, the devil is about to throw some of you into prison, that you may be tested, and for ten days you will have tribulation. Be faithful unto death, and I will give you the crown of life. He who has an ear, let him hear what the Spirit says to the churches. He who conquers shall not be hurt by the second death.' Rev 2:8-11

Smyrna comes from the Greek word *smurna* which means myrrh. Myrrh is an astringent gum which acts as an antiseptic and a stimulant. It is used in perfume and holy anointing oil, primarily for purification and embalming. It was one of the gifts the Magi brought to the baby Jesus. This is quite fitting since the message to this church speaks of death and rebirth – in our consciousness.

These words spoken to Smyrna come from the eternal aspect of our I AM – the first and the last. This I AM died to us when we lost consciousness of it and now through our own initiative we could regain consciousness of it. This is just like the seed in its second phase of growth. It was lifeless to the outside world until it was planted, warmed and watered and now it shows its signs of life by sprouting. So, too, our consciousness starts to regain its eternal essence. It starts to become aware of a wider sphere of consciousness than it had till now. Our consciousness pushes beyond the boundaries just like roots and shoots push beyond the shell of the seed.

At this stage the plant is at its most vulnerable so no wonder we meet Satan and the devil. Our sprouting consciousness encounters the adversary, *satanas*, and the accuser, diabolos. We find these two beings in esoteric teachings described as Ahriman and Lucifer respectively. They each have their own specific qualities and roles and if we are to develop our spiritual consciousness we must learn how to identify them. Otherwise they will kill our sprouting seed. As the roots and sprout gain strength by pushing through the soil, so we are strengthened as we resist the distractions that come from the activity of these forces. St John writes that we must conquer these challenges if our consciousness is to survive the second death.

The second death is when our soul frees itself from its purely earthly consciousness. This is a very vulnerable stage. If we are not in control when our soul begins to experience spiritual consciousness then the adversary and the accuser can take over our soul. This is where the idea of selling our soul to the devil comes from.

Think about the cultivation of plants. If we decide to plant seeds we would not dream of planting them unless the conditions were right; the right time of the year, a suitable location, the soil properly prepared and so on. Otherwise the seeds would not thrive. Do we take this much care with the development of our consciousness? How much do we know about the way our soul processes information? Do we have a working understanding about how our soul-life can be interrupted by our lower being before our higher being can respond? This has to do with all the automatic responses that are 'programmed' into us. These are our unconscious feelings, thoughts and behaviour. We could say that the synagogue represents the ritual in our being, the things we do without thinking, our habits. These are the things that we think are right, but we have never really thought about. Perhaps we do them because our mother told us to. As our new consciousness develops we see new ways of being, new ways of doing things based on our broader understanding.

To give our sprouting consciousness the best chance, we must understand what being conscious really means. We can only do this if we know how our being actually works. In my book, "I Connecting : the Soul's Quest," (Kindle edition "I AM The Mystery") there are clear descriptions of the various ways our lower and higher being interact. This book assists us to become aware of the ways in which our soul sleeps though life. It is a guide to awakening our sleeping soul, so that it can receive our I AM just like the sleeping Snow White received her Prince.

What we often fail to grasp is that our soul likes sleeping. The I AM sends down its roots into our soul and we experience tribulation. This Greek word is *thlipsis* which really means pressure. Through our inner initiative we must resist the feeling of fear from this pressure. We have begun a work and even though we feel poor – and we will because our new consciousness reveals the poverty of our old thinking patterns – we must see the rich resource that is now within our reach. It takes great courage to straddle the two consciousnesses we experience at the Smyrna point in our development. Many people make the mistake of moving too quickly into their spiritual ideas and neglecting their worldly life. This world is the stage for connecting up with I AM, otherwise why would we be here! Through our I AM, without succumbing to the pressure of its presence, we will tap into the riches that are our inheritance and not be hurt by the second death.

"I know your tribulation and your poverty (but you are rich) and the slander of those who say that they are Jews and are not, but are a synagogue of Satan. Rev 2:9

The pressure (tribulation) we experience as our Higher Self tries to educate our lower self manifests in our lives in various ways. Mainly we experience it as discomfort and dissatisfaction. If we don't understand what the pressure is then we are likely to look for an escape. We each have our own way of escaping; noise, activity, even addiction to substances, gambling, shopping, computer games, etc. These activities lower our consciousness so that we become numb and unresponsive to our I AM.

The reference to Jews is not pointing to the Jewish race per se, but to the purpose of this race. This is the race of people who could purify their blood sufficiently to produce Mary who could give birth to the first human being able to connect with his I AM and to then be a vessel for the Cosmic Christ. How many people claim to bring Christ into the world today while at the same time criticizing others who claim to be doing the same thing? This mighty Sun Being is not the exclusive property of any particular religious group just as the sun shines equally on all of us. Also, the I AM unites human beings; belief simply speaks of the different paths to it. To claim right and wrong ways belongs to a synagogue of Satan.

Do not fear what you are about to suffer. Behold, the devil is about to throw some of you into prison, that you may be tested, and for ten days you will have tribulation. Rev 2:10

Notice that the adversary, *Satanas* or Ahriman, gathers people together in a synagogue while the devil, diabolos or Lucifer the accuser, isolates people (in prison). Indeed, there may be times when we feel that we have been thrown together with a group of people or, on the other hand, we are alone, isolated from others. It doesn't matter where we find ourselves, any circumstances are good circumstances for connecting up with our I AM. It isn't a matter of saying that we are Jews, or priests, or leaders or whatever – we have to actually be what we claim. Anything less is a lie and Ahriman is the father of lies. The one who connects up with their I AM demonstrates it for all to see, it requires no explanation.

Above all, we must not fear. Fear immobilises our will making us unable to act. If we are imprisoned in our lower self we are still free to act. We still have the freedom to strive to connect up with our Higher Self. If our prison is our isolation, we can still experience the company of our Higher Self. It doesn't matter what circumstances we are in, we always have the freewill to choose the higher over the lower. This is our test. Ten days probably doesn't mean ten twenty-four hour periods. It could mean ten periods of light and darkness as we struggle to act in higher ways. It could point to a full cycle of numbers - one to nine - with ten starting a new, higher cycle.

Be faithful unto death, and I will give you the crown of life.

To be faithful, *pistos*, does not speak of blind belief but of knowing, of certainty. Those who are faithful live with a growing conviction that they have a Higher Self. Whatever dies and falls away from them, like the blossom dropping its seed, will rise to a new, higher expression. Whatever falls away from us, be it relationships, or possessions, jobs or cherished ideas - if we let them die we create new life. This is the hardest thing to do, we never want to let things die, we instinctively want to resuscitate things.

He who has an ear, let him hear what the Spirit says to the churches. He who conquers shall not be hurt by the second death.' Rev 2:11

Resuscitating is not conquering. Conquering, *nikao*, really means overcoming; to 'come over' from the past into the present. Our soul likes the cosy-bed past, that with which it is familiar. Our soul loves doing things the second time around, it can't always summon the effort required to do something for the first time, something new.

What are we conquering? Ourselves of course! If we look deeply into our souls we will notice that it contains many unsatisfied or yet-to-be satisfied wishes and longings. At some stage in our lives we saw something that we wanted but could not have. The longing lives within our soul as a force of will. What we don't often realise is that we look to the past for its satisfaction which is impossible. We must overcome the urges of the past and bring our longing into the present, using the force of it to create our future. As long as we are unable to overcome – to 'come over' to the present – we will be hurt by the second death. Within us we have the necessary reserves to experience the pressure with equanimity and to wear the crown of life with poise and grace.

Pergamum

"And to the angel of the church in Per'gamum write: 'The words of him who has the sharp two-edged sword. "'I know where you dwell, where Satan's throne is; you hold fast my name and you did not deny my faith even in the days of An'tipas my witness, my faithful one, who was killed among you, where Satan dwells. But I have a few things against you: you have some there who hold the teaching of Balaam, who taught Balak to put a stumbling block before the sons of Israel, that they might eat food sacrificed to idols and practice immorality. So you also have some who hold the teaching of the Nicola'itans. Repent then. If not, I will come to you soon and war against them with the sword of my mouth. He who has an ear, let him hear what the Spirit says to the churches. To him who conquers I will give some of the hidden manna, and I will give him a white stone, with a new name written on the stone which no one knows except him who receives it.' Rev 2:12-17

Pergamum or Pergamos means elevated or heightened. This is the third stage of growth when a plant's shoot elevates itself far above the seed having depleted the seed's substance. Our consciousness, although built on the past, must receive the future openly and with anticipation, like a plant's leaves open out like arms to the sun. If it doesn't, if it looks back to the depleted seed for its sustenance, its growth would be stunted. This would threaten the health of the bud in the next stage.

Each time we do not embrace the future the quality of our

consciousness is compromised and we are vulnerable to the opposing forces.

The sharp two-edged sword aspect of the I AM is now directing proceedings. The thing about this sword is that it can cut both ways and so its use requires skill and balance. The act of removing the sword from its sheath, and wielding it, is intricately tied to motive. How closely do we examine our motives before we act? Motives are like difficult terrain on which we must carefully place each decisive step if we are to safely ascend in consciousness.

What motivates us to do a thing? If we observe our motives closely we will soon discover that self-advantage is high on the list for some, or it is a perceived advantage for the other person. Both these motives are misguided. Our motives must spring from inner morality; from a genuine interest in other people. When our interest in the wellbeing of others is genuine we can see into their lives and experience it as our own. We become one with them and we are motivated by what is best for each of us – not one at the expense of another. This heightens our sense of responsibility because we truly see how our actions can affect others, and how they can be creative or destructive. Born out of an elevated love our motives become increasingly purified.

The one who has the sharp two-edged sword is very aware of their environment; we dwell in Satan's kingdom, where Satan's throne is. In this environment it is our struggle against the adversary that assists us to become more and more conscious. What is it that opposes us when we try to become conscious? Our subconscious impulses from the past – from this life or a past life – cause us to act habitually without thinking. We can also experience illusions about our relationship with other people, especially when we are not able to be 'at one' with them. It is important not to underestimate the forces of opposition that occupy our mind and influence us to think, feel and behave in ways that we would not if we had a stronger connection with our I AM.

Antipas is Greek for 'against all' or 'against everyone' which could refer to the one who stands alone. It is only when we can stand alone and not with the crowd that we can experience the true unity of our 'I'-being. When we see 'I' to 'I' we are the faithful witness, *marturia*. We know the other person deeply, as if we were them. We don't respond to them from the memory of a past experience, but we continually know them anew in the present moment. We also allow them to know us deeply. It takes great courage to enter fully into others, and to allow them to enter fully into us. We cannot, in fact, must not, do this unless we do it from the position of the 'I'. It takes a strong identification with our 'I' to identify any Satan-inspired motives in us or in others.

Satan refers to the myriad of Ahrimanic beings whose own development has been stymied because of wrong motives. We shouldn't be afraid to acknowledge their role in our environment. It is through these opposing forces that we progress, as a kite cannot fly unless it meets the opposing wind. One of the ways in which these Ahrimanic beings works is that they kill Antipas, they kill the one who stands alone. They oppose the individual who dares to stand out from the crowd, who has a different view of the world. These are the ones who are annihilated by all those who mindlessly follow ideas from the media, friends and misguided experts.

If our shooting consciousness is to make it to the bud stage we must hold fast to the name 'I'- "you hold fast my name and you did not deny my faith". Deny means to disown, to reject what is offered. We deny the future continually when we act out of our past ideas; and when we reject the opportunity to know others anew in the present. The 'I' does not do that. The 'I' is the future; it is our purpose for living. We must try every possible way to connect with it and be an example for others to connect to theirs. We elevate ourselves and we elevate others. With our increasingly pure motives we respect each other, never judging, never criticising, never seeking advantage but holding each human soul in our heart as something most precious.

But I have a few things against you: you have some there who hold the teaching of Balaam, who taught Balak to put a stumbling block before the sons of Israel, that they might eat food sacrificed to idols and practice immorality. So you also have some who hold the teaching of the Nicola'itans. Repent then. Rev 2:14-16

It is too easy to place these things externally; these teachers, the sons of Israel, the idols and the immorality. It is a natural response to separate ourselves from the things that are not us. Or we can even regard what is 'not us' as things being mirrored back to us. In each case our attention is directed away from our 'I'. He who has the sharp two-edged sword, this aspect of our I AM, is saying just that. Do not be distracted by all the ideas that come from the things and people that are 'not you'. Do not look to rituals, do not look to teachings from the past, and do not be distracted by other people's ideas and values; only listen to the voice of your own 'I' – "hold fast" to it.

When we decide to work out of our higher nature, this I AM, we begin to experience the power of it long before we are able to control our experience of it. It is like the gangling shoot that must strengthen if it is to support a bud. This, too, was the task of the sons of Israel, to strengthen and purify their blood so that from their race the purest one could be born.

These things are played out within our consciousness as we work towards the firm but pliable connection with our own 'I'. Of course we will be distracted; of course we will find many things to attract our attention, luring us from the main goal. If we read the story of Balaam and King Balak we see that the king tried to impose his will on Balaam but Balaam did whatever he liked. So within our consciousness we should be on alert for the forces that try to overrule us, and the forces that rebel in our soul.

At this stage in the evolution of consciousness we are able to become more conscious of our soul's activity. At the same time, more and more philosophies try to teach us to influence this activity in an unnatural way. Instead of encouraging us to become more conscious of our soul's processes, these philosophies give us tricks to manipulate our soul. Those who can manipulate their soul best are those whose connection with their 'I' is just beginning, they are drunk on the power of it and this results in immorality, *porneuo* – fornication. Fornication happens when the wrong soul forces have intercourse with each other.

There are many ways that this can happen. For instance, if we are making a decision to do something; we begin by infusing our thoughts with a certain amount of feeling to confirm that our thoughts are right. But if will enters into the process too soon we can act prematurely. If strong feelings arise within us which 'fornicate' with our will we can act without thinking.

These are the stumbling blocks that prevent us from purifying our soul so that our 'I' can take its rightful place in our being. It is a process; it can't happen at once just as a seed cannot burst into flower.

Since the Nicola'itans are mentioned again we are again warned to become more aware of how we use our will. Within our soul we are least conscious of our will. Our will lurks below our consciousness influencing our thoughts and feelings. We only become aware of the after we have acted, when we see the results of the use of our will. For instance, if we have imposed this will on others by criticising them or when we want them to agree with us, or when we judge them and think that they should feel, think or act differently. It is not just a matter of refraining from saying these things; it is a matter of refraining from even thinking these things. Each time we think critical thoughts about a person it has an effect on them and an effect on us - a damaging effect. This too is immorality. For morality is found in our ability to experience the other person as if they were us. We only need to realise that if we react to criticism, then obviously so will they.

"Repent then." Repent, *metanoeo*, literally means to perceive afterwards. It implies that we can see the results of our actions before we act. This assists us to change the way we act, think, and feel because we see the after effects. Therefore, we can cut short any injurious thoughts or feelings about others with the sharp two-edged sword. This will contribute to the purification of our soul and assist the birthing process of the 'I'.

But I have a few things against you: you have some there who hold the teaching of Balaam, who taught Balak to put a stumbling block before the sons of Israel, that they might eat food sacrificed to idols and practice immorality. So you also have some who hold the teaching of the Nicola'itans. Repent then. If not, I will come to you soon and war against them with the sword of my mouth. He who has an ear, let him hear what the Spirit says to the churches. To him who conquers I will give some of the hidden manna, and I will give him a white stone, with a new name written on the stone which no one knows except him who receives it.' Rev 2:14-17

Pergamum, representing the vibrant shoot stage in the growth of our consciousness, speaks to us of the energetic forces that we must now harness to create the bud and bloom. These are forces of will in our being which underlie our thinking and feeling. How purposefully are we directing these forces? We are at a stage in the evolution of our consciousness where forces are being freed up to enable us to experience our I AM in our earthly being. We do this first of all by connecting with its earthly expression, the 'I'.

Our modern way of life takes care of many things that in the past we had to do manually. Now we are free to use those forces to develop our higher consciousness. Yet so often this freedom results in dissatisfaction with life. The void is filled with physical thrills like drugs, alcohol, sport, gambling etc. instead of experiencing the thrill, the quickening, that comes from awareness that we are an 'I' in the process of connecting with our Real Self, our I AM.

Furthermore, we must use these newly available forces to create a surplus. The shoot is not just working towards being a beautiful shoot. It must create a surplus of forces that will be available for the bud. What surplus are we creating for the future? We are constantly reminded of how we are depleting our physical resources. Is this just an outer sign of our inability to create surplus spiritual resources for the future? Just as we don't see the forces that are being created for the bud, so we don't realise that it is a spiritual substance we must create upon which our future depends.

The way we waste these resources is placed clearly before us in the letter to Pergamum. We listen to false prophets; the Balaams of this world who tell us that how to find health, happiness and wealth effortlessly. Those who tell us that we can have whatever we want right now if we just sign up for easy (high interest) credit. They distract us from the wise use of our surplus growth forces which in turn affects the substance available for the future bud.

Balak is the emptier, the one who empties our mind so that we don't have to be bothered with the tiresome effort of thinking new consciousness-changing thoughts. Balak encourages us to waste our resources. This surplus energy can be experienced as sexual energy which we must use wisely and creatively and not always for sexual activity.

Nicola'itans will always encourage us to use our will in the wrong areas. Instead of infusing our thinking and feeling with the energy necessary to become more conscious, the Nicola'itans will show us ways of using our will, and they are many. One area that we see more frequently is public protesting. How often is this kind of exhibitionistic behaviour motivated by ego and the feeling of power? Anger is the quickest way to vent ourselves of the surplus will forces. The most effective way of protesting is to change our own consciousness. The more people who do that the more quickly dignity and sanity will be restored to all areas of life.

At this stage of the development of our consciousness many things are weighed in the balance. We can act out of our Higher Self one minute, and then in the next minute the habits of our lower self take over. It requires great vigilance to keep our automatic responses quiet. Our Higher Self is saying: Well, you have put up your hand to take control of your lower self, and if you don't keep up the effort, "I will come to you – not soon but *tachu* which means quickly or swiftly, - and war against them (those lower impulses) with the sword of my mouth". If we thought it was painful to change our consciousness ourselves, imagine how painful it will be to have it changed for us with the sword!

The image of the sword reminds us of the Archangel Michael who draws his sword against the dragon. Michael represents our will-filled thoughts; thinking that is energised and elevated above the dragon who always tries to devour it. These forces drag-on us; they are a gravitational force anchoring us to a material outlook, preventing us from elevating our thinking.

These words to the ekklesia in Pergamum are a reminder that this is not a game. We have a responsibility to individually and energetically work at becoming more conscious. Then we won't be tricked into thinking that global warming will destroy the world. We will know that our lazy thinking and habitual feelings, along with our unconscious will, can be far more destructive than global warming – mostly to ourselves. If these ideas are true they will echo in our inner ear and we will repent, we will change, and we will use the precious resources within us so that the world will also change.

Repent then. If not, I will come to you soon and war against them with the sword of my mouth. He who has an ear, let him hear what the Spirit says to the churches. To him who conquers I will give some of the hidden manna, and I will give him a white stone, with a new name written on the stone which no one knows except him who receives it.' Rev 2:16-17

As we prepare ourselves to receive our I AM consciously it is as if we are preparing our earthly being to be the scabbard for the sharp two-edged sword. Imagine the consequences if this scabbard is not a good fit. This preparation can also be compared with war, or at least the possibility of war. This war arises because to gain access to a greater sense of self we must experience selfishness.

At the same time this experience of self is liberating – we are released from universal consciousness. We are individuated. Through this experience of the lower, the higher is revealed to us. Also, as we experience being separate from what is outside us, the inner is revealed to us. A pattern emerges here forming the symbol of the cross. Note well that the lower and the outer are means to an end.

This process of releasing from the universal to the individual is our greatest challenge. We are likely to underestimate it. Are we up to embracing this newfound freedom? Now that we are not compelled to love others just because they are in our group, can we freely choose to love them? Are we able to make the choice to love, or do we, through fear, hate? If we hate, and there is much more hate in our soul than we realise, then war is the result. This hate, which becomes the catalyst for war, really arises out of fear. Without the security of the group, without the security of experiencing the universal consciousness, and before we connect fully with our I AM, this earth can be a scary place. We have two choices; embrace the process or resist it.

Our initial experience of this individuation is that we inclined to draw things and ideas to ourselves instead of sharing. It is like amassing the spoils of war. However, this feeling of self-centeredness is a good sign, but it should remain just that, a sign. Yet, we see acts of gross selfishness everywhere today. We can observe extremes in this behaviour wherever we look. For instance, the number of hit-and-run drivers is on the increase. It is beyond belief that a human being would not stop and offer assistance to fellow human being.

Does this suggest that some people are experiencing their I AM unconsciously? They feel invincible yet at the same time they are cowardly and secretive. They seem not to have developed the strength and the courage to stand in any circumstance. This invincibility, coupled with cowardice and trickery, is a very nasty war to engage in. Is this the work of the other edge of the sword?

As our 'I' integrates with the rest of our being it becomes a cause that we feel impelled to take up. Can we make it a worthy cause? It should not become a 'me-against-the-world' war. It is not about warring but rather it is about making choices so that we become more conscious of this new dimension of our being. At the same time we must acknowledge that others are in this same process. This can bring us into conflict with them, or bring about a new form of companionship.

The two-edged-swordness of it is that we are drawing things to ourselves while at the same time encountering others drawing things to themselves. Only through the successful integration of our 'I' do we achieve the independence and dignity which renders the battle unnecessary. This would suggest that each time we have the 'battle' experience we should be very watchful not to engage in it for that would mean our lower impulses are trespassing on our higher ones. How does this manifest? It manifests each time we think that our ideas are the best, each time we think that we have reached a full understanding of something and each time we want to convince others to see things our way. We can also recognise it when we don't want to be a companion to others. When we see 'I' to 'I' new developments are always welcome.

Then we are the conquering and receiving the hidden manna - which is a perpetual inner process. This manna points to the spirit part of our body-soul-spirit being. Through our own effort we must develop it and allow it to mature. As we strive to resist being involved in the battle, we refine the forces in our being that nourish us and assist our progress. This manna is a reward for a job well done. It is hidden because we never know when it is going to kick in. When it does kick in it ensures that we stop to render assistance to a fellow-human being even if their injury was caused by our own inattentiveness – and that includes spiritual injuries.

This manna is a community-building substance. It is multiplied by the presence of love. There is no coercion to love others nor do we seek to bind others to us. We love – agape - others freely, whether they love us or not. Indeed, we may not like them, especially if they have been trying to engage us in the battle that we have just managed to resist, but we simply love them as fellow human beings. To be at one with our own 'I' means that we can be at one with the 'I' of others. The 'I' dissolves difference. Those who reject the love that is offered in this way make the choice for separation; the abyss.

If we are conquerors then we earn the right to consciously call ourselves 'I', this name that only we can use when we refer to ourselves. We cannot say 'I' and mean someone else. Hence it is "a new name written on the stone which no one knows except him who receives it." The stone speaks of inner mastery; white indicates purity. Receiving a new name is a sign of attainment; as Abram became Abraham and Saul became Paul.

So it is up to us to resist the war; to resist the very real temptation of pulling things toward us as well as the inclination to push things away from us. This new name 'I' is very powerful and if we can stand in it we will be at one with ourselves and with others.

Thyatira

"And to the angel of the church in Thyati'ra write: 'The words of the Son of God, who has eyes like a flame of fire, and whose feet are like burnished bronze. "'I know your works, your love and faith and service and patient endurance, and that your latter works exceed the first. But I have this against you, that you tolerate the woman Jez'ebel, who calls herself a prophetess and is teaching and beguiling my servants to practice immorality and to eat food sacrificed to idols. I gave her time to repent, but she refuses to repent of her immorality. Behold, I will throw her on a sickbed, and those who commit adultery with her I will throw into great tribulation, unless they repent of her doings; and I will strike her children dead. And all the churches shall know that I am he who searches mind and heart, and I will give to each of you as your works deserve. But to the rest of you in Thyati'ra, who do not hold this teaching, who have not learned what some call the deep things of Satan, to you I say, I do not lay upon you any other burden; only hold fast what you have, until I come. He who conquers and who keeps my works until the end, I will give him power over the nations, and he shall rule them with a rod

of iron, as when earthen pots are broken in pieces, even as I myself have received power from my Father; and I will give him the morning star. He who has an ear, let him hear what the Spirit says to the churches.' Rev 2:18-29

The fourth church, *ekklesia*, is in Thyatira. This is the halfway mark in this consciousness-changing process. It is the pivotal point in the lifecycle; there are three stages either side of it. Thyatira was a city famous for the craft of dying and particularly for its purple dye. In the process of dying there is the suggestion of baptism, both are processes of change. Purple is also said to be a symbol of change. It is interesting that the catchcry of John the Baptist was "Repent". He called us to re-think our understanding, and think ahead, because conditions had changed.

In those days came John the Baptist, preaching in the wilderness of Judea, "Repent, for the kingdom of heaven is at hand." Mt 3:1-2

When Jesus had sufficiently prepared himself it was to John the Baptist that he went to be baptised. This baptism marks the entry of the Cosmic Christ, the mighty Sun God, into the being of Jesus. Therefore the Thyatira stage signals that we have become sufficiently conscious in our 'I' being that we are ready to receive the Christ Impulse into our consciousness.

This is confirmed because John announces that these are the words from the Son of God who is the Christ. If we compare this to the fourth stage in the lifecycle of a plant we also see that something significant is taking place. If the plant is sufficiently strong it stops producing leaves and instead starts to produce the calyx which will support the bud and the petals of the flower. The signal for this to happen is an increased amount of sunlight. In our consciousness, the light of Christ the Sun God assists us to become ever more conscious – enlightened.

This presence of Christ in our consciousness also means that our sight becomes a flame. The light of the sun which enables us to see now turns into a flame. We know that sunlight can become a flame in the presence of a magnifying glass. So our experiences are magnified and we will see everything in more detail. This may not be so comfortable because we may see things that we don't really want to look at. If we start to see things in more detail we also need to have increased understanding. This could be why "the Son of God, has eyes like a flame of fire, and feet (which are under our standing) like burnished bronze." At this level, understanding certainly needs to be as refined as feet of burnished brass.

So this description is a metaphor for what happens within our being as we become increasingly conscious and as we are able to work with the Christ Impulse that awakens within us. Through simple descriptions like 'eyes of flame' and 'feet of brass' we can build powerful images of what to expect on this path of development. We can build on these images if we delve deeper and find out more, for instance, about brass. Brass is an alloy, a combination, of copper and zinc; bronze is an alloy of copper and tin. The addition of zinc or tin hardens the copper while retaining its softness so that it was easily shaped. Each of these metals is formed through smelting at various temperatures. They are refined, usually in clay pots. This could explain why there is mention of breaking earthen pots into pieces at the end of this passage. It isn't enough to know these facts; we also need to use the knowledge to build vivid pictures that assist in the refining of our own consciousness.

The great lesson spelt out very clearly here is that once our consciousness works through our Higher Self we must not revert back to the habitual, familiar behaviour of our lower self. It is very tempting, once we have tasted the freedom and power of our Higher Self to try to drag it down into our old way of life. If we understand that what we experience through our Higher Self can make us feel insecure this knowledge will mean that we will be less inclined to seek refuge in our lower self. At the same time, when we bring the experience of our Higher Self into our lower self we must learn to recognise that our ego is enhanced and often over inflated. It is these changes in our consciousness that we must become more aware of.

Furthermore, we can even stir up superseded abilities that served earlier stages of our development and this is why Jezebel is mentioned. Jezebel is our psychic nature; those premonitions we get which we can't really think through. Those gut feelings that seem to guide many of our decisions. The new consciousness is not about fuzzy premonitions or gut feelings, it is about clear thinking. Thinking that can freely explore new ideas. Thinking that knows, thinking that has a refined understanding and can explain in simple terms the magnified details it sees.

This is why the Son of God says to us, "'I know your works, your love and faith and service and patient endurance, and that your latter works exceed the first." It takes this much effort to produce the bud which will open into a magnificent blossom in the next stage. It is up to us to ensure that we produce blossoms that can create the healthiest possible seeds for our next cycle of development.

'I know your works, your love and faith and service (ministry) and patient endurance, and that your latter (last) works exceed the first. But I have this against you, that you tolerate the woman Jez'ebel, who calls herself a prophetess and is teaching and beguiling (deceives) my servants (slaves) to practice immorality (commit fornication) and to eat food sacrificed to idols (eat idol sacrifices). I gave her time to repent, but she refuses to repent of her immorality (fornication). Behold, I will throw her on a sickbed (bed), and those who commit adultery with her I will throw into great tribulation (affliction), unless they repent of her doings (works); and I will strike her children dead (kill with death). Rev 2:19-23

Quite a few words in this passage can be differently translated to assist us to understand the warnings given by the Son of God. The Son of God, Christ, is speaking to those who are becoming the Son of Man - those who are allowing their Higher Self to educate their lower self. These are the ones who are making themselves priests. This word translated as service is *diakonia* which means ministry. Part of this process means that we are ministering within ourselves - seeing to our own spiritual needs. Even though we are progressing, doing better than when we began, it is clearly not enough just to do good works. In fact, what is promoted as good, or made out to be good, can often be the opposite -especially the so-called good works espoused in our modern culture.

The only way we can know what is good is to become conscious. Particularly we must become conscious of who (or what) we are in bed with. When we are in bed with someone or something we lose our individuality. The boundaries between what is 'me' and what is 'us' become blurred. At the core of these relationships we are dealing with the will, the least conscious of our three basic soul functions, thinking, feeling and will.

In our physical body, will is that unconscious force that keeps us alive. This force is the trigger for us to eat and drink, to breathe, to keep our body at the right temperature and that urges us to reproduce and so on. In our soul the will forces govern our actions and behaviour. In our spirit they become forces of goodwill, the trigger for us to act for the benefit of all. Our works, *erga*, can only be expressed through the use of our will.

This brings us back to the motives that lie behind our will. Our last works may well exceed our first but is that enough? The words spoken by the Son of God, whose magnified vision, and firm understanding, reveals in great detail our inner motivations. We can be so busy thinking we are doing the right thing only to discover that what we do is wrong for this stage of evolution.

For everything there is a season, and a time for every matter under heaven: a time to be born, and a time to die; a time to plant, and a time to pluck up what is planted; a time to kill, and a time to heal; a time to break down, and a time to build up; Ec 3:1-3

How on earth are we to know whether to pluck or plant if we are not conscious? Everywhere in the world there is a lack of patience. When we ignore the right 'season', when we act in the wrong time or place, we feed the hindering forces, those forces within us which seek to distract us and prevent us from becoming conscious. Jezebel represents these unconscious inclinations that slumber within every human being. At its worst it is subhuman behaviour. It is not accurate to say that human beings can act like animals because animals usually act with more dignity than an unconscious subhuman being.

Those who are in bed (the Greek does not say sickbed) with Jezebel are those who abase themselves. They lack the sense of dignity for themselves or for others. This is the degradation of the human spirit. Instead of the body being used for self-development, it is used for self-gratification.

This possibility is an ever present potential within us and it is up to us to keep it in check. Only we can purify these potentials within us – this is the work. It is the striving for the result, not the result itself, that matters. This is why we read the unusual words "unless they repent of her doings" Jezebel's doings, her *ergon*, her works, exist within us. It is up to us to dignify them, not succumb to them. She won't change; she is just doing her job by making it possible for us to make the choice. That is true freedom.

Jezebel is also the abuse in our society, abuse of children, verbally and sexually, abuse of each other's energy, the absence of awe and respect for our fellow human beings, the manipulation, the self-seeking egoism – all of which is there simply to be resisted through our works. Removal of the temptations is no solution; that would make us even more unconscious. What is within us is there to be conquered.

Her children, *tekna*, what she produces, will be killed with death (a more accurate translation) which means that they will be rendered unconscious. This indicates that there are unconscious forces within us that have no possibility of becoming conscious. They are like twilight forces which try to influence our actions. They trick us into judging as good what is really bad. They distract us from the essential truth that human life is sacred. Through a choice of free will we can meet every person with awe and reverence. After all, isn't that how we want others to meet us?

And all the churches shall know that I am he who searches mind and heart, and I will give to each of you as your works deserve. But to the rest of you in Thyati'ra, who do not hold this teaching, who have not learned what some call the deep things of Satan, to you I say, I do not lay upon you any other burden; only hold fast what you have, until I come.' Rev 2:23-25

Our works are our effort to become conscious. We cannot say that we will become more conscious and then not do the work, thinking that no one will really know what goes on within us. "I am he who searches mind and heart", John writes. All the stages of growth within our consciousness are scrutinised by "I am", *ego eimi*, our I AM. The consequences are grave if we say "yes, but ..." or "no, but ...". This is an open invitation to the adversary, the Ahrimanic beings, to darken our consciousness. St Matthew's Gospel speaks about this.

Let what you say be simply 'Yes' or 'No'; anything more than this comes from evil. Mt 5:37

This is exactly what we see every day in the media, especially in politics and public relations spin. What effect does it have on our psyche when, for example, the senior management of toy-making corporation Mattel, forced to recall millions of toys that endanger children's lives, say to us through the media, "We have our arms around the problem"? Does each parent feel as if Mattel is hugging their child? Where are Mattel's priorities? - With the welfare of the children or the welfare of their company and its shareholders? We can then ask, what is their real contribution to the future - our children are the future! Do we cooperate with the spin or do we say, "No, I will not be your customer".

This situation masks the real problem which is a lack of understanding about reincarnation and karma. Too many people see their lives as a one-off event. Some people do think about the future in terms of what they create for their children, but very few people understand that we create the future that we ourselves will occupy when we reincarnate. This also means that the culture we live in today is the result of our own actions in previous lives.

It changes our outlook if we consider that our life has sprung from the seed we created in a previous century. It can be a life changing process to consider what kind of seed are we creating for the future? Our works, the things we put our energy into, can be quite different when we cease to regard our lives as disposable. In fact, it is our works that are recyclable. Our works, what we put our effort and energy into each day, create our future.

If we do not make the effort to understand how it might be possible for our soul and spirit to incarnate in various physical bodies over time then we are involved with the deep things of Satan. *Satana* is the lord of lies, and the biggest lie is that we only live once.

Most of us will probably admit that we are flying a bit blind when we say that we accept the notion of having lived on earth in other bodies, in other countries and circumstances. Most of us certainly do not know what our next life holds in store for us. But if we can "hold what we have" – the Greek does not say "till I come" - if we can hold within us the fruits of our works so that in the future, or in our next life, when we are more conscious, we will see more clearly.

What we don't always understand is that a small step forward in consciousness can often mean a few steps back. We don't keep up the effort. We get distracted and this modern world is a master of distraction. The biggest distractions of all are the personal development techniques that promise to do the work for us – often in one weekend! Only we can do the work and the work can only be done within us in all aspects of our daily life. Not in a flash here and there, but in a sustained way. We say "yes" and our I AM can see that we mean it.

When we start to succeed at this then we hear the tender words, "I do not lay upon you any other burden". All you have to do is just hold what you have, hold what you have developed in yourself so far.

Being told to hold what we have also means that there is the possibility of not holding it. Our works are precious and we must be aware that what we have produced could be removed from us. The Ahrimanic beings are always looking for opportunities to take away the fruits of our works. They succeed, for instance, when we are unconscious of the lies surrounding us. It isn't about fighting the lies, or being cynical, but it is about being aware of them and not letting them take away our fruits. We are like the bud in all its possibility waiting for the right conditions to reveal its full bloom.

He who conquers and who keeps my works until the end, I will give him power over the nations, and he shall rule them with a rod of iron, as when earthen pots are broken in pieces, even as I myself have received power from my Father; and I will give him the morning star. He who has an ear, let him hear what the Spirit says to the churches.' Rev 2:26-29

If these words are expressed a little differently another image arises. One that reveals how in overcoming our lower nature we are like a shepherd watching over – keeping – the works that have been achieved so far. It does not say "rule with a rod of iron" but rather 'shepherd with an iron staff'.

Accompanying this image is the tenderness in Christ's words as he encourages us to be patient in the midst of incredible change. We need only look at a plant as it produces a bud to understand the magnitude of change that takes place at this stage. This plant has been producing green leaf after green leaf and then suddenly there is an inner thickening and instead of green leaves coloured petals begin to form. This is a deeply mysterious process and Christ, like a gentle gardener, is encouraging us to hang on tight, that all will be revealed.

If we can do this he says he will give us power- *exousia* - over our nations, *ethnon*. The various regions of our soul, where thinking, feeling and willing take place, are nations within us. Around the world we can observe the ethnicity of people in different countries and see that they have certain soul moods. Some nationalities have a strong feeling nature, others lean more towards thinking and others are more disposed to action.

In our spiritual development we are striving to connect with our 'I' so that it can have greater power in our 'nations', our thinking, feeling and will – without this connection these faculties are habitual and often unconscious. It is through the involvement of our 'I' in our soul that we can use these faculties with more awareness. We express ourselves more globally through our 'I' and more locally and ethnically through our soul.

This power *exousia* we will receive, *exousia* in Greek is Elohim in Hebrew, the word used in Genesis translated as God. This is a creative power that arises within us when all these things are in place; the overcoming, the shepherding, the holding of the works achieved thus far, the global outlook, the ability to use of the iron staff and so on.

True creation is a process of dying and becoming just as the plant must die to produce the seed to become a new plant. How willing are we to allow things to die away within us so that something new can arise? Only when we can do this will we experience the *exousia* within us. This is a mighty, creative power that can make all things new (Rev 21:5).

We must ask ourselves whether we can withstand the refining process. Can the staff of iron be forged within us? When each refining stage is complete will we allow the clay pots to be destroyed? What are these vessels within us? Are they the containers in which we keep our preconceived ideas, our judgment, our biases, our automatic behaviour, our inability to stick to our word, our reluctance to listen to others, our laziness and so on?

This text in The Revelation echoes the words of David in Psalm

2

I will tell of the decree of the Lord: He said to me, "You are my son; today I have begotten you. Ask of me, and I will make the nations your heritage, and the ends of the earth your possession. You shall break them with a rod of iron, and dash them in pieces like a potter's vessel." Psalm 2:7-9

In The Revelation we find some additional words - "even as I myself have received power from my Father; and I will give him the morning star." The word 'power' is not in the Greek; it could actually be: even as I have received shepherding from my father. Can we be the good shepherd spoken of in Jn 10:11?

If we can we will receive the morning star. At the end of The Revelation we read that Jesus is this morning star.

"I Jesus have sent my angel to you with this testimony for the churches. I am the root and the offspring of David, the bright morning star." Rev 22:16

Can this be the symbol of purity that we need before we can receive Christ into ourselves? Jesus, born of virgin purity, was the first one to connect fully with his I AM and then to receive the full power of the Christ Impulse. This is a truly shattering process and we will certainly need the support of the iron staff. Then the brilliance of the morning star will shine from us to inspire others on their path.

CHAPTER THREE

Sardis

"And to the angel of the church in Sardis write: 'The words of him who has the seven spirits of God and the seven stars. "'I know your works; you have the name of being alive, and you are dead. Awake, and strengthen what remains and is on the point of death, for I have not found your works perfect in the sight of my God. Remember then what you received and heard; keep that, and repent. If you will not awake, I will come like a thief, and you will not know at what hour I will come upon you. Yet you have still a few names in Sardis, people who have not soiled their garments; and they shall walk with me in white, for they are worthy. He who conquers shall be clad thus in white garments, and I will not blot his name out of the book of life; I will confess his name before my Father and before his angels. He who has an ear, let him hear what the Spirit says to the churches.' Rev 3:1-6

Whenever we grow a plant, even though we usually know what kind of flower it will have, there is always wonder associated with our first glimpse of the bloom. This sense of wonder should be part of the fifth stage in the development of our consciousness - the Sardis stage. Here we reach a culmination; we are given the opportunity to experience the fruits of our labour. The thing about becoming more conscious is that we immediately realise just how unconscious we are. This should not discourage us.

On the other hand, when we bloom we can also be tempted to think that we have achieved our goal and this would be why the mighty being says "you have the name of being alive, and you are dead." Oh, thanks a lot! After all that effort, pushing out of the seed, shooting and rooting, strengthening the stalk and producing beautiful leaves, followed by a healthy bud which has finally bloomed we are told that we are only pretending to be alive. Yet we must remember that it is the work that is the point of it all. The bloom is not the point of it all; the bloom, although a thing of beauty, simply produces seeds for the next stage of development.

How often do we get discouraged on this path of development that we walk? How often are we disappointed with our own progress? The pain of failure, the sadness and disappointment only intensifies as we become more conscious simply because we can see so much more. This is why the symbol of the church is used. It doesn't mean a church building it means the ekklesia, the body of forces and impulses that constitute the being of Christ. Our only comfort will come from the firsthand experience of this ekklesia. We are in it, and it is in us. This is what we must awake to. Whenever we experience disappointment, pain or alarm in our soul we must use our imagination to become awake to the ekklesia that we are part of.

We can begin this process by becoming aware of how we view our physical environment. As long as we only see the sharp outline of everything in this physical world we remain asleep to all the spiritual forces that work within everything around us. As long as we only see the flower in all its glory we don't see exactly what forces were at work to produce it. Nor do we see the forces at work producing the seed for the next stage. We can agree that they must be there, these forces of growth, shape, size, smell and colour but as long as we see only the flower we do not really understand how it got to this stage and where it is headed - the same with our own consciousness.

Our consciousness remains dead while we are dead to the way our feelings rise up and hold us in their grip. Our consciousness remains dead when we are continually bothered by a thought that will not go away. When we cannot use our will to think different thoughts and to guide our feelings differently, we are dead. The plethora of advice about tricking our consciousness with mantras or meditations usually provides temporary results. The only solution for lasting change is to become aware of our relationship with our I AM. It is our Higher Self that must educate our lower self, not our lower self engaging in tips and tricks. Only through our I AM can we truly live, without this connection we are dead.

Awake, and strengthen what remains and is on the point of death Rev 3:2

What remains is the seed. We can only strengthen it if we are awake, conscious. This word awake in Greek is *gregoreo* and it means more than being awake, it means to be watchful, to be vigilant. At this stage in human evolution we are straddling two consciousnesses; our earthly every day consciousness and our developing spiritual consciousness. If our works are fruitful then our awareness is heightened. So we can become aware of the motives of others, for instance, which can be hard to handle at times.

When our I AM is able to engage our consciousness we realise that our thinking, feeling and will stop functioning automatically, intertwined with each other out of habit. Now they begin to act alone and it is up to us to combine them according to each situation we are in. This requires great vigilance. In the early stages we can, for instance, become overly sensitive. We can be shocked at some of the thoughts that go through our own mind. We can also be hit by the harshness of some people's words. They may speak the way they have always spoken but we are now more sensitive to what lies behind their words and it can be quite a shock.

In our vigilance we become watchful of the impact that our inner thoughts as well as our words and actions have on ourselves and also on others. Do we give life or are we destructive? We must now accept full responsibility for ourselves; although we are not "perfect in the sight of God" we must at least know that we have potential. Then we have wonder and awe for the flowers that bloom in all the people around us – some blooms maybe small, others maybe bigger and brighter, but they are all blooms worthy of our appreciation. When we experience this we experience how we are all part of the ekklesia which is the body of Christ.

"And to the angel of the church in Sardis write: 'The words of him who has the seven spirits of God and the seven stars.

"'I know your works; you have the name of being alive, and you are dead. Awake, and strengthen what remains and is on the point of death, for I have not found your works perfect in the sight of my God. Remember then what you received and heard; keep that, and repent. Rev 3:1-3

The name Sardis could be derived from the Persian word *sered* which means yellowish-red, i.e. orange, the colour of the sun. It could also be named after *sardion*, a precious stone used to make engravings and seals. Sardis was a wealthy centre of trade famous for manufacturing woollen cloth and carpets.

This letter, like all the others, is written to the *angelos*, the messenger. The angel delivers spiritual images to us in the hope that we can make some sense of them with our earthly consciousness. We could compare this to our dreams which can sometimes have strange images which make sense during the dream but when we awake make no sense. This is part of the new consciousness that we are beginning to experience. However, no longer can we rely on dreamy images, now we must think rigorously to unravel the images that come to us, day or night, so that we can make sense of the future.

It isn't difficult to see that Sardis has a direct connection to the present time. Death is all around us; the earth itself seems to be in the throes of dying. While at the same time a new spiritual awareness is rising up in some people. The sign of major change can be found when the concept of what is 'normal' is continually redefined.

The message the angel brings to our consciousness is from "him who has the seven spirits of God and the seven stars." The seven spirits of God, which we previously identified as the heavenly beings called Elohim can also be regarded as the seven different areas of our own being. These are our physical body; the life-force which sustains our body and gives it shape, our etheric; the centre of motion and emotion which when refined forms our soul, our astral; then the three levels of our spirit which are formed when we refine the former three to spiritual capacities which

Rudolf Steiner and others refer to as Spirit Self, Life Spirit and Spirit Man. The seventh component is our 'I' striving to become the captain of the ship. The highest expression of this 'I' is the I AM - "him who has the seven spirits of God and the seven stars."

In Rev 1:20 we were told that the seven stars refer to the angels. When our I AM becomes active in our soul and spiritualises our earthly expression these angels represent a connectivity between our soul and our spirit. When these messengers are at work in our being our thinking comes to life and we are able to receive new ideas and understanding. Our feelings become deeper and more objective, and we judge less by more freely accepting the choices others make.

These concepts can be difficult to understand unless we create our own images for them. It is the angels who assist us to create the imaginations necessary to make sense of what is happening in our consciousness. Never before in the history of mankind has it been so crucial to understand our own consciousness.

Essentially what is happening is that we are waking up and at the same time we are dying – as if we are the living dead. Our spiritual consciousness is coming to life and our earthly consciousness is dying. This is the life-filled bloom containing the seed-producing death forces. We must come to terms with this process as it occurs in our consciousness. As our spiritual understanding grows, gradually we allow our old concepts to die (hopefully). This does not mean that we should stop our normal conversations and only speak in terms of esoteric principles; this would not be helpful in our daily life. This is a delicate process and we must maintain a continual balance.

If we examine this process a little more closely we see that what dies is the habitual entwining of our thinking, feeling and will. They free themselves from each other so that we can combine them differently. This means that instead of jumping to our usual conclusions we will see different perspectives.

There is a watch point however. When thinking, feeling and will operate independently of each other we not only have the freedom to unite them ourselves to suit each situation, we must unite them. If we do not then we will experience mental lapses. Indeed, the rise of mental problems today can be directly linked to this and therapists who assist their patients to consciously unite their thoughts, feelings and intentions / actions will have great success.

"Remember then what you received and heard; keep that, and repent." Rev 3:3

This encouragement relates directly to our developing spiritual capacities.

Remember: Re-membering our images means that we combine them differently. This is the work of our spiritual Imagination as our Spirit Self comes to life. When we control our thinking we can create images which lead us to new understanding and this raises our feelings from a lower dreaminess to a higher conscious level.

Receive: We allow spiritual Intuitions to enter into us through the activity of our highest spiritual capacity – Spirit Man. We free up our will (freewill) and become open to new possibilities. We are able to enter into the unfamiliar because we can surrender our will like an open flower receives the pollinating bees.

Hear: New ideas, having gained entrance to our consciousness now echo within us as spiritual Inspiration. Our Life Spirit stirs and we inspire and merge within us this new 'air'. This inspiration is not a primitive premonition; this is the capacity for inner hearing our thought processes become more mobile.

Then we must "keep that", we must make it a new habit, not a fleeting experience. Unlike old habits which occur unconsciously, now we are conscious of the new spiritual activity within us and we repent – we change.

Our deep, and often unconscious, aspiration is to be like this being "who has the seven spirits of God and the seven stars." Through cycle after cycle we experience the becoming and dying, the forging and refining that contributes to our being fully conscious one day.

If you will not awake, I will come like a thief, and you will not know at what hour I will come upon you. Yet you have still a few names in Sardis, people who have not soiled their garments; and they shall walk with me in white, for they are worthy. He who conquers shall be clad thus in white garments, and I will not blot his name out of the book of life; I will confess his name before my Father and before his angels. He who has an ear, let him hear what the Spirit says to the churches.' Rev 3:3-6

If we do not watch, *gregoreo*, Christ will come like a thief. It seems such a strange metaphor to use when describing how we will experience the presence of Christ. Alfred Heidenreich in "The Book of Revelation" suggests a different translation for this passage. Change your thinking (repent) and watch otherwise you will not "have known when I have come". The presence of Christ will pass you by. "The effect on your own life will be as if a thief has been and has stolen something, because you will have missed an opportunity." Imagine discovering that we had woken up too late!

The thieves are everywhere; they are the distracting ones, those who do not want us to experience the indwelling Christ. They fill us with abstract thoughts, meaningless activities and useless feelings. They fill us with false ideas so that we either get lost in the world or lost in other people and we cannot find our true self.

Another way of looking at these verses is to consider that perhaps Christ must come like a thief to steal away from us all that is incompatible with his presence; all that is egotistical, judgmental and opinionated within us; all those deadening things within us which cannot exist in the presence of pure love.

Coming like a thief could also be a reference to the second coming which is not a physical event but an event that is difficult to see. It is our task to develop the ability to see the life-force in which Christ will appear. We can only develop the inner sight necessary to "watch" by awakening to our Higher Self.

On the other hand, if Christ came openly to us perhaps we would reject him. Could we bear the pain of what he must remove from us? Those precious possessions that we hoard in our soul, those private thoughts, feelings and intentions that we think are nobody's business yet cause as much damage as they would if we expressed them openly.

To watch means to be attentive. It means that we are able to focus, to concentrate and to pay attention to all the forces in and around us; benevolent and malevolent. In our attentiveness we can keep them in balance. We do not compromise our values and we can stand in our discomfort.

To be a fully attentive does require courage. For when we see the detail we also need the courage to look at it. Especially in our relationships with all the people we encounter daily. This level of watchfulness means that we can find our way into the inner being of others and be with them where they are instead of wanting them to be with us where we are.

Our ability to be attentive and to be with others in this way gives us a name, a worthy reputation. People hold us in high regard because we are able to keep our garments, the various areas of our being, pure. The cleansing of our lower self produces light. Other people can experience this, even if they can't see it. They sense that our motives are pure, that we are trustworthy and dependable.

This purity can only come from being conscious of how we use feelings, thoughts and intentions. We must, with precision, be able to control these functions in our soul. Then we can be objective in all our experiences, not in a cold way or in a sentimental way, but in a genuine and heartfelt way. When we enter into situations objectively and courageously others will feel soothed. Then we have a name for being able to raise situations up to a higher level so that others can experience themselves in a higher way.

To be able to experience true community with others, to be able to stand in all the knowledge that is contained in the book of life, this is the present challenge for each human being. In our present culture many people are isolated from each other, even when they are together. It is as if they live in a book of death; the contribution they make is not worth recording. Each human being must fearlessly ask, "How can I contribute? What can I contribute?" Then their deeds will be worthy of remembering and their reputation will proceed them even in the highest heaven "before my Father and before his angels."

Philadelphia

"And to the angel of the church in Philadelphia write: 'The words of the holy one, the true one, who has the key of David, who opens and no one shall shut, who shuts and no one opens.'"I know your works. Behold, I have set before you an open door, which no one is able to shut; I know that you have but little power, and yet you have kept my word and have not denied my name. Behold, I will make those of the

synagogue of Satan who say that they are Jews and are not, but lie--behold, I will make them come and bow down before your feet, and learn that I have loved you. Because you have kept my word of patient endurance, I will keep you from the hour of trial which is coming on the whole world, to try those who dwell upon the earth. I am coming soon; hold fast what you have, so that no one may seize your crown. He who conquers, I will make him a pillar in the temple of my God; never shall he go out of it, and I will write on him the name of my God, and the name of the city of my God, the new Jerusalem which comes down from my God out of heaven, and my own new name. He who has an ear, let him hear what the Spirit says to the churches.' Rev 3:7-13

Philadelphia means brotherly love and speaks about brotherhood and fraternity. This brotherhood is the basis for a new kind of community with one thing in common; pure love. Out of their own freewill human beings are now called to place pure love at the basis for all their dealings with each other.

This is emphasised when the key of David is mentioned - the name David means beloved – someone who is loved very much. It is our task to learn to love others very much. So many people in this world feel unloved, imagine how different their lives would be if they became beloveds, Davids.

We know if we are loved by others or not don't we? This is because it is really rare to be with someone who really loves us, even in families. This brotherly love we are considering here does not arise through heredity, necessity or lust; it arises between those whose blood carries the Christ Impulse. This is an inclusive kind of love. We feel at one with all those who have this new blood in their veins. When we are with them it is as if we were with Christ. Through being with others who carry the Christ Impulse we increasingly learn how to treat everyone we meet as if they were Christ. This marks our membership of the brotherhood that is Philadelphia.

Having said that, it should be recognised that this state of belovedness is open to those who are actively working to express their higher selves and it is shut to those who do not. Membership of this brotherhood can never be arbitrary; it arises only when

Christ is a reality within our being. This love that rises within us is like the sun which shines on everything equally. Some may use it to warm them, others may use it for pleasure, still others may seek to shade themselves from it – that decision is theirs, not the suns. Would we blame the sun if we get sunburnt?

The sixth cycle in the life of a plant is the death stage. The flower, as if it now has the sun fully within it, droops and the plant's forces change direction from sustaining the flower to producing the seed. The once glorious petals now cocoon this secret work; it is shut away from the world unnoticed just as a dead flower is usually ignored.

We can identify with Christ in these images. Here we see the Cosmic Sun Being who died to create the seed for a new consciousness. His message to Philadelphia reveals another dimension of himself:

'The words of the holy one, the true one, who has the key of David, who opens and no one shall shut, who shuts and no one opens.' Rev 3:7

Remember, this is the one we aspire to be like; holy, true and powerful. However it is only through pure love that we can achieve this.

In his lectures on the Apocalypse, Valentin Tomberg puts forward some powerful ideas and images of what this message to Philadelphia might mean. He paints the picture of the great Sun God now shining from the hearts of men. Through the resurrection the death of the soul has been overcome. This creates in us all the possibility of transformation, especially of our speech. The world is full to the brim with words but they are dead, abstract and compromised. The presence of Christ in our being gives the human voice a Pentecostal power so that our words become a living experience which cannot be misunderstood. The world experienced this power when Martin Luther King said, "I have a dream!"

Then Tomberg uses this resurrection process to express a very powerful idea. He suggests that we no longer need to be guided by the past, now we have access to spiritual insight which can see the future results of what we can create now. This seeing the bloom from today's seed means that we will know exactly what is needed to achieve it.

"...in the old mysteries men looked back into the past at the current of revelation already dwindling to its end, whereas in the Sixth culture-epoch men will be dealing with a current of the ever increasing apocalyptic wisdom of the future. Then men will not look backward to the past to see in what is old the plan and pattern of perfection; they will look forward to the future and seek it there. And that which is fruitful for knowledge and the shaping of the future will take the position held by authority in the past."

It is pure love that casts aside our fear of the future. It is pure love that enables us to embrace everyone we meet as beings who carry within them the seed of resurrection. The experience of this love gives us the courage to experience our weaknesses because we can see in the future what we will become.

'The words of the holy one, the true one, who has the key of David, who opens and no one shall shut, who shuts and no one opens. "'I know your works. Behold, I have set before you an open door, which no one is able to shut; I know that you have but little power, and yet you have kept my word and have not denied my name. Rev 3:7-8

Some key experiences are identified at this stage of the development of our consciousness. This is a crucial phase of our work for we are creating the seed which can produce greater consciousness in the future. It is like an open and shut case. If we are not aware of the consequences of becoming more conscious the door will be shut and we will not be able to open it.

The holy and true one speaks. Holy is *hagios* meaning set apart, purified, the highest; and true is *alethinos* meaning genuine, the real thing. This being gives us a sense of total and utter openness, nothing is obscured. We are called to stand on the threshold of the open door and reveal ourselves. It is impossible to be in the presence of the holy and true and try to mask ourselves in any way. It takes great courage to behold our own holy and true self. For as soon as we do we must also face the self-deception and pretence that has been part of us. It is at this stage that we realise that our development through all the previous stages has paid off and now we have the ability to let all that is not pure and true fall away.

It is interesting to consider how we have cultivated the pretence in our character. We don't have it as young children. It is a learned behaviour based on limited ideas in our culture about what it acceptable and what is not acceptable. These ideas have delusion and deception at their core. We learn that we can think what we like but that we must never put these thoughts into words. We believe that we can keep secrets from others or that our real thoughts can be covered up by so-called positive thinking. This has nothing to do with being holy and true.

To be holy and true means that the words we form in our mind about others are based on a deep knowledge of the human being in all its aspects; body, soul and spirit. To be pure and true means that we can step through the door of self-knowledge and understand our place in eternity. Then we have the courage to speak the truth out of the purest motive.

This open door is the door to eternity and we when we cross its threshold we allow our Higher Self to enter into our earthly life. The state of being that is *alethinos* is created when we experience truth, *alethes*, which means to 'not forget', to reveal what is concealed. What is it that is concealed from our consciousness? Our past lives. The more we act out of our I AM the more conscious we become of how our past actions inform our present life. Instead of being distressed about what comes our way in life now we can have deep feelings of thankfulness. Through this self-knowledge our soul is transformed as we reverently give thanks for every experience that has brought us to this present point in our lives. Through the purest and highest wisdom our I AM guides us through life so that we can make any necessary compensations, as well as create situations for the future, that will assist us to become more conscious than we are now.

We need to be fully prepared to face the truth about ourselves. Each of the messages to the churches is a thanksgiving for what we have achieved and an encouragement to improve in other areas.

The message from the holy and true aspect of our Higher Self acknowledges that when we start to experience our Higher Self, our I AM, we immediately experience a feeling of powerlessness. Now we can see the futility of the cultural ideas that have guided our life till now. We see our superficial judgments and our pretence and a feeling of despair approaches us. This is the point where we must know that we "have kept my word and have not denied my name."

Picture the dying flower as vividly as possible; the plant is powerless to prevent the death of its glorious bloom. If we only see the dying bloom we can be filled with despair, it is only when we experience the resurrection force in the seed that we are filled with hope. This is a similar image to the one that comes to us from the Mystery of Golgotha. If we do not give thanks, even for the most painful of experiences, if we do not allow ourselves to feel powerless, then we deny, that is, we contradict the presence of the living Christ. The image that we have of a man nailed to a cross and giving thanks is so that we recognise similar experiences in our own consciousness as we walk this path to connect with our Real, holy, true Self.

Behold, I will make those of the synagogue of Satan who say that they are Jews and are not, but lie--behold, I will make them come and bow down before your feet, and learn that I have loved you. Because you have kept my word of patient endurance, I will keep you from the hour of trial which is coming on the whole world, to try those who dwell upon the earth. I am coming soon; hold fast what you have, so that no one may seize your crown. Rev 3:9-11

Behold, *idou,* is calling us to be attentive to what may be seen or apprehended. This 'behold' requires us to put effort into being attentive. This is made possible through our connection with our I AM which sharpens our attention so that we are conscious of everything that is going on around us. Our ordinary consciousness is too dreamy to be aware of all the detail. *Idou* is one of twelve different Greek words for behold and it points to seeing beneath the surface of things to the spiritual undercurrents.

This passage is a repetition of the theme introduced in the letter to the Church in Smyrna which says, "the slander of those who say that they are Jews and are not, but are a synagogue of Satan." The synagogue is about a group consciousness which would not recognise the I AM; the individuation and independence that human beings must now embrace.

We could say that the feet represent our lower self and the crown our Higher Self. Within our consciousness are many different forces claiming authority. The forces of *satanas* or

Ahriman will claim to be the chosen ones, the Jews, and unless we are very attentive, continually beholding, we will be deceived by them.

Lies are the deceptions that arise when we are not fully conscious of what we should be doing. For instance, we can be deceived about the amount of work that is required to develop our consciousness. Ideas can arise in our mind suggesting that we can take it easy, we are the chosen ones, we have done as much as necessary for this time in evolution. The trouble is that we cannot see the present moment until it has passed and we can look back on it – then it could be too late. Continually striving and learning is part of patient endurance. We may not experience the fruits of our efforts just yet, which can be disappointing, but we must continually look towards the vision. The so-called chosen ones are in for a shock. At some point they will become aware of the agape, that highest love which is the very substance of the I AM that we have developed in our being, right down to the toes of our lower self. They won't know what has hit them. They will bow down, worship, experience reverence for the power and purity of this love.

When the trials come, those who have a strong relationship with their I AM and have brought to life the Christ Impulse within them will reveal their patience by imposing restraint on all their reactions. It is good to imagine how we will react in "the hour of trial which is coming on the whole world". Rehearsing calmness in adversity means that we will be a living example of the strength of the I AM. This level of calmness will foster a feeling of reverence in all who see it. Those who can remain calm do so because they know that Christ himself delivers adversity. This is the coming, some call the second coming, when the living Christ "comes with a sword" in the hope that those who are ignoring him will wake up to his presence in the world.

It is interesting to consider the difference between the church in Philadelphia and the synagogue of Satan. The synagogue is about fostering the aims of the group rather than developing our own consciousness. Then instead of trying to fit into an already formed group – a synagogue – now a group forms around us. Those who are Philadelphians are attracted to each other; they form a fraternity of love.

You can tell who belongs to these fraternities by their feet. They tread lightly on the earth, ensuring that their transactions don't trespass on others. This is not self-effacing; it is about ensuring that all our activity creates a progressive future for us all. We patiently endure the insight into ourselves which comes from being more conscious. Then we are able to hold fast and continually adjust our activity.

When the door in our being is open we have access to spiritual insight, we can go in and out and find pasture as John puts it in his gospel. When our connection with our I AM is strong we wear the crown signifying that we hold authority in our own being, our kingdom. If we become inflated with our ability to wear this crown it can be seized by other forces. The very reason that we have to work hard for our own progress is so that we can own it fully and completely. It is our own work. If we slacken off and don't hold fast to what we have achieved, to those forces we create within ourselves, other forces can snatch them away from us. We can only endure this stage by knowing that we are loved. If we do not experience the love of Christ then we must create strong images of it. Whatever the image we actively create Christ will occupy it and his presence in our being will become palpable.

He who conquers, I will make him a pillar in the temple of my God; never shall he go out of it, and I will write on him the name of my God, and the name of the city of my God, the new Jerusalem which comes down from my God out of heaven, and my own new name. He who has an ear, let him hear what the Spirit says to the churches.' Rev 3:12-13

Those who conquer *nikao* are the ones who are prevailing - not just once, but continuously. We train ourselves not to succumb to any interference in our consciousness. We also become more skilful at prevailing over all that rises up unconsciously in our being, particularly in our interactions with other people. Each time we conquer, each time we prevail over ourselves in the situations that arise we become a bit stronger. This has nothing to do with suppression or avoidance; it is actually the work of prevailing that creates the strength in our being. Also, we realise that if everything went smoothly we would never have the opportunity to conquer and in our vulnerability our crown could easily be seized.

The work of becoming more connected with our I AM

automatically draws us more deeply into our karma. That is the purpose of karma. Through it we redeem ourselves and through it we become increasingly conscious. Karma is not about settling old accounts; it is our tool of trade assisting us to conquer through doing the works. By reconciling past karma, as well as creating new karma for the future, we become natural conquerors, always prevailing and progressing until we are made "a pillar in the temple of my God".

The pillar is a powerful image of our 'I'. This pillar is not in the church or the synagogue but in the temple, naos, a shrine or sanctuary. In the Jewish temples only the priests could enter the sanctuary of the temple. In his letter to the Corinthians St Paul said that we are the temple.

For we are the temple of the living God; as God said, "I will live in them and move among them, and I will be their God, and they shall be my people. 2 Cor 6:16

If the temple is the sanctuary where only the priest can go then this speaks again about being a priest to ourselves. This means that we express the priestly role within our own being; we preside or prevail over all the forces within us that want to do their own thing, we heal, teach and bless, our actions are sacramental as we hold all things in awe and reverence, we forgive and release and we vow to commit ourselves to the task. The more we are able to do these things within ourselves the more we become the pillar.

The pillar, which connects the floor to the ceiling, also suggests that as pillars we support the spiritual worlds by connecting the earth with the heavens - which is a very priestly role. Therefore if we don't become pillars then there would be a lack of support and connectivity.

The pillar is also an image of being self-supportive, prevailing against the inclination to lean on others. We would also resist encouraging other's to lean on us which can be more about experiencing the power this gives us rather than actually providing support.

Each one who is able to be a pillar in this way is attracted to others who are also acting similarly. A new community of people is formed, all supporting themselves, all prevailing, and all respecting each other in this work. This is the love brotherhood that is

Philadelphia. This is a truly supportive environment where each member's effort is enhanced by the other. Then we are told that new names are given. 1. the name of my God, 2. the name of the city of my God, the new Jerusalem which comes down from my God out of heaven, and 3. my own new name.

Can these three names be speaking about the trinity; the Father, Son and Holy Spirit? It is through the working of the trinity in us that we become aware of our Higher Self. The Trinity has received quite a bit of bad press over the last two centuries, so much so that it is now difficult to give it meaning in our lives.

In his "Karmic Relationship" lectures at the end of his life Rudolf Steiner speaks very clearly about the deep significance of the Trinity as it is revealed in original Christianity (see Lecture given on 12 June 1924 published in Vol 7).

Simply put, the presence of the Father Being can be found in nature where the rule of necessity in natural order operates. This is the basic force that nourishes and sustains our body making it possible for us to live on the earth. Freedom is experienced in the Son Being, the Christ. We are raised out of our body's natural instincts and through our soul we can choose how to feel, think and act. "But it is the power of the Holy Spirit that quickens within us the recognition that we live not [just] in the physical body alone but having been associated with the body through its phases of development, we are awakened as being of Spirit."

When we become aware these new names then we have the reputation of having the Trinity working within us. Those with these names form a very different social community, that of the Philadelphians. It is as if our old self falls away and our true self stands like the pillar; every action we take is a conscious act and we are not afraid to act. We automatically ask three questions; How do my actions affect the earth? How do my actions affect other people? And how do my actions affect the universe and its spiritual community?

When these principles are at work within us we are indeed the temple of the living God. We are self-directed, not directed by other people and forces; those things that can seem to support us but in fact really use us; the false Jews. We have the Key of David when the 'I' finds itself within itself. With this I power we open and shut through our own actions. These are the mysteries which we must hear with our inner ear.

Laodicea

"And to the angel of the church in La-odice'a write: 'The words of the Amen, the faithful and true witness, the beginning of God's creation. "'I know your works: you are neither cold nor hot. Would that you were cold or hot! So, because you are lukewarm, and neither cold nor hot, I will spew you out of my mouth. For you say, I am rich, I have prospered, and I need nothing; not knowing that you are wretched, pitiable, poor, blind, and naked. Therefore I counsel you to buy from me gold refined by fire, that you may be rich, and white garments to clothe you and to keep the shame of your nakedness from being seen, and salve to anoint your eyes, that you may see. Those whom I love, I reprove and chasten; so be zealous and repent. Behold, I stand at the door and knock; if any one hears my voice and opens the door, I will come in to him and eat with him, and he with me. He who conquers, I will grant him to sit with me on my throne, as I myself conquered and sat down with my Father on his throne. He who has an ear, let him hear what the Spirit says to the churches.'" Rev 3:14-22

The seventh and last church is La-odicea. At the time of Christ La-odicea was a prosperous centre of manufacturing and banking. It was famous for its black wool. It was also famous for its medical school and its people worshipped Aesculapius, a god of medicine. The name La-odicea means people of justice.

Justice and judgment are misunderstood and misused concepts today. For the most part, our judging rises out of our polarised soul when it acts instinctively out of its likes and dislikes. It is only when we can engage with our I AM that justice becomes a powerful tool for weighing up truth. In this way justice becomes a continual series of adjustments rather than an instinctual finality. How often are we shackled by past judgments? Even yesterday's judgments! This becomes a lukewarm area of our being. Any warm enthusiasm we might feel about something is restrained by this old judgment. Equally, we can be blasé instead of coldly rational about an inappropriate idea or behaviour. There are many areas in life where we are lukewarm when we really need to be either coldly objective or passionately on fire.

This is why we need to listen to the Amen aspect of our being. It is the presence of the Amen that gives us that inner ring of truth. Some people do acknowledge truth by saying, "Amen to that". When we feel the inner Amen we are confident, we are the pillar – no longer looking to the earth and its mode of thinking for our support. Now our support comes from our eternal being, our I AM, which has experienced all our past lives. Our Amen aspect knows all the choices we have ever made, all our feelings and experiences; all our previous activity is known to it.

When we wake up our soul from its instinctual habits, and allow the light of our eternal self to illuminate us, we connect with the faithful and true witness. This witness knows the deep reasons behind our every thought, word and deed since "the beginning of God's creation." Imagine living with this level of understanding. How free-making. Then we would know when to be hot and cold about life's events instead of blindly ducking and weaving in the hope that we don't upset anyone too much. Or worse, judging people without fully understanding what is behind their actions.

In these first few powerful words to the La-odiceans are captured deep secrets of the human being.

'The words of the Amen, the faithful and true witness, the beginning of God's creation. "

The faithful *pistos* and true *alethinos* witness *martus* emphasises the principles we are considering. To be faithful, *pistos*, means knowing with certainty, not by blind belief. *Alethinos* means not forgetting anything that we have previously known – through all our earthly lives. The witness is the one who re-experiences the event as if it was happening in the present. Now, it is an inner reality. Imagine the intensity and purity of these experiences. It makes sense that anything less than pure could not be part of this being, and would be spewed out.

The word translated as beginning is *arche* and apart from pointing to the beginning or origin it also points to the beings in the spiritual hierarchy called the Archai. These are the same beings referred to in the first words of Genesis, "In the beginning". The

Archai are three levels above us in the cosmic hierarchy and are sometimes called the powers of origin.

Rudolf Steiner speaks graphically about the role of these beings in his 'Anthroposophical Leading Thoughts'. He explains that these are the beings who prepared our human form so that we had an appropriate vehicle to house our soul and spirit on this planet earth. So the Archai have a crucial role in making it possible for us to integrate our I AM. They prepared this body in such a way that we can express ourselves within the force of gravity; standing upright, walking, using our arms and legs with dexterity and so on. It is through the human 'I' that we can stand upright and it is this factor that differentiates us from animals. So it is through their activity that we have the possibility of individual and free self-conscious expression; for we each have differing abilities to use our bodies. In this way the Archai guide the rhythms of our evolutionary development and more.

It is interesting to be reminded of beginnings at this seventh stage because the seventh stage of the plant's growth is the return to the seed. So we have moved through all the stages; germinating, sprouting, growing, unfurling and now the plant contracts into a seed. It is as if the flower spews its seeds out of its mouth heralding the beginning of the next phase of growth; from seed to seed, from *arche* to *arche*.

For you say, I am rich, I have prospered, and I need nothing; not knowing that you are wretched, pitiable, poor, blind, and naked. Therefore I counsel you to buy from me gold refined by fire, that you may be rich, and white garments to clothe you and to keep the shame of your nakedness from being seen, and salve to anoint your eyes, that you may see. Rev 3:17-18

A picture of arrogant selfishness arises from these words, "I am rich and I continue to store up more riches so that I will never need anything." This is happening everywhere in the world today; people want more money, more possessions and more power even when they already have these things. If they were honest these people would admit that no matter how much they have they "can't get no satisfaction" to borrow Mick Jagger's famous phrase. Why would this be? Obviously these inclinations are driven by deep inner fear.

This greed is not restricted to the wealthy and powerful. If we are honest we will find that we often want to hold on to things and to draw things to ourselves. It could be possessions, or it could be our ideas and knowledge or it could even be in our attention-seeking. When we actually recognise this inclination to draw things to ourselves we realise that we are trying to replace something what we feel we lost. We continually try to fill up the void instead of looking into it. We don't realise that unless we feel the loss we can never find what we really need to find – the living Christ within. John recorded this principle in his gospel:

Nevertheless I tell you the truth: it is to your advantage that I go away, for if I do not go away, the Counselor will not come to you; but if I go, I will send him to you. Jn 16:7

This Counselor, *parakletos*, is the Holy Spirit who is the precursor for us to become aware of the living Christ Impulse within our being. In the Revelation the words, "Therefore I counsel you", takes the meaning of the counsellor a step further. The word counsel here is *sumbouleuo* which means counsel which is given, taken and acted upon. This impresses upon us that in this seventh stage of development we have the opportunity to enter fully into our agreement with Christ. At each stage (church) we have experienced a deepening connection with our I AM. We have (mostly) let it displace our old thinking, our old way of being – which means that we have courageously been able to look at all our bad habits. We have openly accepted that we are wrong in certain areas, we have taken the criticism on the chin and now here we are feeling very rich. But it is the wrong kind of rich!

We haven't fully seen the difference between the riches of the earth and the riches of the heavens. The success (riches) we feel when we change our thinking is only part of the work. Then we must make our soul available to think differently – purely. This cannot be explained to us, we must experience it for ourselves. Once we discover it we must be able to replicate the process until it becomes naturally part of our consciousness. When we do discover it we will find that it is directly linked to our inner motives. Then we see for ourselves, and admit to ourselves, that we are "wretched, pitiable, poor, blind and naked".

It is like the story of the Emperor's new clothes which he was told could only be seen by those with special gifts. The emperor himself was prepared to stand naked rather than admit that he couldn't see them. It took the truthfulness of a child to expose the trickster's rort.

Of course we are not fully conscious of our human condition. This is what we are doing; becoming fully aware of where we stand as beings in a vast cosmos. Looking at this list we could easily find seven human experiences; rich, needing nothing, wretched, pitiable, poor, blind and naked. Do they relate to the virtues spoken of by the early Greek philosophers? These philosophers were active at a time when the beings in the spiritual worlds were withdrawing their guidance so that human beings could become individually responsible for their own actions. This transition needed some guiding principles. As we learned to stand in our own consciousness and make choices for ourselves we had get used to weighing all our actions for ourselves. It wasn't so much about getting it right but rather about the process of weighing things up and feeling our way into them. The idea of justice being a series of adjustments comes from this period and this work. The spectrum of the seven virtues swung between two parameters: purity and lust; self-control and gluttony; generosity and greed; industriousness and laziness; patience and anger; satisfaction and envy; humility and pride.

Robert Sardello, in his book "The Power of Soul", relates the virtues to the work we do in our soul not for our own benefit but so that we are better contributors. To what do we contribute? As we saw in the letter to Philadelphia we contribute to the evolution of the earth by considering the effects of our actions on others, on the earth, and on the spiritual fraternity that surrounds us. This form of contributing is not at the expense of self, it is for the benefit of all, including ourselves. In the opening paragraphs of his book Robert Sardello speaks about "doing the good" as a flourishing – "The chief good is the flourishing of the harmonious life of body, soul and spirit."

This is the same challenge given to us by the human archetype that speaks to John; and through John to us. Instead of actions motivated to benefit ourselves, benefits that we are not even conscious of anyway, now we must act out of our connection with the Holy Spirit, with whom we now have a firm contract - to buy gold, garments and eye ointment. These cannot be acquired in any material way to which we are accustomed; we must use spiritual currency to acquire them from the living Christ.

Therefore I counsel you to buy from me gold refined by fire, that you may be rich, and white garments to clothe you and to keep the shame of your nakedness from being seen, and salve to anoint your eyes, that you may see. Those whom I love, I reprove and chasten; so be zealous and repent. Rev 3:18-19

It is no accident that we find contradictory references about being rich in the message to the seventh church. It is important for us to experience what being rich really means. The plant in its seventh phase of growth is a good example. The flower that is dead now drops its seed and can do nothing more than offer up its seed for the next cycle. The quality of the next cycle is tied directly to the quality of the seed. We could say that the plant is rich for having produced the seed but if the seed is not shed the riches are impotent. Our image of being rich through hoarding things is in contrast with the idea of becoming rich by spending.

What is this spiritual currency that is needed for the transaction? Spiritual currency is love; the more we give the more receive. Love is the very substance of the I AM; it begins as a love for self which we continually transform into a love for others. There is no other way but to start from self-love. The minimum requirement is that love must continually flow; it is like a river that is replenished at its source and flows out to refresh all that it touches. It has no hidden motives; it gives to all equally and freely. The health of the river is directly related to the quality of our love - for ourselves and then for others. We know very well the consequences if the river dams up somewhere, or is redirected or not replenished.

When we are able to experience and express this pure love- agape - our being glows like the purest gold when it is refined by fire. Like assaying gold to remove all the base metals, we refine our being of its lower inclinations. The greater the warmth of our love, the more refined we become.

What we may not realise is that this process of purification produces a feeling of shame. When we compare ourselves with the purity of the Christed man we become deeply ashamed. When we are able to see our activities in the light of spiritual perfection our blood rushes to the surface of our body and we blush. While Adam and Eve were still in paradise, at one with perfection, they were not ashamed:

"And the man and his wife were both naked, and were not ashamed." Gen 2:25

Experiencing this shame is an important part of our development; we mustn't try to escape it. The trouble is that the experience of shame is like a burning fire – the evidence of this fire is the heat of our blushing. Since our blood is the vehicle for our I AM the blushing signals that our I AM is calling us to perfection.

The white garment *himartia* is an outer garment, a mantle, and suggests that our being glows white with purity. White in the Greek is *leukos* and comes from *luke* meaning light. So we become light-filled. White is also a balance of the seven colours of the rainbow suggesting that we have achieved harmony in our being. This indicates that we are able to clothe our body with the purified mantle of our soul and spirit. St Paul speaks about this in his second letter to the Corinthians -

For we know that if the earthly tent [earthly body] we live in is destroyed, we have a building from God [spiritual body], a house not made with hands, eternal in the heavens. Here indeed we groan, and long to put on our heavenly dwelling, so that by putting it on we may not be found naked. For while we are still in this tent, we sigh with anxiety; not that we would be unclothed, but that we would be further clothed, 2 Cor 5:1-4

When we are refined and light-filled we must acquire *kollourion*, eyesalve to anoint our eyes. This word comes from the word *kollura* which means cake or bread. It could be a direct reference to the bread as the body of Christ. If we close our eyes and place this bread over them all we have then is our inner sight - *blepo*.

Then we can withstand being rebuked *elencho* which means to be convicted of our faults – of our less than perfect activity; and chastened *paideuo* which means to be trained and disciplined like a child. We will be able to bear this because it is done through the perfect love from Christ.

Then we reach the stage where we are zealous; hot, on fire, and we can repent. Repent *metanoeo* meaning that we can see the results of our actions before we act, but also that we need to rethink everything. We cannot continue to think the way we do, continually placing our limited judgments on everyone and everything in our daily life. Through our ability to experience and express the highest, purest love we shed a glowing light that gives us new sight - to observe, not to judge. We see the good qualities in everyone we meet. We have a new respect for the choices other's make because we know that they are connected with their own karma. We are now able to suspend our judgmental thoughts before they even form in our mind. In our pure love for others we allow them to make their own choices knowing that the One whose task it is to love perfectly will reveal their faults and train them – we don't need to do that for him.

Behold, I stand at the door and knock; if any one hears my voice and opens the door, I will come in to him and eat with him, and he with me. He who conquers, I will grant him to sit with me on my throne, as I myself conquered and sat down with my Father on his throne. He who has an ear, let him hear what the Spirit says to the churches.'" Rev 3:20-22

The closing words of the last message to the churches are so very intimate and deeply moving. If we stand outside these words looking in they hardly make sense; how can we behold a knock which is heard as a voice! We can only experience the reality of this message if we look very closely at the words and stand inside the ideas.

Behold *idou* is our ability to be so attentive that we know exactly what is happening in all its inner and outer detail. Not through vague intuitions or hearing spiritual messages, but through our own fully conscious thoughts.

To stand at the door speaks of a totally independent action. It should be noted that it is the presence of the 'I' in our being that is responsible for our upright stance, thereby differentiating us from the animal kingdom. This leads us to ask: Who is standing at the door? In St John's Gospel one of the seven I AM sayings is "I am the door" - in other words, our I AM is the door.

"Truly, truly, I say to you, I am the door of the sheep. ... I am the door; if any one enters by me, he will be saved, and will go in and out and find pasture. John 10:7 & 9

If our I AM is the door then the one knocking is Christ. Not through vague religious faith but through actual experience will this presence of Christ be a reality for us. We are called to prepare the entrance. While we remain unconscious of the presence of Christ and the way he will enter into our consciousness we will not hear the knocking.

Who hears the knocking? Our small I, the mirrored reflection of our I AM which we refer to as our lower self. Our lower self is that part of our soul when it is in a dream-like sleep and our thinking, feeling and willing are semi-conscious and automatic. It is only when we have awakened these activities from their habitual patterns that our I AM becomes the door. Then we can change the words in the passage in this way:

Behold, Christ stands at the I AM and knocks; if any one (our small I or lower self) hears Christ's voice [*phoné* or sound] and opens the I AM, Christ will come in to our being and eat with us …

Creating an image of our inner being is a challenge yet if we are to know ourselves fully we must work on this image. We know that we call ourselves 'I' but this experience of our I-ness is still developing. When we are self-centred and cannot experience what others are experiencing our lower self, our small I, dominates. Our Higher Self only has an influence to the degree that we have control of our thoughts, feelings and actions. The barometer for this is how we respond to others when they say something that upsets us. If our emotions overwhelm us, clouding our thoughts, then our lower self is eclipsing our Higher Self. If we criticise and judge others putting aside our love for them, our lower self is at work. As long as we cannot control our thinking and feeling at will we cannot hear the knock. How could we hear the knock with so much noise going on inside us? We can only hear the Christ-sound when we experience peace in the turmoil.

It may be helpful to think of the 'I' as a sliding scale from lower to higher – the more conscious we are and the greater control we have, the more we experience our highest self, the I AM. The highest expression of our I AM is outside us, the lowest expression is inside us and we try to make a strong energetic connection between the two. At this stage in human development it is not possible to have a full and constant connection with our I AM.

However, we have reached the stage where we can experience it more often and our most powerful experience of it comes with the presence of Christ. We can describe this as the process of the 'I' finding itself within itself.

Another way to tell this story is to use the images of the mystery of Golgotha. This mystery is all about the human I becoming conscious of itself in the purified soul. There it has supper – bread and wine - with the indwelling Christ. This Christ is the Sun God who journeyed to earth, was born of the purified Mary, then connected with the highly developed human I before being nailed to a cross. This left an everlasting image that that part of us that could be nailed down was not really us. It is when we nail that bit down that the real human being can arise. Then we are self-born, in freedom, and through our own efforts we have conquered and we sit on the throne.

He who conquers, I will grant him to sit with me on my throne, as I myself conquered and sat down with my Father on his throne.

We become the Son of man sitting with the Son of God; the human being who has achieved the potential shown to him by the living Christ. As St Matthew says:

"When the Son of man comes in his glory, and all the angels with him, then he will sit on his glorious throne. Mt 25:31

Summary of the Seven Churches

Our reflections on the seven churches are complete. Before we look at chapter four it would be good to pause and consider our journey so far. We have seen how each church can represent a stage in the growth of a plant; from one seed a new seed is produced for a new cycle of development. It is good to consider how this growth cycles takes place in our own consciousness. What seeds are we creating today for the future? What kind of a future do we face if we do not put a balanced effort into any of the stages?

Throughout each day we can observe the stages of our developing consciousness. If we have been working on thinking more, or feeling more, we can assess our progress as we meet various situations throughout the day. If we are working on guiding our feelings differently are we at the germinating, sprouting, growing or unfurling stage? One way to assess this is to notice how quickly we react? It may not even be an expressed reaction, perhaps we instantly jump to conclusions in our mind. If so, then we know that our eyes are not yet like a flame of fire because we haven't perceived the unseen detail; nor are our feet like white-hot brass, refining and forging our understanding.

The cycles of our developing consciousness can be many and varied. Some of our work can be a series of short cycles while other, more difficult transformations can require a longer cycle. How conscious are we of the stage in the cycle that we are in? Can we identify when we are in a new beginning, in the middle or at the end where some things must be allowed to die away? Understanding these phases in our development means that we can ride the wave instead of being caught in the swell. For instance, it is not helpful if we try to carry into the future what was useful for the last phase of our development. Also, it creates clutter which our new growth must compete with.

The being who instructs John to write to the angel of each church is in fact ourselves. Not as we are now, but as we will be when we forge that connection with our Real Self. In the messages to the churches it is as if this being is remembering the journey it made; the successes and the pitfalls of the 'works'. There is an intimacy in those words that begin most of the messages, "I know your works - as if it is a personal experience. This is also the true I AM experience which doesn't look on from outside but enters into everyone and everything to see how it is for them. This is the I AM that knows the starving child's hunger as if it were its own hunger. This is the I AM that knows firsthand the pain of the mother cradling her dead child. This is the I AM that does not feel death within its self but rather the new birth that immediately follows.

This brings to mind the point and purpose of the Christmas story. That a God took on human form to be a pioneer, showing us the way to become Gods ourselves. Furthermore, through his resurrection he accompanies us as a presence, a life-force; within us as the Christ Impulse and without as the Cosmic Christ. St Paul wrote about this in his letter to the Romans:-

But if Christ is in you, although your bodies are dead

because of sin [error], your spirits are alive because of righteousness [balance]. If the Spirit of him who raised Jesus from the dead dwells in you, he who raised Christ Jesus from the dead will give life to your mortal bodies also through his Spirit which dwells in you. ... ... we are children of God, and if children, then heirs, heirs of God and fellow heirs with Christ, provided we suffer with him in order that we may also be glorified with him. I consider that the sufferings of this present time are not worth comparing with the glory that is to be revealed to us. For the creation waits with eager longing for the revealing of the sons of God; Ro 8:10-11 & 17-19

In the reflections on Chapter One it was noted that "The son of man is our own offspring; our own creation born from our ability to create balance between our lower self and our Higher Self through the indwelling Christ." The messages to the churches reveal this transition and give us guidance for the various stages. We can build a powerful imagination of this being who speaks by putting his seven characteristics side by side. For instance, in the message to Ephesus the being says, "The words of him who holds the seven stars in his right hand, who walks among the seven golden lampstands," In the message to Smyrna he says, "The words of the first and the last, who died and came to life." By taking each statement from each message and adding a brief description from the reflections we have a contemplative prayer. It could be divided into seven parts, one for each day of the week (starting on Saturday).*

One: You are the one who declares the Revelation of what we must become.

May we be able to hold the seven stars, those angels, in our right hand;

no longer confined to a limited form,

and walk in the middle of the seven golden lampstands;

carrying the light of the Holy Spirit within us.

Two: May we experience the first and the last by straddling eternal memory,

May we, like you, pass through death and become the living one; resurrected.

Three: Let our words be a two-edged sword cutting away all illusion;

Four: O, Son of God, may our eyes be like yours, a flame of fire, magnifying unseen detail,

and our feet like white-hot brass, refining and forging our understanding.

Five: May we who have the seven spirits of God make them worthy and pure

to cooperate with the seven stars –

those connecting angels working between our lower and higher being;

Six: Holy one, true one,

who holds the key of David, the I that finds itself within itself,

which opens and no one shuts,

which shuts and no one opens;

Seven: You are the Amen, the seal of consent,

faithful and true witness, capable of re-visioning all works

The *arche* of God's creation.

*This is an expansion of Alfred Heidenreich's idea in his book, "The Book of Revelation" page 52 by adding the meanings put forward in these reflections.

CHAPTER FOUR

John's Vision of God's Throne

After this I looked, and lo, in heaven an open door! And the first voice, which I had heard speaking to me like a trumpet, said, "Come up hither, and I will show you what must take place after this." At once I was in the Spirit, and lo, a throne stood in heaven, with one seated on the throne! And he who sat there appeared like jasper and carnelian, and round the throne was a rainbow that looked like an emerald. Round the throne were twenty-four thrones, and seated on the thrones were twenty-four elders, clad in white garments, with golden crowns upon their heads. Rev 4:1-4

"After this I looked" doesn't quite capture what actually happens at this stage. *Meta tauta eidou kai idou* really says: After these things (happened in my consciousness) I was able to behold and behold! an open door. Behold gives us a sense of being able to see something for the first time. So we acquire the alibility, and then we are able to see things that we have never seen before. Not that they weren't there, but now we have the ability to see them. This means that we can be so attentive that our finer senses came alive, our awareness is heightened, our consciousness operates on a new level. This is what we aim for as we continually repeat the cycles of growth outlined in the messages to the seven churches.

Each time we complete a cycle we become a bit more conscious. We also become a bit more able to bring our whole being into that state of focussed attention. For this is what is required if we are to expand our awareness to see who we really are and understand our purpose. *Idou* sees the hidden detail because it is able to engage the purified faculties of thinking, feeling and will. This is how we find John now - all distraction is quietened, all fear is set aside and in purity of motive John participates fully in his raised consciousness.

John finds himself in heaven – this Greek word *ouranos* means to rise or lift – to heave. Perhaps this is an indication of the effort needed to raise our consciousness to a higher level.

These opening words of chapter four are almost intimidating. They expand John's vision from chapter one. He hears that voice again that he first heard in Revelation 1:10. It speaks within him like a trumpet. This is how we experience the spiritual faculty of Inspiration. An inner voice trumpets within our being saying, "Come up hither, and I will show you what must take place after this." The word 'after' in Greek is *meta* and it doesn't mean 'after this'; it is pointing to what is happening 'behind' the outer physical manifestations that we encounter with our senses. Rudolf Steiner talks about the visual world as a tapestry behind which is a great work. What this verse is really saying is this: Ascend in consciousness! Then you will see what is happening behind the scenes.

As soon as we ascend in consciousness then immediately we experience our spiritual being and gain the use of its facilities. The physical world becomes transparent and we see what is going on spiritually. It could be compared to being backstage at the puppet theatre.

The first thing we see is the throne on which is 'the sitting one'. This is an image of great authority. Could this be us when we rule in our own kingdom? Are we the sitting one? The lack of motion indicated by sitting indicates that we rule over our desires. They are stilled, we are in control. Now our desires will be fulfilled in a timely and appropriate way rather than demanding to be fulfilled the minute they rise up within us.

It is interesting that the two stones mentioned, jasper and

sardius (not carnelian) are the 'first and last' stones on the "priest's breastpiece of judgment" that God instructed Moses to make for his brother Aaron in Exodus 28

These stones are also connected with our original purity when the "word of the Lord spoke to the son of Man in Ezekiel:

You were in Eden, the garden of God; every precious stone was your covering, Ez 28:13

The rainbow is the sign that we have conquered our feelings; they will never flood through us and destroy our ability to think and act clearly.

I have set my rainbow in the clouds, and it will be the sign of the covenant between me and the earth. ... Never again will the waters become a flood to destroy all life. Gen 9:13 & 15

The throne, the stones, the rainbow, the elders clad in white garments, with golden crowns upon their heads reminds us of ruling in our own kingdom and making ourselves priests.

To him who loves us and has freed us from our sins by his blood and made us a kingdom, priests to his God and Father, to him be glory and dominion for ever and ever. Amen. Rev 1:4-6

The throne is the seat of love. When we experience and express love in its most pure form we rule. This love gives us unspeakable power and deep humility. When we rule in our being to the extent that we can control our feelings, thoughts and will, our being shines with a pure light and a golden halo is visible to those who can behold.

From the throne issue flashes of lightning, and voices [sounds] and peals of thunder, and before the throne burn seven torches [lamps] of fire, which are the seven spirits of God; and before the throne there is as it were a sea of glass, like crystal. And round the throne, on each side of the throne, are four living creatures, full of eyes in front and behind: the first living creature like a lion, the second living creature like an ox, the third living creature with the face of a man, and the fourth living creature like a flying eagle. And the four living creatures, each of them with six wings, are full of eyes all round and within, and day and night they never cease to sing, "Holy, holy, holy, is the Lord God Almighty, who was and is and is to come!" And whenever the living creatures give glory and honor and thanks to him who is seated on the throne, who lives for ever and ever, the twenty-four elders fall down before him who is seated on the throne and worship him who lives for ever and ever; they cast their crowns before the throne, singing, "Worthy art thou, our Lord and God, to receive glory and honor and power [thanks], for thou didst create all things, and by thy will they existed and were created." Rev 4:5-11

In this mighty vision we could ask if John is beholding the beginning of human evolution as it unfolds in the Book of Genesis as the Garden of Eden. Or is it the reverse Garden of Eden? A comparison of all the elements in both stories would reveal many similarities. Imagine what it is like for John, having risen in consciousness to a highly aware state, to be beholding the roots of consciousness when human beings were not individually aware? It would be like looking at the plan from within the finished building and having an intimate experience of the wisdom of the architect and builders. This is the moment of crowning glory; a human being has made it. John, the beloved, has broken through the glass ceiling!

What is more, John has brought with him his self-created light. This light has that quality which brings to life, or ignites, other lights; lightning, lamps, glass, eyes – all shining in response to the arrival of a fully conscious human being returning to the source. Not as he left it, but as one who has transformed himself into a glorious being.

Lightning and thunder are signs of our 'I' at work in our blood and our nervous system. This cosmic activity signals the uniting of body, soul and spirit into a vital and highly conscious activity.

The four living creatures in the Greek are zoon which comes from *zoe*. *Zoe* is the life-force that keeps our body alive which we have managed to raise up, to spiritualise, so that it becomes a free living force within us. In its freedom it is available to our consciousness and therefore no longer bound to the basic needs of the physical.

These living creatures, the zoon, are the prototypes of our basic soul functions; of feeling, thinking and will, which are under the control of man, the representative of the I AM. In our journey from the homogenous whole to individuality, from the glassy sea to individual drops of water, we come to that point where we have the freedom to control our own being. The zoon stand as reminders of our responsibility, or the work we must do. They are all seeing; full of eyes in front and behind, all around them and within them.

These creatures should not be taken too literally, they are a resemblance; similar in appearance and behaviour. They could represent many things in our being but when it comes to consciousness our work, first and foremost, is to become very aware of the way we feel, think and use our will. Mostly we are unaware of these activities, they rise up automatically and we behave in repetitive and automatic ways. If we allow our I AM to control these functions we can respond to life uniquely according to each situation we encounter. Then we are truly free, no longer tied to the dictates of our karma, and indeed resolving it more frequently.

One: "the first living creature like a lion," The strongest soul force is our feeling. It leaps on us devouring our thinking, weakening our will, and detrimentally influencing our responses. Its agility and force gives us no time to think and we can quickly be consumed by irritation and anger. This is not the purpose of feeling. From within ourselves we must guide our feeling towards understanding and loving others.

Two: "the second living creature like an ox," The ox is like our will which can be stubborn and unyielding. However the real purpose of the will is to cultivate the soil of our being to be of service of our Higher Self.

Three: "the third living creature with the face of a man," Man stands above the other life forms we classify as mineral, vegetable and animal. We aim to become the Son of Man by fully uniting with our I AM and awakening the Christ Impulse within us. Until our I AM controls our feeling, thinking and will, like a musician masterly plays his three stringed instrument, we are inclined to express the lower characteristics of the lion, the ox and eagle.

Four: "and the fourth living creature like a flying eagle." These are our thinking capacities which can fly around in circles or soar high to give us the broadest perspective.

In chapter four this image that John paints for us gives us an experience of the spiritual company that quietly fosters our efforts to rise above all that prevents us from becoming co-workers of Christ,– the Son of Man united with the Son of God. This possibility is ceaselessly celebrated in the spiritual worlds with cosmic hymns.

When it says, ""Worthy art thou, our Lord and God, to receive glory and honor and power" this word 'power' is really 'thanks' *eucharisteo*, the love feast, the celebration of the transformation of our lower self to its higher counterpart. This takes place when we are able to take the spiritual into our physical being, uniting the two. It is through the Eucharist that we find a real union with Christ. We take the bread and wine into ourselves. It used to be from the outside that we took something consecrated into us.

Now that the living presence of Christ permeates everything, from now on, we must increasingly experience the Eucharist within us. Through our contemplation of spiritual truth, our thoughts and contemplations on the Christ deed, our bodies become the consecrated bread and our blood becomes the consecrated wine. Our conscious feelings, thoughts and will can permeate and spiritualise our inner being – thoughts and feelings as fully consecrated as the bread and wine have been on the altars of churches over the last few thousand years. All external thoughts and external forms are transitory; the Christ-thought lives in ever-new forms in the hearts and souls of humanity – this is the reason for the celebrations John beholds.

CHAPTER FIVE

The Book with the Seven Seals

And I saw in the right hand of him who was seated on the throne a scroll written within and on the back, sealed with seven seals; and I saw a strong angel proclaiming with a loud voice, "Who is worthy to open the scroll and break its seals?" And no one in heaven or on earth or under the earth was able to open the scroll or to look into it, and I wept much that no one was found worthy to open the scroll or to look into it. Then one of the elders said to me, "Weep not; lo, the Lion of the tribe of Judah, the Root of David, has conquered, so that he can open the scroll and its seven seals." And between the throne and the four living creatures and among the elders, I saw a Lamb standing, as though it had been slain, with seven horns and with seven eyes, which are the seven spirits of God sent out into all the earth; and he went and took the scroll from the right hand of him who was seated on the throne. Rev 5:1-7

John's second vision continues into chapter five. To fully contemplate this vision it is best to read chapters four and five in succession. John the Beloved is describing the strange things that he has become able to behold. In his beholding, these beings act and speak. Almost in response to his questions the vision unfolds. What takes place does not fully comply with our understanding of physical laws. Yet we can't dismiss it if we take into account who it is that is relaying this vision to us.

John was the one whom Jesus the Christ was able to love most – not because of Jesus' ability to love but because of John's lovability. This is not about favouritism; this is about compatible spiritual power. St Paul spoke of the power of love, the greatness of love, in his first Letter to the Corinthians.

If I speak in the tongues of men and of angels, but have not love, I am a noisy gong or a clanging cymbal. And if I have prophetic powers, and understand all mysteries and all knowledge, and if I have all faith, so as to remove mountains, but have not love, I am nothing. If I give away all I have, and if I deliver my body to be burned, but have not love, I gain nothing. Love is patient and kind; love is not jealous or boastful; it is not arrogant or rude. Love does not insist on its own way; it is not irritable or resentful; it does not rejoice at wrong, but rejoices in the right. Love bears all things, believes all things, hopes all things, endures all things. 1 Cor 13 1-7

It was John's ability to love so purely that enabled him to see the spiritual reality that surrounds us. It is this purity that gives him, and us, the ability to behold. Many people today see non-physical things which they interpret to be special spiritual visions. Yet if these visions are seen in a semi-conscious state they could simply be darker forces revealing themselves in benevolent images.

What St John and St Paul both stress is that we cannot see the truth unless we have love, the purest, highest love which in Greek is agape.

It is helpful to know about the different Greek words for love.

One: *Eros* - Erotic physical love. The procreative urge arises for survival of the species.

Two: *Phileo* - Brotherly and sisterly love which can be supportive and nurturing but also exclusive. It is usually a gentle, life-giving love

Three: *Storge* - Love of family, tribe and nation. It can be defensive and aggressive to those outside the group. This is the kind of love we also find in the animal kingdom.

Four: *Agape* - Divine love, Christed love, this is the love expressed by those who experience their I AM, they express it without fear or favour. It speaks of unification and intense compassion. It may not always be interpreted as love because in its expression it can cut like a sword.

In his vision John sees a scroll, a *biblion*, with seven seals written within and on the back. This could actually be our own being containing our full biography; a record of all the lives we have ever lived. They are sealed away from us because we are not worthy. Who is worthy? Only those who love.

We get an idea of the fullness of John's ability to love when we read that he wept. *Klaio* speaks about grief, about mourning the dead. John's grief arises when he sees that no one loves. John's challenge is also our challenge. When we are able to see the reality of this present phase of evolution all we will see is death, spiritual death. The only way we will be able to bear this is if we have love. As St Paul says, "Love bears all things, believes all things, hopes all things, endures all things."

Through our Higher Self we begin to behold clearly all the lower expressions both in our own being, as well as in others, and if we don't love we will be in agony, we will be grief stricken. The only thing that will reassure us is if we can behold the "Lion of the tribe of Judah, the Root of David". It seems strange that John did not see him initially for he is the Christ, the one who initiated and loved John. This gives us a further idea of the difficulty we face when we behold spiritual visions. Our only assurance is to become more conscious of our two constant companions; love and Christ.

And between the throne and the four living creatures and among the elders, I saw a Lamb standing, as though it had been slain, with seven horns and with seven eyes, which are the seven spirits of God sent out into all the earth; and he went and took the scroll from the right hand of him who was seated on the throne. And when he had taken the scroll, the four living creatures and the twenty-four elders fell down before the Lamb, each holding a harp, and with golden bowls full of incense, which are the prayers of the saints; and they sang a new song, saying, "Worthy art thou to take the scroll and to open its seals, for thou wast slain and by thy blood didst ransom men for God from every tribe and tongue and people and nation, and hast made them a kingdom and priests to our God, and they shall reign on earth." Rev 5:6-10

In the midst of his vision John's attention is drawn to the lamb. The first two qualities he sees in this Lamb is that it is standing and it is slain. How can we make sense of this contradiction?

The word slain comes from the Greek word *sphage* which means slaughter. It is interesting that this word is used rather than any of the other six Greek words for kill or slay. It suggests a sacrifice; that there is a plan to prepare something for inevitable death. Such a plan was put in place for the being Christ. The new song the creatures and elders sing is about such a plan: "for thou wast slain and by thy blood didst ransom [purchase] men for God".

The vision may make more sense if we place it outside our understanding of time and space and see it as a perpetual event. As if it is happening in a parallel sphere. When time and space are no longer a factor what John beholds is the plan in motion from beginning to end.

This mighty spiritual being who appears like a slaughtered lamb standing could suggest that Christ is continually being slaughtered. Could this mean that the Mystery of Golgotha is a perpetual event?

We might then ask how this is relevant to life in the 21st Century. How can this information be useful in our own lives? When contemplating spiritual information we must always be able to see the relevance in our daily lives otherwise it is nothing more than entertainment or theory.

The relevance of this vision is that since we have already been bought by the blood of the slaughtered one, now it is the Christ within us, and within others, that we crucify. Until we become worthy to break the seals and behold our karma we will continue to slaughter the Christ within. We do this through our criticism and judgment, our lack of interest in each other and our lack of love. This is exactly what happened to Jesus as he made his way to the ultimate slaughter. He was mocked and ridiculed, gossiped about, misunderstood, misinterpreted and suffered disloyalty. The focus was on his errors with no ability to behold his commitment to the mighty plan. John is the first earthly human being to see the panoramic plan and he is trying to warn us not to perpetuate that which has already been taken care of.

If we are to participate in the new consciousness we must try to behold each other differently. We each have the freedom to make individual choices and while some people seem to make strange choices, or behave in unexpected ways, we can't really know the karma that sits behind it. Only those who truly love can open the seals and see what is behind the imprint. In the meantime we must become the interested observer, not judging but loving each other as co-bearers of Christ. Christ is the perfection we strive for; this is our purpose. He is "the one who is and who was and who is to come." Rev 1:4 He was fully connected to his I AM in the beginning and came to show us how it was done. Now, of our own free will, we must follow his example. All the fuss made of him in John's vision is because he made it possible for us to become like him. It is said that, "God is no man's debtor", nor is Christ under any obligation to us. He bought us using the currency of his blood and gives us the freedom to stop slaughtering him in ourselves and in each other.

And hast made them a kingdom and priests to our God, and they shall reign on earth. Rev 5:10

When we rule in our kingdom, and we show real signs of making ourselves priests, we will treat each other as we would treat Christ. As long as we don't treat each other, and ourselves, as if Christ were in our midst then we don't love. Then the lamb, even though it stands in its resurrection power, continues to be slain.

Then I looked and heard the voice of many angels, numbering thousands upon thousands, and ten thousand times ten thousand. They encircled the throne and the living creatures and the elders. In a loud voice they sang: "Worthy is the Lamb, who was slain, to receive power and wealth and wisdom and strength and honor and glory and praise!" Then I heard every creature in heaven and on earth and under the earth and on the sea, and all that is in them, singing: "To him who sits on the throne and to the Lamb be praise and honor and glory and power, for ever and ever!" The four living creatures said, "Amen," and the elders fell down and worshiped. Rev 5:11-14

To fully utilise John's vision we could try to recreate it in our own imagination. We could even create an image of it on paper or perhaps develop a symbol that expresses all the elements it contains. This vision could be of great comfort on our journey through the next chapters when John describes the opening of the seals.

In chapters 4 and 5 John describes the great goal for every human being. He gives us a sense of the importance of this goal, especially in these last verses when he sees and hears so many angels. Imagine what it would be like to see and hear countless angels singing because of what one being did. John is privy to this because that being, here called the Lamb, initiated him. Now we must follow in their footsteps – except now the Lamb is within us.

Once we stop crucifying the Lamb, giving it room to move within us, we become like John, able to behold, able to be conscious. Being conscious means that we must be prepared to experience difficulties and painful realisations. The first thing we behold is ourselves, our own nature. In other words, when we connect up with our Higher Self we see our lower self more clearly. This is a sacrificial act; we must subdue our ego and be strong enough to face our own characteristics. This can be a most difficult experience.

If we are not to be defeated by these difficult experiences then we need something higher to hang on to. The image of John's vision is one support. If we are not convinced that we would need such support just think about how absorbing our pain can be, sometimes to the exclusion of all else. Yet if we are to become more conscious we have to prove, primarily to ourselves, that we can observe our lower self without being thrown by what we see. We must strive to be the interested observer of this lower self. Even if we can't achieve this every time we face some difficulty, as least we should aim to get better and better at it.

The primary difficulty we face is our soul. Even though we are beings of body, soul and spirit an honest assessment will reveal that we identify most strongly with our body. Most of us don't have a conscious experience of our soul and spirit. Yet in reality we are beings of soul and spirit which use the body as a vehicle to dwell on this planet. We could ask whether we are sitting in the back seat as a passenger and letting the car drive itself.

As long as that is the case then our lower self is in charge and our soul is on autopilot. In this unconscious state our soul is caught in a polarity between love and hate, between what we like and what we dislike. Until our Higher Self can have an influence in our soul we swing between what we like and what we don't like and there is little equanimity. Increasingly we must learn how to be the interested observer otherwise we will not be able to bear what we see when our lower self is revealed.

There are many ways to free ourselves from the habitual love-hate polarity. We can learn to become more interested in everything around us. We can see everything with new eyes, as if we are seeing things for the first time. How differently would we relate to each other if we were continually meeting for the first time? How differently would we relate if we listened intently to each other without disagreeing or agreeing with what is said? By developing a quiet appreciation of each other's gifts, of each other's efforts free of judgment, our soul will come alive. The living soul engages with the Higher Self and mediates between the body and the spirit. This is the soul's great secret.

The myriads of angels sing about the qualities of such a person. Having these seven qualities is the sign that they have united their lower and Higher Self. They receive power, *dunamis*, which speaks about motion, nothing is stagnant, everything is flowing and moving like the clouds in the sky. They receive wealth, *ploutos*, which is enrichment, indicating that they are given access to resources which they use creatively. They receive wisdom, *sophia*. They also receive strength, *ischus*, which means ability - they are made able and capable. They receive honor, *timé*, which means they have value and glory, *doxa*, or illumination, so they shine in the darkness. And finally they receive praise eulogia - logia means 'to speak' and *eu* means 'well'. So they are able to speak well so that what they say becomes a blessing to all who hear their words.

It is interesting that the angels sing about all seven and the creatures only sing about four. Perhaps riches, wisdom and ability are gifts belonging to a higher dimension of our consciousness. To the extent that we are worthy of these gifts is the extent to which the Lamb has mobility in our being.

CHAPTER SIX

The Seven Seals

Now I saw when the Lamb opened one of the seven seals, and I heard one of the four living creatures say, as with a voice of thunder, "Come!" And I saw, and behold, a white horse, and its rider had a bow; and a crown was given to him, and he went out conquering and to conquer. Rev 6:1-2

There are various ways to understand the seals. In terms of our developing consciousness we could look at how the seals can be applied to seven different areas of our being. This means that we not only accept theoretically that the human being is more than just a physical body, but that we actually experience how the seven areas of our being function.

John is urging us to see, to behold, *idou*, in more detail who we really are. It is as if the beholding sets off a reaction and one of the four living creatures sounds like a crack of thunder. Come! Act! Move from where you are! Imagine how loud it would have been. Perhaps this was necessary, as if to break open a new ability within John so that he could see what no human being had ever seen before.

John's journey through the seven seals can assist us to experience our whole being more consciously. These are not seven divisions, but rather areas of activity which interweave with each other. If we can experience their different qualities and become aware of how they interact, we can have more influence over them. The more influence we have the more freedom we experience. In fact, true freedom is not about doing whatever we please, it is about having the freedom to control our consciousness. The journey through the seven seals shows how this takes place.

Our first step is to acknowledge that our consciousness consists of our thoughts, our feelings and our intentions or actions (our will). These activities course through our being continually and often unconsciously. Yet it isn't enough just to say that human beings think, feel and act; we all know that every human being has different capacities to express these three functions. Within our own being we express these functions in higher and lower ways according to circumstances and according to how conscious we are. Our aim of course is to be as conscious as possible so that we are in the highest possible control of how we think, feel and act.

If we consider just our physical body for the moment we can say that the domain of thinking is in our head, our feelings are in our heart and the domain of our actions is in our limbs. When we consider the unseen areas of our being we can also see how these three activities have other domains as well, in our soul and spirit. By observing our thoughts, feelings and intentions we can come to know which area of our being is active in any given situation. By breaking open the seven seals within our own being we become increasingly conscious and in control of our lives. However there is a proviso. We must be in the company of the Lamb for only the Lamb, the one who conquered crucifixion, is worthy -

I saw a strong angel proclaiming with a loud voice, "Who is worthy to open the scroll and break its seals?" And no one in heaven or on earth or under the earth was able to open the scroll or to look into it, and I wept much that no one was found worthy to open the scroll or to look into it. Then one of the elders said to me, "Weep not; lo, the Lion of the tribe of Judah, the Root of David, has conquered, so that he can open the scroll and its seven seals." Rev 5:2-5

It is extraordinary to think that no one but one, in heaven or earth, was worthy – does that include God? Can we ever plumb the depths of the mystery of the evolution of mankind? To become worthy it seems that we are continually required to strike the balance between our connection with matter and our connection with the spiritual worlds. If we are too connected with one or the other we are not worthy. Only one, the Lion who became the Lamb, was able to strike the right connection.

It all gets back to the way we think, feel and use our will in the various areas of our being. If we don't quite get this then it helps to imagine how Jesus completed his journey to the cross without becoming depressed, losing his temper, yelling out in pain or even giving up and playing the Roman or Jewish game. This is the kind of conqueror we must become, but now in our consciousness.

Since the Lamb, the only one worthy, is opening the seals then they are shown in their purity. As each seal is opened the innate nature of the different areas of our being is revealed and this becomes a benchmark for us. As we try to imagine these different areas or levels it helps to experience them as forces. This could be why they are described as horses. We could say that the four horses represent the forces that we have developed so far in our evolution. That they have a rider could indicate that our Higher Self has conquered and controls the horse.

Seal One – The White Horse

Now I saw when the Lamb opened one of the seven seals, and I heard one of the four living creatures say, as with a voice of thunder, "Come!" And I saw, and behold, a white horse, and its rider had a bow; and a crown was given to him, and he went out conquering and to conquer. Rev 6:1-2

The first horse is white, *leukos*, which has a sense of brightness about it. This white horse indicates that area of our being where the life-force operates. Rudolf Steiner calls this our etheric body. In chapter one of these reflections this force was described in this way:

"Think of a piece of fruit freshly picked, it is plump and full of vitality. Place it in a bowl and over time watch how it shrivels. The life-force gradually leaves and eventually the fruit will decay. We also have such a life-force in our own body. As long as our life-force is connected with our body we live, if it disconnects, we die."

We have this force in common with the plant world on a physical level, but in the human being it is more developed. Furthermore, the plant does not have its own soul and spirit, it exists in a group or genus. The individualized human being develops higher qualities of this life-force on the soul and spirit level.

On a physical level the etheric is a web of formative forces that builds up and gives shape to our physical body – like an invisible matrix. When we are children it has its greatest vitality which is lost over time and our body sags and wrinkles.

On a soul level these etheric forces contain our thoughts and memories. If our etheric body is too closely bonded to our physical body then our thoughts and memories are habitual. The more lively our etheric body the greater our ability to think new thoughts and combine our memories in new ways. Then we are more open to new ideas and more co-operative with others.

On a spiritual level these etheric forces can assist us to have completely new ideas and insights. Here our thoughts can freely associate and this is how new inventions are discovered. When we experience freedom in our thinking it indicates that our I AM is able to enter into the weaving forces of our etheric body. This gives us a feeling of harmony and balance and a sense of being true to our human nature.

This is a work in progress and we are continually striving to achieve this balance within our being. If we observe the way we think we will identify those thoughts that are closely aligned with our physical being as abstract. These are the second-hand thoughts that are perpetuated in our culture, especially through the media. For example, deodorant causes cancer or gravity makes our body sag. The myth busting television programs are dedicated to exploding this kind of abstract thinking. These are the thoughts we accept from others without testing them. Even spiritual knowledge can be abstract if we accept it without question.

We could say that our thoughts that are too closely bound to the physical body are simply shadows of reality. If our thinking processes are active in our soul our thoughts are lively, they have more movement feed from old patterns. We experience this when we try to introduce new ideas into a group. Some people will always want to do things the way they have always been done, some others will take some convincing to try something new and still others will be willing to embrace the new. This is directly tied to the mobility of a person's etheric body.

If we are able to change a habit, or change the way we think about a thing, then our etheric body will change. These activities lighten our etheric body and give it mobility which in turn keeps us youthful. This sheds some light on what Jesus was saying in the Gospel of St Matthew -

At that time the disciples came to Jesus, saying, "Who is the greatest in the kingdom of heaven?" And calling to him a child, he put him in the midst of them, and said, "Truly, I say to you, unless you turn and become like children, you will never enter the kingdom of heaven. Mt 18:1-3

Observe children to see how their youthful etheric forces are at work in their being. Each day brings changes to their lives as they learn and grow. Observe plant life and see how it adapts to different conditions. If we are willing to accept change, even the smallest change, our own etheric forces will take on new life. But first we must be willing to change the way we think. Not just once but continually. Our lower self will always fight against this. It will convince us that change takes too much effort. This is not true, once we begin to conquer, conquering becomes a perpetual action in our etheric being "and he went out conquering and to conquer." From one small change big changes grow just as an acorn can grow into a mighty oak tree.

This conquering brings nourishment into our being. It loosens the etheric web that wants to cling too closely to our physical body. Then our I AM can engage more easily in our being and enhance our ability to move more harmoniously in life. We will have greater control of our thoughts which can then guide our feelings and influence our actions more easily. We become the conqueror and we are given the crown.

Now I saw when the Lamb opened one of the seven seals, and I heard one of the four living creatures say, as with a voice of thunder, "Come!" And I saw, and behold, a white horse, and its rider had a bow; and a crown was given to him, and he went out conquering and to conquer. Rev 6:1-2

As John looks into the seals with his new ability to behold, he experiences firsthand the panorama of the development of mankind. He sees how human beings individuated from the homogenous whole. As this rider directs his horse out of the pack John follows him and beholds how, step by step, each individual rider learned to take self-responsibility. He beheld what was involved when a human being takes full responsibility for the way they feel, think and act.

So he beheld in the opened seal what it meant to be part of the whole and how every thought immediately affected everything around us. To understand this we need only to think about what happens when we feel personal shame and our skin blushes; then, our thoughts, feelings and actions registered in everything around us for they were more group thoughts, in harmony, or not, with everything in our surroundings.

As John continued to behold the opened seal he saw the conditions change and each human being started to have their own private thoughts and we could think what we liked oblivious of the affect it had on everything around us. Then his vision was directed to the way this condition changed back to the purity it had at first – but now, no longer the homogenous whole but a community of self-realised individuals. Since he is in the presence of the Lamb he would also have understood more deeply the purpose of Christ's incarnation, death and resurrection. He would have seen that the events of Golgotha were the turnkey in human consciousness.

Then John notices that the rider has a bow but there is no mention of any arrows. This could be because arrows or darts are connected with thoughts that we direct at each other. When we were not individuated and we direct a bad thought to someone it was as if our thought became an arrow that tore a wound in that person. This is still the case today but we are not aware of it because we can't see the spiritual results of our thinking. If we did we wouldn't think the thoughts that we do. We must now mount this bright and shining horse and hold our bow not as a weapon but to signify our purity of thought.

Since we no longer have an experience of the homogenous human race which gave us access to all 'memory' now we need to develop our individual memory. Memory lies at the heart of our consciousness to guide us through life. To appreciate the value of memory we need only consider the effects of dementia.

Understanding the relationship of memory to the human life-force (the etheric matrix) will unlock the mystery of this unpleasant medical condition.

So what is memory? Memory is the ability to read earlier sense impressions left behind as imprints in our life-force. We commit things to memory by creating replicas of our sense impressions. Remember seeing something new, like a new computer programme, and then creating a reference point for it. If we don't create the replica we don't remember. Or our inability to remember things previously remembered means that there has been a change in our etheric life-force. Furthermore, if we only store the imprints of memories in our physical body as 'facts' and never open them, like a living book in our soul, then these memories are mere shadows of their reality.

Memory is far more intricate than we are lead to believe. The process of memory has two possible connections within our being. One is connected to our lower self, the other to our Higher Self. The memory belonging to our Higher Self has a broad panorama and therefore is more objective; the lower self's memory images are more subjective and can work against us in many ways. If we are to be released from the grip of some memories we must allow our Higher Self to shine its light into them.

When viewed from the higher perspective we often see that the painful memory has a purpose, it is part of our biography. The pain of the memory can turn into gratitude for the experience that has played an important part in developing our character and capabilities. This 'pain-to-gratitude' is a powerful experience which transforms our etheric body and assists us to bear pain without regret or guilt – those ego-centric experiences that retard our development. When we achieve this Christ is immediately active within us. Like a game of snap, we turn the card from pain to gratitude and we match Christ's Golgotha experience. We become one with him, melded in the sorrow mixed with joy that is the deepest mystery of the human experience. Only then do we go out conquering and to conquer.

Postscript

These words about memory are written on the eve of the apology to Australian Aboriginals for the way they were treated, not only by successive Australian Governments, but also by Australian citizens. The harmful thoughts of indigenous and non-indigenous Australians have shot at each other like arrows from a bow for two centuries. Tomorrow, February 13, 2008, brings the possibility of a mighty 'pain-to-gratitude' experience in the Southern Hemisphere which could have cosmic implications for a renewal of the life-force of this earth. Then the memory of the human journey may be released from its darkness and its dreaming to the light of human purpose and cosmic intelligence. The shining white horse speaks of this.

Now I saw when the Lamb opened one of the seven seals, and I heard one of the four living creatures say, as with a voice of thunder, "Come!" And I saw, and behold, a white horse, and its rider had a bow; and a crown was given to him, and he went out conquering and to conquer. Rev 6:1-2

The gentleness and purity of this description hides the immense significance of the event. Once a seal is broken it can never be restored. Not only that but also "no one in heaven or on earth or under the earth was able to open the scroll or to look into it."

John is drawing our attention to a momentous cosmic event and he is calling us to participate fully in it. This is not a tale from the distant past, or a shadow of the future, this is an event that can occur in our lives just as soon as we are ready. Observation of world events suggests that now would not be too soon.

Our task is to become aware of the Lamb within us whose every deed is dedicated to our awakening. This is the Christ Impulse that, since Golgotha, is part of our inner being. We carry this Lamb within us silently until we reach the same point of despair that John reached when he said:

I saw a strong angel proclaiming with a loud voice, "Who is worthy to open the scroll and break its seals?" And no one in heaven or on earth or under the earth was able to open the scroll or to look into it, and I wept much that no one was found worthy to open the scroll or to look into it. Rev 5:2-4

Surely the seals could be opened if God wanted them opened. It wasn't about what God could do; it was about what John could do, and what we can now do because of the deed of Christ. When Christ is no longer the silent presence within us, when we are able to behold this Christ-Lamb, the first thing he does is open the first seal. How will we know that? We will immediately experience the jolt of the thunderclap. This awakens our inner senses and reveals the secrets of the human being that have been hidden for aeons. Now it is up to us to behold what lies beneath the seals.

Beholding is not a passive activity; it calls for us to experience the living Imagination that is revealed. In this way we become the rider and we know why the horse is white, we know why we have the bow and we know why we are given the crown. Then John says we go forth, our attention turns outwards and we are able to act in the world because we have overcome. Overcome is a better translation for *nikao* than conquer, it suggests that we have 'come over' from the past and can stand in the present and can step into the future as required. We are mobile, not fixed in one position. This is the conqueror, the one who has overcome and continues to overcome the influence of the lower self.

When this bright white horse meets our vision the mystery of the etheric human being is revealed to us. John describes his own vision and he hopes that it will give us the clues for our own discovery. By contemplating his words we can build an understanding of the role of our own etheric life-force. To do this properly we need a basic understanding of the properties of this life-force.

As previously stated, it expresses itself differently in the three different areas of our being. In fact we can see it as a metamorphosis of activity as it moves from body, to soul, to spirit. What in our body is the drive of growth, nutrition and reproduction; in our soul becomes thinking; and in our spirit becomes Inspiration or pure, living thinking.

As this life-force becomes more active in our soul and spirit we become more conscious. We cannot be conscious of the digestive process in our body, and in our soul we are only dreamily conscious of our thinking processes. It is only when we become aware of our thinking as a spiritual activity that we are fully conscious of the work of this life-force in our spirit.

When our thinking comes alive in our spiritual being, freed of its daily, earth-bound, second-hand ways, it becomes a living tool. This new thinking is vital and alive and assists us to reach new solutions, which means to see new connections between ideas.

Furthermore, we don't need a stimulus to think new thoughts; they come to us as if they were a gift 'out of the blue'. When we begin to experience this kind of spiritual thinking, the ideas that come to us have a certain ring of truth. We may not be able to know how we know, we just know. It is this inner knowing that the world cries out for. The demand for scientific proof has reached the point of being ridiculous. Scientists, who say that they can prove that we are only beings of mind and body, at the same time say that they cannot explain the deepest human wonder, which is love. In its highest form this love, agape, is the very substance of our I AM and it pours from us to touch everything and everyone equally. Not until this love exudes from us can we look into the open seal. Then we experience true brotherhood, Philadelphia, and "our life together will be such that we will not disturb one another, such that one soul will work into another soul in complete harmony". Rudolf Steiner "Reading the Pictures of the Apocalypse", May 21, 1909

Seal Two – The Red Horse

When he opened the second seal, I heard the second living creature say, "Come!" And out came another horse, bright red; its rider was permitted to take peace from the earth, so that men should slay one another; and he was given a great sword. Rev 6:3-4

The second horse is fiery red *purrhos* from *pur* which means fire. As the Lamb opens the second seal the essence of the human emotional or desire body is revealed. Emotions, like fire, can glow warmly or flare up uncontrolled. John now saw how mankind had been given the opportunity to individually regulate himself. No longer guided by what is best for the group as a whole, now each person was given control of his or her actions and decide what was best for them. Within this seal are the secrets of our human ability to feel what we should do and what we should refrain from doing. It is obvious that many people in the world today do not take this responsibility seriously. They decide to do whatever they like expressing their emotions inappropriately without regard for the consequences. Nor do they temper their thoughts and actions with a feeling for what is right.

This desire body also controls our inclination to move around which gives us a mobile relationship to the earth. In other words, this is the area of our being which animates us so that we can explore our environment and attempt to make sense of it. In the white horse we have things in common with the plant kingdom; in the red horse we have a connection to the characteristics of the animal kingdom.

It is in this region of our being that we register our perceptions and sensations and create the memories that we store in our life body. The more active this region of our being is the more aware and observant we are.

This body is also the domain of our consciousness and gives us an awareness of our own existence. This awareness gives rise to self-interest. Many of our automatic instincts have their origin here and we need to become increasingly aware of how we put our needs ahead of the needs of others. This results from a feeling that other people will diminish us and gives rise to feelings of strong self-preservation. We are inclined to put boundaries around our interactions with others so that we don't feel threatened by them. Instead of protection, this is experienced as rejection – others feel rejected by us and we in turn feel rejected by them. So it is a false sense of protection and places us at odds with the world.

This paints a bleak picture of the human experience but it is a crucial part of our journey to becoming fully self-conscious beings. If we get stuck in this preparatory cycle we become isolated and alone. This is a trend the world over; many people live alone, do not marry and have few friends. This aloneness points to the evolutionary process of fully experiencing our small earthly self which is followed by the next phase which is to connect up with our Higher Self and experience the brotherhood of mankind.

Knowing this we can make some sense of John's description of the second seal. In comparison, the first rider was given, *edothe*, a crown whereas to the second rider "it was given (not permitted) to him to take peace out of the earth in order that they shall slay one another." This word peace, *eirene*, speaks about the harmonious relationships between men, and refers to friendliness. So one was given a crown, the other was given the ability to remove friendliness. Indeed it is true; our aloneness means that we are without harmonious relationships. This is the only way we can disconnect from the group, and reconnect as self-realised individuals.

We might then ask why it would be necessary to slay one another. In many of our friendships our reliance on the other person hampers our spiritual development. This reliance on others must be slain - especially if our relationships are biased or unbalanced. If we only have relationships with people we like, and reject relationships with people we don't like, then we must question the basis of our relationships. Do we only form relationships with those who can supply our needs? We are at a stage in the development of human consciousness that we must become self-sufficient. We must supply our own needs instead of looking outside ourselves for what we lack. Then our relationships cease to be based on favouritism, we love all people equally.

This is the point when we become very aware that we are beings of soul and spirit. There is another name for this desire body; it is referred to as the astral or starry body. Through it we become conscious that we are citizens of the Cosmos and contributors to human evolution. We understand that it is our responsibility to refine the forces of our astral body by allowing our purest thinking to moderate our feelings. Then we can be trusted with the great sword.

When he opened the second seal, I heard the second living creature say, "Come!" And out came another horse, bright red; its rider was permitted to take peace from the earth, so that men should slay one another; and he was given a great sword. Rev 6:3-4

The red horse speaks vividly about how we might relate to one other. The currency of our relationships is karma. It is our astral, which we can also call our soul body, which gives us the experience of karma. In each incarnation we create this karma through the way we feel, think and act so that in future lives we can reap the rewards. However, we may not always see the situations that are "given to us" – *edothe* – as rewards. We may even blame the rider of the red horse to whom it was given to take peace (friendliness) from our being. Alternatively, which is the whole point of the exercise, we may be able to meet challenging situations so that we restore peace within ourselves.

The red horse represents our astral as the bearer of emotions, images, thoughts; things which are not visible to the eye but which can be felt internally. In comparison, our 'I' which is riding the red horse, is the bearer of Higher Self-consciousness and comprehension. It is our 'I' which rides our inner self into the outer world. It is in this way that our 'I' becomes fully conscious of itself. We will never become conscious of our 'I' if we withdraw from the world, if we shrink back from life's experiences.

Each life brings with it increased responsibility to act, think, and feel in the right way. We could even say that while we act unconsciously our lives are in jeopardy. This is a great incentive to become as conscious as possible so that we make the wisest choices in every area of life. The only way to be conscious is to engage with our 'I' and allow it to override our lower unconscious instincts.

These instincts stem from our karma and are embedded in our soul like a blue print. If we were hurt by someone in a past life our unconscious instinct is to repay the hurt. If we were killed by someone in a past life we may instinctively try to kill them in this life, perhaps not literally, but now we try to kill their ideas or prevent them from expressing themselves fully. If we were judgmental then now we are judged and so on. If these situations are not met with understanding we can be consumed by strong emotional responses, especially anger.

In this way we slay one another with our half formed assessments. For instance, if a person is ill we immediately see it as a punishment for them. Or we can even think that we brought on our own illness through our own actions. Rarely do we see illness as a consciousness-raising transition. When we get ill there are two options; we get better or we die. In both cases we go through a period of inner striving against the dysfunction in our body. This striving builds up our will forces, giving us a surplus of will forces in fact, which we can put to good use after we get better, or after we die.

Healing is also the sign that our life-force is creating a new relationship with our body, soul and our 'I'. This occurs though a breaking down and then a building up. We can only fully understand this by creating an image of the threefold human being. We know what the body looks like but how do we see our soul and spirit in connection with our body? We could see these three areas of our being as being held together through myriads of tiny connections. Our basic functions of thought, feeling and activity connect differently with the different areas of our being; our life-force, our soul-body and our spirit. Remember that it is the 'I' that thinks, feels and acts according to how conscious we are.

So when our consciousness changes through illness some of the connections would need to be adjusted. For instance, if our thoughts increase their moderation of our feelings then this will affect the flow of blood in our body and we will not blush as easily. If our will has a stronger effect on our feelings when we have to speak in public then we are less likely to perspire.

On the other hand, if we manage to change our consciousness because we have engaged more firmly with our 'I' then the relationship of all three regions of our being is changed and this could easily affect the health of our body. Close observation will usually reveal subtle changes in a person's character after a period of illness – something is slain.

As mentioned in chapter five, the word slain comes from the Greek word *sphage* which means slaughter. It suggests a sacrifice; that there is a plan to prepare something for inevitable death. Our consciousness cannot grow if we will not let old thoughts, feelings and modes of behaviour die. At every step we must be prepared to let go of old patterns. Illness can certainly force us to do this. The Lamb is the mighty archetype of our need to engage with the world, to embrace all the experiences given to us, and then to allow them to be nailed to the earth so that we can break free to a state of resurrected consciousness.

When he opened the second seal, I heard the second living creature say, "Come!" And out came another horse, bright red; its rider was permitted to take peace from the earth, so that men should slay one another; and he was given a great sword. Rev 6:3-4

The red horse represents more than just our astral or soul body; in its higher expression it also represents the primary area of our threefold soul. It is here that we have inner feelings about the outside world. Here we are sentient beings; capable of feeling and perception and we respond emotionally rather than intellectually (which happens in the second soul area).

On our path to become self-conscious beings, and distinguishing us from what we have in common with animals, it is in this primary soul region that we begin to personalise our soul. Prior to this we were dependent on an outer group soul – which we could say was divided into four expressions characterised by the four living creatures.

We began developing this area of our soul around 3000 BC and these three areas of soul development can take around 2,160 years (a period Rudolf Steiner and others say is one twelfth of the Platonic Year). Even though human beings developed this area of the soul so long ago we often feel most comfortable experiencing the world in this dreamy, feeling consciousness.

We could also say that here we are dealing with the gateway to our soul. This is where the impulses of the outside world start to mean something to us. It is here that a beautiful rose can arouse a different feeling than a dead possum. We register these images that enter into our consciousness but if we fail to keep images alive by not giving them enough attention they can fade and die into forgetfulness.

Certainly this is the domain of our instincts but they are a level above the instincts we find in the animal kingdom, just as this area is a level higher than our own astral being. Here we can give dignity to our desires and emotions. When we modify our instincts we begin to experience the freedom that comes from the ability to make the choice.

The fundamental experience in this primary soul region is love and hate. Here we find things are pleasant or unpleasant; we are drawn to things or we repel them. If we allow this polarity to dominate us we can be quite irrational in our decisions about what is good and bad. The dream quality of these feelings needs to be guided by our thoughts and will found in the two higher soul regions.

When these feelings arise in us unconsciously we can, for instance, find ourselves rejecting any possibility of friendship with a person because of a karmic undercurrent. How else would we dislike a person that other people like? These unconscious feelings cause us to lean towards people or things, or away from them, without a logical explanation. What we think is logic or an incisive action can simply be overpowering feelings. It is the rider, the 'I', who can awaken our unconscious soul and lead us to a higher response. Indeed, our 'I' must become conscious of itself in this soul region.

Until it does our soul, left to its own natural instincts, can be very misleading. It is here that past life memories arise unconsciously and cause responses that we may regret. This is especially the case with anger. Anger plays a very important role in the life of our soul.

Way back, when we were developing this sentient region of our soul, our anger protected us from any injustice. It gave us the strength and motivation to slay each other if we were threatened. It was also, therefore, a deterrent. As our 'I' being becomes more conscious within us then this anger gives us the opportunity to choose a higher response to an unjust situation.

At the same time, the agitation caused by anger strengthens our soul; it is a kind of rocket-fuel which propels us to a broader understanding. To be able to transmute our anger in this way gives us a tremendous experience of freedom. We become like the rider of the red horse who is given the great sword. Notice that he is not given a shield. He needs no protection; all he needs is the experience of acting out of his 'I' being. This brings with it a certain warm objectivity and gives us the confidence to become a stimulating - and perhaps not always welcome - force in the world.

This sword, *machaira*, is more like a dagger. Such a dagger in the hands of the one who is connected to their 'I' being can excise what is not required. In fact, when our 'I' being becomes conscious of itself in the different levels of our soul, an inner anger rises up within us as we see how unconscious people are. With our dagger we can wake people up from their malaise. Stick the knife in, metaphorically speaking, and take away the fake peace that people try to create. At this stage we have been able to transmute our anger to love. In fact, the role of anger in our being is to give us the highest experience of love. This can only happen through individual choice. If we express our anger, as people so easily do, then we are denied this love experience and instead we feel weakened and empty. If we can ride this red horse, having the conscious understanding of what it means to be given the role of taking peace from the world, then we will experience the love and freedom necessary to receive this great dagger.

Seal Three – The Black Horse

When he opened the third seal, I heard the third living creature say, "Come!" And I saw, and behold, a black horse, and its rider had a balance in his hand; and I heard what seemed to be a voice in the midst of the four living creatures saying, "A quart of wheat for a denarius, and three quarts of barley for a denarius; but do not harm oil and wine!" Rev 6:5-7

The third horse is black and black can either reveal or obscure. It is easier to see a light shining in the darkness than it is to see a light in broad daylight. On the other hand black can hide within its breast that which is yet to be revealed.

The third seal speaks to us of the second soul region; the domain of our mind, our intellect, where our thoughts are active. It is here that we apply reasoning and logic to all that enters our soul through our senses; making sense of things. We weigh things up to see if they are in agreement with each other. We could say that this is the justice department of our being which we began developing during the time of Plato and Aristotle. The foundation of our legal system can be traced back to this time; the balance or scales is its symbol. We worked on developing this area of our being from approximately 750BC up till the fifteenth century.

The weighing and measuring of the fruits of the earth spoken of in the third seal is a good image for the values we place on our thoughts and ideas. As our consciousness evolved we had to be released from the influence of the spiritual worlds by taking responsibility for establishing our own values; wheat is more valuable than barley, oil and wine are absolute necessities. In this process of placing value on things, the first thing that we valued was ourselves. Our instinct was to value ourselves more highly than others. This manifested as a perceived need for self-preservation, physically and in every other way.

While this can be seen to be selfish – and there is always the risk of over-valuing – this experience gave us our first sense of ourselves as individuals living independently from the homogenous spiritual worlds. This also meant that we began to experience thoughts within us, whereas previously we seemed to receive them from outside (although perhaps this perception was a symptom of settling more firmly into our physical being). We soon realised the amount of effort required to think our own thoughts. For instance, what thoughts are we supposed to have about the sound that came from the midst of the four living creatures?

"A quart of wheat for a denarius, and three quarts of barley for a denarius; but do not harm oil and wine!"

When we lived in the thoughts that seemed to be outside our physical body, before we had learned how to form them ourselves, we instinctively knew what they meant. When we have to apply our own logic to these words, on the surface they only seem to tell us some simple things, for example, wheat is more valuable than barley and that it is possible for us to act in a way that could harm the oil and the wine. In fact, our experience of not really understanding the meaning of this statement reveals just how dead our thinking is and what a struggle it is to make sense of it. These thoughts we now experience within us do not have the same quality of life as those thoughts that approached the physical body from outside rather than exist in it. These thoughts actually lived in our etheric body and were not yet experienced in our physical brain as they are today. When we began to experience thinking in our physical brain it was as if it became shadowy and obscure; as if the life was drained from it. We were left to apply methods of reasoning and logic as Aristotle outlined in his various treatises.

Of course, there is always the temptation to revert to a previous state of consciousness, especially if the new consciousness requires effort. Even today many people subconsciously try to re-experience the old thought patterns with their instinctive meanings. This is like reversing the car back into the garage.

What we must come to terms with is that thinking has to die in the physical body (by becoming shadowy) and then be resurrected in our etheric being as the new Imagination. This Imagination is not a spatial sequence of images sitting side by side, it happens in time as a living morphology. The image changes in form as well as in structure; from wheat to barley to oil and to wine. The properties of these substances speak to us as a living Imagination to give us guidance about the right use of our intellect.

With agility of soul we are able to flow into the development of our thoughts with the right amount of feeling and will harmonising our insight and understanding. Then we experience the presence of our Higher Self, the 'I' that stands with the Lamb to make the opening of the seals possible. The darkness of our physical being is necessary to reveal our 'I'. Yet so often we want to escape our physical being and scamper back to our origins without fully passing through the physical earthly conditions necessary for our own resurrection. We mustn't flee from earthly matter; we must strive to give it the appropriate form so that its true spiritual content and purpose is revealed.

When he opened the third seal, I heard the third living creature say, "Come!" And I saw, and behold, a black horse, and its rider had a balance in his hand; and I heard what seemed to be a voice in the midst of the four living creatures saying, "A quart of wheat for a denarius, and three quarts of barley for a denarius; but do not harm oil and wine!" Rev 6:5-7

It is probably just as well that we don't really know how shadowy our intellect is. We might fall into deep despair. Perhaps this is why John gives us such brief sketches of what is revealed within these opened seals. He knows too well the road we must travel in our consciousness.

If we are to become conscious to any degree then this will only occur through our own striving. It is this striving that strengthens our inner being. Our capacity to think things through, to weigh things up, depends entirely on the agility of our soul. The red horse revealed to us the value of experiencing but not expressing anger. The black horse shows us the value of judgment.

When anger takes hold of us it signals our opportunity to broaden our understanding about the person who made us angry. We are not always aware of the catalyst for their behaviour but at least we are open to consider that there may be a reason beyond our immediate view.

When the feeling associated with the red horse works in harmony with the thoughts associated with the black horse we have the opportunity to make a more thorough assessment of the situations we face in our lives. If our anger is too strong it hampers our ability to think clearly. If we can keep the anger at bay then we give ourselves the opportunity to judge a situation more logically.

Our ability to weigh things up depends on the dexterity of the three soul forces; feeling, thinking and will. Since it is the rider, the 'I', who carries the balance, this means that only when our Higher Self is controlling our thoughts are we able to judge correctly. Furthermore, this judging needs to be a continual weighing up rather than a final judgment.

The Greek word for judgment is *krisis* and it means a separating, then a decision. We wouldn't mix the wheat and the barley together before we put them on the scales to assess their value; wheat, which isn't as prolific as barley, costs three times more.

When forming opinions about people how often do we separate out all our thoughts about the way a person acts, and put them back together uniquely for that particular person? Put it to the test. At the mention of the word 'child' many people bring to mind an uncontrollable two year old. People with disabilities are usually considered to be in a wheelchair; women cry, men don't cry and so on. This exemplifies just how shadowy (and lazy) our intellect has become.

Unless we strive to understand that each person's behaviour is motivated by their experiences in all their past lives then our judging is limited by our ability to separate out all their various actions and put them together uniquely for the particular situation. This makes it difficult for us to come to a broader understanding of why they act the way they do. For instance, if a person is talkative perhaps they had a past life in a silent religious order. If they suddenly become silent in the presence of a particular person, perhaps that person was their superior in that life. If a person is quick to anger perhaps they were buried alive and died with the injustice burning like an eternal flame within their being. If a person is short perhaps they looked down on others in the past. If they over eat perhaps they were starved in the past. Each situation gives us the opportunity to broaden our understanding and become more conscious – whether we see it in ourselves or in others.

We don't need to be clairvoyant to see these things, nor should we use such information to judge others. When we see people act in a particular way by simply observing we increase our understanding. If we can involve our Higher Self then, through our clear thinking, we experience a wise knowing. It is our Higher Self that remembers all the lives we have ever lived; all our relationships, all our experiences, and therefore it understands why a person responds to us in the way that they do. It also knows why we respond to the people in our lives differently to the way other people respond to them – sometimes for no obvious reason.

If we can bring some of this into our understanding, even as a possibility, we will begin to see how it stands to reason. Then we will stop our blanket approach to judging the behaviour of others or their situation. Compassion will increasingly rise up within us as we delay our responses to many of life's experiences. Each delay means that we are thinking more, teasing out the facts and putting them together differently. Then we become the rider of the black horse with the balance in our hand.

When he opened the third seal, I heard the third living creature say, "Come!" And I saw, and behold, a black horse, and its rider had a balance in his hand; and I heard what seemed to be a voice in the midst of the four living creatures saying, "A quart of wheat for a denarius, and three quarts of barley for a denarius; but do not harm oil and wine!" Rev 6:5-7

Notice that John describes what he heard by saying that it "seemed to be a voice" or sound, *phoné*, and it was "in the midst of the four living creatures". Could it be a spiritual being sounding forth a message to us all? It may be the guardian angel or archangel of the four living creatures or it could even be an Archai or an even higher ranking member of the spiritual hierarchy.

Notice also that this sound almost has a mocking tone to it. Could this be a warning to us that by claiming control of our intellect certain challenges will arise? When we can think for ourselves, when we have our own personal and private inner thoughts, what affect does this have on our dealings with each other? Vastly different from the providence of the spiritual worlds no doubt!

We should ask why this seal emphasises the trading of goods; one denarius will buy either one measure of wheat or three measures of barley. What has doing business with each other got to do with it? Why warn us about our responsibility not to harm the oil and wine?

Think about the way we do business with each other in the world today? The so-called sophisticated money markets are nothing more than gambling. Everything is couched in acronyms to create the smoke and mirror effect. Of course these mythical structures can come crashing down like a house of cards. Then the innocent people at the bottom of the 'food chain', who have been tricked into borrowing more money than they could ever afford to pay back, become the scapegoats.

Even on a small scale, when we do business we usually seek our own advantage. This is because the thing we value most in life is money; the more we have of it the happier we are. We even think that an excessive amount of money will give us an excessive amount of happiness. Then, self-esteem and money are inextricably linked; we place greater value on those who have a lot of money than we do on those who do not. Consequently we think that money will give us self-esteem. In this way we deny the place of the 'I' in our lives. True self esteem can only come to those who have a strong connection to their own I AM. Perhaps the love of money has a place on the path to this experience – but only a place.

Further to this, we could ask the question: what is more valuable, the wheat or the denarius? Doesn't this question ignore the thing of greatest value? Which is the human labour that planted and harvested the wheat. When our human labour is given its true value then as human beings we experience the dignity that is hidden deeply within us. Then something is ignited within us; like the lamp which has an endless source of oil.

If we give this hidden element its rightful place then we might ask about the true value of the human effort that sowed the wheat and barley seeds, that tended the wheat, harvested it and brought it to us? Now we can begin to love the wise and talented farmer for he is the wine, the love that is poured out for us. We are nourished not just by the food alone but by the gift of his labour.

How much more nourished would we all be if we placed the right value on our business dealings? - or any dealings with each other for that matter. What difference would it make if we got rid of our bargain hunting mentality and we sought out the goods that were produced with love? Would we even be prepared to offer the farmer the amount of money he really needs to produce his wheat or barley? He may say, well we have five children to put through school, and we are caring for my elderly mother, so if you can pay so much my costs will be covered and I will also be able to assist my community in other ways.

These are the ideas Rudolf Steiner put forward under the banner of associative economics and the threefold social order. He explained how production, exchange and consumption could be given new life when we recognised the human being's rightful place. When the human being is strongly connected with their I AM they will never seek to take advantage of another person. The I AM gives us an experience of freedom because our love for each other pours from heart to heart. This is not orchestrated, it just is. The I AM also ignites the eternal flame within us. This flame is fed by the oil that flows when we are truly productive. Like an olive tree we are firmly grounded in the earth and our branches reach up to the heights to absorb the spiritual essence of the sun. In this way no harm can ever come to the oil and the wine.

Seal Four – The Pale Horse

When he opened the fourth seal, I heard the voice of the fourth living creature say, "Come!" And I saw, and behold, a pale horse, and its rider's name was Death, and Hades followed him; and they were given power over a fourth of the earth, to kill with sword and with famine and with pestilence and by wild beasts of the earth. Rev 6:7-9

The fourth seal rings alarm bells. The Lamb reveals to John some very dramatic things that take place within human consciousness as it develops further. These are described to us in signs that we must try to make sense of and apply to the development of our own consciousness. To be able to do this we must increase our knowledge of our own being; not just physically and mentally but by becoming more aware of how our soul and spirit guide our body through life. John sees all that he has written down from "the spirit"; from the perspective of his own spirit. This is a very different view of the world from that which we gain through our body's senses.

Down the ages the wisdom teachers have emphasised the importance of the injunction "Know yourself!" This too, is the purpose of these reflections on the Revelation to John. To know ourselves by applying a few basic principles. To know ourselves is not simply a self-centred awareness of what goes on within us – physically or spiritually - but rather to become conscious of our place in the whole universe. More than that, that we become conscious of our role in the universe; how every emotion, thought, and deed, creates this universe – for better or worse. As our awareness increases we realise the enormous responsibility that we have to ensure that our actions are creative. Furthermore, to realise that what we deem to be creative may actually be destructive, and vice versa.

The fourth seal deals with the will, our soul-will if you like. Of our three soul functions, we are least aware of our will. We can clearly see our thoughts, our feelings rise and fall in a bit of a fog, but we are often blind to the way we use our will. The domain of our will is in the third and highest soul region, the one we are in the throes of developing at present. We can call this region the spiritual soul or Consciousness Soul, the area where our awareness can gain real clarity. It is also the region where the power of the will can be misused. Then our interactions with each other are tinged with manipulative undertones.

If we want to know more detail about this region of our soul we can simply observe modern society. Manipulation is rife. Not just in the media, or in advertising, but in every transaction we make – "will that benefit me" is the unspoken question in our minds. This is how our unconscious will weaves in our being. It is our present task to become aware of it and direct it appropriately.

As John's description so vividly reveals, this is a critical point in the development of the human consciousness. It is not just about the development of our will levels it is also about our ability to involve our I AM in our daily life. It is in this soul region that we first become aware of our individuality, our I AM. Even though we received direct access to our I AM in the preceding period as we developed our intellect, we were hardly aware of it then. We can put this down to the fact that it is difficult to take everything in when an event happens; we become more aware with hindsight.

Freedom from our tribal consciousness has come to full expression today as individuality is everywhere expressed. In essence, individuality is the human experience of freewill. It is a two-edged sword; expressing our freedom regardless of the effect on other people or freely choosing to stand in the other person's shoes to share their experience. As previously mentioned, the former is definitely a step on the path to the latter.

The freedom to make individual choices carries with it a responsibility that we are hardly aware of. We can observe in many places the bravely made choices using an underdeveloped will. In some ways the church tries to circumvent this by encouraging us to follow certain religious tenets which at the same time curtails our freedom and counteracts the deed of Christ. In the words of Judith Von Halle:

"This conception of enlightenment is not held by the churches, because every person who is permeated by this [Christ] spirit will also as a consequence be free from every institution – must basically be able to be a priest in the broadest sense of the word." "And If He Has Not Been Raised" by Judith Von Halle.

John spoke of this in chapter 1

To him who loves us and has freed us from our sins by his blood and made us a kingdom, priests to his God and Father, to him be glory and dominion for ever and ever. Amen. Rev 1:6

As our will becomes conscious we will rule in our kingdom and become priests to reconcile our lower self to our Higher Self, our I AM.

When he opened the fourth seal, I heard the voice of the fourth living creature say, "Come!" And I saw, and behold, a pale horse, and its rider's name was Death, and Hades followed him; and they were given power over a fourth of the earth, to kill with sword and with famine and with pestilence and by wild beasts of the earth. Rev 6:7-9

In his description of the contents of the fourth seal John gives several hints about the mighty deed of Christ, that great sun being who entered into the body of Jesus to be crucified to death, then to resurrect in his etheric body. Until this happened no one was worthy to open the seals.

Notice that none of the other riders was given a name. This rider, the I AM, is given a name; Death. Since the name of a thing depicts its nature why would the rider be given this name? One clue may be that it is only in the highest part of our soul that we can become aware of our I AM. This awareness can call forth the Christ Impulse to the extent that we have made it active within us. For this to happen we must have put to death our unconscious thoughts, feelings and behaviour and resurrect them to give them a new and conscious life.

Why are we so afraid of death? Primarily because we have isolated ourselves from the spiritual worlds. We don't see death as the flipside of life. We ignore the fact that every living thing relies on death. The flower must die if it is to create the seed. Every cell in our body dies to make way for the growth of new cells. If the cells don't die, cancer is the result. Our fear of death will be conquered when we claim the name Death and ride the pale horse.

This colour pale is actually a pale green, *chloros*, which is the colour of foliage, and from which we get the word chlorophyll. Chlorophyll is vital for photosynthesis, which allows plants to obtain energy from sunlight. When the Christ Impulse becomes active in us we align ourselves with the sun's energy because the sun is Christ's home. In other words, we move out of the shadows in which we have been living. We know that when the sunlight is blocked a shadow is cast and nothing much grows.

When we identify ourselves too strongly with our physical body we live in a land of shadows or Hades. Although this is part of the process we do need to be aware of the shadows because we cast them everywhere, with every unconscious thought, action or emotion.

Those who make no effort to improve themselves inhabit Hades; their souls sleep and their 'I' cannot wake it up. It is through striving to become conscious of each thought, each feeling and every motive to act that our soul engages with our 'I' and lets the sun shine into our being casting out the shadows.

When we can assume our name, our nature, as Death it means that we have allowed parts of our consciousness to die. We had to pass through this shadowy consciousness and then let it die. But, of course, that which slept within us accompanies us. It must accompany us, we must own all that was unconscious within us otherwise we would be discarding our refuse indiscriminately. However, we mustn't attempt to revive that which has died within us. This all depends on the calibre of our will.

This period of developing the Consciousness Soul carries with it the great temptation to revive the old. In the heights of our soul, when our spirit begins to work into our consciousness, we are very tempted to turn back. Sometimes we may wonder if we have the stamina to embrace the future. And probably out of our own forces we don't; hence the presence of the Lamb. Only when the Lamb becomes a living presence in our consciousness can we remain fully open to the possibilities.

Think of a lamb; sweet, innocent and totally cooperative. Think of Jesus as the I AM, totally cooperating with the plan for the Christ Impulse to enter into his being. Think of all the painful steps to achieve this; suffering not for sufferings sake but for the opportunity to overcome suffering with an increasingly conscious will.

Our great challenge is to accept that death is an integral part of life. We then look for ways to claim our death-nature so that we may live in our higher being. Then we will be aware of our lower tendencies following us like Hades. We intimately know this lower being that has facilitated our life until now. This lower being that made it possible for us to exist on this earth and develop our consciousness as it can only be developed here. Now we begin to see that only to the extent that we are aware of the presence of Christ on earth can we be aware of him when we die. Only to the extent that we understand why Jesus Christ had to die, and die that way, will we be able to claim the name, the nature, Death.

When he opened the fourth seal, I heard the voice of the fourth living creature say, "Come!" And I saw, and behold, a pale horse, and its rider's name was Death, and Hades followed him; and they were given power over a fourth of the earth, to kill with sword and with famine and with pestilence and by wild beasts of the earth. Rev 6:7-9

Why would Death and Hades be given power over a fourth of the earth? Why would they be given the task of killing in four different ways? This might make more sense if we say that what is here referred to as the earth is not the globe we live on but the earthly being we live within. This earthly being can be either a fourfold or a sevenfold entity. As fourfold beings we are physical, etheric, astral and 'I'. As sevenfold beings we are physical, etheric, astral-Sentient Soul, Mind Soul, Consciousness Soul-Spirit Self, Life

Spirit and Spirit Man.

In our consideration of the seven seals a slightly different configuration emerges; etheric, astral-Sentient Soul; Mind Soul, Consciousness Soul, 'I', Spirit Self and Life Spirit. While this might seem arbitrary, from the perspective of the basic soul functions of feeling, thinking and willing we can see how they fit perfectly into the description of each seal.

As we saw in the description of the first seal, each of these functions is expressed in particular ways in the three levels of our being; body, soul and spirit. So it is not so much the area of our being that we are focussing on, but the way in which we use our feeling, thinking and will.

In our body, feeling, thinking and will have specific functions which are connected with our survival; feeling cold or warm, feeling fearful or safe, pleasure and pain etc. Through our thinking we can combine images and ideas so that we know how to function as human beings. Our will regulates our bodies inner functions; moving fluids around, digesting food and so on.

In our soul these functions become more sophisticated and set us apart from animals so that we function in a higher way. In our soul, feeling, thinking and will are entwined, supporting each other; for example, feelings give warmth to thinking, thinking guides our actions etc. Mostly this happens in an automatic way and we are barely aware of it. Our task is to become more conscious of these soul-functions and as we do, our 'I' is able to take its rightful place in our soul.

When our 'I' connects up with our soul, our feeling, thinking and will begin to operate independently of each other and then it is up to us to combine them ourselves. This requires that we become conscious of our soul-will. This is the stage in the evolution of our consciousness that we are presently working on, the third soul level, which can be called the Consciousness or spiritual soul. Considering this, it makes sense that the rider called Death – because he was able to allow many aspects of his being to die – is now given power. This word is not "power over" but *exousia* which speaks of the freedom to act. The Greek word *exousia* is in the Hebrew language called Elohim. The Elohim are the creator gods in Genesis.

The rider now has the freedom to act within his being, and can be, if you like, a self-creator. The Lamb has revealed to John that twenty-five per cent of our being needs further attention. At the same time that we are becoming more and more conscious, there are still areas of our lower being that continue their habitual ways. There are illusions needing the sword; poorly digested understandings, the famine; a sense of separation from the spiritual worlds, death; and instincts and desires that are too animalistic, the wild beasts.

The only way we can carry out the killing is to become much more finely tuned to the characteristics of our feeling, thinking and will. While in our higher being we can control them more easily, in our lower being they have a life of their own. In our higher being they start to work separately, in our lower being they combine in ways that can be difficult to unravel. Here the strength of our feeling can be mistaken for will and our unconscious thinking mistaken for feeling and so on.

Each of the four ways of killing gives us a clue about the work we must vigilantly, discriminately and continually carry out in our lower being. The sword is *rhomphaia*, the two-edged sharp sword from chapter one. It removes all illusion from our thinking so that our thoughts are will-filled and aligned with the Archangel Michael who rules this age.

The second way is to kill with famine. Our spiritual hunger cannot be satisfied in our lower being; here there is no food to digest. This starvation can only be killed by learning how to use our will forces in our soul. Then we will receive the sustenance necessary to nourish our Higher Self.

The third way of killing is not pestilence but death *thanatos* which in Greek speaks about a separation. We must put to death the death-forces in our lower being - continually. Indeed, the experience of separation from the spiritual worlds in our lower being is killing us; we must strive to experience our higher being and its relationship with the spiritual worlds – while we are incarnated in this earth.

Finally the wild beasts of the earth are those deadly desires and instincts that are the expression of our lower feelings. We must continually give human dignity to these lower feelings so that they are expressed as highest love through our 'I'.

Seal Five – Souls under the altar

When he opened the fifth seal, I saw under the altar the souls of those who had been slain for the word of God and for the witness they had borne; they cried out with a loud voice, "O Sovereign Lord, holy and true, how long before thou wilt judge and avenge our blood on those who dwell upon the earth?" Then they were each given a white robe and told to rest a little longer, until the number of their fellow servants and their brethren should be complete, who were to be killed as they themselves had been. Rev 6:9-11

Could this altar be the table at which Jesus and the disciples shared the Last Supper? Is it a kind of demarcation zone; what took place up till now was the preparation, what will now take place is the deed. What is this deed? It is the gift of the 'I' placed in the heart of each human being as a seed. Human nature as it was known till then had been slain on the altar of Golgotha.

Up till this point in time only a few enlightened initiates had experienced what it was like to have a personal connection with the fourth human element, the 'I'. Everyone else conducted their life with only the first three elements; physical body, life body, and emotional body. We shared the 'I' as a group 'I' as animals have a group soul. This group 'I' is referred to in the Bible as Jehovah.

Before the Christ event no individual person would have referred to themselves as 'I' for it was a deeply sacred name. Only the initiates would use the name 'I' and probably only when they met together in secret. For them to reach this point of being able to use the personal pronoun 'I' they needed the assistance of a teacher or initiator. The sacrificial deed of Christ, the Lamb, meant that now each individual person could, through their own effort, experience their own 'I' and refer to themselves as 'I'. In other words, now they could initiate themselves. This is the goal that we must strive toward. As this passage suggests, it takes great discipline.

So if we didn't have our own 'I', what was it that gave us the human experience? It was our emotional body, our astral body. We can call this part of our being our pseudo-self and still today it often impersonates our 'I'. This emotional body is the region of our being where we experience our desires and it is through personal discipline that we ennoble them. It is to the extent that we raise up these desires that we purify our astral body of its instinctive behaviour. In other words, from its basic state it becomes more refined. As the natural instincts of this astral force become purified, a *morphosis* occurs from which we have our threefold soul. When this happens we begin to be able to control our feeling, thinking and will instead of being controlled by them. We become more and more aware of how these faculties, under the influence of our astral body, are less conscious.

When the text says, "I saw under the altar the souls of those who had been slain" it doesn't necessarily mean people huddled under the altar. The Greek word used here for soul is *psuche* and we could take it to mean the soul in its native state that indwells our body. *Psuche* is the seat of our senses that takes in the outside world and responds to it automatically or instinctively. It is this characteristic of our soul that is slain when we take up the personal connection with our 'I'.

Perhaps we will understand all of this better if see this fifth seal as a play enacted within us. The actors can be divided into two types; heroes and villains. The villains are the pre-'I' memories and habits, our natural inclinations that can work against us. For them the enemy is this newcomer, the 'I' that we must now assimilate. This is not a task to be taken lightly. We must raise up all those natural tendencies in our being so that they work with the 'I' and not against it. This is a real battle and it rages in our soul daily. We have the choice to become conscious of it, and to assist the process, or let it go on unawares. There is no prize for guessing which is the most painful.

We could also say that the altar is our soul. That place where we sacrifice our lower self (villain) so that our Higher Self (hero), the Master, can take its rightful place in our being. Our natural soul, our astral must now be purified by the word of God and the witness, *marturia*, that we bear. The word or logos is not just the word, in the logos the word and the concept become one. We live in the concept that the word describes and we experience a full understanding of it. Witness or *marturia* is a similar experience. When we are the witness we don't describe something that we saw, we re-live it. This is the experience of the 'I'; we experience what happens to others as if it was happening to us. It is bad enough feeling our own pain, as we most certainly do when we become conscious of all that goes on in our being; now we share the experience of others and feel their pain. When this happens the Lamb is also present and he raises up this experience so that we do not fall into despair. This is one of the meanings of those powerful words in St Matthew's Gospel:

For where two or three are gathered in my name, there am I in the midst of them." Mt 18:20

Gathered together, united, in the same experience; feeling the beat of each other's heart, so to speak. This is only possible when we can control all that arises in us out of self-interest and we act in the interests of all those who have allowed their natural soul instincts to be slain.

When he opened the fifth seal, I saw under the altar the souls of those who had been slain for the word of God and for the witness they had borne; they cried out with a loud voice, "O Sovereign Lord, holy and true, how long before thou wilt judge and avenge our blood on those who dwell upon the earth?" Then they were each given a white robe and told to rest a little longer, until the number of their fellow servants and their brethren should be complete, who were to be killed as they themselves had been. Rev 6:9-11

If we rearrange these words slightly, using the Greek a bit more literally, a different view emerges. The verse could say, "When Master – holy and true – will you not judge and [not] avenge the blood of that part of us that is earthly?" This seems to be suggesting that one part of us is making another part of us uncomfortable.

Our master, the *despotes*, is the one who has absolute ownership and uncontrolled power in our being. This is the holy and true one, the transparent one we would call that today. This is the one in whom nothing is concealed or forgotten, *alethes*; and the one who is set apart, *hagios*, or holy. This is our 'I' which wants to have much greater control of our being than it currently has.

The fifth seal is not a story about God or Christ punishing other people because they have been mean to us. This is a story about our own 'I' giving us a hard time so that we will make more room for it in our being. It does this through our karma; judging our past deeds and avenging us for our actions connected with our blood, like anger, for instance. The difficulties in our life arise because we have to face what transpired in our past lives. Moreover, what transpired in a past life was to create the karma we need today to progress our consciousness further. So, if we killed someone then they will seek ways to destroy us. If we used our will to manipulate others in the past then our will in this life will be weak, and so on.

Each episode in life that challenges us is an opportunity to engage with our highest self. This can only happen when we surrender to the situations we find ourselves in each day. If we retaliate, or think harmful thoughts, or allow feelings of hurt to immobilise us, then our lower self dominates. Therefore, the Master has to be more forceful and place greater difficulties before us. This Master, the *despotes*, would never share power with our lower self; this Master seeks absolute ownership and uncontrolled power in our being.

As we engage more and more with our 'I', as we prove that we can face life's difficulties, it is the presence of Christ, the Lamb, in our lives that assists us to see into the detail of the seal and to overcome. Unless and until we have a real awareness of Christ within us and around us, some of life's events will really sting. It is interesting to consider how, in one way, our 'I' is creating difficulties and in another Christ is taking the sting out of the difficulties. Eventually they will merge, as they merged when Jesus took the Christ fully into himself at Golgotha.

In the meantime we are a work in progress. John points out that our lower selves have been slain by the word, the logos, of God. Through this logos we tell the world that we exist. We say, "I" or "I am." The word makes it possible for us to utter our sacred name 'I'. Remember that when we use 'logos' to describe a word we are referring to a word that is utterly understood – the word and the concept the word describes unite (which would make dictionaries redundant). This is so rare today; the world is drowning in words which are mostly misunderstood. When we say "I" we totally understand who we mean. No one else understands this word 'I' when we use it of ourselves. They only understand it when they say "I" when referring to themselves.

Hence today, at this point in human history, total individuation exists in the world; each person for themselves. Yet inherent in the word logos is the uniting, not dividing, of the word and concept. It is only when we connect with our Higher Self that we are united with each other. We are united as self-realised individuals. We deeply understand each other, we feel what the other one feels, and love flows from us. This love is not preconceived, and is not a love that discriminates; loving one person more than another. This love, agape, could also be called logos love. When we experience this logos within us, when the other person ceases to be an abstract human being, and we experience them as if we were them, the Lamb is there. Then we are given the white robe and we wait. We know how precious the word is so we no longer cry out to our Higher Self to stop judging and avenging; we surrender to the process and co-operate.

When he opened the fifth seal, I saw under the altar the souls of those who had been slain for the word of God and for the witness they had borne; they cried out with a loud voice, "O Sovereign Lord, holy and true, how long before thou wilt judge and avenge our blood on those who dwell upon the earth?" Then they were each given a white robe and told to rest a little longer, until the number of their fellow servants and their brethren should be complete, who were to be killed as they themselves had been. Rev 6:9-11

It almost seems as though something is missing between verse 10 and 11. How can the loud crying result in being given a white robe and being told to rest? This resting is like peace; in the midst of trouble remain calm. While facets of our lower self continue to be killed can we remain calm? Therefore the fifth seal speaks about the way we participate in life.

There is something about John's description that is echoed in the Bhagavad Gita. In the first chapter Krishna and Arjuna witness two armies assembling on a plain ready to do battle. Krishna instructs Arjuna to join the fight but when he gets closer he sees all his relatives, "fathers and grandfathers, maternal uncles, brothers, sons, grandsons, companions, fathers-in-law, and teachers." Arjuna immediately wants to withdraw and not participate.

Rudolf Steiner uses this story as an example of what is required of us if we are to develop our consciousness further and higher.

What he says can be found in the lecture series, The Bhagavad Gita and the Epistles of St. Paul, specifically in lecture three.

If we accept the earlier suggestion that the text of the fifth seal is asking "when will you stop judging and stop avenging that part of us that is earthly", then we can compare this with Arjuna not wanting to fight against his relatives. His relatives are all those earthly people who have been related to him throughout all his earthly lives. In other words, all those he has strong karmic relationships with. All the relationships we have had, lifetime after lifetime, inform our character, just as our relationships do today with each person in our current life. One friend today may have been our grandfather, or our partner may have been our wife/husband, child, brother or sister in a past life. Any difficulties in these relationships over aeons can often come to expression in our lower self through our reactions.

Krishna advises Arjuna to participate in the 'battle', but as an onlooker. Only by engaging in life, where our karma comes into play, can we become fully self-aware and connected with the highest expression of our 'I'. It is the nature of this participation that we must become more conscious of. Often we participate either too distantly or too deeply. We either don't engage or we get entangled. The resting that we are told to do at this fifth stage is to do with being impartial. How impartial are we about our inner experiences as well as our relationships? We must strive to observe our lives as though watching someone else living it. Our aim is to see everything for the first time, without prejudice. Then we are not disturbed by the joy or sorrow that we experience through our own actions.

Steiner puts it beautifully when he quotes Krishna advising Arjuna: "if you can rise above all this and not be affected by your own deeds, like a flame which burns quietly in a place protected from the wind, undisturbed by anything external: if your soul, as little disturbed by its own deeds, lives quietly beside them, then does it become wise; then does it free itself from its deeds, and does not inquire what success attends them."

Krishna represents our I AM and Arjuna is its mirrored reflection in our being. Arjuna is 'sent down' to participate in the full spectrum of life's experiences. However, Arjuna can be like our astral / emotional body which directs our participation through sympathy and antipathy; through love or hate.

Arjuna must be open to the promptings of his teacher, Krishna, so that he grows in stature until he merges with Krishna. His participation must be objective, not coldly as we often see today, but observing with interest. Steiner puts it like this: "I perform my deeds, but it matters not whether they are performed by me or by another — I look on at them: that which happens by my hand or is spoken by my mouth, I can look on it as objectively as though I saw a rock being loosened and rolling down the mountain into the depths."

This level of objectivity is mandatory if we are to connect with our Higher Self through our own volition. This is also the story of Pentecost which St John relates in his Gospel, it echoes this same theme. At all costs we must be peaceful. We must strive to still all the forces in our being even in the most difficult moments. To assist us we can imagine Jesus the Christ speaking these words within us continually:

"Peace be with you. As the Father has sent me, even so I send you." And when he had said this, he breathed on them, and said to them, "Receive the Holy Spirit. If you forgive the sins of any, they are forgiven; if you retain the sins of any, they are retained." Jn 20:21-23

When we forgive others we meet them anew each time. When we retain their deeds, working them over constantly in our mind, our lower self is trapped in the earthly subjectivity that cannot participate in life with freedom and love.

Seal Six – Natural destruction

When he opened the sixth seal, I looked, and behold, there was a great earthquake; and the sun became black as sackcloth, the full moon became like blood, and the stars of the sky fell to the earth as the fig tree sheds its winter fruit when shaken by a gale; the sky vanished like a scroll that is rolled up, and every mountain and island was removed from its place. Then the kings of the earth and the great men and the generals and the rich and the strong, and every one, slave and free, hid in the caves and among the rocks of the mountains, calling to the mountains and rocks, "Fall on us and hide us from the face of him who is seated on the throne, and from the wrath of the Lamb; for the great day of their wrath has come, and who can stand before it?" Rev 6:12-17

The description of the sixth seal is very long and continues through the whole of chapter seven. This should alert us to the significance of the next stage of our development. These twenty-two verses will contain important guidance for developing our higher consciousness. The images that arise from the description of the sixth seal are more vivid and more detailed than the descriptions of the first five seals combined. Such vivid images, surely, point to the spiritual faculty of Imagination. Imagination is a much maligned human capacity. It is often referred to as hallucination or fantasy. This can indeed be the case if our 'I' is not involved. The spiritual faculty of Imagination is not a mental aberration it is an astute ability to see beyond the superficial.

There are a few things to consider as we develop our understanding about Imagination. First of all, we only begin to experience this ability when our soul is awakened from its habitual patterns and we become aware of the activity of our 'I' in our consciousness. So not only are we working on our will, we are integrating our 'I' while at the same time experiencing the birth of Imagination. This is a big task and even though it will be many centuries before all human beings develop full use of spiritual Imagination, some people are beginning to experience it now. There are always forerunners who demonstrate the potential of human endeavour.

As we begin to use our higher faculties, as John describes, our whole being is disrupted. It can be very unsettling when our spirit starts to 'intrude' into our being - especially if we are not really aware of it. We are shaken to the core as our previous ideas and conceptions are destroyed. The only way to withstand this natural disaster is to receive our Higher Self. Whenever we achieve this, the kings of the earth, those ideas that rule in our lower self, will want to hide; they do not what to be deposed. Then we will see that all that we counted as powerful, rich and strong within us is really our weakness and our poverty.

Then we see the possibility of following in the footsteps of the Lamb; all that we were in our lower self can now be resurrected to a higher expression. This is the Pentecostal experience. John's words echo Paul's words in the book of Acts. Immediately after the disciples were filled with the Holy Spirit, Peter quotes the prophet Joel:

'And in the last days it shall be, God declares, that I will pour out my Spirit upon all flesh, and your sons and your daughters shall prophesy, and your young men shall see visions, and your old men shall dream dreams; yea, and on my menservants and my maidservants in those days I will pour out my Spirit; and they shall prophesy. And I will show wonders in the heaven above and signs on the earth beneath, blood, and fire, and vapor of smoke; the sun shall be turned into darkness and the moon into blood, before the day of the Lord comes, the great and manifest day. And it shall be that whoever calls on the name of the Lord shall be saved.' Acts 2:17-21

See how this new faculty of Imagination will be revealed. When the Holy Spirit, which is our 'I', is poured out – and we are conscious of it – visions or Imaginations will appear in our minds. They will not be like the images an external stimulus evokes from our memories which we then connect together as our thoughts. These Imaginations will appear without cause, like a dream seems to, and through our 'I' we have new thoughts that 'appear out of nowhere' and seem to take on a life of their own.

John is suggesting that we must stand, steadfastly, accepting that unprovoked ideas such as those come from spiritual Imagination not from hallucination. Furthermore, they are thoughts that can be thought through. They are not psychic feelings difficult to decipher, they are not vague intuitions, these images belong to the domain of our higher 'intellect'. Then we will be able to read the script that reveals what the future will bring to us. At present, in 2008, we stand in the aftermath of the cyclone in Burma and the earthquake in China which together have killed many thousands of people. The lower human mind will see this as the wrath of God and be afraid. Only our spiritual Imagination can assist us to understand that a new consciousness is dawning under the guidance of the Lamb.

When he opened the sixth seal, I looked, and behold, there was a great earthquake; and the sun became black as sackcloth, the full moon became like blood, and the stars of the sky fell to the earth as the fig tree sheds its winter fruit when shaken by a gale; the sky vanished like a scroll that is rolled up, and every mountain and island was removed from its place. Then the kings of the earth and the great men and the generals and the rich and the strong, and every one, slave and free, hid in the caves and among the rocks of the mountains, calling to the mountains and rocks, "Fall on us and hide us from the face of him who is seated on the throne, and from the wrath of the Lamb; for the great day of their wrath has come, and who can stand before it?" Rev 6:12-17

When we read these words where are we standing? Do we see ourselves as a small physical being standing on the earth looking up at the heavens, ducking falling stars and trying to keep our balance as the earth is quaking and changing? What a frightening prospect. Is this what John saw? Or did he see all these things from a different perspective?

Think about an earthquake, *seismos*, that is caused by the movement of the earth's tectonic plates. Then compare the image of these tectonic plates with the bones of our skull. Also, think about how we experience our inner life bound within the perimeter of this skull. Whatever we see outside our body is not part of us.

Could John be describing a vision that extends beyond our conscious perimeter?

If we were to imagine our being enlarged to reach the outer regions of the universe we would then be looking down upon the sun, the moon, the stars and sky. Then all that John describes would be happening within us. Is this what the resurrection is like? Pre-resurrection we are contained within our physical body, our 'universe' is inside our being and our highest experience is of our own skull. Post-resurrection we are freed from the confines of our physical body.

It is quite possible that John is describing the resurrection process. We die to our physical existence as we have experienced it thus far in this life, and we are born to a new vision. Try to imagine looking down on your life. See yourself in your room as if you were looking down from the roof. Then expand this vision to take in your neighbourhood, town or suburb, then your country and so on. This task is made easier since astronauts have sent their images back to earth. Yet John's vision is not quite like that. The astronauts are looking on, John is looking within.

This is the view we come across in the Bagavhad Gita when Krishna advises Arjuna to be the onlooker. The Higher Self speaks to its reflection – the incarnated lower self – saying, "Participate in whatever happens, do not shrink from any experience because each event is an opportunity for us to be together once more." When we have this image of ourselves – the full spectrum of the higher and lower - then everything that happens in our surroundings happens within us. This view, of course, assists us to observe what takes place without overreacting. We experience a new level of courage and a new freedom. Things are no longer 'done' to us; they happen within us.

To the extent that we manage to take this view then our relationships are more harmonious and we are more peaceful. For instance, when someone expresses a different opinion we would no longer say, "That is your opinion, this is mine" but rather, we simply look from different vantage points. This doesn't negate our contribution, or the contribution of others; we simply become more accepting of ourselves and of each other. Then we participate in the Pentecostal understanding, "because each one heard them speaking in his own language." Acts 2:6

The first sign that we stand in our individualised being, as it becomes unified with everything around us, is when we are filled with understanding. Instead of reacting to the person who was rude to us instead we wonder what has happened in their life to cause their rudeness. On a larger scale, when we observe world events our spiritual Imagination reveals what is happening within our own expanded being. For example, conditions of drought can reflect our own parched thoughts. Flooding can be an inundation of misdirected feelings. Anger freely expressed can cause all manner of wild weather, from wind to hurricanes. It is up to each one of us to become the master of our own life; then we are no longer being a slave to outer circumstances which can influence how we think, feel and behave.

The continuing development of our consciousness can only progress as we achieve the inner calm that is part of knowing who we really are. Our 'I', our Higher Self, must become the inner ruler. When the "kings of the earth and the great men and the generals and the rich and the strong, and every one, slave and free," run for cover we can feel the freedom of the resurrection power given by the Lamb – or we can retreat with them.

> *When he opened the sixth seal, I looked, and behold, there was a great earthquake; and the sun became black as sackcloth, the full moon became like blood, and the stars of the sky fell to the earth as the fig tree sheds its winter fruit when shaken by a gale; the sky vanished like a scroll that is rolled up, and every mountain and island was removed from its place. Then the kings of the earth and the great men and the generals and the rich and the strong, and every one, slave and free, hid in the caves and among the rocks of the mountains, calling to the mountains and rocks, "Fall on us and hide us from the face of him who is seated on the throne, and from the wrath of the Lamb; for the great day of their wrath has come, and who can stand before it?" Rev 6:12-17*

Before we move on to the rest of the description of the sixth seal it would be good to contemplate the wrath of these two beings; "him who is seated on the throne" and "the Lamb". The word translated as 'wrath' is *orgé* which is a certain kind of anger. This anger is slow to rise and is associated with indignation. The other word for anger is *thumos* which is more like a fierce outburst.

We considered the nature of anger in the second seal. We looked at how the purpose of anger evolves from one of self-preservation to its highest expression, love. When the lowest expression of our 'I', which we can call our egotistical self, began its earthly journey it needed survival instincts. Now, post-Golgotha, the highest expression of our 'I' is starting to take its place in our being. We could say that we are starting to come face to face with this 'I' that is seated on the throne trying to direct our lives.

If we can place ourselves in the 'shoes' of our highest 'I' we would more than likely experience this wrath, this love-anger, which seeks to raise our ego up. This is the resurrection foreshadowed by Christ that must take place in our being. No matter what we may face in life we must be able to stand. If we succumb to difficulties, allowing them to defeat us, we will not be able to face of our Higher Self.

As the exploration of the messages to the seven churches revealed, new life can only come from death, from destruction. Growth depends on hindrances; when growth is restrained, new and stronger growth can occur. It is as if the pause in our growth gives the spiritual worlds entrance into our being. The tribulation, the pressing down on us of our Higher Self, is the way it enters into us. So when our growth is restrained we come to a point (hopefully) where we allow something new in. In this incremental way our Higher Self becomes more and more influential in our lives.

This wrath, this love-anger, is the spiritual morality that is part of our Spirit Self, part of our spiritual being where spiritual Imagination is active. This is the area of our being where thinking is re-born, resurrected from our physical body and enlivened and freed in our spirit. This pure thinking can experience the other person deeply, knowing them without intruding and without judgment. This pure thinking also guides feelings and influences will in a new way.

Seismic activity can take place in our being if we do not take seriously what it means for our Higher Self to transact within our soul. The only way to withstand it is to be very aware of the Lamb. As John points out, the Lamb too expresses this love-anger. The story of the fig tree in Matthew's Gospel adds some dimension to these ideas.

In the morning, as he was returning to the city, he was hungry. And seeing a fig tree by the wayside he went to it, and found nothing on it but leaves only. And he said to it, "May no fruit ever come from you again!" And the fig tree withered at once. When the disciples saw it they marveled, saying, "How did the fig tree wither at once?" And Jesus answered them, "Truly, I say to you, if you have faith and never doubt, you will not only do what has been done to the fig tree, but even if you say to this mountain, 'Be taken up and cast into the sea,' it will be done. And whatever you ask in prayer, you will receive, if you have faith." Mt 21:18-22

At the first hint of this love-anger we need to be able to speak to the Lamb, the living, resurrected Christ who is our constant companion. We can ask him for the strength to stand and if we know that he will do it, he will do it. There is no prescribed way to do this; each one of us will do it in our own way. All we need to do is create an image of the risen Christ, any image, and he will inhabit it. We know that we have succeeded in doing this when we feel an inner quickening; the more we do it, the more often we will become aware of him who loves us so much that he can express his wrath knowing that we will be able to stand.

CHAPTER SEVEN

Seal Six continues

After this I saw four angels standing at the four corners of the earth, holding back the four winds of the earth, that no wind might blow on earth or sea or against any tree. Then I saw another angel ascend from the rising of the sun, with the seal of the living God, and he called with a loud voice to the four angels who had been given power to harm earth and sea, saying, "Do not harm the earth or the sea or the trees, till we have sealed the servants of our God upon their foreheads." Rev7:1-3

Now John sees a very different panorama; after the seismic activity everything is stilled, almost blissful. It is reminiscent of Jesus calming the storm which St Mark relates in his Gospel.

And he awoke and rebuked the wind, and said to the sea, "Peace! Be still!" And the wind ceased, and there was a great calm. Mk 4:39

How calm are we? How much control do we have over our feelings when we become irritable? How often do we think things through thoroughly before we act? Are we able to cheer ourselves up when we are feeling low? Or do we respond predictably in a given situation? John is witnessing what happens in our being when our soul and spirit are enlivened. When our spiritual being becomes active it is up to us to control and combine our thinking, feeling and will. They no longer operate automatically as they did in the past. While this is a good thing, and we become free of certain habitual actions, thoughts and emotions, it can also be quite unnerving.

If someone speaks to us harshly, where in the past we may have been inclined to let it go, now we have to actively guide our emotions with our thoughts. Until we do that our emotions can become a raging storm within us. When we can still them, through understanding the other person's position, this self-won calm is bliss. This extraordinary bliss arises through our own inner effort to create stillness within our being. The more often we can do it, the easier it is to do - again and again like a seal stamping on our foreheads. Its effect is like many injections of Botox; our frown lines are gone and our face has a serene glow.

Our foreheads also mark the place where our etheric body, our life-force, can protrude from our physical body (giving us the image of a horse's head). This can happen when we have deep spiritual love for the other person, when, through spiritual insight, we understand them. When this happens those with spiritual sight will see a halo around our head. This loosening of our etheric body is significant because our etheric body contains our memory bank.

As we begin to take charge of our own thinking, feeling and actions we need the stillness, the space to respond differently than we have in the past. This is like de-programming our memory. We stop functioning out of unconscious habits that have developed over lifetimes. We are able to respond in new ways to the karmic situations we encounter. It is the presence of Christ in our being that assists us to be the onlooker as we engage in the harmonising of our past deeds. This too gives us an experience of bliss. We have, through our own efforts, created stillness within our being.

So if we are achieving this ourselves then what are the four angels doing? Well, they assist us. Like the parent who assists their child to take its first steps; they wait till we do some of the work and then they act in a supportive way so that we can win our independence. John sees them standing at the four corners of the earth; the north, east, south and west corners. These four points could also be the four temperaments that colour our soul. These temperaments are the fire, air, water and earth elements in our being. Usually one dominates but all four can unconsciously influence the way we express ourselves in the world.

It is helpful for us to recognise how we express these temperaments and in this way we will understand how to handle them in other people. This is going to be crucial in the future when these four angels are allowed to express their power, potentially harmfully. In other words, those of us whose spiritual being comes into play, who are able to hold the rawness of these moods in balance, will need to develop ways of communicating with those who do not.

In 200 AD Galen identified these four temperaments and many others have studied them and written about them since then. In brief overview they are:

Choleric; fire: passionate, quick to react and bad tempered, determined, assertive, energetic

Sanguine; air: optimistic, cheerful, warm and pleasant, changeable, superficial

Phlegmatic; water: unemotional, slow moving and indifferent, placid, patient, cautious

Melancholic; earth: sad and depressed, long-suffering, self-centred, reserved.

These four can also be associated with our fourfold being; our 'I' – fire; our astral body – air; our etheric body – water and our physical body – earth. Those who can weave them together in harmony are then identified and sealed as the servants of God.

After this I saw four angels standing at the four corners of the earth, holding back the four winds of the earth, that no wind might blow on earth or sea or against any tree. Then I saw another angel ascend from the rising of the sun, with the seal of the living God, and he called with a loud voice to the four angels who had been given power to harm earth and sea, saying, "Do not harm the earth or the sea or the trees, till we have sealed the servants of our God upon their foreheads." And I heard the number of the sealed, a hundred and forty-four thousand sealed, out of every tribe of the sons of Israel, twelve thousand sealed out of the tribe of Judah, twelve thousand of the tribe of Reuben, twelve thousand of the tribe of Gad, twelve thousand of the tribe of Asher, twelve thousand of the tribe of Naph'tali, twelve thousand of the tribe of Manas'seh, twelve thousand of the tribe of Simeon, twelve thousand of the tribe of Levi, twelve thousand of the tribe of Is'sachar, twelve thousand of the tribe of Zeb'ulun, twelve thousand of the tribe of Joseph, twelve thousand sealed out of the tribe of Benjamin. Rev 7:1-8

Angels and Archangels are such an important part of our earthly life but what do we really know about them? The word 'angel' is the English translation of the Greek word messenger. As beings outside us these messengers are guardians of evolution carrying the ideas of the highest spiritual beings to those of us who can hear them. They also communicate the outcome of human activity to the spiritual hierarchy of which they are a part. It is said that the angels are will-less beings thereby enabling them to maintain their purity. There are, however, angels who are not benevolent. Like humans, who are one level below them, they can become stuck if they do not take every opportunity to evolve. In this trapped and dormant condition angels, and humans for that matter, can become the puppets of the Luciferic beings.

The mysteries of Lucifer are detailed and deep; far beyond the level of our current contemplation. However, we do need to know that if we see an angel we must be able to know which side it is on. Furthermore, we need to realise that they can change sides according to our own activity. If we are striving to connect with our 'I' the Luciferic beings can assist us. If we fail to use life's opportunities to increase our spiritual awareness, then these beings will play harmful tricks on us.

This is what John sees; angels whose actions of harming the earth, sea or trees are frozen. Here they are in assisting-mode so that some of us can receive the seal of approval. So why would John only see the earth, sea and trees? Perhaps the earth represents our physical body, the sea our astral body, and the trees our etheric body. Or the trees could be our vascular system which has a tree-like formation as does our nervous system. The sea could be our emotions. The fact remains that if we do not take charge of our own development these angelic beings will cause us harm;

physically, mentally and spiritually. Each time we counterbalance the work of the Luciferic angels; which we can do, for instance, when we overcome nervousness, we receive the stamp of approval on our forehead. When we prevail in life's many challenges these angels can guard and guide us.

Who is this being John sees "ascend from the rising of the sun, with the seal of the living God". It must be the mighty Archangel Michael who not only commands the Luciferic beings but also fights the dragon, the Ahrimanic beings responsible for spiritually blindfolding humanity. Michael is the ruling Archangel of our time. He waits for human beings to awaken their soul forces and learn how to use them consciously. When we can change a thought instantly through the use of our will we have power over our habitual responses to life. This ability places us in a position of great power indeed. We could act without morals and conscience. To make the right choices in life we need the presence of the Lamb. Through our own initiative we must awaken this presence within us. Then we will behold the full extent of our spiritual being – we will know who we really are.

Then we can look both ways; outside ourselves to the activity of these spiritual beings and within us to see their influence there. Unless we see the whole picture our knowledge is abstract and all abstraction is the work of the Ahrimanic beings.

Within us the angels represent the communication between our higher and lower self. When our lower thoughts and emotions rule this means that we are overwhelmed by the influence of the Luciferic beings. They try to drag the past into the present. For instance, they are always behind those nagging thoughts that want us to relive, over and over, some bad experience. Through our Higher Self, our 'I', we are able to recognise that the events of our life contribute to our unique biography. It is our acceptance of our unique path that creates harmony in our being and makes us sealable. This is what Archangel Michael and his co-workers look for; the ones who conquer within their own being and find the living God, the etheric presence of Christ.

Then John relates to us the list of the twelve tribes of Israel. This is the first time the number twelve is mentioned in The Revelation. Twelve is a very divisible number and produces many combinations; groups of three and four, six and two and so on.

Many things are grouped into twelve, not the least of which are the tribes of Israel, the disciples and the zodiac. It would suggest that each of the twelve has a certain quality which, when combined, complete the group. At the same time smaller groups can work together for particular purposes. Twelve suggests a state of completeness and so it is not the actual number that concerns us but that the group is complete, all its facets are present. So it is within us, we must develop all the facets of our being so that we become completely human and completely divine.

After this I looked, and behold, a great multitude which no man could number, from every nation, from all tribes and peoples and tongues, standing before the throne and before the Lamb, clothed in white robes, with palm branches in their hands, and crying out with a loud voice, "Salvation belongs to our God who sits upon the throne, and to the Lamb!" And all the angels stood round the throne and round the elders and the four living creatures, and they fell on their faces before the throne and worshiped God, saying, "Amen! Blessing and glory and wisdom and thanksgiving and honor and power and might be to our God for ever and ever! Amen." Rev 7:9-12

The four images John sees within the sixth seal are like a symphony in four movements; now we enter into the third movement. It could be that each movement reveals how we can purify the four areas of our being; physical, etheric, astral before the finale of fully connecting up with our 'I'. This is, of course, the ultimate purpose of this round of evolution for the human being. It is also a unique cosmic event because human beings are the first beings to take into themselves this mighty 'I' of their own free will. The secrets of the 'I' cannot be fully known at this stage of our development because that would give us power which we are not capable of wielding. Those who try to break open its secrets come to grief as we shall see in later chapters of the Revelation.

When considering the development and evolution of the human being it is important to remind ourselves again and again that the journey is more important than the destination. Today we are so results oriented that we underestimate the importance of the effort that contributes to the result. We are continually tempted with shortcuts and instant results and this deprives us of the opportunity to develop ourselves fully and appropriately.

Furthermore, it is not who we are that is important but rather how we do what we do. Is the CEO of a corporation on a level footing with a garbage collector? Or is it equally important how the garbage is collected and how the corporation is governed? If we continually want to be something, or someone that we are not then we miss the point and purpose of our incarnation. If we continually promote our own views over others, as religious organisations are prone to do, then we miss the point. The multitude is made up of every different type of person in the world and they are all equal; they have all been "invested with a white stole" - which is one way of interpreting *peribolaion*, stole (translated as "clothed in white robes").

Those who are worthy to be invested are the ones who do whatever is placed before them each day with love and devotion. Each task is equally important and all thought of being finished with one task so that something more pleasing or important could occupy us does not enter our minds. For each person in the multitude every task is a privilege; every difficulty is faced with equanimity and the living Christ is seen in every person. Those who achieve this purity are recognised by the luminosity of their being marked on their forehead and by the presence of the white stole.

They also carry palm branches. The word palm in Greek is *phoinikes* which has a connection to the word phoenix and is a symbol of victory. This could be in association with the resurrection of Jesus, but also the resurrection of Lazarus which, as St John tells it in his Gospel, was the reason for the greeting of Jesus with palm branches as he entered Jerusalem sitting on as ass (conquering his astral).

So they took branches of palm trees and went out to meet him, crying, "Hosanna! Blessed is he who comes in the name of the Lord, even the King of Israel!" Jn 12:13

Then the multitude says the strangest thing, "Salvation (belongs) to our God". The word belongs is not in the Greek. Why would our God need salvation, deliverance? We might make more sense of it if we ask who this God might be. In chapter four we met this 'sitting one', the ruler over our lower desires and emotions. If we say that our God is our I AM, the highest expression of our 'I' then it does make sense that our 'I' is delivered from all that prevents it from experiencing the resurrection.

Then the great chorus of worshipping voices recognise the purity and resurrection of the human being in all its parts:

"Amen! Blessing and glory and wisdom and thanksgiving and honor and power and might be to our God for ever and ever! Amen." Rev 7:12

Alfred Heidenreich puts it perfectly in his reflections published as "The Book of Revelation" (page 82). "[Here] we have in these seven words the seven ideal qualities applicable to the sevenfold being of man — reading not from the bottom upwards, from the physical to the spirit man, but from the top downwards. Eulogia, blessing, is the highest that man's transformed physical body, as Spirit-Man, Atma, can achieve. Then we come to the transformed etheric body, the Budhi, the Life-Spirit; its quality is *doxa*, glory, radiance. Further down is what will develop just above our Ego ['I'], the higher soul-being, the Spirit-Self, Manas; its content, its finest achievement, is wisdom, sophia. Then comes the ego, and *eucharistia*, thanksgiving or self-giving, is its highest ideal; the self grows by giving itself. Coming further down into the soul region, or astral body, *timé*, dignity, is the highest quality. Of the life-body, or etheric body, *dynamis*, vitality, is the best quality, and then, finally, of the physical body, *ischys*, strength, power, stability. So, in such a hymn which otherwise seems rather like celestial sound and fury signifying nothing, we can discover some real content."

Then one of the elders addressed me, saying, "Who are these, clothed in white robes, and whence have they come?" I said to him, "Sir, you know." And he said to me, "These are they who have come out of the great tribulation; they have washed their robes and made them white in the blood of the Lamb. Therefore are they before the throne of God, and serve him day and night within his temple; and he who sits upon the throne will shelter them with his presence. They shall hunger no more, neither thirst any more; the sun shall not strike them, nor any scorching heat. For the Lamb in the midst of the throne will be their shepherd, and he will guide them to springs of living water; and God will wipe away every tear from their eyes." Rev 7:13-17

Something new happens at the end of the sixth seal. John responds to the elder's question. This two-way conversation signals a new phase of consciousness. Conversing with images that we become aware of spiritually indicates that the faculty of Inspiration is entering into Imagination. So at the end of the sixth seal John announces that we will reach a point where we can respond to, not necessarily a vision that we see before us, but certainly to the voice which we hear within us. This probably won't be an audible conversation for that would cause others to question our sanity. We are simply interacting with the images that arise within our being. We are now able to hear what they say and respond to them. This is only possible when we make the conscious connection with our 'I'.

These conversations happen within us now, perhaps much more than we realise. An idea rises up within us that we think about and act upon (or not). Often we think this process is of own doing and we are not aware of the way our Higher Self speaks within us to motivate us to carry out certain actions and interactions. We can become so bound up in our ego, our lower self, that we don't hear the voice, or if we hear it we don't respond to it. When significant ideas rise up within us, seemingly out of nowhere, we can be pretty sure that our 'I' is knocking on our door.

If we hear the 'voice' and we are able to respond then we are on the same wavelength with the elder. Elders are those who have connected to their Higher Self already and who wait for us to do the same. To the extent that we can, we are automatically connected to all those who have already achieved this state. This is why John answers in this way, "My Lord (not sir), you know" – because you yourself are clothed in this same luminous way. It almost seems like a test message - as if a new microphone is being tested by asking a rhetorical question.

Then the elder continues the conversation, confirming that he knew the answer to all along, by saying: "These are they who have come out of the great tribulation". These are the ones who have passed through the ordeal of *thlipsis*. Tribulation or *thlipsis* is the pressure exerted on us by our 'I' as it tries to enter into our lives more fully. The first person to pass through this ordeal was Jesus. If we wonder what this pressure is like then we need only read the gospel stories of Jesus' life. In the final stages we find the seven phases of this rite of passage; foot washing, scourging, crowning with thorns, crucifixion, death, burial and resurrection.

As the elder explains, "they have washed their robes and made them white in the blood of the Lamb." They appear purified and luminous because of the experience of the Lamb, Christ, who now lives within them. Jesus showed us how to bear these seven stages of pressure and prevail over them. These stages refer directly to the spiritualising of our consciousness.

When we achieve the state of Spiritual Imagination, and when we hear the words of Spiritual Intuition within our being, we know that we are born again into the spiritual worlds – not in death but while we live in this incarnation on earth. We have become the self-born; we give birth to our Higher Self through our own inner activity.

This is cause for great celebration among all the beings in the spiritual worlds, just as we today celebrate the birth of a baby. As we gaze on the tiny body of a newborn we are filled with awe; recognising its purity and its potential. At these moments we recognise the unity of heaven and earth. This is exactly what happens within us when we experience our own higher Imagination; heaven and earth unite. This is one of meanings behind the words of Jesus in the Gospel of St Matthew: "Truly, I say to you, unless you turn and become like children, you will never enter the kingdom of heaven." Mt 18:1-3

Whenever we feel the pressure of our 'I' we should sit down and deeply contemplate the glorious words of the elder. It is as if he holds us in his arms and tells us of his own experience. We are sheltered, never hungry nor thirsty. The sun shall not strike us, nor any scorching heat because now we dwell with Christ within the sun, no longer experiencing it as something external to us. The Lamb is now within us (in the midst of the throne) shepherding us, and he will guide us to springs of living water; and God will wipe away every tear from our eyes. This is the great gift of the living Christ as he is within and around us today in his risen power. In moments when we can experience the grace and peace of the beautiful words of the elder, we are at one with Christ.

CHAPTER EIGHT

Seal Seven – Prayers of the Saints

When the Lamb opened the seventh seal, there was silence in heaven for about half an hour. Then I saw the seven angels who stand before God, and seven trumpets were given to them. And another angel came and stood at the altar with a golden censer; and he was given much incense to mingle with the prayers of all the saints upon the golden altar before the throne; and the smoke of the incense rose with the prayers of the saints from the hand of the angel before God. Then the angel took the censer and filled it with fire from the altar and threw it on the earth; and there were peals of thunder, voices, flashes of lightning, and an earthquake. Now the seven angels who had the seven trumpets made ready to blow them. Rev 8:1-6

Contained within the seventh seal are the seven trumpets. We could wonder if these trumpets sound the seven different tones of the musical scale; each note carrying the melody to reveal the harmony when the seventh note sounds. Certainly the descriptions of the six trumpets seem to be most discordant.

These trumpets give us a real clue about what develops in our consciousness next. Since we are considering how the seventh seal reveals the qualities of our higher faculty of Inspiration then it stands to reason that the faculty of hearing is introduced. What is now added to our faculty of Imagination - our ability to observe spiritually in images - is an extra dimension of sound. We could compare this to the difference of looking at a trumpet and hearing it being played.

The entry of the spiritual faculty of Inspiration into our Imagination could go unnoticed if we are not observant. We certainly would not hear it if we doubted that images can emit sound. Perhaps this is why John tells us that "there was silence in heaven (our higher consciousness) for about half an hour." Probably the silence is necessary so that we are able to get used to this new kind of hearing.

The silence could also indicate that we have to quieten the babble which continually goes on in our being. For what we are about to hear is a completely different form of sound, on a different wave length. This kind of sound goes unnoticed in our daily lives; like the sound of a stick hitting an object which automatically informs us of the size of the stick. Or the sound of a knock that automatically tells us about the density of the thing being knocked. Many of us don't pay particular attention to these things because our mind is too full of the day's events.

Unless we are able to experience silence, we will never experience Inspiration. Silence is a very uncomfortable experience. Try sitting with friends in silence, it is excruciating. Try thinking of nothing, even for five minutes. Then try paying attention to every detail that meets the senses; sound, sight, smell, for just five minutes of the day – especially while you are busy doing something.

This is so much more difficult today because the world is so full of noise – not just sounds, but words and ideas. We are continually filled with these second hand ideas – which these reflections are by the way – that we can't hear the truth that lies within us. If we can experience the silence, we will hear the truth rising up within us through the presence of the active Lamb.

So what is this Inspiration? Is it just the sudden brilliant idea as defined by the dictionary or is it more? We experience this Inspiration when our life-force, our etheric force, is purified by our 'I'. This means that our etheric forces have been resurrected from lower activities.

Inspiration signals our capacity for independent thought. While we are bound to our lower nature our etheric activity is constrained by our physical brain preventing it from unfolding its higher functions of pure thought, which is inspired thought or living thought.

Then we might ask what this has to do with the very religious scene that John describes; the altar, the golden censor, the angels and the prayers of the saints. Is this the altar mentioned in the fifth seal? the altar that stands between our lower and higher being? Religion is the most misunderstood notion in the world today. It creates chasms between people when it really should bring all people together. Perhaps this is why our lower and Higher Self are so separate because modern religion separates rather than unites.

The purpose of religion is to awaken the presence of Christ within us, within every single person on this earth regardless of creed or culture. John's emphasis on the core symbols of religion supports the idea that many spiritual teachers put forward; religious impulses work on the etheric body so that part of it is separated and transformed into Inspiration. It is in this purified etheric force that we meet the etheric presence of Christ. It is also in this region of our being that we can hear the Word, the Logos, which lies at the core of Inspiration - but only if we experience the silence first.

Afterwards, the silence is shattered by the action of the angels. They cause a great disturbance in our lower being uprooting all our habitual thoughts, feelings and behaviour. If we have said yes to the experience of Inspiration then we must also be able to withstand the destruction of all that is lower within us. Only our lower ego can prevent us from experiencing the spiritualisation and resurrection of all that we do unconsciously. We have to let go of all that is old and trust the living Christ within us – the Lamb.

When the Lamb opened the seventh seal, there was silence in heaven for about half an hour. Then I saw the seven angels who stand before God, and seven trumpets were given to them. And another angel came and stood at the altar with a golden censer; and he was given much incense to mingle with the prayers of all the saints upon the golden altar before the throne; and the smoke of the incense rose with the prayers of the saints from the hand of the angel before God. Then the angel took the censer and filled it with fire from the altar and threw it on the earth; and there were peals of thunder, voices, flashes of lightning, and an earthquake. Now the seven angels who had the seven trumpets made ready to blow them. Rev 8:1-6

The introduction to the seventh seal paints a vivid picture which could apply to our present global condition. We know that we stand in the balance when the arctic ice melts; when violence rages unabated; when millions of people starve while farmers choose to grow narcotic producing plants instead of food; when the financial markets are in turmoil, and when human values are debated. Even those who claim to be the religious experts on what is right and wrong fall on their sword. Doesn't it seem odd to hear that men are the rightful priests and bishops and at the same time some members of this same gender sexually abuse those in their care? Surely the alarm bells are ringing loudly enough.

John describes a drama; angels participating in heavenly bliss or causing earthly fury. He straddles the two as if to advise us to become more aware of what is happening. Nothing changes by demanding apologies or pointing fingers. What is urgently required is a new understanding of the human being. The Lamb is ready to reveal the deepest mysteries to anyone who can prepare themselves to look at them. The privileges that were once given to our leaders are now available to anyone who becomes aware of the presence of the Lamb within them. We must no longer look outside ourselves to others, no matter how high and mighty they are, to do for us what we can now do for ourselves.

This is a mighty work we are called to do. The Lamb knows this. That is why he continually reveals the presence of the angels who wait to assist us. If we ignore them we could get caught up in the wild weather. What John describes here gives us a real sense of the angels celebrating if we are aware of them, and causing us grief if we ignore them.

In his lectures published as "Old and New Methods of Initiation" given at the end of World War I Rudolf Steiner makes some urgent comments about world affairs. Since the time that these comments were made we have had another World War and we now live in a world that rages with war in many regions. Not to mention the wars that can personally rage within us and between us. Therefore Steiner's advice could be even more pertinent today. He urges us to create a relationship with the spiritual beings directly above us; the angels and archangels. These are the beings that most directly guard and guide us, just as we guard and guide the animal and plant kingdoms so that the world is safe and habitable.

Steiner urges us to develop a loving relationship with these higher beings so that we can cooperate with them. It is their task to direct higher human development, to assist us to use our soul and spirit which will give us clear spiritual insight. They cannot do it for us; the impetus must come from us. Steiner further suggests that if we remain unconscious of angelic beings then they lead us into situations by coercion which can give rise to disagreements and nations fighting against nations. Steiner suggests that this would not happen if human beings loved these beings and created images of them. Furthermore, this lack of love can throw us together with those with whom we have deep karmic bonds. Karma is always exacerbated when there is a lack of love - even among those who seem to be following the same spiritual path of development.

Saying that we love doesn't mean that we love; love is an action which pours from those who have a real relationship with the angels and archangels. In turn our love is food for these spiritual beings, without it they are not nourished. The ways we love and hate then become the catalyst for the actions of the angels as John describes. The first step is to become more aware of how and why we love others. In the movie "Suddenly Last Summer", a play written by Tennessee Williams, Elizabeth Taylor speaks these deeply unfortunate words about human nature. She says, "Isn't that what love is? Using people? Maybe that is what hate is – not being able to use people."

It is possible that we don't love the angels and archangels because we have no use for them – that we are aware of. We could ask if this is why they are throwing fire down on the earth which causes "peals of thunder, voices, flashes of lightning, and an earthquake"? Is this a wakeup call? Perhaps the best course of action is to spend some time each day, and possibly at the beginning and end of the day, acknowledging the participation of these spiritual beings in our lives. We could thank them for their guarding and guiding, we could create images of them and we could work on developing our love for them. This should strengthen us to withstand their violent actions while at the same time giving us access to participate in their heavenly ceremony.

When the Lamb opened the seventh seal, there was silence in heaven for about half an hour. Then I saw the seven angels who stand before God, and seven trumpets were given to them. And another angel came and stood at the altar with a golden censer; and he was given much incense to mingle with the prayers of all the saints upon the golden altar before the throne; and the smoke of the incense rose with the prayers of the saints from the hand of the angel before God. Then the angel took the censer and filled it with fire from the altar and threw it on the earth; and there were peals of thunder, voices, flashes of lightning, and an earthquake. Now the seven angels who had the seven trumpets made ready to blow them. Rev 8:1-6

Imagine standing beside the Lamb when the seventh seal is opened. The Greek doesn't actually say 'when' he opened the seal but 'whenever' he opened it. So this might not be a once only event, it could mean that the seals can be opened again and again. Whenever they are opened we are able to behold the mighty imaginations that come to life. Like John we can look in and find guidance and understanding for the development of our own consciousness. Then we gaze on the face of spirit in these images; just as our own face reveals what goes on within us. Then, if we can look behind these images we may see more than was initially obvious.

John sees God, but which God? It is simply a God or the God. The Greek actually says 'the' angels and 'the' god *tous angelous... tou theou*. A literal translation would be: And behold the seven angels stood in view of the God. *Theos* means a deity, a divine being, a holy being. The divine being within us is our Christed I AM.

This ceremony is actually celebrating the birth of Christ within us. This event takes place when we begin to use the spiritual faculty of Inspiration. Our life-force, our etheric, is raised; its earthly function meets its spiritual potential. How do we know that a birth is celebrated? because of the presence of gold, frankincense and myrrh.

The altar is gold; the censor *libanotos* is derived from *libanos* which is Greek for frankincense; and the presence of myrrh is indicated by the altar; the place of sacrifice which today is the symbol of the resurrection - dying to our lower life and resurrecting to a higher life.

Gold is also the symbol of our purified thoughts, frankincense is the symbol of the holiness of our feelings and myrrh represents the mastery of our will. Christ cannot come to life within us until we purposefully combine these facilities in a new way, and at will. When the Magi brought these gifts to the baby Jesus it was an outward expression of what would later take place within us. When it does there is a great celebration in the spiritual worlds.

Our modern lives are so full of external images that it becomes increasingly difficult for us to be aware of our inner experiences. Our attention is continually drawn into the outer world. Also, we are bombarded by ideas that prevent us from taking full responsibility for the events in our own lives. How often do we hear, or think, these words, "It's your fault, it's not my fault"? Each time we are drawn out of ourselves in this way we turn away from what takes place within us and we turn our back on the birth of Christ.

This ceremony takes place because some human beings have given birth. When this happens for us, not only do we experience the gifts of the Magi within us but we are also surrounded by the prayers of the saints. The saints, hagios, are the holy ones who have perfected themselves before us. They know what an amazing achievement it is when the infant stirs within us. Imagine the incense and the prayers pouring from the hand of the angel. This is reminiscent of the power that can be seen pouring from the hand of the crucified Christ which is described by those who have the stigmata. In her book on this subject, "If He Had Not Been Raised", Judith Von Halle says that the stigmata isn't always a wound but can be a sensation of energy streaming from the place of the wounds of Christ.

Of course the birth of Christ within us would be accompanied by inner disruption. For a start our blood is changed, no longer the blood that we received through heredity, now we share Christ's blood. Our blood is the fire, the warmth, in our body. The angel throws this new blood down from the sacrificial altar into the earth of our being.

When this fiery new blood meets our airy nervous system, thunder and lightning result. This would clear the air, so to speak, in our thinking - it isn't too hard to imagine that when we think there is a dynamic interaction between our blood (fire) and our nervous system (air). Then the noise (voices) and the earthquake are felt as habitual thoughts, feelings and behaviour are thrown from their comfort zone. When we experience the breakup of old patterns we can be assured of the presence of our newborn Christ which is about to be trumpeted throughout the universe.

The Seven Trumpets

The first angel blew his trumpet, and there followed hail and fire, mixed with blood, which fell on the earth; and a third of the earth was burnt up, and a third of the trees were burnt up, and all green grass was burnt up. Rev 8:7

We could expect to encounter a rhythm when an angel trumpets. Timing would be very important. The thing with rhythm is that it is open to interpretation. For instance, a familiar tune played to the wrong rhythm can be unrecognisable. Being out of rhythm can be uncomfortable. Not that we should be thinking about the modern trumpet. Ancient trumpets were a signalling device with only a few tones with much more emphasis placed on the rhythm. They signalled an announcement, a command or were used for ceremonial purposes. The original trumpet was probably the conch shell; its sound was an emblem of power, authority and sovereignty.

This gives us an idea of the place and importance of these angels trumpeting. An overview of the seven trumpetings can indicate that the first three create disturbances in our body, the pivotal fourth directs our attention to the heavens where eclipses take place accompanied by the announcement of the three woes. The last three trumpetings are the woes which take place in those who do not establish the right rhythm during the first three trumpetings.

The first angel's trumpet calls us to pay attention to a series of events. Hail and fire, mixed with blood was cast into (not fell on) the earth, in other words, was cast into our body. Fire and ice, extremes of heat and cold mixed with the warmth of blood; these three are cast into us and we must create the right rhythm between them. If we don't we will probably experience discomfort.

We must never underestimate the response from the spiritual worlds when we commit to our spiritual development. We cannot resume our regular, comfortable way of life, not even for a second. Perhaps these trumpeting angels deliver a shock each time we repeat an unconscious action. So when we repeat old patterns of behaviour the trumpet blasts within us giving us the choice to take the necessary action. This would not invoke feelings of self-pity but rather an objective self-evaluation. We are assisted to see our personality more clearly and we become more forgiving of ourselves and resist blaming others for bringing out the worst in us. These are often the very situations that give us a greater degree of self-awareness, they are a gift.

This self-awareness is awareness of our 'I', our Higher Self. When we start to experience the strength of our 'I' then we must stand in it. We can't stand in it sometimes and then exclude it at other times. It doesn't work that way. Once we commence the work of consciously connecting with our 'I' it is a commitment for all eternity. That is the example of the Lamb.

Perhaps the hail, the frozen water, is to cool our overheated emotions. The fire could be to warm our cold thoughts. The blood, the new blood permeated by the Christ force, could assist to regulate our will, our activity. These three are like a three-note tune; notes which can be played in various combinations. In the past they combined themselves according to what we were used to. Now, we must combine them ourselves into a smooth rhythm.

The burning up of the earth, the trees and the green grass could represent a purification of the landscape within our being. The Greek indicates a burning down, not a burning up – *katakaio*. It may not be a third that is burnt, the burning or purifying could take place three times or for a third time - *tritos*. It could also be done in three different ways, perhaps by the Father, Son and the Holy Spirit.

What is it that will be purified within us? For each of us it will be different, individual. It is an inner work, out of the reach of those who like to place their judgement on such things. This work is between ourselves and the angel and should be kept privately within our hearts as we grow and change. Yet this is not our inclination. If someone causes a reaction in us we are often prompted to point it out to them, or to tell a friend or therapist about our bad experience. This dissipates the experience and robs us of the benefits.

These three areas that are burnt could be represented in this way:

Earth, *ge*, our body: our metabolism and mobility – the vehicle of our will

Trees, *dendron*, our nerves and senses: the vehicle of our thinking

Green grass, *chortos* (a feeding enclosure where animals graze), our rhythmic system of breath and circulation: the vehicle of our feelings.

When the fire and ice land in our being, upsetting the status quo, we must be very tender with ourselves. Think of the tenderness of the landscape; the rich earth, the strong green trees and rolling grass. This is the gift of nature that accompanies us during our earthly sojourn; it can feed our soul and free us from anxiety. This nature can fill us with an invigorated life-force that echoes the etheric presence of Christ. Here we find the rhythm established in the tone of the first angel trumpeter. We silently experience our inner strength, no matter how painful, and stand ready for the second blast.

The second angel blew his trumpet, and something like a great mountain, burning with fire, was thrown into the sea; and a third of the sea became blood, a third of the living creatures in the sea died, and a third of the ships were destroyed. Rev 8:8-9

When we actively and purposefully change our patterns of thinking, feeling and behaviour it is a signal to our higher 'I' that we are making room for it in our being. We can only do this when we become aware that we have two different expressions of this 'I' being. We have the small 'i' through which we become aware of ourselves as earthly individuals. It is through this part of our being that we respond subjectively to life's situations. This is when our emotions can overpower our responses. Then we have the higher 'I' when we can use our will to control the way we think and feel about things; this is when we can be objective. It is the higher 'I' that gives us the mountaintop view.

There is so much confusion in the world today about finding our real or Higher Self. Some say we have to fully experience what is within us; others say that we must experience ourselves at one with the universe. This polarity of selfishness and selflessness is like a tug-of-war. There is a third position and that is to be able to experience both at once.

We can only come to this third option when we can experience the other two. First we must be able to fully experience our small self, alone and cut off from the cosmos. Most of the time, when we approach this feeling of aloneness, we pull back because we can't bear feeling this powerless. Yet this is the powerlessness that lives in the image of Jesus Christ nailed to a cross. When we are able to experience this powerlessness fully, it is in that instant that we become aware of the Lamb standing beside us. The lamb is the epitome of powerlessness. It is the world-symbol of sacrifice.

What are we sacrificing? We sacrifice all our earthly experiences that have assisted us to become a confident, egotistical, citizen of the world. When we have 'fattened up' our small self, when we have experienced our worldly ego fully, then we must allow it to be slaughtered. Here lies the problem. We are not willing to let go of all that we regard as valuable in our character. We don't see that it only had value up till this point and that now something new is required. To make the transition we begin to see how much of our behaviour is based on fear, and how often we act out of defensiveness. Now we must become more able to see our lives objectively. So when others do not respect us, when they trample on us in a battle of egos, we mustn't wallow in a sea of subjective feelings which obscure the real issues.

If we can stand on top of the mountain and look down on our lives objectively a very different picture emerges. If, at the end of each day, we review our day backwards, not from within ourselves but from the vantage point of the mountain, we can be much more circumspect about the day's events. There is a profound difference when we view the day's events in reverse from two different perspectives; in the valley with the small 'i' and from the mountain top with the higher 'I'.

So what do the ships, the sea and the creatures represent? The Greek actually says "the creatures having souls - *psuche*". If we take the ships to be our physical vessel, and the sea to be our life-force which keeps our ship afloat, and the living creatures to be our soul, then we can build an Imagination of what will take place in our being. These are the three parts of our being that have sustained our life on earth till now. We are preparing to connect up with our fourth part, the 'I'.

When the fiery mountain is thrown down into the sea - our life-force or etheric body – it means that we have become conscious. In this instance, we have become conscious of the way we think and what is stored in our memory because thinking and memory have their home in our etheric body. When our higher 'I' is cast into our etheric body it is as if the fire burns away all the rubbish-memories that we have accumulated there over lifetimes. This purification of our life-force frees our thinking from our physical body and spiritualises it. Then, from the higher perspective our awakened memory reveals why we have to experience certain things in our life. We see our life as a biography that we have written, and we see why we had to write it the way we did. This brings a great release from all our regrets, frustrations, guilt, etc. We can see how our Higher Self continually led us into situations to give us the opportunity to balance deeds of our past lives.

When a third of the sea becomes blood our etheric force is purified by the presence of the Lamb. The etheric presence of Christ the Lamb becomes a reality within us. We have accepted that all that we have worked for must experience the death and destruction necessary to make way for a new and higher life. We become aware of the resurrection force which now works in our being. For John, this is the image of "something like a great mountain, burning with fire being thrown into the sea" and changing our blood into Christ's blood.

The third angel blew his trumpet, and a great star fell from heaven, blazing like a torch, and it fell on a third of the rivers and on the fountains of water. The name of the star is Wormwood. A third of the waters became wormwood, and many men died of the water, because it was made bitter. Rev 8:10-11

This star that fell from heaven, blazing like a torch, is an image of a comet. Rudolf Steiner talks about how comets work on our physical and etheric bodies preparing them to work with our 'I'. A star, aster, in the Greek, can refer to our astral body - our starry body.

If we place this image inside us then we can see that this shooting star blazes with light into the foundation of our being; our etheric and physical bodies. For this contemplation it is good to remember that our etheric body, our life body, gives life to our physical substance by constantly preventing it from decaying like an apple decays when removed from its life-force, the tree.

Our life-force can be found in the rhythmic processes in our bodies which are linked to the fluids which circulate to sustain our life. It is remarkable to think that more than two thirds of our body is water. Furthermore, our etheric body appears as fine jets or sprays – fountains we could say.

So what is happening here when we hear the third trumpeter? A great force passes from our astral to our etheric preparing the way for our 'I'. It is very suggestive of a baptism. The blazing torch, lampas, is a torch that is frequently fed with oil. It symbolises the fire of the Holy Spirit which we feed with oil to prepare us for the presence of Christ.

Why would this star be called Wormwood? Wormwood, *apsinthos*, is absinth, a bitter and harmful plant. It is one of the bitterest substances known to man. The essence of wormwood is poisonous and should never be ingested. Calling the star Wormwood could be to emphasise that we are going to experience a lot of bitterness within our being. Since the etheric is the storehouse of our memories perhaps all our bitter memories from this life and all our past lives will be revealed to us which is a consequence of being conscious of our 'I'. It is our 'I' that knows what takes place in each of our incarnations. Through conscious awareness of our 'I' we come to remember our past lives.

So why don't we remember our past lives as a matter of course? This is because we are not fully aware of ourselves; we live our life as if in a mirrored reflection. This is quite a strange idea which can only really understand when learn to be conscious through our 'I'. What we don't fully realise is that being, our vehicle; our physical, etheric and astral bodies, are inherited from the universe. In this sense they are not fully us. It is like looking in the mirror; we recognise our image but the image doesn't have a life of its own, it is controlled by the universe. Through our spiritual development we are assuming a life of our own. This takes place as we strive to become conscious of the workings of our whole being. Then we can regulate it ourselves under the direction of our 'I'. This is the work in progress, and we are at a crucial point in that work at the moment.

So we must prepare ourselves for the great blazing star, the Holy Spirit, which is our purified astral. How can we tell if our astral is purified? In its lowest expression our astral can be quite animalistic; as we refine our impulses we raise our astral forces to their highest expression. It is these raised astral forces that we call the human soul where our feeling, thinking and will are active.

The core expression of our astral is emotion and passion. The core expression of our soul is feeling. Feelings, as distinct from emotions, are the barometer by which we decide what is good and what is bad. The purpose of feeling at this level is to keep us safe from harm. Then at the core of our feeling activity is love and hate. In their most basic state they polarise us; we either love or we hate. What is more, we experience these feelings only semi-consciously. Through our own volition – and this is where the 'I' comes in – we must develop a new barometer, one that overrides these dreamy instincts of love and hate so that we can make a new and conscious decision in every situation rather than falling back on our habitual responses.

If we are to deal with the bitter and poisonous Wormwood then we will need strength to handle our emotions of bitterness, anger, resentfulness, mental pain; things that we have difficulty accepting and generally find unpleasant.

This is exactly what we experience when our 'I' influences our astral. Our astral or lower soul prefers all our experiences to be comfortable. Any discomfort is met with an angry or bitter response. This is what we must overcome. We must resist feelings of annoyance and use every ounce of strength to moderate our emotions and awaken our feelings. In this way, through our thinking, and employing our will, all that we feel is ennobled. If we are to heed the signal of the third trumpet we cannot continue our automatic responses to life. If we cling to 'the way things were' we will not receive our 'I' for the Holy Spirit and Christ can find no place in our being.

The fourth angel blew his trumpet, and a third of the sun

was struck, and a third of the moon, and a third of the stars, so that a third of their light was darkened; a third of the day was kept from shining, and likewise a third of the night. Then I looked, and I heard an eagle crying with a loud voice, as it flew in midheaven, "Woe, woe, woe to those who dwell on the earth, at the blasts of the other trumpets which the three angels are about to blow!" Rev 8:12-13

The fourth trumpeting is the pivotal point in this series of seven. This is the final call to those who are committed to their spiritual development. Those who fail to take this task seriously, or fail to grasp what the task actually is, will experience the three woes that are to follow.

The primary task in our spiritual development, especially at this stage in human development, is to give new life to the way we think. The only way to change the way we think is to transform our thoughts into spiritual Imaginations. So how do we do this?

Take, as an example, a flowering plant. We know that it needs soil, water, sunlight and nourishment to produce a flower from a seed. Some gardeners are even guided by the phases of moonlight when they plant seeds. Through the growth cycle many changes occur in the plant until it finally flowers. When the plant is in full bloom, we see the coloured petals and we smell the scent of the flowers. These are the results of our physical observation. What about the forces behind the shape of the plant and the colour of the flower? Is this just genetics or are there unseen forces influencing the plant? If so, wouldn't these forces be different for different plant shapes, and different coloured petals? What about the forces behind the different perfumes? What about the force that assists the flower to face the sun, or turn away from the sun? Time lapsed photography has given us quite different ideas about the way physical growth occurs; we must use our spiritual Imagination to create thought images of how the different forces work within and around the plant to create its shape, colour and smell. It is in this way that Goethe came to his idea of the archetypal plant. These imaginations can be like watching a film, seeing different energies flaring at certain points in the plant, and how the images move and change - but at this stage they are silent.

When we are used to experiencing these vivid pictures that seem to work and weave 'behind' the physical image, then we begin to have an auditory experience, as if the images speak to us. This is our spiritual Inspiration at work. These sounds or tones enter into us as if we breathe them in, inspire them, and hear them not with our ears but within us.

In the third and final stage we become part of the image and know it intimately. We surrender our self and become one with it - we know and are known. This happens when our thoughts are transformed from Imaginations to Intuitions. This could be called virtual reality by some; but those who experience this interaction, even if only fleetingly, realise that it is the physically observed life that is the virtual reality.

The crucial thing for us is to recognise these aspects of our consciousness, and that even though it will be some time in the future when we will experience our consciousness in this way, we are beginning to experience it today, if only momentarily. If we don't have these experiences yet, at least we can think about what it will be like when our consciousness is elevated to this level of purity. We do need to do this preparation now.

The fourth trumpeting is directing our attention away from the bitterness we can experience within our being to the greater universal expansiveness of which we are a part. Instead of crouching within our bodies, as a frightened animal may crouch in a cave, we must be able to view our lives more objectively and expansively. Then we see ourselves as unique contributors to the development of the whole of mankind. Sometimes we may be the protagonist in someone else's karma, sometimes they in ours. When we can see a larger playing field we will play a better game.

From this view we will also see how certain elements in our being eclipse each other in certain situations. As our 'I' increases its influence in our being, our astral, or small 'i', becomes territorial. It becomes like a giant eclipse which hides our soul and spirit from view. Our emotions, instincts and lower impulses will rise up and cast a shadow over all that is higher within us. We will not be able to think rationally and we will certainly not behave with awareness. Our higher soul functions have been blocked. Our still higher, spiritual functions of Imagination, Inspiration and Intuition are totally off the radar. This is what could be meant by a third of the light being darkened. That third part of our being, our spirit, cannot shine.

If we can share the eagle's view we will start to become aware of what transpires in our consciousness. Then we can objectively assess why our thinking, feeling and willing can be dark. These are the blind spots in our being. This is when we have 'black outs' and act habitually and unconsciously. Yet we resist looking at these darkened places because we fear what we will see. We think that it is safer to "dwell on the earth." This fear of looking at ourselves objectively is nothing compared to the fear that we will experience if we don't shine the light into the darkness – of our own volition, now. If we don't leave our earthly position and develop our higher consciousness then we will experience the three woes. Fortunately John was able to see and report on these woes to give us the incentive to act differently now. Then we can stand with the Lamb and experience the deep importance for us of the Mystery of Golgotha.

CHAPTER NINE

The Seven Trumpets continued

And the fifth angel blew his trumpet, and I saw a star fallen from heaven to earth, and he was given the key of the shaft of the bottomless pit; he opened the shaft of the bottomless pit, and from the shaft rose smoke like the smoke of a great furnace, and the sun and the air were darkened with the smoke from the shaft. Then from the smoke came locusts on the earth, and they were given power like the power of scorpions of the earth; they were told not to harm the grass of the earth or any green growth or any tree, but only those of mankind who have not the seal of God upon their foreheads; they were allowed to torture them for five months, but not to kill them, and their torture was like the torture of a scorpion, when it stings a man. And in those days men will seek death and will not find it; they will long to die, and death will fly from them. Rev 9:1-6

At the fifth trumpeting John seems to be telling the story of Christ's deed; the heavenly 'star' who, having fallen onto the earth, was given entrance into the depths of the earth. The Gospels don't clearly describe Christ's so-called descent into the depths of the earth after his crucifixion. In St Matthew we can see some of the parallels with John's vision.

Now from the sixth hour there was darkness over all the land until the ninth hour. ... And Jesus cried again with a loud voice and yielded up his spirit. And behold, the curtain of the temple was torn in two, from top to bottom; and the earth shook, and the rocks were split; the tombs also were opened, and many bodies of the saints who had fallen asleep were raised, Mt 27:45, & 50-52

What does this abyss mean in terms of our consciousness? A better translation for the shaft of the bottomless pit, *phrear ho abussou*, would be the deep well. In terms of our place in the cosmos it is as if we are in a deep well. This is the reason Christ incarnated in the body of Jesus; to assist us to get out of the well unscathed. After the crucifixion Christ enters into the depths of our being and releases all that is trapped in there.

This fifth image also tells the alarming story of how we can incarnate too deeply. The purpose for our incarnations on this earth has become obscured. We are not here to enjoy all that the earth offers us, or to be miserable when it doesn't offer us enough; we are here to become self-realised individuals. This work of freeing ourselves from the abyss connects us with our 'I'. We climb the consciousness-ladder whose rungs are Imagination, Inspiration and Intuition.

While we are in the abyss our consciousness is dull. We cannot see the workings of spirit in us and around us. We struggle to get a foothold on the first rung; spiritual Imagination. If we do experience it to some extent we may not then hear Inspiration speaking into these Imaginations. Our inner senses are obscured by smoke and a darkened sun, and we are threatened by ravenous grasshoppers that will devour that which is plant-like in our being. They will consume all the etheric life-forces in their path.

This etheric force is an airy water-filled sheath which surrounds this earth and from which all things receive life. This same substance is within each of us; it is the life-giving substance within our bodies. Through our own effort we can keep these forces 'green' and lively like a healthy garden. The primary way we do this is through the way we think. Do we strive for lively insightful thoughts or do we perpetuate the dead wood of abstract thinking so prevalent in society today. Do we think carefully before we speak or does an automatic banter roll from our tongues?

Furthermore, do we take full possession of our thinking ability? If we let thoughts flow through our mind without direction we become like mobile phone towers. Thoughts that originate elsewhere can enter our minds and we can find ourselves thinking about the strangest things. Worse still, we may not even be aware of these thoughts. If we do become aware of these rogue thoughts a healthy mind will dismiss them immediately. If the grasshoppers have been chomping away in our etheric then we may think that the ideas that come to us are real and this will manifest in various degrees of psychotic behaviour.

We can avoid this situation through our determination to strengthen our connection with our 'I'. Only by cultivating a sincere interest in other human beings, by having a loving interest in the people around us, can our 'I' make the right connection with our etheric forces. How do we measure this? Do we ask people how they are because we are as interested in their welfare as we are in our own? Do we wish them a nice day because we want them to have the same nice day that we want for ourselves? When someone is sad do we feel the depth of their sadness? If not then we can always make a beginning by using our thinking to create an Imagination which makes these experiences as real as possible. Gradually they will happen naturally.

Why would the grasshoppers be given scorpion power? What happens when a scorpion stings a person? The scorpion's poison causes numbness. This highlights that we are numb to the experiences of other people. We read about a mother losing her child and we say that it's sad, but we don't feel that mother's pain, we are numb to her experience.

If we become aware of this numbness we start to become aware of how deeply we have incarnated. It is like our foot going to sleep – which actually indicates that our etheric forces have left that area of our body. When this happens, think about how heavy our foot feels. As soon as we experience the heaviness we have the opportunity to understand the effect of our etheric forces on our physical body.

We also notice that we can't walk on a foot that has gone to sleep. This realisation assists us to become aware of the force that makes us mobile. This is our astral body which gives the human being motion and emotion. It is also through our astral force that we experience passion and compassion.

What becomes clear here is that we have choices. We can be numb to world events or we can experience true compassion. We can think new thoughts or swallow the media-influenced thinking that infiltrates modern life. We can have the seal of God on our foreheads or suffer the torture that comes from dwelling too deeply on the earth. We can reach out and touch the world and then experience that deeply within us. Then we won't long for an elusive death, we will value all our experiences as an opportunity to stand with Christ in his risen etheric presence.

In appearance the locusts were like horses arrayed for battle; on their heads were what looked like crowns of gold; their faces were like human faces, their hair like women's hair, and their teeth like lions' teeth; they had scales like iron breastplates, and the noise of their wings was like the noise of many chariots with horses rushing into battle. They have tails like scorpions, and stings, and their power of hurting men for five months lies in their tails. They have as king over them the angel of the bottomless pit; his name in Hebrew is Abad'don, and in Greek he is called Apol'lyon. The first woe has passed; behold, two woes are still to come. Rev 9:7-12

John's image reveals to us the nature of the person who has not managed to strengthen their connection with their 'I' but tries to make out that they have. This should not be seen as a permanent condition. Every human being has the opportunity to stand in the strength of their 'I'; they must simply choose to do so. This fact lies at the core of human freedom.

Those of us who have connected with our 'I', even to a small extent, have to live side by side with people who live under the illusion that they work from their 'I'. As John points out it only looks like they do. The word 'like' *homoioo*, that John repeatedly uses alerts us to this.

Look at the characteristics that John saw in the locusts: like horses; like crowns of gold; like human faces, like women's hair, like lions' teeth, like iron breastplates, like the noise of many chariots and like scorpion's stings. It isn't too hard to work out how each of these characteristics are displayed within ourselves and in our interactions with others every day.

The essential characteristic of these pretenders is that they work in groups; they like to be with others who are the same. Locusts always swarm in groups, they never act individually. Furthermore, they are not self-directed. They have a king over them meaning that they must receive external orders. Whenever we seek external advice it means that we don't rule within our own being. When we look like horses arrayed for battle we are giving an inflated impression of ourselves. When we wear what looks like a golden crown we are pretending that we are our own sovereign.

In the Nordic legend, Ring of the Nibelungs, Siegfried the dragon slayer fearlessly confronts some neighbouring Kings who seek his gold. They say, "It takes more than gold to make a man worthy to fight a king." To which Siegfried replies, "It takes more than a crown to make a man be a king."

The wonderful thing about the nature of our 'I' is that it is self-evident. We don't need to impress others with our 'I' qualities, these qualities are experienced by everyone we meet. In fact, the more a person is connected with their 'I' the harder they try to be part of their surrounding community. This can be difficult when we are challenged by the imposters. However, the more we connect with our 'I' the easier it is to meet this challenge.

The primary characteristic of a strong connection with our 'I' is that we love. Like a natural spring this love pours from us. It is not ours to direct it according to what we think might bring us the greatest advantage. This love just pours into the hearts of others. The reason this love pours out of us is because its barrier, fear, has dissolved. This love is a simple outpouring of goodness. If we are asked to do something, and we are able to do it, we do it without thinking of any inconvenience. We are also able to say yes or no to situations and accept that our decision is the right one, regardless.

We need to be clear about what is the 'I' and what is an imitation. There are some interesting facts about locusts which can give us some further clues to unravelling John's vision. They have no pupa stage of metamorphosis; instead, to reach adult size, they shed their skin five times. They only live for about five months and they have no known natural enemy. They can be heard up to ten kilometres away and we could say that they turn paradise into wilderness. Their angel-king is Abaddon which means destruction or Apollyon which means destroyer.

In John's vision these locust-beings are warlike, arrayed for battle. There is angriness about them. This anger is not righteous anger that gives birth to love; this is anger born from fear. They look fearsome because they are riddled with fear.

When we begin to see the reality of our present human condition; that we dwell in the bottomless pit, then we realise that we must use each situation to become strong and wise. No matter how frightening a situation is we know that we can never be defeated. Remember that we are always in the presence of the Lamb, we just have to know it.

Hans-Werner Schroeder in his wonderful book, Necessary Evil, repeatedly points out that modern life presents us with situations that are very necessary for our development. Whatever locusts come our way, they are simply opportunities. "Lucifer himself supplies the sword for his overcoming." It is all about acting freely out of our own personal impulses. As Schroeder says, "freedom is an inner quality, an inner 'taking hold of oneself' and 'developing oneself'". He quotes Steiner, "The characteristic common to all evil is nothing other than egotism," and, "fundamentally speaking all human evil proceeds from that we call egotism." This egotism was necessary so that we could experience ourselves as individuals, taken too far we can become locusts.

Then the sixth angel blew his trumpet, and I heard a voice from the four horns of the golden altar before God, saying to the sixth angel who had the trumpet, "Release the four angels who are bound at the great river Euphra'tes." So the four angels were released, who had been held ready for the hour, the day, the month, and the year, to kill a third of mankind. Rev 9:13-15

When John hears the sixth trumpeting he describes the second woe. Woe is an interjection, an interruption. It could be seen as a challenge to our developing consciousness; a challenge that we accept or that we succumb to.

John hears a conversation; a voice or sound coming from the four horns, or from within the altar, that instructs the trumpeting angel to release the four angels who are bound at the great river

Euphrates (sometimes known as an Eden River). The angels are probably the four angels mentioned in chapter seven.

After this I saw four angels standing at the four corners of the earth, holding back the four winds of the earth, that no wind might blow on earth or sea or against any tree. Rev 7:1

It was suggested that these four angels controlled the four temperaments that colour our human soul. These temperaments have a correlation to the four elements; fire, air, water and earth. If we analyse our personality we will find that one of these elements is predominant while the other three make varying contributions to the way we express ourselves. If they are unleashed in our personality we could assume that a certain volatility would result.

In his lectures to Young Doctors in 1924 Rudolf Steiner aligned these elements in this way: fire is active, working will; air or the blowing wind is a revelation of courage; water is an expression of feeling; and the earth resembles our thoughts because they have weight. There are also other ways to identify the four elements in our being. The development of our consciousness is helped if we are able to recognise when we are being fiery, airy, watery or earthy. If these elements are unrestrained, and are expressed as natural instincts, this means that we have rejected our 'I', therefore we are beings without an 'I'.

This is what is meant by a third of mankind being killed. One third of mankind will not be able to integrate their 'I' into their being. This means that they are not individuals, they are not self-reliant, they have no ideals, no original talent and no love; like locusts they devour the forces of others. We can be inclined to think that this will only happen to someone else and not to us. However, if we manage to recognise the four elements in our nature we will quickly see how close we are at times to being a locust.

This passage is in fact a warning. The images speak directly to the Garden of Eden when human beings were freed from the spiritual worlds. The first indication of this is the golden altar with four horns? An altar, *thusiasterion*, probably means the place of sacrifice because *thusia* means sacrifice. This golden altar could be the Ark of the Covenant, the sacred chest Jehovah instructed Moses to build. This 'chest' was a symbol of the purity the human being could attain. We could say that it contained the calibrator by which we can measure our purification.

When we embarked on our earthly journey, signified by the story of Adam and Eve, we sacrificed our heavenly consciousness, and for good reason. We were given the freedom to create our own consciousness according to the experiences that we encountered in daily life.

The purpose of the first part of this journey was to become self-conscious; to experience ourselves as individuals; beings separate from other beings. This meant that we had to taste selfishness. When we managed to express ourselves out of deep selfishness then we had to sacrifice it. Not by becoming selfless, for that would be returning to our previous condition, but by standing side by side with all the other selfish beings and realising that each human being is equally important. This is a profound experience and its highest expression is the I AM. We know that we are experiencing this condition when we can be completely objective about our inner life while at the same time completely subjective about the life that surrounds us. This is what an inner experience of the Mystery of Golgotha reveals to us.

To be objective about our inner life means that when our interactions with others disturb us, we remain neutral about it. Equally, when we speak to others, perhaps forthrightly, we have no regrets. But! at the same time, we deeply care about the other person. This means that we won't deliberately cause distress, nor will we shrink from it if the opportunity arises to be honest. If what we hear, and what we say, is guided by Inspiration - that purified life-force within us - great healing will occur.

We develop a deep awe and respect for our surroundings and all that it contains. We won't dismiss the ideas of others because they don't agree with our own, and we will freely speak about our own ideas knowing that they won't be dismissed or judged. This is the purity represented by the Ark of the Covenant, the altar with the four horns. We are able to sacrifice our hard earned selfishness and courageously stand in our true self. We have an active working will, our feelings are appropriately guided and our thinking is suitably weighted. This speaks about the deeds of Eden and Golgotha, the deed of integrating our 'I', that we can choose to work on each moment of each hour, each day, each month and each year.

The number of the troops of cavalry was twice ten thousand times ten thousand; I heard their number. And this was how I saw the horses in my vision: the riders wore breastplates the color of fire and of sapphire and of sulphur, and the heads of the horses were like lions' heads, and fire and smoke and sulphur issued from their mouths. By these three plagues a third of mankind was killed, by the fire and smoke and sulphur issuing from their mouths. For the power of the horses is in their mouths and in their tails; their tails are like serpents, with heads, and by means of them they wound. The rest of mankind, who were not killed by these plagues, did not repent of the works of their hands nor give up worshiping demons and idols of gold and silver and bronze and stone and wood, which cannot either see or hear or walk; nor did they repent of their murders or their sorceries or their immorality or their thefts. Rev 9:16-21

This is a mighty vision of war. Is this war taking place within us? In twice ten thousand times ten thousand ways? How many of our daily encounters produce a war within our being? The horse with the lion's head issuing fire, smoke and sulphur from its mouth can be an image of the way we can respond to others, and the way they can respond to us. Even if we don't express our disagreement, we can think it. What is it within us that can't bear being wrong and the other person being right? Why do we become so indignant? And why do we want everyone to agree with us? John notes that the mighty power, *exousia*, issuing from the mouth and the tail causes wounds.

We carry many wounds don't we? There is so much disagreement in the world, which never seems to abate. Those who have the most powerful influence, especially in government, set such a bad example. For instance, they discuss how to deal with bullying in schools while they themselves continually bully each other in their so-called parliamentary debate. Fire, smoke and sulphur issue so easily from people's mouths today. When we are surrounded by this behaviour it can easily influence our own. This air of disagreement is everywhere while at the same time we yearn to be with those who agree with us. In this very unsettling environment we expect agreement to come from outside us when all the while we don't see that it must come from within us.

The only way to experience this state of 'agreement' is to experience our 'I'. From the perspective of the human 'I' all the ideas that approach us in this world are for our consideration. None of these ideas need to be rejected as wrong, but they can be used to continually weigh up our own ideas. Of course, at the same time, it is important to recognise that every idea that enters our consciousness is from the past. Even ideas we thought of a second ago are from the past. We can only embrace the present and the future if we remain open to new ideas. Unless we do this there is an unsettling war going on within us.

The fire, smoke and sulphur could also represent our thoughts, feeling and will, probably in that order. If our thoughts, our emotions and our actions are the tools of our 'I' we will not be wounded. But if we reject new ideas because they disagree with our own, usually because we are too lazy to understand something new, our soul is in a crippled state. It continually relies on crutches for support, the crutches of other people's ideas; preferably ideas that waft through our soul like a gentle breeze; none of those unsettling ideas that need to be worked on.

This is all about our will. At this present time in the evolution of mankind's consciousness we are to become aware of our will. This is an initiation process for each of us. It is as if we are in a dark forest and we must find our way to the light through the correct use of our will. The map to freedom is drawn through the effort we put in to comprehend spiritual truth. As each ring of truth etches into our being we vigilantly ensure that it stands the test of time. It is by putting our will into action in our lives that we conquer our urge to go to war with all those who disagree with us. We accept all their ideas as fodder for our continual search for truth.

By dropping our defences it doesn't mean that we become lethargic; it means that our anger is transformed to love, to the highest expression of love which in the Greek is agape. This love dissolves differences and through it we are able to accept all the experiences of life. Even though we may have the seal of God on our forehead, we still have to navigate the woes.

Here lies the mystery of the escalation of events as each trumpet sounds; the more people who have the seal, the more ferocious the vision becomes. If human beings are to win their freedom and stand alongside Christ as co-creators, we must master our will. With every advance we make we are faced with a new set of circumstances to enable us to put the mastery of our will to the test. What we call evil is really just the resistance that calls forth goodness in us.

In this way we can see how goodness calls evil into existence. As we master our will, stronger tests are required. Then it follows that the more goodness there is, the more evil there is. Isn't this the image of Judas at the Last Supper? Jesus sets the example; to continue to love in the face of betrayal. This is the task of every human being. This is why we must use our will to become ever more impartial about the war continually raging within us. At the same time to become much more personally concerned about what happens in the world around us. If we deeply experience that we are part of the human race whose actions create this world, moment by moment, we will probably change the way we contribute. We won't fight for peace; we will be peaceful regardless of the wars within us and around us.

The number of the troops of cavalry was twice ten thousand times ten thousand; I heard their number. And this was how I saw the horses in my vision: the riders wore breastplates the color of fire and of sapphire and of sulphur, and the heads of the horses were like lions' heads, and fire and smoke and sulphur issued from their mouths. By these three plagues a third of mankind was killed, by the fire and smoke and sulphur issuing from their mouths. For the power of the horses is in their mouths and in their tails; their tails are like serpents, with heads, and by means of them they wound. The rest of mankind, who were not killed by these plagues, did not repent of the works of their hands nor give up worshiping demons and idols of gold and silver and bronze and stone and wood, which cannot either see or hear or walk; nor did they repent of their murders or their sorceries or their immorality or their thefts. Rev 9:16-21

There are some interesting facts about the things in John's vision. "the riders wore breastplates the color of fire and of sapphire and of sulphur", – sulphur is yellow but turns red when melted and blue when burned. Sulphur dioxide is a preservative (220) which compensates for the loss of the life-force in food. So it keeps food alive artificially. Rudolf Steiner suggested that an increased supply of sulphur to the organism gives rise to feelings of giddiness, and a reduction of consciousness. We can see some parallels here with the work of the dragon and therefore the critical need to become more aware of the work of Michael.

Michael's sword must pierce us, wound us. We find Michael's sword in the so-called plagues. The Greek word is *pléges* which means stripes or wounds. Michael's wounding can seem to be a hindrance to our consciousness, but the reverse is true. By killing the thirty per cent of our consciousness that has been conquered by Ahriman, Michael assists us to connect up with our Higher Self and its cosmic perspective.

It is Michael's sword at work when we think for ourselves, daring to have new thoughts which may contradict the thoughts around us. It is Michael's sword that assists us to change our thoughts instantly when we are offended, or hurt. It is also Michael's sword that assists us to feel compassion instead of feeling revengeful or dismissive. It is Michael's sword that turns hatred to love.

It is a contradiction that to be inflicted by plagues or wounds indicates that we are conquerors. Instinctively we would avoid these wounds without realising that through them we divest ourselves of that part of our consciousness that is not spiritually helpful. Hence John's strange words, "The rest of mankind, who were not killed by these plagues, [and who] did not repent of the works of their hands". He is speaking about those who didn't accept the wounds and thereby continued to cling to abstract, lifeless thoughts and refused to use their will, ie, they did not repent.

Repent, *metanoeo*, literally means to perceive afterwards. This is an ability we are acquiring as we connect with our 'I'. So even though we see the detrimental results of our thoughts and actions we continue to think and act in the way we always have. If we accept that human consciousness changes then perhaps we should consider when and how this change occurs. Of course it is happening continually. Our consciousness has grown since yesterday (hopefully). The thing about noticing change is that we can only see it after the fact. Archangel Michael calls us to realise that we are living the change. Every moment is an opportunity to become aware of the change. We must try to see that in our consciousness Michael is continually sticking the sword into all that 'drags on' us. Each time we don't see it, the sword wounds us a little more deeply.

The rest of mankind, who were not killed by these plagues, did not repent of the works of their hands nor give up worshiping demons and idols of gold and silver and bronze and stone and wood, which cannot either see or hear or walk; nor did they repent of their murders or their sorceries or their immorality or their thefts. Rev 9:20-21

We live in critical times. Our values are continually challenged and our leaders grope for solutions to the many and varied crises that arise. Why do these crises continually arise, each one worse than the next? One answer would be that our values are misplaced.

To worship demons and idols who neither see, nor hear, nor walk, instead of valuing human life, could be at the heart of the problem. Demons, *daimonion,* are the spiritual agents acting in all idolatry. They could be nature spirits, especially if they are working through natural elements. Science, with its demands for physical proof, has removed all knowledge of these beings from us. These are not the only spiritual agents at work in this world. While we remain unconscious of any of them, ignorant (ignore-ant) of them, they play with us and distract us from things of real value.

Not that we should embark on a study of these beings. The single most valuable thing for us is to experience our 'I'. In everything we do we must strive to become aware of all that elevates us above the mineral, plant and animal kingdoms. It is not just a matter of reading descriptions of the four members of our being; it is about experiencing how these members work in us every moment of the day.

Our 'I' being is of such cosmic importance that a God took on human form so that we could have a full experience of it. If the full meaning of this truth lived in our consciousness we would never underestimate ourselves again. Nor would we devalue others. We would experience our ability to preside in our own being, where we can rule in our own kingdom. We no longer need the external king and priest but now we become the king and priest, firstly to ourselves. We considered this concept in chapter one.

... and from Jesus Christ the faithful witness, the first-born of the dead, and the ruler of kings on earth. To him who loves us and has freed us from our sins by his blood and made us a kingdom, priests to his God and Father, to him be glory and dominion for ever and ever. Amen. Rev 1:5-6

So it is not about trying to analyse what we should and shouldn't do. Having lists of what is wrong and what is right. Invariably what we think is wrong is actually right and vice versa. The point about worshipping demons and idols is that they are outside us. We must come to worship what is within us. We are the ones who can see, hear and walk.

There is a powerful story about some old monks whose order is facing extinction. One monk decides to seek the advice of a rabbi nearby. No solutions came out in their conversation but as the monk leaves the rabbi said to him, "all I can say is that the Messiah is one of you".

When we come to the realisation that the Messiah, Christ, is one of us, we see ourselves differently and we see each other differently. We don't look outside, placing importance on idols made "of gold and silver and bronze and stone and wood, which cannot either see or hear or walk". We value what is within us and within others. Christ is in each one of us; that is the mystery of Golgotha. We just have to see it.

We must uncover the importance of being the ones who are able to see and hear and walk. The word used for 'able' is *dunamai*. The *dunamai* are highly developed spiritual beings who are able to experience earthly matters through us. This happens more fully when we acknowledge that without them we could not see, hear or walk. Again, it is not so much about knowing the intricate detail of the works of the *dunamai*, it is about being aware that Christ could not have incarnated in the man Jesus without the assistance, nay sacrifice, of these beings. As we experience our 'I' more fully we will come to value the order of the spiritual worlds and the work they do behind the scenes. Most of all we will value the fact that we are in a physical body and they are not.

When we understand what it really means to have our human

gifts - to see and hear and walk - we cease to have external 'idols'.

Seeing, *blepo*, is about inner sight, insight. This could be our spiritual Imagination that only human beings can experience on earth.

Hearing, akouo, is not about the something audible entering our consciousness from outside; it is about hearing and understanding the inner meaning within us. This is our spiritual Inspiration.

Walking, *peripateo*, is about living in a particular way, entering into a particular walk of life. When we experience our own sacredness and the sacredness of others we enter into them and walk with them as if we were them.

When we experience our 'I' we will never murder which means to take life from others, for we will have sufficient life of our own. We will not be sorcerers which means to manipulate others to give our life more value. We won't be immoral which, among other things, means to use our spiritual development to advance our physical life. We won't be thieves; which means that we take what is not ours. When we experience our 'I' we won't look outside for our value, we will experience our own Christ-given value and this, in turn, will make those around us feel valued.

CHAPTER TEN

The Seventh Trumpet

Then I saw another mighty angel coming down from heaven, wrapped in a cloud, with a rainbow over his head, and his face was like the sun, and his legs like pillars of fire. He had a little scroll open in his hand. And he set his right foot on the sea, and his left foot on the land, and called out with a loud voice, like a lion roaring; when he called out, the seven thunders sounded. And when the seven thunders had sounded, I was about to write, but I heard a voice from heaven saying, "Seal up what the seven thunders have said, and do not write it down." And the angel whom I saw standing on sea and land lifted up his right hand to heaven and swore by him who lives for ever and ever, who created heaven and what is in it, the earth and what is in it, and the sea and what is in it, that there should be no more delay, but that in the days of the trumpet call to be sounded by the seventh angel, the mystery of God, as he announced to his servants the prophets, should be fulfilled. Rev 10:1-7

Since angels are messengers then we could assume that this strong, *ischus*, angel is portraying a weighty idea to us. What emerges in our mind when we paint the image of this strong being with a cloud cast, *periballo*, around it, with a sun-like face, a rainbow halo and fiery legs? What message does this image carry?

Rudolf Steiner puts forward an interesting concept about this in his lectures to the first Christian Community Priests in 1924, five months before his death. The lectures are published as "The Book of Revelation and the Work of the Priest" (see page 197ff).

Steiner describes this being as "the most significant appearance that present-day humanity ought to be contemplating." This image has much to reveal about the current state of human consciousness. It is our task at present to work on our ability to become aware, conscious, of the mystery of the human being. Yet all around us there is evidence that humanity is groping in the dark. When our financial markets are in such crisis, as they are at present (2008 Global Financial Crisis), we face the great question of what is our purpose. Money is the god of this world and when its value is diminished it leaves us wondering where true value may lie.

Furthermore, alarms bells surely ring when manufacturers of baby food water down milk and then add the chemical melamine, which is used to produce plastic, to make the milk appear richer in protein than it actually is. What value do these manufacturers place on human life?

Or is it not about that? Does it have to do with consciousness? Are business decisions being made in an unbalanced way in both these examples? To answer this question we must look more closely at our developing consciousness.

Steiner says that humanity as a whole is crossing the threshold into the spiritual worlds. This means that we now have the opportunity to see the hidden spiritual forces at work in the world. We have been groping around but now we have the opportunity to see. What some human beings have achieved in the past in terms of raising their consciousness, humanity as a whole is now experiencing. This is a rite of passage which occurs as we experience the influence of our 'I' in our being. Some of us are aware of this to a lesser or greater extent, others are totally unconscious of it. One of the signs of having access to our 'I', but not being conscious of it, is that we have the courage to do things that no one has dared to do before. For example, daring to manipulate the financial markets to the point where they tumble like a house of cards, and daring to manufacture poisonous baby food. Other signs are the degradation of the human being through drugs, violence and sex.

Another consequence of crossing the threshold is that thinking, feeling and will work independently. In our earthly consciousness these three more or less balance and moderate each other; in spiritual consciousness it is up to us to put them together appropriately. To be able to do this means that we must have sufficient will power. One of the missions of this current phase of evolution is to develop good will. While we do this work individually, at the same time humanity as a whole is challenged to do it too. We are working towards a collective goodwill. While we don't see much evidence of it yet, a start is always being made somewhere on this earth.

What Steiner observed was that people form into three distinct groups; cloud people, rainbow people and fiery footed people. With our own increased awareness we can identify groups of people whose thinking is well developed but their feeling and will are stunted – these are the cloud people. The rainbow people are feelers whose thinking and will is stunted and those with feet of fire use their will with restricted thinking and feeling. When these three faculties work alone they are unbalanced and alarming.

In our own spiritual development we must consciously combine these facilities within our own consciousness. The human race as a whole must figure out how the three different groups can work together. How difficult is it for the thinkers to work with the feelers who have stunted, and probably conservative, thinking? The feelers have just as much difficulty with the thinkers whose ability to feel is limited. Those with dominant wills, expressing their rage unabated, create an even greater difficulty.

The only way to establish a common ground is through the 'I'. Where there are divisions the 'I' is weak. The more we can integrate our 'I' the greater our ability to work together. This is not something that should be written down as a guide for people to follow. It is up to each person to do the work individually then collectively we will all benefit. This leaves us to contemplate our personal contribution which happens through our ability to hold each other in our hearts whether we be cloud or rainbow or fiery footed people.

Then I saw another mighty angel coming down from

heaven, wrapped in a cloud, with a rainbow over his head, and his face was like the sun, and his legs like pillars of fire. He had a little scroll open in his hand. And he set his right foot on the sea, and his left foot on the land, and called out with a loud voice, like a lion roaring; when he called out, the seven thunders sounded. And when the seven thunders had sounded, I was about to write, but I heard a voice from heaven saying, "Seal up what the seven thunders have said, and do not write it down." And the angel whom I saw standing on sea and land lifted up his right hand to heaven and swore by him who lives for ever and ever, who created heaven and what is in it, the earth and what is in it, and the sea and what is in it, that there should be no more delay, but that in the days of the trumpet call to be sounded by the seventh angel, the mystery of God, as he announced to his servants the prophets, should be fulfilled. Rev 10:1-7

John's account of The Revelation, as revealed to him by Jesus Christ, takes a surprising turn in chapter ten. The blood, fire, locusts, plagues and other gruesome images are intercepted by this mighty vista. All through The Revelation it is as if both sides of the coin are presented at once. The good and the bad co-exist, and we have the freedom to choose which one to experience. Furthermore, we have the opportunity to experience both. In other words, we are invited to be more conscious of the full reality of life, not just one side of it. The presence of this strong angel, roaring like a lion, jolts us away from the fury of the last two chapters and we are awakened to the other side of the coin.

The pre-requisite for understanding the intricacies of life is that we have self-knowledge. The more aware we are of our own consciousness, the more we will be able to make sense of what helps and what hinders human evolution. Often what we think will help actually hinders, and vice versa.

Can this angel be revealing to us that when we reach a certain point in our own spiritual development we become angel-like? To become angel-like means that we begin to rise above that state of human beingness that is ignorant of the spiritual worlds. Many people are at this stage now, either consciously or unconsciously.

The present stage of the development of human consciousness

is complex; three things are happening. Firstly, as the highest level of our soul awakens and we become more conscious of the way our will works. We then become more aware of all our actions and motives, especially those actions which previously happened automatically. This area of our soul is known as the Consciousness Soul or Spiritual Soul. It is characterised by a new level of awareness, and an ability to make better choices.

Secondly, when our Consciousness Soul levels break through to a certain point, we become aware of our 'I'. Through our 'I' we are able to make more informed choices, choices that will affect more than just this one life that we are living now. These choices may not be the most comfortable, but they will be significant for us and for others in future the lives that we must live on this earth.

Thirdly, when our Consciousness Soul begins to be more active, and we begin to experience our 'I', this activates our Spirit Self (our angel-like consciousness). In other words, we have access to a higher human consciousness which reveals itself in spiritual Imaginations that form in our minds. The kind of spiritual Imagination that John is experiencing here.

What John describes could be a conversation with his Higher Self. John could be alerting us to an event that we can experience. Perhaps in a dream-like state, or even a nightmare, we could see a more complete view of ourselves. We could see how our thoughts originate in the clouds of the spiritual worlds. We could see the seven different rainbow hues of our feelings. And we could also become aware of the fiery heat of our will.

In other words, our consciousness breaks through the barrier between earth and spirit. This could be what is meant by having one foot on the earth and one foot on the sea; the sea being a metaphor for the great spiritual expanse that surrounds us. When this happens we will find courage by identifying with the strength of the being we see. Otherwise, if we remain identified with our small earthly existence, we could be scared out of our wits.

This strong being has in his hand an open book. This could be our blueprint, the plan for our incarnation which we are now able to read. In this way we can know ourselves more fully. The purpose of spiritual insight is not so that we have insight into other people, but that we have insight into our own nature. Sensing things about others is a psychic consciousness from the past. Being able to see clearly into our own nature is the great gift of the new consciousness. This ability puts us in charge of ourselves, we rule in our own kingdom.

What, then, are these seven thunders? Rudolf Steiner describes how our thinking is like thunder; the warmth in our blood meets the air in our nervous system whenever we have a thought or idea.

Then John is told not to write them down. Is it 'do not write them down' or 'you cannot write them down'? Our insights cannot always be put into words. Spiritual insights need to gestate before we really understand them. As the insight grows within us it becomes part of us and then we do not need to write it down. We don't write down many of the things we know. We don't write down how to make a cup of tea, or how to make the bed.

When we come to this stage in our spiritual development we can know many things but at the same time feel that we know nothing. This kind of knowing isn't set out within us like a book but rather it is as if we have access to a vast library - but only when the occasion arises. In this way we can't possess the knowledge, it only comes our way on a need to know basis. With the right combination of fire and air in our being, lightning will flash and thunder will roll, and we will know what we need to know. When we identify with this glorious being we will have the courage to step into the future knowing that we are part of the mystery of God.

And the angel whom I saw standing on sea and land lifted up his right hand to heaven and swore by him who lives for ever and ever, who created heaven and what is in it, the earth and what is in it, and the sea and what is in it, that there should be no more delay, but that in the days of the trumpet call to be sounded by the seventh angel, the mystery of God, as he announced to his servants the prophets, should be fulfilled. Then the voice which I had heard from heaven spoke to me again, saying, "Go, take the scroll which is open in the hand of the angel who is standing on the sea and on the land." So I went to the angel and told him to give me the little scroll; and he said to me, "Take it and eat; it will be bitter to your stomach, but sweet as honey in your mouth." And I took the little scroll from the hand of the angel and ate it; it was sweet as honey in my mouth, but when I had eaten it my stomach was made bitter. And I was told, "You must again prophesy about many peoples and nations and tongues and kings." Rev 10:5-11

There are many indications, even in these few verses, that this angel is the Imagination of our I AM – the highest expression of our 'I', our sense of self. If we create this image in our minds, or even draw it on paper, we are immediately elevated above our sense of being a body standing on a particular point of this earth. Since the Greek word for angel means messenger, then what is this being telling us? It could be telling us to identify with it as a means of tapping into our full potential? It is a messenger between our Higher self and our earthly self.

The time has come for us to stop seeing ourselves as beings limited to our physical bodies. So when this being stands with one foot on the sea and one on the land, and one hand reaching the heavens and the other, no doubt, reaching as far in the opposite direction, we have a sense of an all-encompassing presence. This image can then become our goal; each day we can try to imagine what it would be like to experience ourselves as beings with a consciousness that is not limited to our physical body. This is when we begin to experience the perspective of our I AM. This is part of the mystery of God.

It is our I AM that experiences each life that we have ever lived. It is our I AM that is conscious of all that we experience between birth and death, as well as between death and re-birth. Our I AM is conscious of all that lies behind our inclinations. Our I AM seeks to influence our souls by guiding our thinking, feeling and will. It is our I AM that is the one who lives forever and ever. So it is our I AM that gives us the book; now we have inner knowledge, no longer drawing knowledge from external sources. Then we know and then we are the prophets.

What is it like to experience our Higher Self that lives forever and ever? Simply put, limits are removed. The words translated as, "there should be no more delay" *chronos ouketi estoi* really mean that time no longer shall be. When we no longer experience time then we are in eternity. Eternity is timeless, without beginning or end. We experience eternity when we remove the boundaries placed on us by time. Then we can view our lives as part of a series of lives. This gives us new goals accompanied by a different sense of achievement, which brings with it a new level of understanding as well as a greater satisfaction with our life.

Then we come to an important question. Did God create heaven, earth and sea? Or did we? Don't we create our environment through our deeds, through all the choices we have made - in this life and all previous lives? Sure, God gives us the raw materials, but if God created everything wouldn't this cosmos be paradise? We were kicked out of paradise and given freedom. So now we are the creators, for better or worse. In fact the biggest illusion of all is not seeing that we have created this world. All the choices made by human beings, life after life, make our world what it is. To say that this physical world is maya, as many metaphysicians do, distorts the truth. The maya, the illusion, is our failure to recognise that we have created this world through the use of our will. When we realise the truth of this we face the full weight of our responsibility.

To experience our limitlessness is at the same time to experience our creative power. We become much more objective and impartial about our inner life. Then, when we are not so self-absorbed, we develop a deep and personal concern for all that takes place in the world. Our self-centred inclinations are transposed into compassion for all life. Then we become one with the Christ deed; this mighty deed that is the mystery of God. The mystery of a god becoming man to show us what is possible if we strive to experience our I AM. When we experience this truth we will be able to bear the bitterness of knowing what limits us. Then, by example we will again be a living prophecy before "the peoples, nations, tongues and kings".

CHAPTER ELEVEN

The Seventh Trumpet Continues

Then I was given a measuring rod like a staff, and I was told: "Rise and measure the temple of God and the altar and those who worship there, but do not measure the court outside the temple; leave that out, for it is given over to the nations, and they will trample over the holy city for forty-two months. And I will grant my two witnesses power to prophesy for one thousand two hundred and sixty days, clothed in sackcloth." These are the two olive trees and the two lampstands which stand before the Lord of the earth. And if any one would harm them, fire pours out from their mouth and consumes their foes; if any one would harm them, thus he is doomed to be killed. They have power to shut the sky, that no rain may fall during the days of their prophesying, and they have power over the waters to turn them into blood, and to smite the earth with every plague, as often as they desire. Rev 11:1-6

We are the temple of God as St Paul reminds us in 2 Corinthians – "For we are the temple of the living God; as God said, "I will live in them and move among them, and I will be their God, and they shall be my people." 2Co 6:16 This idea was explored in chapter three.

How do we measure up? This is the burning question for those of us who have committed to developing our consciousness. As we reach the point where our higher selves can influence our souls we must measure our success to ensure that we keep our eyes on the prize. There are places within our consciousness that are altars and places that are outer courts. We are advised to measure that which is holy and not to measure what is outside. This is because all that we have developed within us that is holy, all that is influenced by our 'I', all that has received the touch of Christ, is tender and fragile and can be trampled by what is in the outer court.

In life the opposite happens. We are willing to measure our superficial character flaws but we rarely measure that which is deeply spiritual within us. Perhaps we have no measuring rod until we reach a certain point in our development. One measuring rod that we do have is the life of Jesus revealed to us in the four gospels. If we want a bench mark for our progress we can place ourselves within these stories and gauge how we would respond to the events.

Chapter eleven often alludes to the processes in the life of Jesus as he gradually took the Cosmic Christ into his being. Not the least of which is the power to turn water into blood, reminiscent of turning the water into wine - the symbol of Christ's blood. We could use this chapter as a guide for our own experiences of making our souls ready for the dramatic changes; from outer court to altar. This is what must happen if our 'I' is to take its rightful place in our being in preparation for the Christ presence. This necessarily involves a battle between our lower and higher selves.

We are warned not to measure, not to analyse, our lower nature (or the lower nature of others for that matter). One reason for this is that we are going to be able to see the lower more clearly. As the light of our Higher Self illumines us, we will see how spiritual truth is the opposite of all that we have learned through life. The values of our community or country often contradict spiritual reality. Human value cannot be judged by the size of a bank account or the number of university degrees. This notion of the 'haves' and 'have-nots' is misplaced. Only when this measurement is applied to spiritual development does it stand. Then, the 'haves' do not shun the 'have-nots', and vice versa; they cherish and encourage them. Love pours from those who have attained a level of spiritual development. This love is not hoarded and only given to those who are in favour, it is freely available to all who want it.

Not all, however, want it. The life of Jesus is testimony to this. When his love flowed he was met with derision and hatred. When this love begins to flow within us many things are revealed. For ourselves this means that we see the source of our temperaments. We see the drives and desires that colour our nature. We see how they can be instinctual and how we ennoble them. We see how we are driven to prevail against all that threatens us. We see how our drives become desires which, without wisdom, can do great harm. We are faced with the distinction between the altar and the outer court, and we must turn our attention to the temple and the altar.

Our drives and desires are one of the areas of our being we could assign to the two witnesses. Our drives are associated with our life-force, our etheric; and our desires are associated with our emotional body, our astral. When one is harmed or damaged the fiery emotion of anger pours out; when the other is damaged life is killed. How are they harmed? By all that is contained in our lower selves. This is why it is important for us to become very aware of our drives. They rise up from deep within our organs to ensure that we take care of our physical body. It is possible that when these drives are not managed properly obesity or anorexia is the result. When our desires are not ennobled anger and violence are expressed without constraint. These are some of the reasons that we must "Rise and measure the temple of God and the altar and those (characteristics within us) who worship there".

And when they have finished their testimony, the beast that ascends from the bottomless pit will make war upon them and conquer them and kill them, and their dead bodies will lie in the street of the great city which is allegorically called Sodom and Egypt, where their Lord was crucified. For three days and a half men from the peoples and tribes and tongues and nations gaze at their dead bodies and refuse to let them be placed in a tomb, and those who dwell on the earth will rejoice over them and make merry and exchange presents, because these two prophets had been a torment to those who dwell on the earth. But after the three and a half days a breath of life from God entered them, and they stood up on their feet, and great fear fell on those who saw them. Rev 11: 7-11

The whole of The Revelation given to John is about awareness. This awareness is not only awareness of the spiritual worlds that interpenetrate this earth, but also awareness of what goes on in our own consciousness. This word 'testimony' is marturia which means to witness. Witnessing is a favourite human pastime; it is the way we make sense of the world. Our preference can be to witness things from a distance and this has given rise to the popularity of reality television.

Vicarious observation is a very elemental way of experiencing ourselves. As long as we are the onlooker we do not self-witness. Now self-witnessing isn't a process of psychoanalysis, self-witnessing is being able to see our place in the world and stand firmly in it. We are not swayed by what others think of us, or what we think of ourselves – which is usually coloured by what others think of us anyway. We are not concerned with our failures; we objectively observe the biography of our own life.

Self-witnessing means that we are connecting with our purpose and contribution to human evolution. This may not be accompanied by a great fanfare and, indeed, we often do not see what we do until we are able to look back on it – which may not even be possible till after we die. Nor is it necessary to be able to see what we are doing, for if we manage to fully occupy our place in the world we are great contributors. This means that we put our will to good use by creating the right future. This is a resurrection process. This is what John alludes to when he says, "… after the three and a half days a breath of life from God entered them, and they stood up on their feet."

In preparation for this moment, we have had to become aware of ourselves as separate, individual beings. Separate from the homogenous whole and from each other. We have had to develop a healthy ego and experience selfishness. Now all this must die. All those egotistical feelings, thoughts and actions that were the tools of self-awareness must die. We must now give up all ideas of being separated from others. At the same time, we must continue to develop our individualism. All the distinguishing features that separated us into tribes and tongues and nations must die; no longer can we gather in groups because we share these distinctions.

Now the distinctions are within each of us which makes us unique individuals. This means that we have to make an effort to get along with each other. We are no longer drawn together through similar soul moods, nor do we reject people who appear to be foreign. Now we find ways to value all human beings and hold them in our hearts with great respect. In fact, we see the Christ is each person and we relate to them as if they were Christ. At first this is most difficult.

The difficulty arises because the beast is a necessary part of this process. Here, of course, lies the danger. The beast always likes to overdo things. Only through our own vigilance can everything be kept in balance. In our newly resurrected state this is not always easy; just like it is not easy to keep our balance when we first learn to ride a bike.

The crucial factor in this work is our ability to be a reliable self-witness. This takes great courage for we must admit to ourselves our egotistical thoughts. After we speak rudely to someone we remember that we would never speak that way to Christ. We must be able to identify those raw feelings – instincts – as they rise from the depths of our being and take them for what they are; unrefined drives and desires. The only way we can deal with this is to remember that we are in the presence of the Lamb, the risen Christ, who once lived on this earth as we do. It is the Lamb who is opening these seals. This too is part of self-witnessing.

We must accept that the more self-aware we become the more pain we will experience through what we witness. However, at the same time we will experience the elation that comes from conquering. To be able to conquer the habitual ideas etched in our memories is the sweetest thing. To be able to see things in a new light is to have the breath of life from God enter into us so that we can stand.

Standing is one of the three special gifts given to human beings to set us apart from the animal kingdom. Our ability to stand on two feet comes to us through the human 'I'. When a human being stands in the power of the I AM, the highest expression of the 'I', a great fear falls on those who see it.

We meet this fear from people in our environment, and we meet it within ourselves when we doubt ourselves. This fear rises up out of our regrets, feelings of guilt, our disappointments and all those thoughts and feelings that make us feel small. Only through self-witnessing can we see who we really are – co-creators with the living Lamb.

And when they have finished their testimony, the beast that ascends from the bottomless pit will make war upon them and conquer them and kill them, and their dead bodies will lie in the street of the great city which is allegorically called Sodom and Egypt, where their Lord was crucified. For three days and a half men from the peoples and tribes and tongues and nations gaze at their dead bodies and refuse to let them be placed in a tomb, and those who dwell on the earth will rejoice over them and make merry and exchange presents, because these two prophets had been a torment to those who dwell on the earth. But after the three and a half days a breath of life from God entered them, and they stood up on their feet, and great fear fell on those who saw them. Then they heard a loud voice from heaven saying to them, "Come up hither!" And in the sight of their foes they went up to heaven in a cloud. And at that hour there was a great earthquake, and a tenth of the city fell; seven thousand people were killed in the earthquake, and the rest were terrified and gave glory to the God of heaven. The second woe has passed; behold, the third woe is soon to come. Rev 11:7-14

If we read the whole story of the two witnesses / prophets in Rev 11:1 - 14 there are apparent contradictions. This could be the result of a mistranslation or perhaps viewing John's description from the wrong perspective. If we take the story to be an explanation of what we can experience when we connect with our I AM, the story could be retold in this way.

Those of us who have prepared our bodies to be the temple of God will begin to experience ourselves in two ways; one as a spiritual person and the other as an earthly person. The two olive trees and the two lampstands could be expressions of this. These two could be standing either side of a gateway. Perhaps when we look from one side we see olive trees, and from the other we see lampstands. Furthermore, the lamps rely on oil, which olive trees produce – this was considered in Rev 1:12-16.

A gateway suggests an initiation and this story makes reference to the period of initiation. Initiation is essentially the transition of our consciousness to a higher level. In ancient temples the initiator placed the neophyte into a deep sleep for three and half days. The biblical story of Lazarus marks the end of that form of initiation. Now we self-initiate through life's events. It is interesting to note that the periods of time mentioned earlier in chapter 11 also point to this 'three and half' period; forty two months, or one thousand, two hundred and sixty days, are approximately three and half years.

John could be giving us an Imagination of what we will experience as we self-initiate when he describes the dead bodies not being placed in a tomb, and the subsequent rejoicing. The ultimate initiation is for us to experience our Real Selves hidden within our soul; this is the soul's secret. The challenge is to do this while we live on this earth separated from the spiritual worlds. We stand between the I AM and its mirrored reflection, our earthly ego. It is our earthly consciousness that must go through many small deaths, to be resurrected ever higher and higher. These changes in consciousness are continual events in the lives of those of us who are committed to the work of becoming conscious of our I AM. The more we measure up, the more the Lamb can stand within us.

If we identify ourselves with the two witnesses then we are given the authority to prophesy. *Propheteia* means to speak our mind, to speak our thoughts. We are no longer able to hide our thoughts in the privacy of our minds. This bears with it a tremendous responsibility because to speak our mind can do great harm. However, if we are provoked, fire will proceed from our mouths and devour whatever opposes us. When we stand in the truth of our Real Self we fearlessly deal with whatever opposes the truth. Fire is the element associated with the I AM as we are told in Exodus 3:2 in the story of the burning bush. We become beings of fire without being destroyed by the fire.

The witnesses wear sackcloth, the garment worn by mourners. So they will prophesy in mourning for three and a half years. This confirms the many deaths and misfortunes that take place during this time – both within our own consciousnesses and within the consciousnesses of those around us who are naturally affected by the changes in us. When it says that they have the authority, this word *exousia* infers the influence of spiritual beings that share in the work of Christ.

The demonstration of this authority evokes the beast. The beast is the one who opposes, and if there is nothing to oppose then the beast has no task. When our thoughts, feelings or actions are at odds with truth the beast rises up to try and conquer us. If we are conscious of the work of the beast, our unconscious habits die and lie in the street of the great city which spiritually, *pneumaticos*, (not allegorically) is called Sodom, the consciousness destroyed by fire, and Egypt, the consciousness released from bondage.

The rejoicing and gift-giving are suggestive of the birth of Jesus, the supreme model for the I AM process. These gifts are given because these two prophets had been a torment to our earthly consciousness. Torment, *basanismos*, refers to the acts of testing and judgment that must continually occur in our consciousness if it is to be raised. Hence, they went up to heaven in a cloud which is the ascension Paul describes in the Book of Acts.

But you shall receive power when the Holy Spirit has come upon you; and you shall be my witnesses in Jerusalem and in all Judea and Sama'ria and to the end of the earth." And when he had said this, as they were looking on, he was lifted up, and a cloud took him out of their sight. And while they were gazing into heaven as he went, behold, two men stood by them in white robes, and said, "Men of Galilee, why do you stand looking into heaven? This Jesus, who was taken up from you into heaven, will come in the same way as you saw him go into heaven." Acts 1:8-11

Contemplating John's words will prepare us for the shift in consciousness that must happen, is happening, and will continue to happen into the future. While we look outside ourselves for authority, and for the impetus to become more aware of what is going on, we will never see it. The authority is now within us. It is up to us to hear the voice say, "Come up hither!" Come up to your higher consciousness. This will cause difficulties in our lives, but with the authority that comes with the I AM we will be able to deal with them wisely.

But after the three and a half days a breath of life from God entered them, and they stood up on their feet, and great

fear fell on those who saw them. Then they heard a loud voice from heaven saying to them, "Come up hither!" And in the sight of their foes they went up to heaven in a cloud. And at that hour there was a great earthquake, and a tenth of the city fell; seven thousand people were killed in the earthquake, and the rest were terrified and gave glory to the God of heaven. The second woe has passed; behold, the third woe is soon to come. Rev 11:11-14

For the duration of the sixth trumpeting we are dealing with the second woe. The second woe accentuates the divisions between people. These divisions can be found within us also. It is as if we need an injection of friendliness both within and without. How can we experience the separateness that is an essential part of present human evolution without feeling separated?

This feeling of separateness causes animosity and anti-social feelings as people instinctively put themselves ahead of others. It is obvious that individualism gives rise to avaricious selfishness and greed. Has this separation between human beings gone too far? Or are we meant to be standing at the precipice of the bottomless pit? Does the temptation of greed give us true freedom? Ironically we think that greed is the ticket to freedom. So we each face the personal decision to stand as an individual among individuals. We choose to love the other person and to love ourselves.

This freedom is so near, and yet so far. Two basic principles hold sway within us; do we like the other person, or do we dislike them. We swing between these two feelings in everything we do. It is like a pendulum swinging in our soul; I love this, I hate that. Furthermore, we go to great lengths to avoid using the 'h' word. This is proof that we avoid facing the truth of what transpires in our soul. The fact remains that the unawakened soul oscillates between love and hate, like and dislike. Not using the word 'hate' doesn't lessen the experience of it.

While we remain polarised between love and hate it means that we are ruled by our instinctual feelings. It is only when our thoughts can influence our feelings that we can love the other person. Till then we are fearful and antisocial regardless of how well we hide it – and we are not free.

Steiner speaks about this very clearly in his lectures given in

1918, published as "The Challenge of the Times". Specifically in the fifth lecture, called "Social and Antisocial Instincts", he goes so far as to say that when we love another person we are really loving ourselves. This love is then egotistical and exclusive which makes us antisocial beings. While this has a place, especially in relationships and families, we need to recognise this self-love and not mistake it as loving others.

What does this say for the increasing numbers of single people? Wouldn't this mean that more people have to learn to love themselves directly without the impetus coming from another person? This too is freedom.

So, unconsciously we seek out people we like as a means to love ourselves better when, in fact, it is the ones who challenge us that assist us to exercise our freedom; to love them as well as ourselves. It is this freedom that leads us to our Real Self.

What about when people hate each other? What effect does that have? The fear we have for others is experienced by them, for our consciousness connects us with each other. When we think loving thoughts about a person, it affects them. When we hate them, they experience this hatred – even if they are on the other side of the world.

Do we pray for others confident that our blessings will have an affect but then forget to apply this principle to our judgmental thoughts about others? If we want to experience true freedom then we must be able to suspend our opinions about others at will. We never know the full story behind why people act the way they do. In freedom we can be the observers while resisting premature conclusions. We can open ourselves to accept that people and organisations can change and they do.

This freedom that we can experience within us, guiding our feelings, invigorating our thoughts and using our will, indicates that the Holy Spirit works within us. When John says, "But after the three and a half days a breath of life from God entered them," the word 'breath' is *pneuma* or spirit. This spirit of life that enters into us is the Holy Spirit. This is reminiscent of the events in the upper room in John's Gospel.

Again Jesus said, "Peace be with you! As the Father has sent me, I am sending you." And with that he breathed on

them and said, "Receive the Holy Spirit. If you forgive anyone his sins, they are forgiven; if you do not forgive them, they are not forgiven." Jn 20:21-23

When this Holy Spirit, the I AM infused life-force, *zoe*, enters into us, we stand. We take our position of confidence and authority. We could say that we become true freedom workers. We are fully able to exercise freedom within our own being so that we are able to forgive ourselves and forgive others. This forgiving is judgment-free observation. Blessing, giving glory, flows from our being as if from a kind of freedom-priest. We are no longer bound to the repetitive patterns of our thinking, feeling and will, we let things be. The freedom that we have been able to achieve flows from us as love. Through this love some difficulties are removed, some stay. This is not through our own earthly judging but rather because we can stand in harmony with the cosmos through our inner freedom. It is like an earthquake this unbinding of our automatic thoughts, feelings and actions that always have opinions. They always want to act towards others instead of acting within. When we exercise this true freedom within us we love, a love that pours from our hearts in every direction giving glory to the God of heaven and blessing those around us.

But after the three and a half days a breath of life from God entered them, and they stood up on their feet, and great fear fell on those who saw them. Then they heard a loud voice from heaven saying to them, "Come up hither!" And in the sight of their foes they went up to heaven in a cloud. And at that hour there was a great earthquake, and a tenth of the city fell; seven thousand people were killed in the earthquake, and the rest were terrified and gave glory to the God of heaven. The second woe has passed; behold, the third woe is soon to come. Rev 11:11-14

If we take this story as an account of the changes within our consciousness, we can see how fear and anxiety are a natural part of the process. When the breath of life from God enters into us we experience our 'I' being because it stands up in us. We could say that there is the feeling of movement from fear to inner courage. Then we become aware that not all the forces within us feel this courage. Some parts of us experience great fear. This would be especially true of our habitual thoughts and feelings which are about to become redundant.

It is when we get a taste of the future that fear arises within us. We get a glimpse of new ways of expressing ourselves, new ways of thinking, of feeling, and we also see that our behaviour will change. We know that this will change our personality and therefore will have an impact on our relationships.

When such pictures of the future flow towards us and enter into the present moment, fear rises up. If we live our life in the moment, if we are only able to take in what is happening now, we will face some difficulties. To be able to manage fear and anxiety we need to take into account all that lies behind us, and all that is to come. This is our biography, encompassing all the events that make us who we are. Sure, we will have some regrets. With hindsight we can see what we have left undone. We can see the spare capacity that we could have used. What we must realise is that this spare capacity is still at our disposal. This spare capacity is our 'I' being. When we realise that we could have achieved more in the past, and that we can achieve more in the future, we experience our 'I' being. When we can view events from the perspective of our 'I' being we stand with God, and we experience time, not as a moment now, but as an eternal moment.

Then, we can embrace the changes that the future brings, and our feelings of fear and anxiety can be used in another way. Instead of experiencing fear and anxiety as many people do; either as an adrenalin rush or being paralysed by it, there is a third way. We only find this third way when we realise that fear is not a thing in itself; fear is an opportunity.

This brings us to the true meaning of prayer. When John reports that "… the rest were terrified and gave glory to the God of heaven" he is saying that if we become prayerful - giving glory to God - in this moment we experience how our terror, phobos, (fear) brings us to the experience of our 'I'.

When religious leaders use fear as a vehicle for making demands on our behaviour they miss the point entirely. Fear is not the tool of guilt; fear is the path to God. Of our own accord, when we feel the fear within us, we have the opportunity to experience our 'I'. Furthermore, what isn't often realised is that our 'I' is the root cause of this fear. Without fear we become satisfied and secure and don't look outside ourselves to our potential. Then, as we become more conscious of our 'I', our anxiety levels rise because our 'I' leads us towards an unknown future. This is the modern initiation experience.

Initiation, which now happens in even the smallest events in our lives, calls us to resist being overwhelmed by fear. We must learn how to stand in the tension produced by fear. We can do this by becoming the observer. As we observe the fear rising within us, and then begin to experience the resulting anxiety, we can hear the voice, "Come up hither!" This is the call to raise our fear from its natural, overwhelming state, to a place where the energy of it can be used differently. Not for thrill seeking, or for feeling defeated, but as wind in the sails of our higher consciousness. Then fear becomes the freedom-force. We link the past, present and future together in our soul enabling us to look beyond the passing moment to eternity.

When we are able to use the feelings of fear and anxiety that come to us from so many directions in modern life, it is as if we upset all the forces within us. These are the forces we create within our being according to how we think, feel and become motivated to act. It isn't hard to imagine the turbulence that fear creates.

Fear causes the etheric body to retract. Just like the earth's crust, our body is divided into plates; physical substance and etheric and astral forces. These move together and apart in the different areas of our body as we respond to life. These 'plates' move against each other, and can build up tension just like they do in the earth's globe. Sometimes the tension can be released in a sudden and often violent jerk. This sudden jerk creates an earthquake. This confirms that we have prevailed through the second woe causing the third woe to come quickly.

Then the seventh angel blew his trumpet, and there were loud voices in heaven, saying, "The kingdom of the world has become the kingdom of our Lord and of his Christ, and he shall reign for ever and ever." And the twenty-four elders who sit on their thrones before God fell on their faces and worshiped God, saying, "We give thanks to thee, Lord God Almighty, who art and who wast, that thou hast taken thy great power and begun to reign. The nations raged, but thy

wrath came, and the time for the dead to be judged, for rewarding thy servants, the prophets and saints, and those who fear thy name, both small and great, and for destroying the destroyers of the earth." Then God's temple in heaven was opened, and the ark of his covenant was seen within his temple; and there were flashes of lightning, voices, peals of thunder, an earthquake, and heavy hail. Rev 11:15-19

The seventh trumpeting announces that something has been accomplished. Now there is to be a celebration. Those who rule in their own kingdom are acknowledged for the mighty work they have achieved. We could even imagine that these trumpets sound simultaneously rather than consecutively. The raising of consciousness is a not about working on one thing after another, it is a simultaneous process within us. While the first trumpet sounds as we begin to reign over one difficult area, the seventh trumpet may sound as we achieve in another area.

Loud voices in heaven can refer to our higher spiritual faculty of Inspiration; when spiritual truth resounds within us. Inner voices or sounds, phone, are loud; like the echo produced when sound waves reflect off a surface. Do we always hear them in this noisy world?

Seeing the twenty-four elders fall on their faces indicates that the physical eyes are no longer necessary. The Greek word faces, *prosopon*, means towards - pros the eyes - ops. When our spiritual Imagination is active we are able to see what takes place within our own being. Seeing the twenty-four elders can be part of an archetypal process indicating that we are connecting with our 'I'. Becoming aware of them can assist us to take the final steps in our development. It is as if they are watching us in our progress but when we become aware of them they no longer need to watch us, and they bow their faces in reverence and praise.

The two kingdoms are our lower and higher being. The kingdom of the world or *kosmos*, is that place in our being where our astral's force rules. The kingdom of our Lord, *kurios*, is that place in our being where our 'I's force rules. Our Lord is our I AM. Like Jesus, we prepare our being by refining the worldly astral's force so that the spiritual 'I's force can now guide our consciousness. This is the preparation required for the birth of the Christ force within our being.

We are so used to our astral's force providing us with an understanding of who we are and what we are meant to be doing with our life. Lifetime after lifetime our astral's force had this function, it is very practised. In the past these forces allowed the cosmos to play into our being and thereby gave us knowledge of creation and our role in it. However, since the time of Christ, the astral's force has been superseded. This task has been handed over to our 'I's force which is actually too weak to give us knowledge of creation, and hence knowledge of who we are and what we are meant to be doing.

It is only when we can strengthen our 'I's force that we will be able to make sense of everything. Paul refers to this in his Letter to the Romans;

I consider that the sufferings of this present time are not worth comparing with the glory that is to be revealed to us. For the creation waits with eager longing for the revealing of the sons of God; Ro 8:18-19

The sons of God are those who have strengthened their connection to their 'I's force that it becomes a more continuous influence in our earthly being. If we are to do this we must first be able to recognise how it affects us. The only way to become aware of this is to become better acquainted with the nature of our feelings, our thoughts and the way we act. Whenever we are swayed by our likes and dislikes we know that our feelings are governed by our astral's force. Whenever we feel repelled by something, or automatically drawn to it, our astral's force has control of us. If we are able to intercept such instinctive responses then our 'I's force is at work.

We can tell ourselves repeatedly that we have strengthened our 'I' connection, but we can only test our progress in our interactions with other people. Only when we encounter a wide variety of people can our ability to prevail over our astral's force be put to the test. Remember that it is very strong, very experienced and territorial. We need a determined will to be able to change the way we respond to some situations. Driving a car in congested traffic would be an excellent testing ground, or phoning the call centre about our bank account.

Even though we may wonder if we would ever be able to rule in the kingdom of our being, sometimes it only takes a split second for a new response to replace an old one. It is like loosening the rope on a sail and the whole sail unfurls to catch the wind. Our task is to loosen the rope in the right way, at the right time.

The rope, the sail and the wind can represent our thinking, feeling and will which must work together in harmony and with intensity. This is often not the case. We think things about others that cause great harm, especially other drivers on the road, or call centre employees. Our intense feelings rise up in protest when we hear what others say to us. We can act wildly in response to this, even if we think of killing the person with no intention of carrying it out. We think that things said and done in private have no effect, this could not be further from the truth. Furthermore, the more our 'I' shines in our being the more light is shed on our unhelpful tendencies. This causes great suffering and we can be tempted to retreat from our development. However, we must be confident that the Lord of our being reigns for ever and ever, and is available to us if we just turn towards it.

Then the seventh angel blew his trumpet, and there were loud voices in heaven, saying, "The kingdom of the world has become the kingdom of our Lord and of his Christ, and he shall reign for ever and ever." And the twenty-four elders who sit on their thrones before God fell on their faces and worshiped God, saying, "We give thanks to thee, Lord God Almighty, who art and who wast, that thou hast taken thy great power and begun to reign. The nations raged, but thy wrath came, and the time for the dead to be judged, for rewarding thy servants, the prophets and saints, and those who fear thy name, both small and great, and for destroying the destroyers of the earth." Then God's temple in heaven was opened, and the ark of his covenant was seen within his temple; and there were flashes of lightning, voices, peals of thunder, an earthquake, and heavy hail. Rev 11:15-19

It is not easy to make sense of what the twenty four elders say. They are sitting on their thrones indicating that they also reign or rule within self. When they fall on their faces their eyes no longer take in what is outside them. They worship God and give thanks. Worship, *proskuneo* means 'towards kiss'. Imagine kissing God. In their deep reverence they give thanks, *eucharistia*, from which we have the term Eucharist used to describe the bread and wine symbolic of Christ's sacrifice.

This is a moment of holy awe, full of religious feeling. The word religion means to bind, to reunite the physical with the spiritual. When the kingdom of the earth, which is our material existence, comes under the rulership of our 'I', it is an experience shared with all those who achieved it previously. It cannot be private and personal. When one of us "hast taken thy great power and begun to reign" those who have been there before now re-experience it. This is the true meaning of spiritual morality.

Spiritual morality is pure, sense-free, will. When we act morally we are very aware of our motives. This can only be revealed through our Higher Self. Our actions arise out of our interest for the highest human potential. This pure morality means that nothing is acquired at the expense of others, and the spiritual achievements of others are felt as if they were our own.

When we reach this level of self-knowledge the nations do rage within us. The nations are those divisive instincts that tie us to our nationality. Then we usually favour people and things that come from our place of birth. If we have German, Dutch or French heritage we usually have a bias in that direction. Our I AM has no such feelings, for it has experienced all the nations of the earth through many incarnations.

Then the wrath comes. The word translated as 'rage' and 'wrath' is *orgé* which is the kind of anger that is slow to rise. We experience it when we are indignant. (The other word for anger is *thumos* which is more like a fierce outburst.) We seem to live in an atmosphere of anger today. Perhaps it is building up within us because of the tension between our lower and higher selves. It could come from a deep seated dissatisfaction caused when our I AM shines into our being. We mustn't be consumed by this anger; it must burst from us as love. If we express this anger our lower instincts reign.

Instincts are patterns of behaviour created by past memories. These memories are formed when our sense impressions are imprinted on our etheric body, all day, every day. If we act unconsciously then we can certainly be basing our actions on this store of past information. We could call it our lower memory which is at odds with the cosmic memory of our I AM. Our I AM could be trying to work through some karma while our lower memory could activate patterns of behaviour that have worked out the best resistance. This is the time "for the dead to be judged". Our shadowy dead memories need to be seen in the right light, the I AM light.

Then John hears the elders list all those who should be rewarded. More likely it means that with spiritual insight we can see the benefits of each one's work. Servants, prophets, saints, fearers; each one contributing in their own way to human evolution. When it says, "destroying the destroyers of the earth" the word 'destroying' diaphtheiro, is really corrupting. This indicates that the wrong energies are combined; the earthly corrupting the spiritual or the anti-forces working against our progress.

Then God's temple in heaven was opened, and the ark of his covenant was seen within his temple; and there were flashes of lightning, voices, peals of thunder, an earthquake, and heavy hail. Rev 11:19

With these words we reach the end of chapter 11 and the first half of the Revelation concludes. We are God's temple. His covenant is our pure being untarnished by a sojourn on the earth. We see the archetypal pattern to which we aspire. When this truth is revealed we will never be the same again. The wild weather is a sign that our whole being is shaken to the core by this revelation.

Before stepping into chapter 12 it would be good to think back over the 11 chapters we have travelled through. This map of the development of human consciousness began right at the beginning of The Revelation with these three verses.

The revelation of Jesus Christ, which God gave him to show to his servants what must soon take place; and he made it known by sending his angel to his servant John, who bore witness to the word of God and to the testimony of Jesus Christ, even to all that he saw. Blessed is he who reads aloud the words of the prophecy, and blessed are those who hear, and who keep what is written therein; for the time is near. Rev 1:1-3

In essence, the Revelation is about seeing and applying. We are asked to behold and then act. How we see is important, we don't just look. This word is *idou*, one of twelve different Greek words for behold, and it means to see beneath the surface of things. Being able to see in this way then informs the way we act.

If our consciousness is to develop in the right way it is vital that our behaviour is appropriate. Every action and every motive must be informed by spiritual insight. How can we be sure that we are acting in the right way? This is the dilemma that faces every person who steps onto the spiritual path. All our actions arise out of the force of our will and at this stage in human evolution we are still developing our will. We could read every verse in these 11 chapters as guidance for the use of our will. Conquering and ruling are emphasised throughout.

So how does this will work? The will forces in our physical body are beyond our consciousness. This will force underlies all the movement in our body; the movement of air through breathing, the circulating blood and other fluids, food digestion, the movement of our limbs and so on.

We also find will impulses in our wishes and desires. These are strong forces that do not rest until they are satisfied. We know this force best in our hunger and thirst. There are still other will forces that we experience as motive, our reason for behaving in a specific way. These are the will forces that we must become much more aware of, for behind them lie the impulses of karma.

Karma is one of the most important components of our existence, and on the whole, the most misunderstood. Essentially karma assists us to become conscious of our 'I' being. Every time we meet up with other human beings our karma is drawn into play. In this way our 'I' being gives us the opportunity to resolve and harmonise our relationships. This means that we must face the way we expressed our will in our past lives. Were we forceful? or unable to be forceful? If we lacked the ability to express ourselves then, now we will probably want to do so. If we were overly wilful in a past life, in this life our physical mobility may be compromised and so on.

The will is a very complex matter. We are often unaware of the many ways we impose our will on others. It could be through wanting others to accept our ideas or advice. We can even be wilful when we resist the advice of others. Often we use our will to compensate for a sense of losing control, or feeling overwhelmed by the will of another person. Being able to impose our will helps us to feel safe again. We can, of course, even be wilful when we don't act.

Will is usually experienced as a tension in our lives; we seem to oscillate between the need to act on the one hand, and the inability to act on the other. We experience this as a need to move towards, or to move away, from this or that. It is as if we want to have too much control of our will processes even though we are hardly conscious of them. The more wilful we are the less we can know our will. We have to let go and observe to become truly conscious of our will.

Reviewing our day backwards is the very best way to disengage with our will so that we can see it. Then our will can become conscious in our soul and spirit – which is the goal if we are to become 'I' conscious. This review of our day allows us to objectively see how we used our will. Not so that we can regret our actions – for what's done is done - but so that we can know ourselves better. In this way we become aware of our 'I' being. In this awareness we experience strength and certainty which in turn leaves us less inclined to be wilful.

The wonderful passage in the "Bhagavad Gita" that deals with this issue is where Krishna gives advice to Arjuna about the use of his will: "if you can rise above all this and not be affected by your own deeds, like a flame which burns quietly in a place protected from the wind, undisturbed by anything external: if your soul, as little disturbed by its own deeds, lives quietly beside them, then does it become wise; then does it free itself from its deeds, and does not inquire what success attends them."

If we can cultivate the ability to live quietly beside our own deeds, which usually arise out of past life events, then we will tread more lightly on the earth. Then our will becomes goodwill which nourishes the earth. Just on that, a true understanding of climate change can only be reached by understanding the way human beings use their will – this is the real Inconvenient Truth. Not that we should be tempted to examine how other's use their will, however, otherwise we would fall into the trap of misusing our own will.

Our task is to become aware of our own will. For this we need a certain amount of strength for we will quickly see how often we trespass on others with our will. Our quest is to behave towards others as we would behave towards Christ. Then our will becomes at the same time freewill and goodwill.

In this freedom we establish a new atmosphere of respect which blesses others as it gives blessing to us. This is the love that Jesus revealed when he walked on this earth. He used his will wisely, not to impose it on his accusers, but to receive into himself the mighty Christ forces that saved this world from the destructive will forces that were gathering like a mighty storm in the cosmos. These are the things that we must behold so that we act out of our highest will forces which are both free and good.

CHAPTER TWELVE

A Woman Clothed with the Sun

And a great portent appeared in heaven, a woman clothed with the sun, with the moon under her feet, and on her head a crown of twelve stars; she was with child and she cried out in her pangs of birth, in anguish for delivery. And another portent appeared in heaven; behold, a great red dragon, with seven heads and ten horns, and seven diadems upon his heads. His tail swept down a third of the stars of heaven, and cast them to the earth. And the dragon stood before the woman who was about to bear a child, that he might devour her child when she brought it forth; she brought forth a male child, one who is to rule all the nations with a rod of iron, but her child was caught up to God and to his throne, and the woman fled into the wilderness, where she has a place prepared by God, in which to be nourished for one thousand two hundred and sixty days. Rev 12:1-7

Now we come to a mighty image that has puzzled many great thinkers. While we can look up at the sky and imagine a huge being clothed with the sun and so on, we also should think about how this image might apply to our own being as we stand on this earth.

When would we contain within our being the sun, moon and stars? When the limits of our being expand beyond our skin. When we are able to experience our spiritual being that is not limited to our physical body; then we will be in labour. The seed within us, its gestation complete, is ready to be delivered. This seed is our I AM which first appeared on the earth in the Jesus child, born in Bethlehem two thousand years ago. Why does childbirth herald this great event? Why not stone tablets or a flood and an ark? Why is the deepest secret hidden in the birth of a male child? And where are the shepherds and the kings? Why are they replaced by the fiery, *purrhos,* dragon?

When we see this portent, the *semeion*, the sign, we know that our soul is giving birth to our I AM. From within the womb of our soul, our I AM is a rod of iron forged from our purest will. The fire is forging our pure feeling, and the rod is shaped by our pure thinking. These faculties are pure because they do not arise from any outer stimulus. They are founded in our experience of truth, beauty and goodness. They are the very opposite of the way modern human beings think, feel and behave today.

When we achieve this new state of being our interaction with others changes; for out of the purity of our feeling, thinking and will we evoke the dragon. This is the dragon who wants to drag things out of the highest heaven into the lowest earth. He is our creation. He attends every higher birth within us and takes away a third of what we have produced with the sweep of his tail. This is the normal course of events of which we must become conscious. Then we handle our relationships with a new understanding.

At the time of this writing, it is the threshold of Christmas 2008 in the midst of a global financial crisis when a third of the value was swept from stock markets the world over. During such an event can we stop to look at the child? If we had kept our eyes on the child all along we would not be in this position, a position of fear without hope for so many. We are living The Revelation now. We are in labour continually and our focus should be on the child not the pain. We should also try not to make the birth more painful than it needs to be.

In the atmosphere of Christmas it is tempting to become intoxicated by the rituals; the cards with their messages of love and appreciation, the presents, everything that comes from outside us.

These are the dragons seeking to devour our inner work. These dragons are the distracters; they say look at this, look at that, and forget yourself. Drown yourself in all that you see outside you and then you won't have labour pains - no labour pains but a stillbirth.

Whenever we look outside ourselves for that which we feel we are lacking we have created a dragon. Since the birth of the Jesus child we have been given the ability to be self-born. The I-being that dwells within us seeks to grow to full term and doesn't necessarily want to cause labour pains. These pains arise from our resistance. They arise each time we misapply spiritual truth, and each time we think we've got the truth when in reality we have only just seen the tip of the iceberg. They arise when we try to apply our earthly understanding to a spiritual situation and vice versa.

These pains intensify each time we look outside ourselves thinking that others can give us something that we think we don't have. When we think that others are elevated above us, we deny the divinity within us. Indeed, if we think that we are more elevated than others, we kill the child and feed the dragon.

The greatest pain of all is when we don't see God, blindly accepting that he is there just in case. If we allow our soul to give birth, without holding anything back, it will not fear the desolation of the wilderness, it will not feel bereft of all that it ever knew, it will be nourished in that place prepared by God – this earth. This desolate, lonely, greed-filled earth where truth is a lie, beauty is ugly and goodness is utterly bad.

Only when we have the rod of iron can we rule in our own kingdom. The nations, the group consciousness that surrounds us will not touch us, yet we can be in it with equanimity. It is as if we crawl into the skin of the dragon, knowingly becoming part of it, and finding there the wisdom of the three kings and the love of the shepherds. This is the peace that passes understanding that lives in the hearts of those who know the eternal. Then can the child be continually born, transforming our being into its cosmic destiny, to be co-workers with the living Christ in our midst.

And a great portent appeared in heaven, a woman clothed with the sun, with the moon under her feet, and on her head a crown of twelve stars; she was with child and she cried out in her pangs of birth, in anguish for delivery. And another portent appeared in heaven; behold, a great red dragon, with seven heads and ten horns, and seven diadems upon his heads. His tail swept down a third of the stars of heaven, and cast them to the earth. And the dragon stood before the woman who was about to bear a child, that he might devour her child when she brought it forth; she brought forth a male child, one who is to rule all the nations with a rod of iron, but her child was caught up to God and to his throne, and the woman fled into the wilderness, where she has a place prepared by God, in which to be nourished for one thousand two hundred and sixty days. Rev 12:1-7

The human soul cries out to be delivered from the material view of human life. Yet at the same time it is bound to it through all that has been learnt throughout life. Innately we know that we have something precious within us that seeks to be released, something that will bring about enormous change.

The material view of life invades our soul at every level. While we know that we are so much more than our physical appearance, the first things we say to each other when we meet are about how we look; if we look well, or not, what we are wearing, what we are eating, or not eating, and if we are going to the gym or not and so on. Rarely is it about how we are thinking and feeling, and what is affecting our behaviour. When someone asks, "How are you?" if, instead of responding with the expected, "good", we say that we are unhappy, the other person will usually say, "good." This is an automatic response that confines our soul in continual labour. Deep dissatisfaction arises from this desolation in our soul.

This material view of life is so limited that it disregards the role of the sun, moon and stars in human life. Any discussion beyond their mechanistic functions is regarded as superstition. In some respects perhaps this is a good thing for some ideas about the sun, moon and stars can certainly be misleading; taking us back into a past consciousness that clouds the new vision that is in anguish for delivery.

The sign that John sees is the new vision. The contemplation of this sign is urgent for it holds the clue to our release from the limits of materialism -matter-realism as Sevak Gulbekian puts it in his book, "In the Belly of the Beast". While we can apply this vision to external events, we can equally apply it to our own consciousness. We could take the simple approach and say that this male child is Christ causing labour pains in our being or we could say that Christ has already been born in us and perhaps this vision is really about the woman. Who is she?

The Bible can be very fruitful when we know what we are looking for. Certainly the meaning of the Greek words opens up new possibilities. For instance, the word 'heaven' *ouranos* indicates elevation; John sees this sign in his elevated consciousness. Heaven is also where we find the clouds into which Christ disappeared as Paul describes in Acts 1.

But you shall receive power when the Holy Spirit has come upon you; ... And when he had said this, as they were looking on, he was lifted up, and a cloud took him out of their sight. And while they were gazing into heaven as he went, etc. Acts 1:8-10

This echoes Christ's words to his disciples as he prepares himself, and them, for his impending crucifixion.

Nevertheless I tell you the truth: it is to your advantage that I go away, for if I do not go away, the Counselor will not come to you; but if I go, I will send him to you. John 16:7

This counselor, the comforter, the *parakletos,* is the Holy Spirit. So Christ disappeared into heaven and now, out of this heaven comes the woman. She is Sophia who brings the new wisdom to us. This wisdom will give us the self-knowledge that we seek. We will move beyond philo-sophia that uses our earthly mind to make sense of the world, and enter into a living philosophy to experience the virgin birth in our own soul. This virgin birth is simply a DIY conception; we do it ourselves without outside assistance. This is what the term 'only begotten son from the father' means; to be self-born, *monogenes*.

Our task is to become aware of these events within our consciousness. The pre-requisite is to consciously engage in the purification of our feeling, thinking and will. Only we can do this work, Christ cannot assist us at all. He can only come to us afterwards. This purification takes place when we engage with our Higher Self, when we allow our I AM to elevate our habitual and instinctual thoughts, feelings and actions. When we begin to discipline our unconscious soul activity we will become aware of the presence of Sophia in our soul. She will be our constant companion.

When this purification has taken place our soul will be clothed with the sun so that the feelings of our heart will radiate pure love. Our will forces will irradiate our understanding like a moon under our feet, and we will wear our thinking like a crown because we will always consider all twelve aspects of an issue, not just the one that attracts us. This incredible sign, so vividly painted in the mind of John, can be of great comfort to us as we pass through this next phase of our work.

And a great portent appeared in heaven, a woman clothed with the sun, with the moon under her feet, and on her head a crown of twelve stars; she was with child and she cried out in her pangs of birth, in anguish for delivery. And another portent appeared in heaven; behold, a great red dragon, with seven heads and ten horns, and seven diadems upon his heads. His tail swept down a third of the stars of heaven, and cast them to the earth. And the dragon stood before the woman who was about to bear a child, that he might devour her child when she brought it forth; she brought forth a male child, one who is to rule all the nations with a rod of iron, but her child was caught up to God and to his throne, and the woman fled into the wilderness, where she has a place prepared by God, in which to be nourished for one thousand two hundred and sixty days. Rev 12:1-7

This presence of Sophia, as John saw her in The Revelation, dwarfs our known universe. She makes the sun, moon and zodiac seem like just a small part of heaven. Why would such a mighty being cry out in distress? Are we causing this distress? This is quite likely. For as long as we do not purify our inner being Sophia's labour continues.

This purification, which begins in our lower soul levels, is an urgent task for all human beings. This task involves restoring the pure virgin forces to our soul so that Christ may emerge from his enclosure within us. So how do we cleanse and purify our lower soul levels? This work can only be fully understood if we examine, in detail, the characteristics of our own feeling, thinking and will.

For the most part, these three function automatically as we respond to each moment in our day. For example, we usually feel warm and secure if someone smiles at us, and we feel cold and insecure if someone ignores us. These are natural responses that we are used to feeling because of our experiences through life so far.

Some people have no response to being smiled at or ignored; it is as if they are numb to these nuances of life. This can point to a disconnected soul, and in its extreme this can be an indication of autism. We might wonder if there isn't some degree of soul disconnection in many people. While on the one hand this can be recognised by a certain numbness; it can also be recognised by impulsiveness. In the extreme, the unbridled expression of anger that is becoming more prevalent in society also indicates soul disconnections.

We can find a similar thing happening in the area of human reasoning. On the one hand we have human beings capable of thinking the most complicated things, on the other we have people who don't think at all. A prominent Australian scientist in his eighties said that when he was young it was possible to know everything. In just eighty years knowledge has become so specialised that it is a challenge to know everything about one area of knowledge. At the other extreme, our thinking is dampened down by the media and our work is guided by procedure manuals.

When we examine the human will expressed in human activity or inactivity; on the one hand we see people living their lives by proxy in front of the television. On the other hand we see the extremes of behaviour in risky physical pursuits or in drug or alcohol induced socialising, extreme sexual activity and an alarming increase in the level of violence. Put in this way, we may be able to understand Sophia's distress.

How do these three areas play out within our own consciousness and how do we purify them? Isolation and a lack of openness with others is one area where we find the expression of our will forces. Not that we should immediately speak every thought and spend no time alone; it is about balance. It is about being able to gently share something that we have been inclined to hide in the past. It is about being more trusting of others and allowing them to experience us more fully. It is also about becoming more aware of what we set in motion through our own actions, or lack of them. The highest expression of will embraces others, and quietens our own fears.

In our thinking we can intercept the anxious tirade of thoughts that seem to invent even the most impossible possibilities. Or we can counteract our lazy thinking by trying to think things through a bit further than we usually do. We can intercept our judgemental thoughts about others, while at the same time increasing our thoughtfulness of others. It is through logic, through disciplining the mind, ruling it with an iron rod that one becomes the independent being that Sophia gives birth to.

When it comes to our feelings, we can stop feeling hurt by the words or actions of others. On the other side we can empathise more for someone who is experiencing difficulties. We can resist becoming irritated by others, and increasingly let others be themselves. We can accept our actions without regret or embarrassment and resist feeling embarrassed when others do things in a less than perfect way.

It becomes clear that we need great discernment if we are to purify our soul levels. It is not so much about being pure and good, it is really about the actual activity of tempering some of our natural inclinations and enhancing others. For each person it will be different, and the responsibility of it lies with each individual. The purification of our soul cannot arise through external rules or expectations. We must experience the play of the forces within us and know that we can move these forces in one way or another. When we achieve this, it is a signal to Sophia to share her cosmic wisdom with us. This does not come to us as an obscure premonition, but as a clear and bright sense of knowing.

Then John says, "behold, a great red dragon". He doesn't just tell us about the dragon, he tells us that we must see it. Behold, *idou*, be attentive, see more than what meets the eye. The situation is like a child learning to walk. At times the balance is right and many steps can be taken, at other times we fall. The key is not to retreat into familiar patterns, but to strive to be more and more conscious of the inner workings of our own consciousness. We find our feet when we can identify old patterns, and perhaps still use them, but now with full consciousness. This is when the nourishment kicks in. "where she [in this case, our soul] has a place prepared by God, in which to be nourished." God, that cosmic creator, waits for us to show signs of self-purification, of discipline, and then he enfolds us, nourishes us and keeps us safe.

War Arose in Heaven

And another portent appeared in heaven; behold, a great red dragon, with seven heads and ten horns, and seven diadems upon his heads. His tail swept down a third of the stars of heaven, and cast them to the earth. And the dragon stood before the woman who was about to bear a child, that he might devour her child when she brought it forth; ...

Now war arose in heaven, Michael and his angels fighting against the dragon; and the dragon and his angels fought, but they were defeated and there was no longer any place for them in heaven. And the great dragon was thrown down, that ancient serpent, who is called the Devil and Satan, the deceiver of the whole world - he was thrown down to the earth, and his angels were thrown down with him. Rev 12:3-4 & 7-9

Imagine this fiery dragon with seven heads, ten horns and seven diadems. That makes up to twenty-four items altogether. We associate the head with thinking, with knowledge and the intellect and we could probably identify seven different types of thinking, or seven different ways to introduce feeling and will into thinking perhaps. It isn't clear where the horns are, however, a horn is a weapon, and a symbol of strength. The diadems could be on the heads because a diadem is a head band that binds on a crown indicating royalty and rulership. This is some dragon and now he has been cast down to the earth, that is, into our lower consciousness. Every time our consciousness is lowered he rules in our being. Every time we do not think things through to the end, the dragon rules.

It is not the presence of the dragon in our being that should be of concern; what should concern us is our awareness of his activity. Only our pride will suggest that we are too pure and good to have such a being within us. In fact, he is our own creation. He comes into being through all the negativity and misinformed thoughts that we have; through all our unconscious and misguided feelings; and through all our premature actions and misbehaviour. Most of all he comes into being through all our misjudgements about what is good and what is bad. This is not the only way the dragon becomes active.

We should remember that all this is happening when the seventh trumpeting sounds after the Lamb has opened the seventh seal. So through the action of the risen Christ, John, who has purified himself sufficiently so that his spiritual faculties are seeing, hearing and understanding, is given access to the mystery of his own being. He sees that when earthly consciousness stirs to the presence of the I AM and the risen Christ, the dragon becomes active. This is a warning to take our pursuit of spiritual knowledge very seriously. In fact, it is very dangerous to be half hearted about attaining spiritual knowledge. The dragon sees our half-heartedness when we do not put enough effort into becoming conscious of the way we feel, think and use our will. It really boils down to that.

It is interesting to note that while the dragon is in the heavens he is one being, when he is cast down to earth he becomes two different beings. One is "that ancient serpent, who is called the Devil" which we identified as Lucifer in Chapter 2 when considering the Letter to Smyrna. The other is "Satan, the deceiver of the whole world" who is Ahriman. So it seems that the dual nature of evil manifests when the Archangel Michael is at work.

In general, these dragon-beings connect with us through our intellect, fragmenting it. Making intellectual matters so specialised that people with knowledge of specific fields cannot communicate with each other. For instance, a computer scientist and a medical scientist may struggle to find a common language. The proliferation of acronyms and the tricky terms used to describe the simplest of things are other examples.

In particular, Ahriman tries to confound our knowledge so that we feel confused and stupid. He is the father of lies and encourages us to accept half-truths. He also discourages us from cross referencing our understandings so that we arrive at truth through our inner effort. Lucifer is the master of the lazy shortcut; he prefers to drag the past into the present. Lucifer encourages us to apply the spiritual knowledge of the past to our present experiences and has us believe that this is the only truth. If this were the case spiritual knowledge would never evolve and there would be no such thing as freedom.

More than any time in the entire history of mankind are we called to become aware of what goes on within us. Even the most fleeting, antagonistic thoughts and feelings about others must be observed and apprehended. They often come from the inner dragon who wants to keep us away from true spiritual communion with others. We must come to terms with the fact that many of our habits of soul arise from fear of each other. The mighty vision of the Cosmic Sophia, Archangel Michael and the Ancient Serpent *Ophis ho archaios* – which could be more accurately described as the archetypal serpent who manifested in the Garden of Eden – together form the Holy Spirit. These are the comforters; Christ has sent them to prepare us for his full manifestation within us. Our quest is to become aware of the way they work in our own being.

Now war arose in heaven, Michael and his angels fighting against the dragon; and the dragon and his angels fought, but they were defeated and there was no longer any place for them in heaven. And the great dragon was thrown down, that ancient serpent, who is called the Devil and Satan, the deceiver of the whole world--he was thrown down to the earth, and his angels were thrown down with him. And I heard a loud voice in heaven, saying, "Now the salvation and the power and the kingdom of our God and the authority of his Christ have come, for the accuser of our brethren has been thrown down, who accuses them day and night before our God. And they have conquered him by the blood of the Lamb and by the word of their testimony, for they loved not their lives even unto death. Rev 12:7-11

Does this war occur just once, or is it continually happening? The answer is linked to our understanding of space and time. In the physical world we think of things happening in a particular place, at a particular time. This assists us to orient ourselves in the world so that we not only know our location but also have an expectation of what should be taking place. For instance, the light from the sun, and its movement across the sky, guides us in this process. If the sun is shining we expect to be awake, if it is not shining we prepare to sleep – well that is the general idea, teenagers might think differently. In this sense our lives in this physical world are black and white.

If we are able to free ourselves from these concepts that space contains three-dimensional matter and the concept of linear time, we would see a different picture. We could see, as if in a giant film strip, all things taking place, as if at once. This film strip would show us what has already transpired, and what will transpire. But when we look at what has yet to transpire we would only see possibilities. This is what it would have been like for John. As he looks at the war between so many angels and the beings who lead them, his imagination must have been working overtime as he wondered how human beings could possibly live with this tumultuous activity; this atmosphere of angels, some led by the Devil and Satan and some led by Michael.

Immediately the voice of his Inspiration echoes within him as if to remind him about the presence of Christ. Not Christ alone but in the company of the three members of the second Hierarchy. These are the mighty beings of wisdom, motion and form. This is what the words 'power, kingdom and authority' indicate. These are beings regulating this universe through their wisdom, and those who ensure that everything moves in an orderly way - the stars and planets, the air and clouds; and those whose force gives form to the things in universe.

How aware are we of these spiritual beings? If we are to prevail over the dragon-beings we need to forge a closer relationship with these beings of salvation. If we can include them in our lives as a real presence they will assist us to conquer the accuser. One way to make these beings real would be to think about the certainty of the sun rising and setting each day, or the movement of the clouds, or the myriad of different forms and shapes in the world. If we take notice of these things and acknowledge them with awe, instead of taking them for granted, the beings governing all this may reveal more of themselves to us. They will speak into our Inspiration giving us new understandings.

If such mighty beings are involved in this war then we can assume that there is wise guidance underpinning the events. Michael, therefore, is meant to clear the heavens of the activity of the Devil, and Satan the deceiver, and their angels, and throw them down to the earth. In response to this we must become the conqueror – for what is a conqueror without anything to conquer?

We might think that Michael should be here on earth to assist us, but no, he stays in the heavens calling us to raise ourselves up to him.

So here we are with the accuser, the cosmic whistle blower, who day and night makes accusations about us. Probably giving God a blow by blow account of how we succumb to the pull of the earth and fail to raise up our consciousness. This, of course, is not how it works. On the surface it might look like we fail in our attempts to connect with our I-being, but if in that moment that we fail, we actually recognise our failure, then it counts as a success. If we forget to acknowledge the presence of the hierarchy when we feel a gentle breeze on our cheeks, but quite soon afterwards correct our thinking, we have prevailed. The dragon does not get that.

Then we read this strange sentence:

And they have conquered him by the blood of the Lamb and by the word of their testimony, for they loved not their lives even unto death.

Paraphrasing this we could say; we have prevailed over the lower forces because we recognise that Christ's blood flowed into this earth making it his body. In our recognition of this action we hear the higher word, the *logos*, enabling us to witness, *marturia* – have a firsthand experience of Christ's deed. This is made possible because we experienced the highest love *agape* and thereby resisted our soul's *psuche* death forces. Through the love and wise guidance of Christ and the spiritual Hierarchy we can prevail over all that we encounter. We must remember that in the blink of an eye our failures become our success.

Rejoice then, O heaven and you that dwell therein! But woe to you, O earth and sea, for the devil has come down to you in great wrath, because he knows that his time is short!" And when the dragon saw that he had been thrown down to the earth, he pursued the woman who had borne the male child. But the woman was given the two wings of the great eagle that she might fly from the serpent into the wilderness, to the place where she is to be nourished for a time, and times, and half a time. The serpent poured water like a river out of his mouth after the woman, to sweep her away with the flood. But the earth came to the help of the woman, and the earth

opened its mouth and swallowed the river which the dragon had poured from his mouth. Then the dragon was angry with the woman, and went off to make war on the rest of her offspring, on those who keep the commandments of God and bear testimony to Jesus. And he stood on the sand of the sea. Rev 12:12-17

We can clearly identify the three elements of air, earth and water in this story. Allegorically these can refer to thinking, will and feeling in that order. John reports that we should rejoice - be glad - if we have been able to raise our thinking out of our body so that it tabernacles in the heavens. This word tabernacle refers to a temporary and mobile dwelling; a tent is such a dwelling. The more mobile our thinking, the more easily we can respond to the antics of the serpent, the devil and the dragon. It becomes increasingly important for us to think on our feet as we encounter the increased activity of these hindering forces - then we can put their gifts to good use.

We must also be able to free ourselves from those unconscious and habitual thoughts which prevent us from seeing things in a new way. Lucifer and Ahriman occupy all that is unconscious within us so that it can be their ideas we express, not our own. It takes great vigilance to be aware of which thoughts are our own, and which are not. We can loosely say that when our ideas are stuck in the past, in the good old days, then Lucifer is active. When our thoughts discard the past and look for untested solutions, Ahriman is active. Christ stands between these two urging us to continually test assumptions. We often resist this position because it can be very tiring. It is often far easier to think the same old thing, and resist the innovative ideas; or on the other hand to ignore the past and engage with some illusive fantasy.

Meanwhile, we have our lives to live, moment by moment, each day. The woman, our soul, is giving birth to our I-being. This process is continually under theat. It seems odd that the woman is borne upwards on eagle wings, while at the same time dealing with the threat of being swept away by a flood of water. This is what can happen in our lives, sometimes many times during the day. Our thoughts can carry us up to lofty places and then, in a flash, our emotions sweep us away. We need the earth, our solid will forces, to swallow up such a flood of emotions. Only through our will can we be saved from drowning in our emotions.

This story contains a dire warning; unless we become more conscious of the way we think, feel and behave the dragon will have a field day in our consciousness. If we contemplate the following information, and put it to the test daily, we should be in much better shape to deal with the increasing activity of the hindering forces, within us, and within society.

Our thinking is our most conscious faculty, but not always. Our feelings are only semi-conscious, and therefore much harder to control. Our will forces are mostly unconscious. This means that we are often not conscious of our motives and our intent. Our feelings and our will cause us the most grief. As we work to become more conscious, the angry devil takes advantage of all that remains unconscious within us. He knows that it won't be long before those who have discovered the secret of becoming conscious will have transformed all that remains unconscious.

In my book "I Connecting : The Soul's Quest" (Kindle edition "I AM The Mystery"), I put it this way.

"So it is not a simple matter of being told that we have a soul; it is entirely up to each of us to give our soul its rightful place within our being. We can only do this when we recognise how we feel, think and will and how these soul faculties interact with each other. We explored these faculties in some detail in chapter 3.

One of the first things we need to do is to become aware of which soul regions we use the most. If we are a feeling person then we need to try to add thoughts to our feelings as often as possible, always remembering that feelings cannot be changed; they can only be guided. If we are a thinking person then we must seek every opportunity to allow feeling to warm our thoughts. We need also to become aware of the nature of our thoughts. We can only transform our thinking through concentration which requires the use of our will. We need to become more aware of the role will plays in our soul life. How strong is our will? How do we apply it? We can only transform our will through meditation.

Remember that it is our 'I' which feels, thinks and wills in our soul. If our feeling, thinking and willing function automatically then our I-connection is weak. Our soul uses our body to express these feelings, thoughts and actions. Our soul has enough learned responses to carry on with life automatically but at this stage in evolution our 'I' is demanding a more prominent place in our soul. While we remain unconscious of the activities of our 'I' in our soul we experience the 'I' as an unknown pressure. This pressure causes anxiety that some people are inclined to relieve with stimulants like alcohol, drugs, computer games and gambling."

If we fully experience how we cannot change our feelings, but can only guide them like the Dutch guide water using dykes, then we will be more accepting of the feelings that rise up within us in the course of our lives. We will also accept the responsibility of guiding these feelings ourselves rather than blaming others for how we feel. Over time we can develop new ways of concentrating so that our thoughts are raised on eagle's wings. Through meditation our will becomes more malleable and we can find ways to open the right path for our emotions to flow without causing damage. When we are conscious of the movement of these soul faculties then we stand "on the sand of the sea" – that is, on the threshold between the physical and spiritual worlds.

CHAPTER THIRTEEN

A Beast Rising out of the Sea

*And I saw a beast rising out of the sea, with ten horns and seven heads, with ten diadems upon its horns and a blasphemous name upon its heads. And the beast that I saw was like a leopard, its feet were like a bear's, and its mouth was like a lion's mouth. And to it the dragon gave his power and his throne and great authority. One of its heads seemed to have a mortal wound, but its mortal wound was healed, and the whole earth followed the beast with wonder. Men worshiped the dragon, for he had given his authority to the beast, and they worshiped the beast, saying, "Who is like the beast, and who can fight against it?" And the beast was given a mouth uttering haughty and blasphemous words, and it was allowed to exercise authority for forty-two months; it opened its mouth to utter blasphemies against God, blaspheming his name and his dwelling, that is, those who dwell in heaven.
Rev 13:1-6*

In some versions of the Bible chapter thirteen begins with the words: "And he stood on the sand of the sea." It is almost as if these words belong to the space between the two chapters. This sand which separates the sea from the land is a threshold of consciousness. It is that place in our consciousness where we become aware of our spiritual faculties of Imagination, Inspiration and Intuition. It indicates that our experience of our I AM is intensifying and our feeling, thinking and will are freed from their habitual patterns.

What we must realise is that it is not something that is immediately familiar to us. If, in our kitchen, we move the kettle to a different place, for a while we will continue to reach for the kettle in the place where it used to be. So it is with our consciousness. All our lives we have been exposed to explanations about man, the earth and the universe based on the notion of physical proof; if you can't touch it and test it in the laboratory, then it isn't real. We cannot abandon this knowledge instantaneously, just like we can't stop ourselves from reaching for the kettle where it used to be.

We could compare this threshold of consciousness to being on a vast open beach. Here we can free up our old way of thinking and play with new ideas that come to us. When we experience this openness in our consciousness we will be able to see the beast rising out of the sea. This beast, *therion,* is a wild beast. So out of the sea of our emotions we will now have the strength to face the contents of our soul. We will see the various animal or astral expressions that have dominated our soul over lifetimes.

The leopard with its black spots can represent truth mixed with error. The strength and speed of these contaminated truths can devour our quest for real truth. In Isaiah 11:6 we read that the leopard will lie down with the kid in peace during the Messiah's rule. This leopard has bear's feet indicating that it stands on instinctive passions and illusions distracting us from our spiritual consciousness. Having a mouth like a lion's mouth would indicate the devouring of newborn spiritual ideas.

This beast has "ten horns and seven heads, with ten diadems upon its horns and a blasphemous name upon its heads." The great red dragon we met in chapter twelve had "seven heads and ten horns, and seven diadems upon his heads." Perhaps it is a mistranslation, perhaps not. What stands out is that diadems have moved from the heads to the horns and there is a blasphemous name on its heads. To blaspheme is to speak injuriously; could these be the names we have called others when we haven't been able to control our emotions? Indeed, we must face all our thoughts and deeds when they are illuminated by the light of pure truth. Blasphemy is a serious matter and when we are able to see the spiritual effects of our blasphemy on others we will never blaspheme again. Oddly enough this week in Australia we read this headline in the press: The Anglican Church of Australia and atheists agree on one thing - that blasphemy should no longer be a criminal offence. Hopefully they mean that people no longer need an external law to moderate their behaviour.

Then John says: And to it the dragon gave his power *dunami* and his throne *thonon* and great authority *exousia*. Why are these groups of spiritual beings mentioned here? The seventh hierarchy, the thrones, are the will forces behind the creation of this earth. They gave of their substance so that human beings could take on physical form; the powers or dunami gave this substance motion; and the exousia gave it form. One of the reason's these levels of hierarchy are mentioned here could be that at some stage in our evolution these gods could see that, to quote Rudolf Steiner from a lecture given 14th November, 1911, "If we keep going in this way ... beings will never arise who are able to act freely out of their own personal impulses." In other words, we would remain puppets of the gods and would never be able to connect with our I AM to become co-workers with Christ.

What happened is an extraordinary story and one which we should deeply contemplate. These spiritual beings who poured out their forces of substance, motion and form began to feel that their gifts were being rejected. This feeling of rejection isolated them. They could no longer continue their same old task and they became disgruntled and probably formed a union to protest that they weren't being valued. Now their forces gathered as a kind of hindrance which we must overcome. In fact, their hindering is a gift to us so that we may rise up out of our own striving, rather than being raised up automatically by the actions of higher beings.

As long as we rest in our lower being with its animal instincts – which are in fact the base forces in our astral body – we are a playground for the beast. Tempers can flare, insults can fly, passions rage. We are self-absorbed and unable to express higher love. We give people blasphemous labels showing our disrespect for our fellow human beings – sometimes publically but especially privately. However, when we stand on the sand of sea all this is revealed to us and we must quickly turn to the Lamb who stands at our side reminding us that seeing it, heals it.

One of its heads seemed to have a mortal wound, but its mortal wound was healed, and the whole earth followed the beast with wonder. Men worshiped the dragon, for he had given his authority to the beast, and they worshiped the beast, saying, "Who is like the beast, and who can fight against it?" And the beast was given a mouth uttering haughty and blasphemous words, and it was allowed to exercise authority for forty-two months; it opened its mouth to utter blasphemies against God, blaspheming his name and his dwelling, that is, those who dwell in heaven. Rev 13:3-6

This beast gives us the impression of impulsiveness. It looked like a leopard but the feet and mouth of a leopard were unsuitable, so it took bear's feet and a lion's mouth. One of its heads had suffered a deadly blow but was miraculously healed and all the earth held it in awe and wonder and worshipped it.

Doesn't this point to the way of this world? We are driven to constantly interfere with things in an attempt to make them better, or more functional, or more profitable. Young minds are encouraged to manipulate in virtually every area of life. If you can't think of ways to manipulate then you are nobody. Children are masters of this, just take them shopping.

Even in our simplest interactions with others we can manipulate things in our own favour. This could be to give ourselves a greater sense of control, or it could be to renounce control completely. This feeds an instinctive wilfulness which courses through our lives like a serpent. The healing of the mortal wound is the greatest manipulation of all.

In the Bhagavad Gita there is a story about the mighty serpent Kali twining around Krishna, but he was able to tread on the head of the serpent and in so doing it wounded his heel. Krishna represents our I AM and the serpent represents the ancient knowledge that was available to us involuntarily. If we are to connect up with our I AM then we must inflict this deadly wound on the flow of ancient knowledge into our being.

Each time we see the healed wound, allowing us to breach our sacred contract with the gods who guide our evolution, we devour this ancient knowledge. This is what it means to follow the beast with wonder. Why would we find ancient knowledge so wonderfull when we have our I AM at our disposal? Never before in evolution have beings had the personal freedom to use the very power of God. For that is what the I AM is.

I and the Father are one. ... [and] ... 'I said, you are gods' Jn 10:30 & 34

No wonder such fearsome beasts try to prevent us from accessing our I AM. No wonder they want to heal up, to restore, what Krishna killed. The actual Greek translation is, "wounded to death; and his deadly wound was healed." The beast is bringing back to life something that was killed in a bygone age in an attempt to subvert our attention from our I AM.

So we are tempted to worship the dragon and hold the beast in awe and wonder. We inherently want to hold things in awe and wonder, and we long to worship. It is our responsibility to ensure that we do not satisfy this deep longing within us prematurely.

In fact, we should cultivate reverence at every opportunity, especially in our children. This is difficult today because it isn't cool to look up to other people. Looking up to people suggests that we might be inadequate. If we are able to generate feelings of reverence within us we nourish our soul so that it becomes fertile ground for our I AM. Each time we show disrespect or dislike for others our I AM has no access to our soul. Each time our reverence is misplaced, when we are manipulated by outer impressions, mesmerised by healed wounds, unable to experience inner awe for the simplest thing, the beast has got us.

We will only experience our higher consciousness when we can fully appreciate with awe the beauty in the world, the beauty in nature, and in each human being. When we take into ourselves the impressions we encounter each day in our environment, and hold them in awe, we will discover the divine within ourselves. Even when we have a disagreement with someone and afterwards we are able to admire something about them that we observed during the heated discussion, we will discover the divine within us. Then, as we are able to do this more and more easily, we will meet the divine in others, and in the world, more frequently. The work of this beast will be revealed to our spiritual insight and it will be redeemed. This is a grave responsibility which we must respond to in our own way.

Post Script: In Australia we are trying to make sense of the ferocious fires that have taken hundreds of lives and homes and obliterated whole towns (February 2009). It is helpful to remember that fire lies sleeping in everything. The fire in our blood that warms us contains Christ, the same fire of the burning bush. Fire is the element of our I AM. These are intense times and we are definitely called to see beneath the surface to the esoteric meaning of world events.

Men worshiped the dragon, for he had given his authority to the beast, and they worshiped the beast, saying, "Who is like the beast, and who can fight against it?" And the beast was given a mouth uttering haughty and blasphemous words, and it was allowed to exercise authority for forty-two months; it opened its mouth to utter blasphemies against God, blaspheming his name and his dwelling, that is, those who dwell in heaven. Also it was allowed to make war on the saints and to conquer them. And authority was given it over every tribe and people and tongue and nation, and all who dwell on earth will worship it, every one whose name has not been written before the foundation of the world in the book of life of the Lamb that was slain. If any one has an ear, let him hear: If any one is to be taken captive, to captivity he goes; if any one slays with the sword, with the sword must he be slain. Here is a call for the endurance and faith of the saints. Rev 13:4-10

We need to be very discerning about the forces at work in us, and in the world. Apart from the influences of the dragon and the beast, what about the influence of past memories? How can we be sure that our consciousness is never influenced by knowledge from previous incarnations? What relevance would this knowledge have in the present? Would what we knew in a bygone era have any application in this modern world? At present we are called to rigorously use our thinking to develop spiritual awareness. Further, we must use our thinking in a living way to create images or Imaginations that assist us to understand truth. We don't need to ask others for their interpretations of our images, nor do we need to agree or disagree with the images of others; we just need to test them continually. We develop our own logic, our own reasoning while at the same time remaining open to a new or different angle from which to see our ideas.

This causes difficulties in our lives because much of what we have been taught prevents us from pursuing this living thinking. And this is exactly what the dragon and the beast want. It can't be stressed enough that we live in confusing times. Some people who have studied esoteric knowledge for many years still apply it in a materialistic way. This fits nicely with the training and education they have received all their lives but it is like trying to fit our left hand into an imprint made by our right hand.

To fully understand this dilemma we must come to terms with the fact that we have lived for many thousands of years virtually unconsciously. We had no capacity to be conscious because we can only be fully conscious through our I AM. We are only now in that period of evolution where we can interact individually and personally with our I-being and become personally responsible for our lives rather than part of the tribe or the nation. This process gives us an immense amount of freedom before we are fully ready to handle it. Daily we make decisions based on shaky assumptions. The responsibility of decision-making can weigh heavily on us. Therefore it is very attractive to be able to trust an authority that appears qualified to make decisions for us.

So what decisions are made for us? They are contained in the mountains of advice given to us by our governments, our media, our family and friends. They can be summarised into three areas; how we should act, when we should think, and what we should feel – and never ask why! Furthermore, there are many conflicting ideas in these three areas. In the confusion many of us find that it is better not to think for ourselves, not to feel too much, and to act minimally. Or, if we are forced to act in a particular area, perhaps because we are ill, and when the medical advice we receive is inadequate, then we begin an endless search for alternative remedies. It is so easy to run from one solution to the next, there is no better distraction. The same thing can happen in our search for spiritual truth and then we become a spiritual tourist, staying a short while at many different destinations.

All of this is blasphemy. Blasphemy is when we have the wrong ideas, or confused ideas about the truth. Blasphemy is when we accept the status quo and we don't have the courage or the strength to contribute to change. The beast was given a mouth, a *stoma,* which is an opening, from which came great things (not haughty), impressive things that were wrong. Perhaps John was having a vision of today's news coverage by the media. It seems that the media have no concern for the truth, as long as what they publish is impressive. And we are often easily impressed!

What is more, there is rarely any point in trying to correct the errors. John says, "Who is like the beast, and who can fight against it?" It is futile to fight, and in any case, it is not our task to fight the beast or the dragon, all we have to do is to calmly identify it.

By fostering our own consciousness to become increasingly aware through sharp and mobile thinking we will find our own personal truth, and that truth is our I-being. The dragon and the beast work hard to confuse us with their blasphemous errors so that we don't discover the name of God which is 'I', and his dwelling place which is us!

Those who dwell in heaven are those of us who are managing to maintain a connection with our I. The emphasis is on maintaining for John clearly says that the beast "was allowed to make war on the saints and to conquer (overcome) them." The saints are those who have reached a certain level of consciousness but they are not out of the woods, the beast has permission to ambush them and try and overcome them.

And authority was given it over every tribe and people and tongue and nation, and all who dwell on earth will worship it, every one whose name has not been written before the foundation of the world in the book of life of the Lamb that was slain. If any one has an ear, let him hear: If any one is to be taken captive, to captivity he goes; if any one slays with the sword, with the sword must he be slain. Here is a call for the endurance and faith of the saints. Rev 13:7-10

For as long as we align ourselves with a tribe or people, or language or nation then we assist the beast and work against the lamb. This is a hard teaching for we are always more interested in connections with our own neighbourhood, family, profession etc. We are also more interested in the affairs of places we have visited than of those we haven't. Regardless of where we live, if our family background is Dutch or Jewish, Russian or Catholic, we will always be more interested in the affairs of these places and people.

Nevertheless, if we could remember all our past lives we would see that we have lived in many different parts of the globe. Furthermore, in the history of humankind many different nations have been at the forefront of human development at one time or another. In this period now, after the event of Golgotha, we have reached a point where the whole earth should become a single nation. This is being facilitated in many ways, especially through the internet but also with the ease of travel. Imagine a globe with one language, one currency, a unified legal system and a transparent government!

We might think that this is a pipe dream but if we understand anything about the Archangel Michael, who is the spiritual regent of our time, we know that this is his aim. As he works silently in the background he has already achieved much in this area through the rise of global corporations over the previous decades. The task of the Archangels is to rule over nations and Michael is a one-global-nation guy. Michael, of course, is the one who conquers the dragon.

If we think about the advantages of this so-called global village, and if we take this idea seriously, we contribute to its creation. It is easy to think that as individuals we could not possibly have any influence in creating global unity, yet, if we think about it, each human being already creates global disunity with their national pride and alliances. They fall in behind the beast and the dragon who want followers, and followers always need leaders. The beast and dragon put themselves forward as qualified leaders thereby preventing people from having any sense of power or responsibility. Yet, if each person on the earth realised that they could change the world, wouldn't it be changed?

Those who connect with their 'I' change the world. Essentially because the world needs to be a different place if it is to be the dwelling place of I-connected individuals. So, as more and more people express themselves through their 'I', and, as a consequence, take responsibility for their actions, the more saints we will have. At the same time, those who want to be led by the beast will appear in stark contrast.

Then we read these mysterious words, "And authority was

given it (the beast) over ... every one whose name has not been written before the foundation of the world in the book of life of the Lamb that was slain." Surely this doesn't refer to a chosen few who are destined to navigate the difficult road to salvation, while the rest are not? If we remember that our name is 'I', then we realise that every person has their 'I' written in the Lamb's book of life. What happens to those who do not claim their name? And what happens to those who claim their 'I' but do not follow through with claiming it? The latter are the holy ones, the saints, who are overcome by the beast. The beast and his minions take over the human beings who fail to claim their heredity. Wouldn't this mean that their names are no longer written in the book of life, the book of *zoe* - that life-force associated with the resurrection? This is a sad tale but true.

This is why it is so important, at this point in our evolution, to have knowledge about our 'I' and how to incorporate it into our soul. The two vital qualities that we need are "endurance and faith" *hupomone* and *pistis*. *Hupomone* is more about patience than endurance. The hallmark of the ones who connect with their 'I' is that they have a patient understanding of others. They are not offended or annoyed by others, and if they feel annoyance rising, they are quickly able to take on the role of the 'interested observer'. Alienation, for any reason, is never part of those whose 'I' is active.

Pistis, faith, is not about blind belief. Faith is the knowingness experienced through our 'I'. Faith is not belief in ideas but it is the level of understanding that rises out of conscious feeling, thinking and will. Through faith we see spiritual reality as it unfolds in the various situations of life. It is through faith that we identify the activity of the dragon thereby robbing him of his power. It is through faith that we create the future that we see – one global community standing with the Lamb.

If any one has an ear, let him hear: If any one is to be taken captive, to captivity he goes; if any one slays with the sword, with the sword must he be slain. Here is a call for the endurance and faith of the saints. Rev 13:9-10

Our lives are going to become increasingly difficult in the years ahead, not so much because of the increased activity of the dragon and the beast, but because of the increased activity of Christ. Whenever Christ steps up his activity, in us as well as in the cosmos, the forces of resistance come to meet him. Christ will prevail; how quickly depends on us. Each human being has the personal responsibility to awaken the Christ force within them. John reminds us that this can only be done through endurance and faith, through patience with self and others, and through the faith that knows what the future requires of us.

John's words here speak of karma, of the cause and consequence that underpins each moment of our lives. The Greek words do not say "is to be taken into", they say, if anyone is for captivity then he must experience captivity; not that we need to take this literally. Captivity is about restraint. If we want to restrain someone from acting in a certain way, or from feeling something, or from thinking certain thoughts, then at some later stage we will be unable to act or feel or think. If we kill others, perhaps by acting towards them as if they didn't exist, or speaking about them in a deadly way, then we can expect to be ignored. There are so many moments in our lives each day where the consequences of our actions in this life or past lives are replayed. In these moments we have the opportunity to be patient because our faith tells us that the future depends on our passing the test. Whenever we respond to a situation with understanding we balance out the karmic moments in our lives. As Orland Bishop, founder of the Shade Tree Foundation, puts it, "How must I be in order for you to be free, how do I host the freedom of the other, the development of the other and the greater truth of the other?"

Sergei Prokofieff, in his book, "The Occult Significance of Forgiveness", writes about the epitome of patience, faith and freedom through the experiences of George Richie, an American Psychiatrist, who visited a Nazi concentration camp in 1945 after the liberation, and came across Wild Bill Cody. "But though Wild Bill worked 15 and 16 hours a day, he showed no signs of weariness. While the rest of us were dropping with fatigue, he seemed to gain strength. 'We have time for this old fellow,' he'd say. 'He's been waiting for us all day.' His compassion for his fellow-prisoners glowed on his face ... For six years he had lived on the same starvation diet, slept in the same airless and disease-ridden barracks as everyone else, but without the least physical or mental deterioration."

George Richie discovered the secret of Bill Cody's patience and faith, which explained why he seemed so free even though he had been imprisoned by the Nazis. It is a most powerful story about karma. The Nazis shot Bill's wife, two daughters and three sons right before his eyes. They didn't kill him because he spoke German and would be an asset in the concentration camps.

George Richie recorded Bill's conversation in this way: "He paused, perhaps seeing again his wife and five children. 'I had to decide right then,' he continued, 'whether to let myself hate the soldiers who had done this. It was an easy decision, really. I was a lawyer. In my practice I had seen too often what hate could do to people's minds and bodies. Hate had just killed the six people who mattered most to me in the world. I decided then that I would spend the rest of my life – whether it was a few days or many years – loving every person I came in contact with.'" George G. Ritchie, Elizabeth Sherill, "Return from Tomorrow".

While this is a story of great forgiveness, it is also a story of karma. In the Bible there are quite a few quotes similar to the Revelation text we are considering. They speak vividly about karma. In Genesis we find: "Whoever sheds the blood of man, by man shall his blood be shed; for God made man in his own image." Gen 9:6 Matthew says, "Then Jesus said to him, "Put your sword back into its place; for all who take the sword will perish by the sword." " Mt 26:52

Note that in the Revelation text John hears the risen Christ say, "If any one has an ear, let him hear:" So what is there to hear in George Richie's story about Bill Cody? One possibility is the likelihood that Bill Cody violently put people to death in a past life, either physically or mentally. What needs to be heard here is that if he hadn't, he might never have been able to forgive the Nazis in that instant. He might never have been the example of compassion and freedom that undoubtedly upheld hundreds of people in the appalling conditions of the Nazi concentration camps. Indeed, at the very time that the risen Christ was manifesting himself, at least some people could see him through the presence of Bill Cody.

We could ask ourselves whether we are committed to exemplifying the risen presence of Christ in our lives. For in this way others may catch a glimpse of him through our patience and faith, prompting them to seek their own personal experience of him. We have the opportunity to do this whenever we feel badly treated, disrespected, devalued, misunderstood, ignored and so forth. Unimaginable freedom awaits us if we have the ear to hear this story and put it into action in our lives.

Then I saw another beast which rose out of the earth; it had two horns like a lamb and it spoke like a dragon. It exercises all the authority of the first beast in its presence, and makes the earth and its inhabitants worship the first beast, whose mortal wound was healed. It works great signs, even making fire come down from heaven to earth in the sight of men; and by the signs which it is allowed to work in the presence of the beast, it deceives those who dwell on earth, bidding them make an image for the beast which was wounded by the sword and yet lived; and it was allowed to give breath to the image of the beast so that the image of the beast should even speak, and to cause those who would not worship the image of the beast to be slain. Rev 13:11-15

This new beast rises out of the earth, in other words, on this side of the "sand of the sea" - the sand being the threshold between the physical and the spiritual. The earth is also the place where Christ can now be found since his crucifixion and resurrection. This beast also looks like Christ, that is, the risen Christ who John refers to as the lamb. It bids other beings to make images, replicas. We can sense an increasing atmosphere of deception from this beast. It doesn't have its own appearance but takes on the appearance of other beings. We might ask if it is created through the actions of others beings. Or, does it actually control, or seek to control, other beings?

If we think about Christ, the being who left the sun and made his way to this planet earth, who was ultimately crucified but then hung around and appeared to various people in his spiritual body, perhaps we can understand something more about the appearance of these beasts. Take into consideration that Rudolf Steiner said that Christ's descent was made possible by human beings – especially by those who recited the prologue of the Gospel of St John (John 1: 1-14). "In the beginning was the word, and the word was with god and the word was [a] god. Etc." Similarly, the reappearance of Christ also depends on human beings awakening his presence within them. Otherwise his presence could go unnoticed.

Therefore, would the same principles apply to these beasts? Can we say that through human activity situations are created to facilitate the presence of these beasts? In fact, isn't John suggesting that this beast in verse 11 is able to realise the extent of its power according to the activity of Christ – it mirrors Christ's image? Given that Christ's activity depends more and more on human beings awakening to his presence within them and within the etheric atmosphere of this earth, we must assume that this beast is equally our creation. So at the same time that it is our creation it is also the powerful being who orchestrates the activity of all the other hindering forces as the text describes. It is imperative that we become more conscious of our role in the activity of all spiritual beings. This fact lies at the heart of what it means to be human.

We are in the midst of a great awakening taking place in the world. This awakening rises out of the chaos created by human beings claiming the freedom to act out of their own personal volition. One barometer of the amount of freedom that human beings are claiming is the amount of fear in our society. Even the banks use a fear factor to analyse the economy!

Governments, Institutions and Corporations lead us to believe that we are free if we want for nothing. They tell us that the more money we have the more freedom we will have. Then, just when everyone thinks they have easy access to money and unlimited possessions, and therefore real freedom, the global financial system reveals the extent to which it is an image - smoke and mirrors. Immediately an atmosphere of fear is generated. Many people have had to face the reality that having money and possessions is a false freedom founded on fleeting feelings of self-importance. This is followed by a sense of wondering who we really are if we are not defined by what we own. Ironically, the fear we experience for the loss of our freedom actually causes the loss of our freedom.

We should never underestimate the power of fear. When we are fearful our skin turns white because our blood contracts into the interior of our being. Since our blood is the vehicle for our 'I' then we could assume that fear reduces the ability of our 'I' to connect to our body thereby making it impossible for us to arrest our fear. In the overcoming of fear we strengthen and purify ourselves and create a stronger connection with our 'I'. This is exactly what the beast works against. Each time we overcome our fear we create the atmosphere Christ needs to reveal himself to us. Through a strengthened connection to our 'I' we contain our fear and we experience Christ. All that works against this is the Antichrist. Christ is here, now, and it is easy to imagine that he is sick of being ignored. Perhaps he is behind the fear factor thereby prompting us to exercise our freedom to actively reduce the impact of fear in our beings.

A recently released book, Christ & the Maya Calendar - 2012 & the Coming of the Antichrist by Robert Powell and Kevin Dann, places into perspective the interplay between Christ and the Antichrist. There are various categories of beings who work against Christ; one of them is Ahriman or Satan who is expected to incarnate soon into a human body, as Christ incarnated into the human body of Jesus. In the Afterword of this book, Robert Powell says, "Ahriman cannot be overcome either by *attacking* the Ahrimanic element or by trying to convert it externally. The Ahrimanic influence can neither be coerced by force nor inwardly transformed. The point is to *recognize* the Ahrimanic element, not fear it. A courageous glance of recognition is the sword that limits Ahriman in the outer world, and the courage of self-knowledge is the force that renders the Ahrimanic nature powerless in the human subconsciousness. As for Ahriman, the point is not to grant him power over the soul, and – with the weapon of recognition – to destroy all his attacks through uncompromising human courage." Page 214

It is love that conquers fear. The kind of love that carried a high spiritual being into the limits of a human body to then be humiliated and slain. We must contemplate the work of the beast who will "cause those who would not worship the image of the beast to be slain." If we recognise this work we will not fear and we will experience Christ's empowering love.

Then I saw another beast which rose out of the earth; it had two horns like a lamb and it spoke like a dragon. It exercises all the authority of the first beast in its presence, and makes the earth and its inhabitants worship the first beast, whose mortal wound was healed. It works great signs, even making fire come down from heaven to earth in the sight of men; and by the signs which it is allowed to work in the

presence of the beast, it deceives those who dwell on earth, bidding them make an image for the beast which was wounded by the sword and yet lived; and it was allowed to give breath to the image of the beast so that the image of the beast should even speak, and to cause those who would not worship the image of the beast to be slain. Rev 13:11-15

It is noteworthy that John's first observation of this beast is its two horns. In two we find duality, and the possibility of opposition or polarity. The essential tone of our soul is the polarity of sympathy and antipathy; love or hate. This is the soul's natural inclination so that in every moment of our lives we can swing from one to the other, drawn to some things and repelled by others. If we remain unconscious of this natural response we are tossed to and fro causing us to become bound to earthly matters and obscuring our spiritual capacities. Then we are inhabitants of the earth and we will "worship the first beast, whose mortal wound was healed."

If we are to fully experience our 'I' it is essential that we arrest these feelings of approval or disapproval. We can do this in the smallest areas of our lives by becoming more accepting of the things that occur around us. It might simply be about the weather; we can stop ourselves from complaining about the heat, or the cold, or that it is too dry or too wet, too sunny or two cloudy. Or it could be about accepting a traffic or transport delay and receiving the unexpected gift of time rather than becoming impatient. If we become angry about things like this, imposed upon us by outside circumstances beyond our control, we are bound to the earth and in the hands of the beast. Not that this should then be labelled a good or bad situation but we should simply recognise it for it is probably the work of the beast in some unconscious action that caused the delay.

The binding hinders our experience of freedom. One of the greatest experiences of freedom that we can have is to overcome the tension of love or hate, like and dislike. If we can prevail over our inclination to dislike a person who annoys us, or a situation that distresses us, we conquer ourselves. Through our own inner ability to remain warmly neutral we create harmony which gives us the opportunity to experience the bliss of freedom. We reach a point of understanding that assists us to balance the polarity of like and dislike. Our understanding becomes the third element that removes the tension from the disparity.

The key to experiencing this level of freedom is to achieve the balance as an inner activity that we do by ourselves. There are many areas that work against this, the church, the state and even our friends and family. Take the church for instance. It exercises its authority by telling its members what they can and cannot do (usually by misinterpreting the Bible or other sacred writings). The church, or any other doctrine for that matter, that imposes ideas ON human beings reveals that it does not know that Christ is IN each and every human being. The point and purpose of the Mystery of Golgotha is that each individual must discover this for themselves; they discover it when they become aware of their 'I'.

Having an 'I' makes us human and sets us above the mineral, plant and animal kingdoms. Having an 'I' doesn't imply that we are able to act out of it fully. In fact, we only become fully human when we can act out of our 'I' continuously. Therefore our humanity is a work in progress. The beast thinks that he has the authority to make beings what they are, as John reports, "and it was allowed to give breath to the image of the beast so that the image of the beast should even speak". So the beast tries to make human beings the image of the beast! He regards himself as having the only authority, authority which counteracts any kind of freedom. We can identify these 'beasts' in so many areas of modern life. We could go so far as to ask ourselves whether people are turning away from the church because they are turning away from God, or because God is misrepresented.

The two horned beast can also be found in all the dualities within us and around us. It can be found in our own behaviour when, for example, we say that we will do a thing and then procrastinate. Or we say one thing and think another. Or when we think our ideas are right and can't find a place within our thinking for the other person's ideas. It can be found when we excel in life - which is usually when we reveal our talent by acting out of our 'I' - and then we seek recognition for it. Duality can also be found when we study spiritual principles but don't apply them, or misapply them, in our lives.

One of the areas where this duality is very apparent is when we favour some people over others, especially in groups where cliques are formed from which some people are excluded. These excluded ones experience a kind of death. They don't 'worship life's dualities' for they have a tolerance arising from their experience of being repelled because of their difference. Perhaps they are placed in certain circles to give everyone the opportunity of overcoming their antipathy and also, perhaps they are different so that they have the opportunity to overcome past expressions of duality. The ultimate experience for each individual is to experience the Christ principle which is in every human being. If we treat each other as we would treat Christ, if we look for the Christ in each other, we will find him in ourselves. Then we will rise above life's dualities and understand something of the mystery of the Trinity; Father, Son and Holy Spirit.

Then I saw another beast which rose out of the earth; it had two horns like a lamb and it spoke like a dragon. It exercises all the authority of the first beast in its presence, and makes the earth and its inhabitants worship the first beast, whose mortal wound was healed. It works great signs, even making fire come down from heaven to earth in the sight of men; and by the signs which it is allowed to work in the presence of the beast, it deceives those who dwell on earth, bidding them make an image for the beast which was wounded by the sword and yet lived; and it was allowed to give breath to the image of the beast so that the image of the beast should even speak, and to cause those who would not worship the image of the beast to be slain. Rev 13:11-15

We live in a world of deception. It is very difficult to know what is real and what is not real. Even when we decide to develop our higher consciousness we are constantly faced with the difficulty of knowing what is true and what is not true. Even the loftiest spiritual information that we may read or hear is not truth for us until we are able to confirm it within our own being and test it continually. Even so, we must still remain vigilant for deception; even the most basic deception clouding our vision and preventing us from seeing the spiritual reality in us and around us each day.

One of the biggest deceptions is the notion of maya. Maya is not simply about the illusion of the physical world we live in; maya is our own failure to recognise that we have created this world through the use of our own will. If we fully experience the truth of this we will cease to complain about the modern world we find ourselves living in. This realisation of what maya really is changes our behaviour because we realise that it is not up to governments, or even groups of people to change the world, we can change it, from today, through our own ideas and behaviour.

With this new attitude we begin to see through the deceptions created by the second beast. We see how this second beast is the greatest of all deceivers as he operates covertly behind all the manifestations of the hindering forces and their deceptive images.

What are some of the deceptions in modern life? Money is one; we are led to believe that money will give us power. That we should amass it without thinking about the fact that if we have more, others will have less, is part of the deception. Positive thinking is another great deception. We think that by expressing everything positively, even if it isn't, we create a force for good. If we attempt to train our minds to think that there is only good, and no evil, then evil is at work. Our task is to see the polarity of good and evil and learn to balance them. These deceptions are the work of the second beast at its unseen best. It hides behind all facets of modern life. The only way we will see it is if we become conscious. The only way to become conscious is to allow our 'I' to influence the activity of our soul.

This may sound simple but we must accept that our soul can be a beast. This is certainly true when its lower instincts govern our behaviour; when our thinking, feeling and will operate unconsciously. We can even deceive ourselves about what is conscious and what is unconscious. Often what we think is conscious is actually unconscious and vice versa. Being focussed and alert is not necessarily being conscious. We can easily be alert and still act out of our habitual behaviour which has formed from blurry past experiences.

All unconscious activity has memory at its foundation; the kind of engrained memory of how to respond to the various situations in life. If we can identify in each of our thoughts, feelings and actions some learned behaviour then we know that something unconscious informs our expression. If we are able to act in an imaginative, inspired or intuited way, which will be experienced as a new response to a situation, we have acted consciously and freely.

It is as if we can stand in situations free from karma, fear and any other restriction. We have a sense of standing outside ourselves at the same time that we are within the boundaries of our being. This is the experience of our 'I' that straddles the sand of the sea.

When we are able to do this there is a sense that our actions or expressions are true and aligned with what is right. There is a watch point however, and this is to be aware of any decisions founded on sympathy or antipathy. Spiritual truth is not a matter of what we like or do not like, spiritual truth just is. The clue to understanding this fully is to deeply experience the Mystery of Golgotha. How could a human being withstand the agony of this deed? This is why the risen Christ is called the lamb; without resistance Jesus, the man, gave up his hard-earned 'I' so that he could carry within him the Cosmic Christ. This whole passage we are considering refers to the pseudo Christ who forces the first beast to join it in a luciferic religious fervour, restoring that which is dead, whipping up a false Pentecost by making fire come down from above without regard for individual and personal effort. Even manipulating the crucifixion image where Christ Jesus was pierced by a sword and yet lived. And then to give breath *pneuma,* which is the inbreathing of the 'I', so that the deceptive image could then speak (another 'I' function). And those who fell for this deception showed that they were dead to the spiritual worlds (not, as the translation puts it: slaying those who didn't fall for the deception). John's image is for deep contemplation so that we have the courage to see the truth and experience the lamb through our own striving while at the same time courageously resisting the seduction of what is presented to us from outside ourselves.

Also it causes all, both small and great, both rich and poor, both free and slave, to be marked on the right hand or the forehead, so that no one can buy or sell unless he has the mark, that is, the name of the beast or the number of its name. This calls for wisdom: let him who has understanding reckon the number of the beast, for it is a human number, its number is six hundred and sixty-six. Rev 13:16-18

Not one of us is free from the influence of the beast. If we think that we have achieved a level of purity that excludes us from its influence then we must think again. In so many different ways John expresses the vision to enable us to identify the work of the beast. That, in fact, is our task. We do not have the task of analysing the behaviour of others and pointing to the beast operating in them. Our task is to analyse our own behaviour and identify how he works in us. Furthermore, this task involves identifying the ways that we create the beast. If we remain *ignore-ant* of how our behaviour, thoughts and feelings create the beast, the more powerful he will be.

The effect of the beast can be likened to a cheering crowd; the more people who cheer and the louder they cheer, the more powerful is the effect of the cheer. If we have ever been in a large cheering crowd we know what an effect this has on our consciousness. Within our own consciousness we continually cheer for the beast – unconsciously of course. We urge on all the animal expressions in our lower being; to be comfortable, to have all our appetites satisfied, to express our anger, to have our way, to be defensive, etc. So, the more human beings in the world who are unconscious, or not fully conscious, of their animal nature, the greater the activity of the beast will be in the human population.

Similarly, as we move around in this modern world, the mood of the people we encounter has an affect on us, sometimes more deeply than we realise. The less conscious we are when we are in public places, for instance, the more the thoughts of those around us enter into our minds. Then we can't be sure if we are thinking our own thoughts or the thoughts of others. Some people regard this as the high art of mind-reading but, in fact, it is often the influence of other beings on our lowered consciousness.

Should this alarm us? Of course, but not in the way we might think. The reason for us to become increasingly aware of the content of our thoughts is so that we can identify those thoughts that are our own and resist the stray thoughts that occupy the vacant spaces in our minds. As we become more adept at this there will be fewer vacant spaces and our mind will be fully occupied with its own business.

What is our business? Buying and selling, exchanging one thing for another. This is the primary activity of every human being on the earth. When exchanges between human beings take place, our primary concern is value. Are we fully aware of how we value things? Value is directly tied to meeting our physical needs. We would pay a very high price for a glass of water if we had been without water for a whole day than if we had drunk many glasses of water throughout the day.

When we buy and sell our attention is usually on the transaction rather than on the people making the transaction. This usually means that we don't value the labour that has created the commodity being exchanged and therefore we want to pay as little as possible for the commodity. In this way we actually devalue human effort. We want more from others than we are prepared to give of ourselves. When we seek the advantage we devalue others. This is the mark of the beast. If we are to step outside his influence then we take on the responsibility of recognising the real value of things. There is a place where we do this and that is when we consciously give a tip for good service in hotels and restaurants etc..

Our exchanges are not limited to meeting our bodily needs of course. We can be quite needy in other areas; our need for love and appreciation from others, our need for power and control over others, all driven by our reliance on others to boost our self-esteem. Regardless of how successful we are at attracting what we need from others, all that we receive is never fully satisfying. When we buy and sell as human beings we always want more. This is the work of the beast.

The satisfaction we seek is only to be found when we connect with our 'I'. This is wisdom, this is Sophia. We must become more conscious of Sophia the eternal mother who accompanies all those who walk the path of developing a higher consciousness. Like any mother, all Sophia wants to do is show us her child. Like any mother she encourages the best from us, and loves us regardless. Through her we come to true self knowledge, facade falls away and we are free to be ourselves. In uniting with Sophia we can then give birth to Christ. Through Sophia we purify our astral or animal nature of the effects of the beast.

CHAPTER FOURTEEN

The Lamb and the Angels

Then I looked, and lo, on Mount Zion stood the Lamb, and with him a hundred and forty-four thousand who had his name and his Father's name written on their foreheads. And I heard a voice from heaven like the sound of many waters and like the sound of loud thunder; the voice I heard was like the sound of harpers playing on their harps, and they sing a new song before the throne and before the four living creatures and before the elders. No one could learn that song except the hundred and forty-four thousand who had been redeemed from the earth. It is these who have not defiled themselves with women, for they are chaste; it is these who follow the Lamb wherever he goes; these have been redeemed from mankind as first fruits for God and the Lamb, and in their mouth no lie was found, for they are spotless. Rev 14:1-5

Imagine being John who had been looking at the intricacies of the work of the beast and then, as if he blinked and looked again, saw the Lamb standing on Mount Zion. John's two visions are like the two sides of a measuring scale with John as the fulcrum. Isn't that our own position as we navigate modern life? We walk the line between what is good and what is bad, trying to be sure that what is bad is not masquerading as good, and what is good doesn't appear to us as something bad. Perhaps our lack of confidence in knowing what is good and what is bad leads us to find satisfaction in judging whether others are good or bad. This could well be the proving ground but if we dwell there we neglect our task of identifying the two within ourselves.

Our contemplation of the beasts through chapter thirteen and before has shown us what a necessary part of the plan they are. Hans-Werner Schroeder, in his wonderful book Necessary Evil, paints picture after picture of the rightful place of evil in our lives. He suggests that only through our ability to distinguish between good and evil are we fully human. This fact is displayed before us again as we journey through Holy Week (2009) and gaze upon the three crosses on the mount of Golgotha which St John in his gospel describes as follows:

So they took Jesus, and he went out, bearing his own cross, to the place called the place of a skull, which is called in Hebrew Gol'gotha. There they crucified him, and with him two others, one on either side, and Jesus between them. Jn 19:17-18

So Jesus is crucified on a cross with two others on either side of him. Who are these two others? Could they be anything else other than Lucifer and Ahriman? This would mean that at the moment Jesus takes the Cosmic Christ into his being, Lucifer and Ahriman enter into the two people on either side of him? Since the purpose of the crucifixion is to make the full power of the human 'I' available to humanity in general, then obviously it cannot happen without the presence of Lucifer and Ahriman. These two forces are necessary to create the tension in us that enables us to walk the straight line to our destination.

John sees the Lamb now standing on Mt Zion. It is as if Golgotha and Zion are two pillars at the entrance to a new temple. Golgotha marks the point where humanity received the freedom to choose between good and bad. Zion, where the Ark of the Covenant was kept, represents the purity of humanity when there was no choice but to be good – meaning that we were unfree. In 1 Kings we find the story of Mt Zion which is echoed in the Revelation text we are contemplating.

Then King Solomon summoned into his presence at Jerusalem the elders of Israel, all the heads of the tribes and the chiefs of the Israelite families, to bring up the ark of the Lord's covenant from Zion, the City of David. 1 Ki 8:1

Do we only see Jesus hanging on the cross on Golgotha? Or at the same time do we see what preceded it? Do we see the many sacrifices in the spiritual worlds, by the spiritual hierarchies, that contributed to the deed of Golgotha? Do we see only Jesus hanging there and not the entry of the Cosmic Christ into his willing being? Do we see only Jesus hanging there and ignore the other two vital components of the process? If we are quick to think that we are part of the one hundred and forty four thousand we could create an illusion. We can only understand the mystery of the Lamb if we are open to all possibilities.

The one hundred and forty four thousand (twelve times twelve suggesting a connection with the twelve tribes of Israel) are those who have connected with their 'I', who cannot rest until they are with others who do the same, for these are the ones who follow the Lamb. By the way, these are the first fruits, not the only crop! Those who are able to do this work will become the example for all those who will, no doubt, find it easier because the way has been paved. This is what Jesus did, he paved the way for us, and during this Holy Week we can retrace his steps right to the point of becoming aware of the company we are in. Like him we can stand in the face of what seems to be insurmountable odds, and thereby complete the task that sets humanity free to achieve God's plan - become gods ourselves.

In the final chapter of "Necessary Evil", Schroeder says this: "With the forces of good acquired through the struggle with evil together with Christ, mankind is to lead the Adversaries back into the ranks of the angels, from which they were torn to help with the evolution of humanity." This is the gift we can receive anew as we accompany the Lamb.

Then I looked, and lo, on Mount Zion stood the Lamb, and with him a hundred and forty-four thousand who had his name and his Father's name written on their foreheads. And I heard a voice from heaven like the sound of many waters and like the sound of loud thunder; the voice I heard was like the sound of harpers playing on their harps, and they sing a new song before the throne and before the four living creatures and before the elders. No one could learn that song except the hundred and forty-four thousand who had been redeemed from the earth. It is these who have not defiled themselves with women, for they are chaste; it is these who follow the Lamb wherever he goes; these have been redeemed from mankind as first fruits for God and the Lamb, and in their mouth no lie was found, for they are spotless. Rev 14:1-5

The Lamb and the Father share the same name; I AM. This, too, is the name that we will call ourselves when we have completed our cycle of development by perfecting our being and achieving complete spiritual awareness. When this work is done we are then continually aware of the presence of the standing Lamb, the conquering Lamb. John's words here echo the words from his Gospel which record Jesus' pre-crucifixion prayers;

And now I am no more in the world, but they are in the world, and I am coming to thee. Holy Father, keep them in thy name, which thou hast given me, that they may be one, even as we are one. Jn 17:11

Out of John's experience of this oneness he is able to hint at what we will experience when we have achieved it. However, as John points out in his Gospel, we can begin this experience while we are still "in the world", on this side of the threshold. Even though we live on the earth we need to become more aware of how often our consciousness crosses the threshold. Each time we connect with our real 'I' we straddle the threshold and participate in heavenly things. Not that we should compartmentalise our earthly life and our heavenly life – a mistake made by many who follow the spiritual path. We must learn to live with a foot in both worlds which is a difficult task when we are contending with the activities of the 'beasts'.

We might wonder why this name would be written on the forehead. One reason has to do with the change in our being that was necessary for us to become self-aware. When we experienced ourselves as un-individuated cosmic beings we were not confined to our physical body as we are now. When the fullness of our being drew into our physical body, that part of our life body (etheric) that was outside us contracted to a point behind our forehead between our eyes – perhaps like a kind of spiritual umbilical cord.

Until this had occurred we were unable to say 'I' when referring to ourselves. Still today there are indigenous people connected to the cosmos in an ancient way and who do not refer to themselves as 'I', as independent personalities. Their 'I' is vested in the tribal elder. We find a similar thing occurring in young children when they refer to themselves by their given name rather than saying 'I'. Their 'I' is vested in the parents. When they do say 'I' to refer to themselves it is an indication that they have disconnected from the spiritual worlds and experience themselves as an individual. It should be mentioned that even though we have this experience of our 'I' from early childhood, it is only as a 'mirrored reflection' of the fullness of our real 'I'. Through each incarnation we develop a stronger and stronger connection with our 'I' until finally we can stand fully in it and then our name is I AM. Then we have no need to say, "I am female or male, have this or that occupation, country, job, etc.

As we increasingly experience our real I-ness, rather than its reflection, we reconnect with the cosmos as individuated beings. Then the contracted point within our foreheads expands thus displaying our true name. As we continue the work the name becomes increasingly visible. During this process, the more we become conscious on the other side of the threshold, the more we will hear the sounds from heaven which are frequently called the music of the spheres. We will recognise the different sounds and we will come to know the creative influences behind them and our contribution to them.

The harpers new song can be a reference to the perfection of our own being. The Greek word translated as harp is *kithara*, lyre. The lyre is a small harp which usually had four, seven or ten strings, and it is played like a guitar rather than a harp. The free hand can silence any unwanted notes. The lyre is a good metaphor for the human being in its various aspects of body, soul and spirit and how we create harmony as we become more and more conscious of the interrelationship between them.

If, for instance, we visualise our 'I' as the musician playing the strings of our thinking, feeling and will in our soul, then we can imagine the harmony and even disharmony that could arise. We can also see how the 'free hand' could silence, for example, our feeling to allow thinking to introduce some logic to the matter. Or feeling could warm a thought or prompt an action. So, of course, only when we have connected with our 'I' allowing it to conduct our earthly life, can we sing the new song as part of the one hundred and forty four thousand. Then as virginal, undefiled by our lower astral feelings, we are no longer discordant with heavenly harmonies. All falseness, *pseudos,* will be unnecessary; we will express ourselves in purity and freedom, for we will be flawless.

Then I saw another angel flying in midheaven, with an eternal gospel to proclaim to those who dwell on earth, to every nation and tribe and tongue and people; and he said with a loud voice, "Fear God and give him glory, for the hour of his judgment has come; and worship him who made heaven and earth, the sea and the fountains of water." Rev 14:6-7

John's attention is now drawn to a series of angels, messengers, who speak loudly from mid heaven. So they are speaking from a high perspective, not the highest, but in the middle between highest heaven and the earth. It is possible that these so-called angels are the spiritual beings from the middle hierarchy where we find the Elohim; the creator gods of Genesis. This idea would be supported by the fact that they speak of the creation story.

In chapter 15 we can identify seven messages which remind us of the seven visions John was instructed to write to the seven angels of the seven churches at the beginning of The Revelation. Then, each message was specific to a church in a particular location. Now, these seven messages are for everyone regardless of culture, family, language or group.

These messages are not written in a book as the messages to the churches were; these messages flow eternally from these angels. This is the eternal gospel available to everyone, the eternal *euangelion,* the good news about truth. Most of us will admit that it is our deepest wish to know the truth about creation and human existence. One of the most powerful promises from Jesus, reported in John's Gospel, is about truth.

"If you continue in my word, you are truly my disciples, and you will know the truth, and the truth will make you free." Jn 8:31-32

So now John is hearing the words of truth from the eternal gospel. This gospel does not need to be confined to a book; it is available to all who raise their consciousness. Then, from these angels come ideas about the meaning of sacred writings like The Revelation to John. It is like tapping into the creative stream of consciousness that orders the world. This is the order resulting from all the activity of all the beings in the cosmos, including human beings.

Those who are no longer confined to their earthly consciousness can now hear the seven messages and understand what is taking place moment by moment. These messages are not whispered; they come as a *mega* sound. We are in no doubt about them.

"Fear God and give him glory". Why is it important for us to experience fear? Fear is not encouraged in our modern lives, in fact we are taught to avoid it. Perhaps if we look at the purpose of fear these words may make more sense. The purpose of the feeling of fear is so that we can overcome it. To understand this we need to look at what happens within us during the experience of fear.

When we experience fear our life-force, our etheric body, retracts. As soon as the retraction begins we can interrupt the process by not succumbing to the feeling of fear which then indicates that we personally control the movement of our etheric body. The ability to do this comes from the strength of our connection with our 'I'. The more often we can experience the fear, and interrupt the feeling, the stronger and more conscious we become. At the same time the glory, the *doxa,* radiates from our astral body because our 'I' is able to influence our emotional life.

When we develop some mastery in this way it means that "the hour of his judgment *krisis* has come". This hour of *krisis* is cathartic or purifying. When we experience this we worship. Inner reverence rises up within us and we have feelings of deep respect for the wisdom of creation. This is not something we are asked to do by another person, ie. through church doctrine; this is a response that rises up from deep within us as a natural result of our experience of fear, glory and purity.

When we have this experience we begin to see the reality of creation and we see it most powerfully in each other. When we are to fully see the truth that heaven and earth, sea and fountains of water - which probably mean fresh life-giving water – have been created to serve human wellbeing we are filled with awe and reverence. We see that all this was created so that humans could exist on earth. What an amazing thing! When we turn our full attention to our fellow humans, "created in the image of God," our reverence is expressed in our respect for each one. Is this how we see each other? How differently we would all feel if it were; if everyone respected us as the creation of God and treated us accordingly.

Another angel, a second, followed, saying, "Fallen, fallen is Babylon the great, she who made all nations drink the wine of her impure passion." Rev 14:8

Babylon is a later name for Babel, one of the first cities built after the great flood. Bab-el means gate of God. We could say that humanity stood at the gate of God and waved him goodbye as they took the first steps toward self-responsibility. In fact, the tower of Babel was mankind's first political statement; no longer governed by God, now a self-governing people. Babel also marks a point in human evolution when we no longer understood each other, and if we look at today's Governments we can see that not much has changed in that regard. The story is told in Genesis 11.

Therefore its name was called Ba'bel, because there the LORD confused the language of all the earth; and from there the LORD scattered them abroad over the face of all the earth. Gen 11:9

Babylon was an important and holy city existing between approximately 2250BC until the night it fell in 539BC. It was during this time that humanity first become conscious of its soul forces. Until then we had only developed our physical expression in the world. Our soul and spirit were held in the spiritual worlds until we reached the appropriate stage to take possession of them. So at the Babylon stage of human history it was through our physical senses that we began to notice the contrast between what was physical and what was spiritual. For the first time, through our own individual senses, we experienced our environment. We were able to internalise beauty and relive what we saw as an inner experience. That is, we could replicate an image of what appeared before us. If we saw a beautiful flower we could recreate an image of the flower in our soul and enjoy it again and again. This meant that our experiences now became personal and private.

At this period of our development we had no personal experience of our 'I' and this awakening of our soul, which arose out of our astral forces, meant that egotistical passions could emerge. Our sense of justice and fairness could be overshadowed by our own needs. As we mastered the use of this soul force we were able to ennoble our instincts and refine our feelings. This also meant that we became aware of our ability to make choices. However, we still could not think for ourselves.

Instead of thinking, we received ideas from the spiritual worlds that assisted us to understand the physical world. We were also ruled by kings, pharaohs and priests. We certainly had no experience of individual human will. It is only now that we are learning to use our personal will.

Against this backdrop of human development we can place the message of the second angel. We know too well that there are many things that occur in modern life that belong to the distant past. This becomes very evident when we observe how people live in their feeling levels, barely using their thinking capacity, let alone their will. We could even say that modern Governments suppress the thoughts and actions of the people it governs. So it makes sense that the angel would use Babylon as an example.

It is said that Babylon was considered to be a golden cup in the hand of Jehovah to pour out indignation on the unfaithful. This means that human beings did the right thing because of a threat hanging over their heads. However, when they were given access to their soul forces hand in hand with the personal responsibility to act in a higher way, there was also the possibility of misusing these forces. They become drunk on the power of it which results in *porneuo* – impure passion. This word *porneuo* can also be rendered fornication indicating that the wrong forces have intercourse with each other.

Since this area of our soul is the one that we have experienced for the longest time, we are tempted to fall back on it when the pressure is on. And at no time in our history has the pressure been on human beings to develop their consciousness as it is at present. So we can be very tempted to drink the wine of Babylon's impure passions.

One of the first signs of this happening is when we become

defensive. This defensiveness arose at the time of Babylon when we became aware of ourselves as separate from our environment. The need to protect ourselves would have been a consuming experience. Now, we no longer need to protect ourselves. What we are called to do now is to become conscious of all the forces around us that lure us back into past conditions of consciousness. The less aware of them we are, the stronger they are. It is likely that the angels use the metaphor of wine to draw our attention to the use of alcohol to relieve the pressure of the work we are called to do with our consciousness. Wine always reduces are consciousness.

The purpose for scattering humanity and separating them through language no longer exists. Now we are called to dissolve divisions and speak one language again – the language of pure compassion. In this way we can listen to each other, feel into each other. In this way we continually test and progress our own consciousness. In this way we are open to the future flowing towards us and we meet each other in the middle ground, in the place occupied by the Lamb.

And another angel, a third, followed them, saying with a loud voice, "If any one worships the beast and its image, and receives a mark on his forehead or on his hand, he also shall drink the wine of God's wrath, poured unmixed into the cup of his anger, and he shall be tormented with fire and sulphur in the presence of the holy angels and in the presence of the Lamb. And the smoke of their torment goes up for ever and ever; and they have no rest, day or night, these worshipers of the beast and its image, and whoever receives the mark of its name." Here is a call for the endurance of the saints, those who keep the commandments of God and the faith of Jesus. Rev 14:9-12

The third message has increased in intensity and in detail. We are called to become conscious of much more. It starts with actions; worshipping, receiving a mark, and drinking. Then it moves into feelings of torment followed by a state of unrest twenty-four/seven. In a state of unrest our minds are continually occupied by thoughts. So in this message we can identify a story about the basic faculties of will, feeling and thinking that are the very foundation of the human soul.

If we are to know ourselves as human beings then we must start here. Until we are fully aware of how we will, feel and think, we will remain a mystery to ourselves. The complicating factor is that we are barely conscious of the way we will, we are only dreamily conscious of the activity of our feelings and it is only in our thinking are we awake and aware. We could also say that we are barely conscious of God, we are hardly conscious of why we feel tormented at times, and we often get no rest from our thinking. Each one of these conditions describes the boundaries of physical life on this earth, a life that is hardly aware of the reality of our spiritual home.

So the third message calls us to face this question of how well we really know ourselves. We often hear the human cry, "You don't know me, you don't understand me!" as we try to justify our behaviour. We could also ask why human beings consult psychics, astrologers and even psychologists. All because we long to know ourselves! And all the while the tools for knowing ourselves are within us. The human personality can only be known through becoming conscious of the way we will, feel and think.

In fact, the whole purpose of the Lamb is so that we can know ourselves, so that we can inwardly grasp the person that we are. Before Golgotha the human personality was obscured by our spiritual consciousness. We were not self-aware; self-awareness is something that we must work towards. To make this possible, the Lamb, God's son, left his father, went through the 'gates' and experienced human life and human death and is now in our presence as a life-force. The less we strive for self-awareness, "in the presence of the holy angels and in the presence of the Lamb", the more active is the beast.

Our task is to become more conscious of all this activity. Closing our eyes and saying that we don't want the mark of the beast on our forehead or hand, and pretending that we don't drink the wine of God's wrath, *thumou*, his boiling anger, just won't do it. When, at the Last Supper, Jesus used the bread and wine as a symbol of the renewal of human existence, he gave us something concrete to do. The wine is mixed with water and taken with the bread. These three elements can represent thinking, feeling and will. When we are aware of this we recognise that we have the ability to mix them consciously within us. It is such nonsense that the church decrees who is worthy to take communion and who is not, and for that matter who is worthy to give it and who is not. We can have this communion with the Lamb every time we eat, whatever we are eating, and wherever we are.

We are at a very critical point in the evolution of human consciousness. It is urgent that we identify the characteristics of our own will, our own feeling, and our own thinking. We don't need others to tell us, for they can only guess anyway. How can another person know us if we don't know ourselves? In fact the more we know ourselves, the more others will know us and love us.

We can only know ourselves when we are able to consciously mix these three faculties in an appropriate way according to all that we encounter in daily life. Each time we uncontrollably lose our temper they are unmixed. Each time we are offended, they are unmixed. Each time our thinking keeps us awake at night they are unmixed.

Human consciousness evolves regardless of human beings being aware of their own consciousness. When these changes occur unconsciously the beast has access to our soul. This gives rise to God's wrath indicating that will, feeling and thinking are poured unmixed. There is no greater torment than thinking day and night without the will to change the thoughts and the feeling to know which thoughts are right and which are not.

Human beings have journeyed through many stages of development, from Babylon to the present day, now we must use our faculties or lose them - to the beast. It is up to us to create the right mix within our soul. Those who do are the saints; they are the ones who have been able to endure the task of mixing the God-given gifts of will, feeling and thinking within their own being and according to their own individuality.

And another angel, a third, followed them, saying with a loud voice, "If any one worships the beast and its image, and receives a mark on his forehead or on his hand, he also shall drink the wine of God's wrath, poured unmixed into the cup of his anger, and he shall be tormented with fire and sulphur in the presence of the holy angels and in the presence of the Lamb. And the smoke of their torment goes up for ever and ever; and they have no rest, day or night, these worshipers of the beast and its image, and whoever receives the mark of its name." Here is a call for the endurance of the saints, those who keep the commandments of God and the faith of Jesus. Rev 14:9-12

It can't be stressed enough that the whole of humanity, at this stage of its development, is called upon to work on their will faculty. Of course, we cannot be aware of the will forces regulating movement in our body, but we can become aware of the working of will in our soul, and perhaps even to some extent in our spirit. Will is a directive force in our soul; we strengthen it through our thinking and we express it according to our feelings of enthusiasm. Obviously the quality of our actions will depend on the quality of our thinking and feeling. We can often observe these three faculties playing off each other in our indecisiveness as we oscillate between acting and not acting.

As we strive to refine these faculties, and our control of them, we move closer and closer to spiritual awareness. This is the secret of the will. We could say that we approach a certain level of purity which allows us to see things which could present a certain danger if we were not in full control of our will. In October 1918 Rudolf Steiner gave a series of lectures, published as Three Streams in Human Evolution, which emphasise the work we must do to develop our will in the current environment in which we are placed to do it.

He explains that one of the reasons the beast is referred to as 666 is because in the year 666 AD the beast tried to inoculate us with pre-developed will. This meant that we would not have to work to claim our own will forces; they would be freely given to us 'at no extra cost.' If this had happened it would have created a counter-force to the deed of Golgotha; all that had been achieved through the Christ being would have amounted to nothing. Humanity would have been captured in these alien will forces unable to develop our consciousness to a higher level. It would have meant that we would be unable to connect up with our I AM and consequently unable to develop our higher spiritual faculties of Imagination, Inspiration and Intuition.

Do we really understand what a privilege it is to develop our consciousness? Whenever we think that the task of developing and purifying our will forces is difficult we can remind ourselves of the privilege that is ours to do this work in freedom. Anyone who is not doing this work has the mark of the beast on them. They are neither thinking with their forehead, nor using their hands creatively to prevail against the motives of the beast. These human beings give themselves up for the pre-prepared consciousness of the beast, which can be likened to putting a frozen meal in the microwave oven.

As we live in these times of the initiation of the will we must realise that this means that our will is tested. In so many different ways we must face these tests – it isn't about the detail of the test so much as it is the test itself. We can certainly be side-tracked into working out what the detail might mean, and miss the purpose of the test completely. Think about how we can test our physical strength by picking up something heavy, or pushing a large object – in this way we meet the measure of our strength. In a similar way we can meet the strength of our will in our striving for the knowledge and understanding of the spiritual reality underpinning this world and our lives. Just like the physical test, we must meet obstacles with awareness, resisting defeat or distraction. If truth is not immediately revealed, then we must have the endurance to become aware of the full revelation. This is what John did when he wrote down these words that we are considering. We must also be aware that sometimes we grasp onto revelations too quickly, and it is only through our will that we can test these ideas over and over by applying them to many situations to see just how true they really are.

All this happens in an environment where the beast wants us to believe that we are all part of one great benevolent cosmic consciousness. That we can, without effort, experience the great group soul, this heavenly state where goodness always prevails. In this way, individual consciousness gained through refining our will, while connecting with our 'I', is sidestepped for a greater glorious state of being. This is an illusion and malevolent to the core. We have work to do and we must do it with each other regardless of the friction, because it is only in our relationships that we can express and observe our will. Some of our observations may be very uncomfortable, these are the tests of our will, and it calls for endurance by keeping the commandment, the new commandment that Jesus spoke of in John's Gospel.

"This is my commandment, that you love one another as I have loved you. Jn 15:12

The faith, *pistis,* of Jesus was his ability to see and experience how capable human beings are of refining their will. The indwelling Christ experienced this refinement of the will through the man Jesus. We too can have this faith, not simply a belief in ideas, but a real experience of what we are capable of if we just keep testing our will, facing the tests of life, and stretching our endurance little by little till we experience the new reality that John sees – a band of angels flying in mid-heaven with this most important message.

And another angel, a third, followed them, saying with a loud voice, "If any one worships the beast and its image, and receives a mark on his forehead or on his hand, he also shall drink the wine of God's wrath, poured unmixed into the cup of his anger, and he shall be tormented with fire and sulphur in the presence of the holy angels and in the presence of the Lamb. And the smoke of their torment goes up for ever and ever; and they have no rest, day or night, these worshipers of the beast and its image, and whoever receives the mark of its name." Here is a call for the endurance of the saints, those who keep the commandments of God and the faith of Jesus. Rev 14:9-12

These angels are following each other. There are many words in the Greek for 'follow', this one is *akoloutheo* which means that they are companions going the same way as each other. *Akoloutheo* is also the word used in the gospels to describe the disciples as followers of Jesus. These following angels are probably followers of the Lamb. They "fly in the midst of heaven" could refer to the etheric worlds surrounding this earth and giving it life, which is where the Lamb dwells. As they fly they are booming out these messages which we could assume that they do continually or eternally, that is, outside the confines of time.

If this is the case then we too should be able to hear their messages whenever we wish. For this to happen we will need to become aware of our inner hearing, our faculty of Inspiration which is only available to us when our 'I' is active in our soul. We might wonder why it needs to be loud *mega*. Perhaps this is so that we are able to hear it over the noisiness of our modern life. Not just outer noisiness, but also inner noisiness from the grinding of our materialistic thinking which can drown out higher ideas.

This third message is literally one of fire and brimstone - brimstone, *theion*, is found in places on the earth which are touched by lightning, which leaves a sulphurous smell. This image of the cup of wine pouring out in the presence of fire and brimstone is reminiscent of a bubbling, frothing cauldron. In the mist of it arises great torment. As we read John's words it is easy to place ourselves outside as an onlooker, thinking that all this is happening to others, but then we come to the last verse calling us to endure. In others words, we can't be saints unless we endure.

Therefore we can assume that this message is telling us about experiences that we ourselves may have; moments of torment that we must overcome. When we feel tormented it is easy to focus on the object of the torment and completely ignore the importance of the process of overcoming. If we are able to observe the ways in which we overcome these torments we will be strengthened. If we can look over past torments and not be drawn into re-experiencing them, we will be strengthened. This strengthening happens a bit at a time, so that eventually we will be able to prevail over certain torments that come our way while they are actually happening. If we dig up old torments then the cauldron will froth and bubble.

When we consider the torments that we face in our lives we should not think of it as punishment for not keeping commandments, or excuses about why we can't keep them, but rather as opportunities to become fully human. Do we really experience the enormous privilege of being human? Of all the beings in the universe The Creator designated us to be human. It is indeed a privilege to be human! Paul speaks of this in Romans chapter 8;

For the creation waits with eager longing for the revealing of the sons of God; Ro 8:19

Who are these sons of God? They are human beings who are fully developed because they were able to observe the torments and not get caught up in them. We might then ask ourselves the question: How human are we now? As Nietzsche famously said, "You have made your way from worm to man, and much in you is still worm." Not that we should take literally the idea of man being worm, but more the idea that we are crawling around in the materialistic nature of the earth, which of course gives us the opportunity to connect with our I. For it is only here on the earth that we can do this work, we cannot do it after death when we are in the spiritual worlds; we have to do it here. We have been created with the ability to raise ourselves up to the full stature of saint and to become sons of God. Of all the beings in the universe, we have the task of integrating the forces of the 'I', and so to become sons of THE God.

No wonder that while we remain earthbound, like the worm, then God's love appears to us as wrath. No wonder we have an innate sense that we are not doing the right thing. Of course this prompts us to look around us for the cause. If our eyes don't rest on a fellow human being, then they will often rest on God's wrath. But then this wrath is actually an illusion! What appears to us as wrath is really God's love, love that gives us the opportunity to observe the torments. This love manifests through our fellow human beings as they give us the opportunity to observe the torments. Yet sometimes we torment them back instead of observing. It is only in the observing that we have the opportunity to become sons of God.

When we remain in the illusion of wrath then we receive the mark of the beast and his image. Remember that in verse 1 there were a "hundred and forty-four thousand who had his (the Lamb's) name and his Father's name written on their foreheads." It is interesting to note the difference between what appears on their foreheads with the mark the beast's name leaves. The beast's mark is *charagma* which means carved, engraved, stamped, like branding a cow - it is an indelible mark and perhaps a premature mark. The word used for the Lamb and the Father's name is *grapho* which means written, scripted, and is similar to *graphe* which means scripture – in this case there is a sense of achievement arising from individuality and freedom.

When we look deeply into this Revelation it becomes clear that we are still trying to grasp the purpose for which we are placed on this earth. What we think is a burden is often a gift and vice versa. If we can just delay our judgements a bit longer, playing out our observations, we may see what John sees.

And I heard a voice from heaven saying, "Write this: Blessed are the dead who die in the Lord henceforth." "Blessed indeed," says the Spirit, "that they may rest from their labors, for their deeds follow them!" Then I looked, and lo, a white cloud, and seated on the cloud one like a son of man, with a golden crown on his head, and a sharp sickle in his hand. Rev 14:13-14

How appropriate to reach this verse at the time of Ascension and Pentecost – these festivals which are the climax of Christ's Deed. It is not too difficult to find the mystery of Golgotha woven into John's experience in these two verses pivoted between three angels on both sides.

We can begin by considering in brief the reason for the Deed of Golgotha; to reverse the entry of human souls into matter. From the perspective of the spiritual worlds the dead are those who leave the spiritual worlds to dwell in physical bodies on the earth. Humanity is so engrossed in matter that it is commonly thought that our lives begin and end in our physical bodies; that we have no pre-birth life or post-death existence.

To know the error of this we must conquer death, just like Jesus did. The only way he was able to do this was to fully integrate his 'I' into his being as an earthly human being. In this way he became fully human; body, soul and spirit firing on all cylinders here on earth. Then, at the crucial point, he was able to give up his 'I', his Lord, he was able to die to his Lord and make way for Christ, the Cosmic I AM, the Son of God, to fully enter into his being. As Paul puts it in Galatians, "I have been crucified with Christ; it is no longer I who live, but Christ who lives in me;" Ga 2:20

This sounds simple enough, however there are many traps along the way. We can identify many of them by reading the Gospels and applying all the events to our own inner life. It becomes obvious that we often want a shortcut to Christ without doing the work necessary to integrate our 'I'. We are drawn to old faculties of spiritual vision instead of using the new ones grounded in thinking. We even turn back to old Gods, like Buddha for instance, instead of recognising Buddha's new role as a Christ facilitator. After all, these are old friends and much easier to be with than making new ones.

If we use the capacities of our soul - thinking, feeling and will - with full awareness, then we will see that we can only claim our 'I' if we accept that we are dead – that we have no life in us. If we accept that we are dead and experience this death consciously, we live in a state of resurrection and have life in us. This means that our soul faculties are spiritualised, which begins when our thinking is freed from dead concepts to living ideas, new insights which we can think through logically. Spiritual ideas which can be integrated into modern life without being written off as whacky because of a reliance on terminology or practices that belong to the past.

If we deny that we are dead and think that this deathly state is life, we turn our back on our 'I'. Then we have no option but to take up the life of our astral being or animal-like state. This is a false life of comfort and instincts; we only need to look at our animal companions to identify the characteristics. If we choose to remain dead it also means that we are trying to claim our rest before we have earned it.

In John's description we also find the flipside of the beatitude, "Blessed are the poor in spirit, for theirs is the kingdom of heaven." Mt 5:3 The poor in spirit were those who left behind their awareness of the spiritual worlds, and their dependence on them, and fully immersed themselves into this earthly, limited understanding of things. We could say that this journey we are all making is from being spiritually unconscious, to being earthly conscious, to then becoming spiritually conscious. In this way, through our own efforts we claim our freedom.

There is much to contemplate in this fourth phase of John's experience. First John hears and then he sees. Through his spiritual faculty of Inspiration, that deep inner hearing, John hears a sound *phone* and then with his faculty of Imagination he sees *eidou* a man sitting on a cloud wearing a crown and holding a sharp sickle.

Is this the same cloud that took the resurrected Jesus out of sight? Paul tells us about this in Acts, and we considered it in chapter 11. (Note the reference to Pentecost when the Holy Spirit can come upon us.)

But you shall receive power when the Holy Spirit has come upon you; and you shall be my witnesses in Jerusalem and in all Judea and Sama'ria and to the end of the earth." And when he had said this, as they were looking on, he was lifted up, and a cloud took him out of their sight. Acts1:8-9

Could it be that if we manage to engage with our 'I' that we complete the act of resurrection? Are we the "one like the son of man" that John saw in his Revelation? Are we like the farmer or gardener who has sown the seed that can now be harvested with the sharp sickle?

Read what John reported in his Gospel about the son of man.

For as the Father has life in himself, so he has granted the Son also to have life in himself and has given him authority to execute judgment, because he is the Son of man. Jn 5:26-27

We must work diligently to have this resurrected life, this *zoe*, of which the cloud is a metaphor. When our thinking is freed from its earthbound concepts, when it is trained to understand how spirit works here in this world of matter, we will wear the golden crown and there will be much to harvest in our being. Till then, we have to labour and tend the garden. Who is this gardener? It is our 'I'. Without our 'I' there will be nothing to harvest and nothing blessed.

And another angel came out of the temple, calling with a loud voice to him who sat upon the cloud, "Put in your sickle, and reap, for the hour to reap has come, for the harvest of the earth is fully ripe." So he who sat upon the cloud swung his sickle on the earth, and the earth was reaped. Rev 14:15-16

Why did this angel come out of the temple? The others were flying in mid heaven. The last time the temple was mentioned was in chapter 11 right after the seventh angel began to blow his trumpet – which he is probably still blowing. It said, "Then God's temple in heaven was opened, and within his temple was seen the ark of his covenant." Rev 11:19

The word used for temple is *naos* which means shrine or sanctuary, a place where only the priest could enter. The whole of John's Revelation calls for us to become a priest, not the kinds of priest that we encounter in the church today but a new kind of priest. This kind of priest was discussed at the beginning of our contemplations in Rev 1:5-6;

...it is not so much about having a sense of being a priest but of how we are functioning as a priest. This new priest first presides within themselves. These are the ones who have an innate sense of awe and reverence for their own being and for every other human being they encounter. They express love and forgiveness for themselves and others, creating a sense of community that does not depend on membership of an external organisation. Furthermore, it can straddle belief systems. Those who are functioning as this new priest are an example for others to experience the kingdom and the priest within themselves.

We can tie these ideas in with the first mention of the word temple in The Revelation which can be found in chapter 3.

Him who overcomes I will make a pillar in the temple of my God. Never again will he leave it. I will write on him the name of my God and the name of the city of my God, the new Jerusalem, which is coming down out of heaven from my God; and I will also write on him my new name. Rev 3:12

This work of overcoming, as previously discussed, means to 'come over' from the past and stand in the present so that we can step into the future as required. To a great extent we live in the past, shackled by our karma and afraid to step into the future for fear of unleashing any further karma. The new priest is the one who 'comes over' and can then reap the harvest.

If we are to know what is to be harvested don't we need to know what has been sown? We can become so focussed on our personal issues that we forget to look at all that has gone into making the human being what he is today, and what he will be in the future? Even if we don't know the details of how the creator God set in motion all that was necessary for us to achieve what we have achieved so far, we can at least stand in awe of it from time to time.

How often do we stand in awe of the miracle that is our human body? Not only the physical component, which is built up of all that comes from the earth as we consume the earthly harvest; grain, fruit, vegetables, meat etc. turning them into the physical substance of our body. All of which is able to exist on the earth because of the force of gravity, but also that force that makes it possible for us to counteract the decay of physical substances, the life-force, the weaving formative forces, which can also be called the etheric body. This is the force which gives our physical substance shape and life preventing it from decaying. It is these forces that leave our body at death. It is these forces that leave when a piece of fruit rots. These forces come from the outer reaches of the cosmos and are often referred to as cloud. As the physical component of our being is pulled down by gravity, this life-force pulls towards the cosmos. The health of our being depends on these two forces being in perfect harmony. When they are we shine with vitality and can often look younger. This can even be the case when we are physically ill.

John's reference to reaping the harvest could be pointing to those people who have an abundance of these life-giving life-forces. They are not weighed down by the physical forces of gravity; they have a certain amount of levity in their being because their life-force is vibrant.

Rev Mario Schoenmaker made an unusual comment not long before he died. At this time he was deeply contemplating the need for a new kind of priest in the world. The kind we have been exploring here. He spoke the following words in a similar manner to the way The Revelation was received by John:

The field is ripe unto harvest but where are my servants, my anointed ones? Are they getting fat on the goods of others? Are they walking around in rich robes, in mighty buildings? Where are my servants who must preach and teach in humility? September 4, 1996

The new priest is the one who works quietly on themselves, and sees the richness in others that is often overlooked in a world so obsessed with money and power. In the seeing comes the harvest.

Another angel came out of the temple in heaven, and he too had a sharp sickle. Still another angel, who had charge of the fire, came from the altar and called in a loud voice to him who had the sharp sickle, "Take your sharp sickle and gather the clusters of grapes from the earth's vine, because its grapes are ripe." The angel swung his sickle on the earth, gathered its grapes and threw them into the great winepress of God's wrath. They were trampled in the winepress outside the city, and blood flowed out of the press, rising as high as the horses' bridles for a distance of 1,600 stadia. Rev 14:17-20

These last three angels (messengers) seem to be working as a team; they are all in the temple and the seventh angel is in charge of the fire on the altar. In ancient times the priest kept the fire on the altar burning continually. The flame was a symbol of the priest's sacrificial offering to the gods which was carried upwards with the smoke. His prayer was that the offering of the flame would be returned as a blessing of divine creative power. This is mentioned in Leviticus.

The fire on the altar shall be kept burning on it, it shall not go out; the priest shall burn wood on it every morning, Lev 6:12

Now the fire is within us, in our blood. This fire, this warmth, contains Christ, who is, after all the God from the fiery sun. Now we, as the new priest, must keep the flame burning on our internal altar. Tending the flame is a great responsibility for each one of us. We may think that if we are too tired or too busy that no one will know if we have let the flame grow dim. Of course, it isn't about anyone else knowing, we no longer live in an age where we act in a certain way to please others. Now it is our own responsibility to do what is right; not right according to rules but right because Christ is waiting for us to become his co-workers. The light from our flame brightens his flame and the brighter this flame, the more noticeable it is.

The last time our attention was drawn to the altar was in chapter 6 as part of the fifth seal where it said, "When he opened the fifth seal, I saw under the altar the souls of those who had been slain for the word of God and for the witness they had borne;" Rev 6:9

In our contemplation of these words the following was put forward:

Could this altar be the table at which Jesus and the disciples shared the Last Supper? Is it a kind of demarcation zone; what took place up till now was the preparation, what will now take place is the deed. What is this deed? It is the gift of the 'I' placed in the heart of each human being as a seed. Human nature as it was known up till then was slain on the altar of Golgotha.

These images weave into the text we are now considering as John sees the fire on the altar and the harvesting of grapes. This could be the internal altar where the last supper occurs continually as we prepare to sacrifice all that is lower within us, that it may be crucified and resurrected as our Higher Self? This is in line with

John's words in his Gospel "he who eats my flesh and drinks my blood has eternal life," 6:54.

Also in John's gospel, in the seventh I AM saying, Jesus tells us about bearing fruit.

I am the vine, you are the branches. He who abides in me, and I in him, he it is that bears much fruit, for apart from me you can do nothing. Jn 15:5

Do we really give Christ the central role in our life that we should? It isn't easy to untangle ourselves from the ideas perpetrated by the Church over the last few thousand years, and especially in our own lifetime. Even those of us who strive to find the hidden truth in the sacred mysteries can often taint our understanding with superficial theological ideas.

It is these ideas that keep Jesus nailed to the cross in perpetual crucifixion and prevent the resurrection of the living Christ. If Jesus remains on the cross then his blood would continually flow. Could this be what is meant by "blood flowed out of the press, rising as high as the horses' bridles for a distance of 1,600 stadia."? Or perhaps it means that our lower self is being continually crucified and we do not rise from the grave. This would aggravate God's wrath; wrath, of course, meaning God's intense love for us.

One of our greatest challenges is to see that sacred deeds are not trapped in time or space. We must open our minds to the implications of this. The revelation of Jesus Christ depends on it. The angels are sent to reveal to us the truth of the living Christ and give us clues about how things will pan out in our individual lives. Consider again the opening words of The Revelation.

The revelation of Jesus Christ, which God gave him to show to his servants what must soon take place; and he made it known by sending his angel to his servant John, Rev 1:1

Another angel came out of the temple in heaven, and he too had a sharp sickle. Still another angel, who had charge of the fire, came from the altar and called in a loud voice to him who had the sharp sickle, "Take your sharp sickle and gather the clusters of grapes from the earth's vine, because its grapes are ripe." They were trampled in the winepress outside the city, and blood flowed out of the press, rising as high as the horses' bridles for a distance of 1,600 stadia. Rev 14:17-20

We could wonder if these angels, these messengers, are actually angels or whether they are higher members of the spiritual hierarchy. Or it could be that the higher members are working through the angels. One clue about this is that John saw that the seventh angel had charge of the fire. This word 'charge' is *exousia* which means authority or power and is the name of the fourth group of spiritual beings above mankind. These are the beings known in Hebrew as Elohim; the gods who created heaven and earth. They are the Spirits of Form and they work through heat and would therefore have "power over fire" as the King James Version of the Bible puts it.

These creators are very interested in the progress of their creation; they wait in eager longing St Paul told us in the Romans 8. Their goal is for human beings to become like them - creators. The only way for this to happen is for us to become aware of the work of the spiritual worlds in this earth sphere. This is our current task as we try to become fully active in all our soul levels. We have developed our feeling and thinking levels, now we work on our will. This area of the soul is about consciousness, awareness and we cannot develop it in a semi-conscious state.

Contemplating a mysterious text like this can enhance our awareness. If we try to evoke our spiritual Imagination and bring the scene to life, creative ideas about its meaning can be revealed. What we see are angels with sickles harvesting grapes to be trampled so that their liquid floods a vast area of the land.

One way to make sense of it is by reading the spiritual script that it represents. This script is not something that can be taught, it must be personally experienced as we gaze upon the images. One example of this script is when we recognise that the crescent moon looks like a sickle. If we look closely we can see the faint circular outline of the full moon now obscured by the movement of the earth and sun. This is an image of the communion host resting in the sickle shaped moon and reminds us of the Sun-God, the Lamb whom the angels follow.

Grapes are also part of the spiritual script because they are ripened by the sun and their juice is a symbol of the blood of Christ. It is our task to become grapes ripened by the presence of Christ so that our blood becomes his blood - then the blood of

Christ flows in our veins. Perhaps a certain quantity of this blood is required before this earth can be redeemed. As our blood becomes the blood of Christ we become part of a fraternity which John saw at the beginning of this chapter, the one hundred and forty four thousand; the new priests.

Imagine that much blood flowing over that much land. Perhaps there were so many grapes that the horses had to assist with the press vats. When we contemplate the image of the horse's bridle it speaks to us of control, of management. All that is below the neck is now washed in Christ's blood and the head, which represents our thinking, is controlled by the bridle which can represent the will. This brings us back to the importance of our present human development as we work on the final stages of developing our soul. This stage is about the awareness and management of our will. The world today is so highly mechanised that we must use our will to resist the diminishing of our consciousness. This *is* the task. There is no use fleeing from machines or going back to nature, we must realise that the mechanisation is there so that we can actually develop our consciousness. We only become conscious in the striving to overcome all that makes us semi-conscious.

This new awareness which rises out of the depths of our soul connects us with our I AM the possibility for which was given when Christ connected with Jesus during the Mystery of Golgotha. It is a new form of awareness, it is not the old clairvoyance which can be difficult to decipher with the modern mind, this is the new clairvoyance, that awareness that comes when we free our thinking from its base in our body. This is the kind of thinking that understands John's vision. It may not follow logical sequences, methods of reasoning developed by the various sciences, but it can take these sciences a step further, over the threshold into spiritual truth as revealed by the cosmic spiritual script. Then the angels can speak into our awareness about the next steps.

CHAPTER FIFTEEN

The Seven Bowls of Wrath

Then I saw another portent in heaven, great and wonderful, seven angels with seven plagues, which are the last, for with them the wrath of God is ended. And I saw what appeared to be a sea of glass mingled with fire, and those who had conquered the beast and its image and the number of its name, standing beside the sea of glass with harps of God in their hands. And they sing the song of Moses, the servant of God, and the song of the Lamb, saying, "Great and wonderful are thy deeds, O Lord God the Almighty! Just and true are thy ways, O King of the ages! Who shall not fear and glorify thy name, O Lord? For thou alone art holy. All nations shall come and worship thee, for thy judgments have been revealed." Rev 15:1-4

The next four chapters take us into another realm of the development of our consciousness. John sees the details of this phase in the image of the seven angels with bowls of wrath and the judgement of Babylon.

Could this sea of glass mean that it is our task to become

completely transparent? In this transparency we would have the courage to be open about our motives and the ability to face all the influences of our lower self. Before we can embark on this we need a strong sense of community. To develop this new community requires a level of trust that we do not very often see today. It also requires that we set aside personal opinions and prejudices and meet each other with selfless love.

The first step to experiencing this new community is to stand on our own feet and become self-sufficient. We don't look to this new community for support, or leadership from others, nor do we try to lead and support others. Hierarchical systems like this prevent us from awakening our will and using our Consciousness / Awareness Soul levels. It is in the making of our own decisions that we enliven these higher levels of our soul. If we continually defer to others we give up the right to be fully human. On the other hand, we should not reject this new community-building because of the inherent difficulties.

Rudolf Steiner has a lot to say about this stage of our development, which we are experiencing intensely at the present, in his lecture series From Symptom to Reality in Modern History. These lectures were given in October 1918 a year before the end of World War I. His extraordinary insight and commentary about the struggle of human nature addresses many of the issues we face today.

Long gone is the era of soul development when we awakened our personal intellect and ability to reason. Plato and Aristotle were the forefathers of this development. At that time we needed the leadership of elders, the church, royalty and government because our will was not sufficiently active. This development was complete by the early fifteenth century when we began to take affairs into our own hands. This was the dawning of our ability to make our own decisions. That the church still tries to subordinate people with rules and doctrines is an attempt to quarantine them in the age of reason which culminated over five hundred years ago. Essentially what this means is that the church tries to hold people back from developing their own awareness. Even today we see so many very old notions influencing many areas of our lives. We look to history to justify our actions when what is recorded as history is merely the symptom of a deeper reality. The reality is in the viewing of the past actions of others to see how events have changed human consciousness and vice versa. Then some events, even disastrous ones, can be seen to have a higher purpose.

In this lecture series, Steiner revealed the real meaning of Fraternity, Liberty and Equality and pointed to its importance for us today. Not as it was wrongly applied in the French Revolution, by applying it to society in general, but rather to apply these three principles to our own inner development of body, soul and spirit.

- In our physical life, true fraternity is fundamental to the new community, especially in our individual behaviour. This means that the responsibility lies within each person to express themselves through the Consciousness Soul by awakening their will.

- In our soul, we experience liberty when we free ourselves from our semi-conscious feeling levels.

- Only in our spirit do we experience equality. The spiritual nature of the human being is a state of equality.

It isn't difficult to see how these concepts have been misapplied creating disharmony and confusion for both inner and outer life.

Unless we understand the development of human consciousness then the Consciousness Soul is anaesthetised. Only through major upheavals like the 2008 Global Financial Crisis can we wake up to the requirements of the new community. The mere fact that a person with a lot of money is regarded to be more important than a person with no money shows us how far we are from this new community. When money is far more highly valued than creativity and innovation human development is arrested.

There is much to understand about the development of our Consciousness Soul. Our capacity to develop it depends on befriending the forces of death by recognising the impermanence of things. Perhaps our study of these plagues will reveal how God needs to kill a few things off so that we can become spiritually conscious. Then the new community can arise. Steiner puts it this way, "Only a genuine concern of each man for his neighbour can bring salvation to mankind in the future ... [we must] devote ourselves increasingly and with loving care to the shortcomings of our neighbours." Furthermore, "in the epoch of the Consciousness Soul nothing is more dangerous than to surrender to, or show a predilection for personal opinions or prejudices." Here lies our great challenge and our great reward.

Then I saw another portent in heaven, great and wonderful, seven angels with seven plagues, which are the last, for with them the wrath of God is ended. And I saw what appeared to be a sea of glass mingled with fire, and those who had conquered the beast and its image and the number of its name, standing beside the sea of glass with harps of God in their hands. And they sing the song of Moses, the servant of God, and the song of the Lamb, saying, "Great and wonderful are thy deeds, O Lord God the Almighty! Just and true are thy ways, O King of the ages! Who shall not fear and glorify thy name, O Lord? For thou alone art holy. All nations shall come and worship thee, for thy judgments have been revealed." Rev 15:1-4

There is something a bit odd about the introduction to chapter 15. Normally we would use words like 'great' and 'wonderful' to indicate something good but John is linking them with plagues and the wrath of God. Perhaps this sentence would make more sense if it said *mega* mighty, enormous, and *thaumaton* amazing, something to marvel at. Powerful and dynamic might be another way of putting it. Then, we could assume that the members of the fourth and fifth spiritual hierarchy are at work here. The fourth are those who created form, the Powers, and fifth are those who give motion to form, the Dunamai, the dynamic ones.

We might think that our connection with these spiritual beings who guide creation is so far removed from us that we can have no thoughts about them. This is far from the truth. Each time we admire the form of a rock, a tree, a cat, a human, etc. we are admiring the work of the Exousia, the Powers. Each time we see clouds moving across the sky and feel the wind moving over the landscape we experience the work of the Dunamis or Mights. It is up to us to engage with this and not let it pass us by unnoticed. When we engage with the work of these beings, which usually means that we have to overcome half-baked scientific ideas about the creation of the world, then our soul comes alive. It is a sign, a portent - *semeion*, a mark in our lives.

It could be like the mark in chapter 12 where John stood on the sand of the sea, between the spiritual and physical worlds. It also speaks about the demarcation zone of the souls under the altar in the fifth seal in chapter 6 which can represent the pre- and post-Last Supper. We face these marks or zones in our lives continually. It would be naive of us to think that there were only two zones; earth and heaven. It is equally naive to think that these two zones are here or there. Furthermore, we must experience the reality that we are spiritual beings who move in and out of the formed world through birth and death. The formed world and the unformed world are one and the same place – we are just not fully aware of the unformed when we are formed.

If we can grasp this idea then it is easy to see that there would be lots of demarcation zones. Even if we look around our immediate environment we find many demarcation zones. People trained for certain jobs are allowed in certain areas from which others are excluded. Therefore those who have trained their consciousness to be more aware of the work of the spirits of form in the various shapes of things, and the spirits of movement in the movement we associate with weather, for instance, will have earned the right to step over the mark, to move in another zone.

One of the most important zones in our lives is where we have to work out relationships with others. The difficulty some people experience in their relationships could be called the wrath of God. In other words, the karmic relationships that God, through his tough love, hopes we will resolve. God sees that lifetime after lifetime people have the same kinds of relationships with each other, as if they are on a round-about. Not only that, but in this life, people are locked into certain repetitions. There is no forward movement; patterns of behaviour are continually repeated. Then the peacemakers come in, the deal makers, whether it is on a global political level in the Middle East or Afghanistan, or on a professional level with psychologists, or on a personal level seeking the advice of a friend. In this way we keep the wrath of God in perpetual motion so that it can never end.

The only peace can be inner peace. This is not about turning to others to make a deal for us; it is about inner change personally directed. A good place to start is to change our focus and look for the activity of the spiritual beings in this formed world. Just by acknowledging their work we step into their zone – as we feel others are 'in our zone' when they acknowledge our work.

When we acknowledge the work of the beings of the spiritual hierarchy it awakens our soul from its robotic slumber. Then we are able to place many things into perspective; the way we relate to others, the way we function in the world, and most of all, the great contribution that we can make to the creative process that is still being played out. If we don't do this then we are holding everything and everyone back. This is the enormous and amazing story of the seven plagues.

Then I saw another portent in heaven, great and wonderful, seven angels with seven plagues, which are the last, for with them the wrath of God is ended. And I saw what appeared to be a sea of glass mingled with fire, and those who had conquered the beast and its image and the number of its name, standing beside the sea of glass with harps of God in their hands. And they sing the song of Moses, the servant of God, and the song of the Lamb, saying, "Great and wonderful are thy deeds, O Lord God the Almighty! Just and true are thy ways, O King of the ages! Who shall not fear and glorify thy name, O Lord? For thou alone art holy. All nations shall come and worship thee, for thy judgments have been revealed." Rev 15:1-4

What would a sea of glass look like? A sea is quite a large body of water and usually not at all transparent. It is also usually in motion - from swells below or wind above. It is coloured according the reflection of the sky overhead and what it contains beneath the surface. In other words, its appearance is caused by its response to outer influences. This is a picture of our own lives isn't it?

Every outer influence changes us constantly throughout the day. Even when we are alone, our memories and thoughts that have come to us from outside have a similar effect. Yet if we are to mature as human beings we must aim for the sea of glass state. This stillness can only arise from within us through no other influence but our own. It cannot come from techniques or meditations either for they are only temporary solutions; it can only come from the conscious use of our feeling, thinking and will. Left to their own devices these elements of our soul can, in an instant, turn our being from a sea of glass into choppy, turgid, watery foam.

John tells us how this can happen. It is when we are not

conquerors. We can only be conquerors if we overcome, if we come over from where we were and can stand in each new situation that comes our way. It is as if there is no rest for us. What is it about change that brings on a feeling of tiredness? Essentially it is our resistance to new developments. If we were able to move steadily forward, responding to changing circumstances without resistance we would probably not tire. This is the secret of overcoming, or being able to come over and conquer our natural inclinations.

So why do we resist? Again John tells us that it is because of the beast, the beast's image and the number of the beast's name. It is odd that John lists these three characteristics instead of just generalising about being conquerors of the beast. It obviously points to the need to conquer three different aspects of the beast. How are we to recognise these three aspects of the beast? Should we launch into a detailed study of all the manifestations of the beast? We could feel defeated before we start trying to identify the beast, its image and its name or nature? Or is it just a matter of striving to be calm, striving for the sea of glass state? Wouldn't that be far easier and far more certain? For after all, to do this, we only need to be aware of the nature of our own soul. There is much more certainty in dealing with our own soul than trying to identify three or more aspects of the beast's activity. Perhaps this is the challenge the beast puts before us, trying to distract us from creating our sea of glass.

This is where the fire comes in. This fire indicates the presence of the sun god; this is the fire that Christ planted deep within our being at Pentecost through the vehicle of the Holy Spirit which we read about in John's Gospel chapter 20:19ff. This fire descended from the heights of the spiritual worlds and it slumbers within our hearts until we kindle it. The essence of this fire is love. When we are able to fan its flames by loving others in the right way we achieve the perfect balance of fire and sea within us. This balance can only come about through perfecting our control of our feelings, thoughts and intentions; the three strings of the harps of God.

This is the third time John has seen these harps. Each time they appear the Lamb is there. The first time they appeared, in chapter 5:6-10, there is a sense that they are singing the human being into the creation. Then in chapter 14:1-3 they sing because some human beings have been able to conquer the materialistic conditions of the earth by overcoming its negative aspects. The story of Moses leading the Israelites out of Egypt by controlling the sea is a metaphor for this journey. Now, in chapter 15, the human beings themselves are actually playing the harps. They are the ones who can pluck at the feeling string to harmonise it with the strings of thinking and intention and so on.

The only way for us to 'come over' into a conscious experience of the way our feeling, thinking and will interact is to connect up with our Higher Self, our I AM, that human core through which we can know who we really are. When we are ready, when we have control of our soul faculties, when we play the harp in perfect harmony, our being will be transparent. We will know why we have had to take the journey that we are on. Even though it may have been difficult at times, we will see that we would not have swapped this journey with anyone else – for it is the journey that gives us the greatest possibility to create our own harmony. This is another reason why we resist coming over into new situations, and why we feel tired at times, because we experience the comfort of our own journey which we imagine will be taken away by a movement forward. If we can take the movement in our stride we will experience greater and greater harmony and we will "sing the song of Moses, the servant of God, and the song of the Lamb".

Then I saw another portent in heaven, great and wonderful, seven angels with seven plagues, which are the last, for with them the wrath of God is ended. And I saw what appeared to be a sea of glass mingled with fire, and those who had conquered the beast and its image and the number of its name, standing beside the sea of glass with harps of God in their hands. And they sing the song of Moses, the servant of God, and the song of the Lamb, saying, "Great and wonderful are thy deeds, O Lord God the Almighty! Just and true are thy ways, O King of the ages! Who shall not fear and glorify thy name, O Lord? For thou alone art holy. All nations shall come and worship thee, for thy judgments have been revealed." Rev 15:1-4

This is a song of love sung by the transparent ones. It is not about loving someone, something, or even some deity. It is about experiencing the fullness of love in itself which can only be experienced through our I AM. This is the task and purpose of the human being, to be able to withstand the intensity of love as it pours from God the Almighty, the *pantokrator*, the one who holds all, the one who has the strength to hold everything. Imagine the scope of his love if this god is to hold absolutely everything! Compare this to how we reject so many things because we can't bear them.

Such love as this can only be experienced by human beings through a certain level of purity. Only in the purest possible transparency, only in the perfect harmony, and only in the ability to withstand the revealing of judgements, can we know anything of this perfect love. However, we can have glimpses of it, of course, we must have glimpses of it otherwise we would be staring at our own defeat. These glimpses come to us through spiritual insights. We get a taste of this love through our contemplations of truth, in the confirmation of what is just and true, and also what awakens in us when judgements have been revealed. However, if we turn away from these then we are denied the experience of this highest love. It is this highest love that is actually the substance of our I AM, our holy name.

This word translated as judgment is a bit misleading; *dikaioma* more accurately refers to an ordinance, a law or rule. We don't see the rules that we are meant to live by, otherwise we would not live the way we do. This law could be expressed in the way John recorded it in his Gospel:

A new commandment I give to you, that you love one another; even as I have loved you, that you also love one another. Jn 13:34

The fire that is mixed into the sea of glass is this kind of love that Jesus speaks of here. This highest love calls us to experience it and express it. Yet at the same time we feel that it will, like fire, consume us. It will deprive us of the self-love that we have become so used to. So we flee from this love as we would flee from a consuming fire. We prefer to wallow in our self-love and all our opportunities to progress become fodder for the beast.

So what can we do today, in our lives, to change this? One simple thing we can do is to try to experience what others experience. If a child cries for its mother we can try to feel, as fully as possible, what that child is experiencing. If a friend tells us of their misfortune we can try to step inside them and really experience their disappointment and loss as if it is our own. Our initial response often finds us turning away from them back into the safety of our own being. Or we simply can't even leave our own being in the first place and we stay there absorbed by our own pain.

So it is a catch twenty-two situation. We are polarised between self-love and selfless love. Of our own accord we must experience the difference between these two and take the step across the abyss more often to experience selfless love. Each time we falter the beast is waiting. This is an urgent task every human being on this earth is called to embrace. And there is a watch-point; selfless love does not mean abandoning self-love – the two must co-exist.

We should also watch for that form of love which binds groups of people together through a common ideal but which actually only exists when there is an opposing group supporting another ideal. This is love based on hatred, it is everywhere. Our I AM can have nothing to do with it.

This song of love is really a song to our I AM:

"Great and wonderful are thy deeds, O I AM, the one who holds the fullness of our being!

Just and true are thy ways, O I AM of the ages who has experienced all our earthly lives!

Who shall not fear and glorify you, I AM?

For you alone art holy (*hosios*, pure and observant of god's will - which is to love).

All nations shall come and worship the I AM, for the I AM's judgments have been revealed."

After this I looked, and the temple of the tent of witness in heaven was opened, and out of the temple came the seven angels with the seven plagues, robed in pure bright linen, and their breasts girded with golden girdles. And one of the four living creatures gave the seven angels seven golden bowls full of the wrath of God; and the temple was filled with smoke from the glory of God and from his power, and no one could enter the temple until the seven plagues of the seven angels were ended. Rev 15:5-8

It is good to imagine John looking at this scene. If we place ourselves in his position we can try to recreate what he is looking at, perhaps as if in a dream. But this is not a dreamy consciousness that John has, he really looks. This Greek word for looked is *eidon* and indicates perceiving the spiritual reality of a situation. This looking is not one dimensional as our physical sight is; this looking sees the inner meaning of everything in the scene. It knows why each element is present and understands why the events take place.

The first thing that John perceives is "the temple of the tent of witness" - *naos tns skenes tou marturion*. What kind of strange temple is this? A temple suggests a substantial building and a tent suggests something flimsy and temporary. We could wonder about the accuracy of the translation, however, if we think of this in terms of our human condition it makes more sense. The *naos* is the shrine within the temple that only the priest can enter. The *skenes* is a temporary dwelling, just as our body is the temporary dwelling of our soul each time we incarnate. *Marturion* is witnessing a thing not from a distance but firsthand by entering right into what is happening and experiencing it in the moment.

So what John is seeing is that those who can enter where only the priest can go, when they experience their inner priestly nature, they are able to experience their karma. They are able to enter into this special place, the temple of the tent of witness, and re-experience all that has brought them to this point, life after life. Because of their priestly nature they are able to objectively observe everything that has contributed to who they are today. Until we can become this inner priest we will not have the courage or the strength to relive certain events from our past lives. When we can become this priest there will be a certain equilibrium as we have to face what we have done to others, and what they have done to us. When we look we will know why.

We may not be able to be fully composed as we face certain karmic issues, but we will be able to quite quickly regain our composure. This is the nature of the priest; they are the ones who forgive and place every situation before Christ. We could call these priests natural priests; it is in their inner nature to raise any situation up from the depths of instinctive reactions to a place of understanding and equilibrium. This happens in the sacred place within us, the *naos*, where the true priestly nature is found.

While in the world today the church promotes the authority of the priest over its people, and places great store on bestowing ordination, they seem not to understand this ability of people to experience their own priestly nature. While the church is busy with its pomp and ceremony these natural priests are being ordained from within. They are discovering the *naos* within their own being and realising that by being a priest to themselves and developing their priestly nature the power of Christ streams from them. We get a sense of this purity from the angels that John sees coming out of our inner shrine "robed in pure bright linen, and their breasts girded with golden girdles."

There is something sublime about these angels, even though they have the plagues and carry the bowls full of the wrath of God. It says that no one or no thing could enter the temple while they are doing their job. Perhaps this means that at this point in our development the forces of opposition, the beasts, cannot interfere as long as we do this work.

At this point in human evolution the activity of Christ is escalating. We must raise our vision to see him as he dwells in the life-forces of this planet since he experienced the crucifixion. It isn't about waiting for a vision to appear before our eyes, it is about creating our own vision of this Christ. Whatever image we create Christ will enter it. Rev Mario Schoenmaker spoke about this at the end of his life.

"I believe that you cannot love the Christ properly without having seen him. I think I have said that before. But if you create within your soul a picture of the Christ in accordance to your own imagination, hold that picture before you in your brain when you contemplate, then you will find that your love becomes stronger.

The wonder of the Christ spirit is that he is not fastened to a particular manifestation. So even if you create that picture within your consciousness, with all the beauty you can give it - and each picture from each person can be different, and probably is - the manifestation of the Christ is not limited, he manifests himself through the picture that you create. Then you start loving him better, deeper, greater. Then your devotions are no longer a duty, then they are a joy. Then your prayers are a deep need for communication, then your love will be extended and become manifest in all areas of your life." 19.09.1995

This is the work that we do in our naos, in that inner sanctuary which is then "filled with smoke from the glory of God and from his power, and no one could enter the temple".

After this I looked, and the temple of the tent of witness in heaven was opened, and out of the temple came the seven angels with the seven plagues, robed in pure bright linen, and their breasts girded with golden girdles. And one of the four living creatures gave the seven angels seven golden bowls full of the wrath of God; and the temple was filled with smoke from the glory of God and from his power, and no one could enter the temple until the seven plagues of the seven angels were ended. Rev 15:5-8

If we look at this temple as our dwelling place, which means not only our physical body but our whole being of body, soul and spirit, an interesting story unfolds. Within the temple are seven angels robed in pure, cleansed, luminous linen with golden girdles and seven plagues. John sees them leaving the temple with the plagues and taking seven bowls of wrath from one of the four living creatures. John is giving us a picture of what goes on within us and what takes place outside us at a certain stage in our development.

So we share our temple with these angels and at some point they leave us. How aware are we of these angels dwelling within us? or around us for that matter? To recognise their activity we need to contemplate their role both in the cosmos and in our lives. Angels, being one stage above human beings, as animals are one stage below human beings, have experienced the human condition albeit under different circumstances. Of all the beings in the cosmos angels would know best what we are going through.

Another way to look at the role of angels is to consider how we look after our pets and ensure that they are safe, comfortable, well fed and content, so do angels watch over us. They guide us and work with us lifetime after lifetime. They witness of all our deeds and they know why certain experiences come our way. They know us intimately and they offer guidance to us to make the best use of every opportunity in life. While they experience our freedom to make decisions, for good or bad, they have no such freedom. They are the messengers who must deliver what they are given to deliver. In this case, seven plagues and seven bowls full of the wrath of God.

If we are to make any sense of all of this we must revisit our purposes as human beings. We cannot fully grasp human purpose unless we attempt to experience the reality of reincarnation in our lives. There is no point saying that we do or do not know about reincarnation, we must actually experience the truth of it. One simple way is to ask ourselves why we instantly dislike someone we have just met. Or, for that matter, instantly like someone we have never met before. There are many ways to explore knowledge of reincarnation and it is important that we each do this work.

Then we might ask why we live repeated lives on earth? Put simply, it is so that we can become more highly developed beings. Higher development entails thinking, feeling and acting consciously. Not only that, but to be able to direct our thoughts, feelings and activity in ways that suit whatever situation we find ourselves in. We can become quite accomplished at this until we meet the consequences of our actions in a past life. Then all our good work can fly out the window and we act unconsciously and sometimes inappropriately towards others. This is more proof of the fact of reincarnation.

Furthermore, we should realise that the person we are now interacting with may not be the person involved in that past life incident, they may just be triggering a response in us that we must deal with inwardly. Of course, often we don't deal with it inwardly and then the plagues manifest in our outer life.

The more highly developed we are, the more conscious and aware we are of all these details in our lives. Countless details escape our attention often because we don't recognise what we see. Are we aware of the angels in our temple or even the angels we meet in daily life? As the author of The Letter to the Hebrews said,

Do not neglect to show hospitality to strangers, for by doing that some have entertained angels without knowing it. Heb 13:2

Our purpose is to become more aware of the reality in which we live. As we develop ourselves we become ready to experience the work of the angels whose only task it is to assist us with our higher awareness. They are "robed in pure bright linen, and their breasts girded with golden girdles". In other words, they leave the *naos,* the inner shrine of the temple, wearing the priestly linen which is not bright but rather shiningly luminous, *lampros,* and adorned with golden girdles.

The Greek word for girdle is *zone* and would perhaps suggest a level of achievement or a zone of consciousness. In fact, the consciousness of angels can be likened to our spiritual consciousness, that level of consciousness we can reach when our soul is awakened on all levels (or in all its zones) and we are able to activate our Spirit Self, that region just above our soul where images come to life - just as these images live in John's mind.

We are called to be much more aware of all that operates in our lives. When we are faced with difficulties we must observe, observe, observe and leave all judgement aside – for how can we know all that contributes to a situation when we are not fully conscious of angels or past life circumstances or even the state of our own inner development. If we don't know what to make of a situation then one good thing to do would be to ask our guardian angel for advice. This is one way that our being can be filled with the glory of God.

After this I looked, and the temple of the tent of witness in heaven was opened, and out of the temple came the seven angels with the seven plagues, robed in pure bright linen, and their breasts girded with golden girdles. And one of the four living creatures gave the seven angels seven golden bowls full of the wrath of God; and the temple was filled with smoke from the glory of God and from his power, and no one could enter the temple until the seven plagues of the seven angels were ended. Rev 15:5-8

Is this smoke a smoke-screen to protect us from the glory of God and his power? Do we think about what it would be like to see God? Could we withstand it? Or is the smoke indicating the presence of fire, purifying fire which burns away everything to make room for new growth?

We should also ask which God John might be referring to. He may just be referring to the higher spiritual beings, which, from our perspective, are so far above us we can call them gods. He does mention the word power which in the Greek is *dunamis*, and Dunamis are the spiritual beings whose task it is to preside over all motion in the cosmos. They give motion to the forms that are created by the beings just below them, the Elohim. It is the Elohim who are called God in the first verse of Genesis as discussed in Chapter 2 of these reflections - "In the beginning Elohim created the heavens and the earth." Gen 1:1

The presence of wrath definitely indicates a meeting with beings higher than ourselves, beings who have purified themselves in previous times. When we have reached a certain level of purity we are able to see how we have underperformed. We need to be strong enough to be able to look at the ways in which we have missed the mark. Missing the mark is actually the right way to speak about sin. We sin when we are not able to act according to the creative intent of the cosmos.

When this happens there is darkness in our being. Love is obscured because we have not been able to experience and express the pure love that is the very expression of our I AM. This means that love appears to us as wrath. As we become increasingly able to express our I AM, even some of the time, then we are able to withstand the purity of love, this experience creates light in our being. This is the glory of God. Glory in Greek is *doxa* or illumination and this light is the outward appearance of the purity of love.

God is also the being who epitomises oneness, there is no duality. This is also the nature of our I AM. We experience this I AM nature when we are able to make individuality of the duality within us. Hence there are no divisions within us or among us. For if we see God at work in self and others we cannot be divided within self, or from others, we are at one. John speaks about this in his first Letter.

Beloved, let us love one another; for love is of God, and he who loves is born of God and knows God. He who does not love does not know God; for God is love. 1 Jn 4:7-8

If we are to purify our love then one of the best places to start is to refrain from liking some things and not liking other things. This antipathy and sympathy that is so ingrained in modern life keeps us from experiencing our I AM. Like and dislike is primarily anchored in our opinions which are, for the most part, misguided. If we become very conscious of the basis for our opinions we quickly realise that they are based on hearsay and half formed ideas. These opinions keep us from knowing truth because when we have opinions we rest on them. Only when we are open to knowing more do we realise that our opinions do not encompass the whole truth, only the part of it that we have been exposed to so far. Perhaps we can't bear the whole truth just as we can't bear the presence of God, and for that matter the presence of our I AM.

We can make good progress in this task if we resolve to resist having opinions about things. Each time an opinion forms in our minds we could ask ourselves if we are fully informed about the issue we are forming our opinion about. Perhaps we could say that there is too much smoke around the issue for us to see it clearly. Perhaps God is at work and obscures reasons and motives from us. The fact remains that each time we suspend an opinion we will have a bit more of the glory and power of God in our temple, in the inner shine of our being, our *naos*.

CHAPTER SIXTEEN

The Seven Bowls of Wrath continued

Then I heard a loud voice from the temple telling the seven angels, "Go and pour out on the earth the seven bowls of the wrath of God." So the first angel went and poured his bowl on the earth, and foul and evil sores came upon the men who bore the mark of the beast and worshiped its image. Rev 16:1-3

The sphere of operation for the first angel is the earth. This could indicate that its task has to do with the physical body. Through its actions diseases appear in the physical bodies of certain people. These people are those who see the human being as a kind of higher animal, in other words, as a beast. This is a hard thing to avoid in a world full of concepts that support this notion. After all, there are many similarities between human beings and animals, but there are also many differences. These differences are not usually recognised because many people are at pains to show how clever and human-like animals are.

The essential difference between human beings and animals is that human beings have individual souls and animals have group souls. To form an idea of what this actually means in terms of functioning in the physical world we need to realise that each human being has the capacity to guide their feelings, thoughts and activity personally (although many people do not take up this option) while animals are guided from the spiritual worlds by their group soul. Hence, dogs chase cats, cats chase mice and so forth. It is the group soul which informs the instinct of the animal to act in certain ways to ensure their survival. It is up to human beings to use their personal soul to inform themselves of the most dignified ways to survive life in this physical world.

Whenever human beings act instinctively they are showing animal tendencies and in so doing they bear the mark of the beast and reveal that they worship its image. For this very reason it is crucial that each human being, of their own accord, becomes more and more aware of the thoughts and feelings that course through their soul. Not only that, but we also need to fully occupy all the thoughts, feelings and intentions of our soul as much as we possibly can.

If there is one prime cause for the increase of disease in the world today it is because people do not take control of all that flows through their souls. These soul forces can be preoccupied with ideas and feelings that should be left alone. On the other hand, our soul's forces can be under occupied leaving them at the disposal of other beings. If we say to a person, "What possessed you to say or do that?" we have recognised a real truth. If the beast finds an 'unoccupied' soul running on auto-pilot, he will take possession of it and make mischief. Whenever our consciousness is lowered through laziness or through stimulants other beings can possess us and express themselves through us.

Our task is to be able to identify all that prevents us from becoming a fully developed human being. There are so many areas where materialistic thinking obscures spiritual concepts. A simple example would be the idea that death is an end instead of a new beginning. We accept that of the plant world, why not of the human being? Why don't we attend funerals to celebrate the beginning of a journey to a new incarnation? It would be of tremendous help to the spirit of the person if we did. By not doing this we create sores, not just for ourselves but for future generations.

We could say that these sores are like cancer. There is increasing evidence that cancer is the result of cells not dying fast enough - rather than multiplying out of control. This supports the notion that we don't let things die, we want to revive that which has passed its use by date. We don't want to move on from certain points in the past and we drag them into the present. This is the mark of the beast. This principle doesn't just apply to events in this life; it also applies to events in past lives which inform our behaviour unconsciously. This is another very good reason to strive to become more conscious of our feelings, thoughts and motives to act.

There are many areas in our souls where cancerous activities take place. We could say that our thoughts are cancerous when we resuscitate past events by thinking about them over and over again. This means that we cannot forgive and forget certain difficult moments in our lives. We don't see that the experience was our opportunity to become more fully human. If we stop and observe the feelings we had when an upsetting event occurs and compare that with how we feel about it today we quickly see that these feelings lessen in intensity over time, yet if we cannot forgive we thereby renew their intensity. This is the how the beast works, taking advantage of an undisciplined will and bringing to life that which should die. Of course, if we don't make use of life's challenging opportunities they will be presented to us again and again until we do. Then we will be very sore indeed.

The second angel poured his bowl into the sea, and it became like the blood of a dead man, and every living thing died that was in the sea. Rev 16:4

The second angel's actions work on our etheric forces. The etheric has an association with the element of water - although, we can never be too prescriptive about this because in other situations water can indicate something else. If we take the sea to mean the etheric environment that surrounds us then it is from this environment that we receive all that enters into us through our senses. The more alive this environment is the more stimulated we are. If we visit a park, for instance, because of all the beautiful plants, which are etheric, our own etheric being is revitalised. The same thing happens when we work on our relationship with Christ, meditating on him and his work in the etheric worlds.

So what is the effect on this etheric environment when it

becomes like the blood of a dead man? The word used here for death is *nekron* which is related to the medical term necrosis. Necrosis is the death of cells in a tissue or organ caused by disease or injury. There is finality about it as there is at the death of a person. When a human being dies, the point of death is when our etheric body is completely disconnected from our physical body. The etheric, life-force completely leaves our body and all that is left is the physical part of us which quickly becomes necrotic.

So when the second angel pours the second bowl of God's wrath it could indicate the removal of the vitality of the etheric environment of the earth. This would have a devastating effect on human life. All those people who depended on this etheric vitality would become shrivelled and depleted like an old apple. On the other hand, all those who had the source of this vitality within them would not be affected. This would indicate how important it is for us to create within us the deepest possible relationship with the Lamb. Perhaps John is suggesting that if we are always looking outside ourselves for this sustenance then, at some point, the supply will dry up.

The next phrase is mistranslated, "and every living thing died that was in the sea." *kai pasa psuche zoe aphethanen* should read 'and all soul life died' - p*suche* is soul and *zoe* is life. *Zoe* is that etheric life-force that is infused with the forces of our I AM. In other words, the etheric presence of Christ infuses into our own etheric force placing it at the disposal of our higher being. The Greek word for died is *aphethanen* and speaks about renewal, the passing over to a new phase.

So again there are two options. Those who have worked on awakening their soul and connecting with their 'I' will benefit from the death of their soul life because there will be an immediate resurrection of their faculties of feeling, thinking and will, they will be raised to their higher expression; Imagination, Inspiration and Intuition. Those who have not developed an awareness of the activity of their soul will be thrown back into their instincts, which is the realm of the beast. While we might hope that the first option is open to us, witnessing those who are subject to the second option will be most painful. We will be virtually helpless to change the situation because we can't develop another person's spiritual consciousness for them, each one of us must do it for ourselves. It is pointless thinking that we can teach others, we can't! We can only 'teach' ourselves through striving to become more aware of what lies right before our eyes. In this way we are the example.

As with all sacred texts many meanings can be hidden within the words. God's wrath has to do with our karma. We associate our karma with all that is unpleasant, yet each karmic situation we encounter gives us the opportunity to achieve our goal of becoming more conscious. It could be that this passage is also saying that the activity of the angel, by pouring God's wrath into our etheric body, will kill our connection to karmic memories that we haven't been able to free ourselves from. Again we can see that it has to do with our preparedness to have these experiences. It is up to us to experience the work of the angels as helpful or hindering, as love or wrath. If we think that we could be let off lightly we are mistaken. We will still have to do the work of releasing ourselves, it might just happen more quickly – but only if we are aware of what is taking place.

There are some other considerations here because John has seen the connection with the blood. On one level blood binds us to some people at the exclusion of others. Christ poured out his blood as an act of inclusion; he didn't keep it to himself and his favoured ones. He made it available to all thereby showing us that we have the possibility of uniting with everyone beyond race or creed. We can move beyond our family or tribal blood ties, beyond our karmic ties of whether people please us or displease us to embrace all human beings as kindred spirits. This has to become a real experience for us, not just something we say we will do. Each time we reject others, or feel rejected by them, we live in the environment of the blood of a dead man.

The third angel poured his bowl into the rivers and the fountains of water, and they became blood. And I heard the angel of water say, "Just art thou in these thy judgments, thou who art and wast, O Holy One. For men have shed the blood of saints and prophets, and thou hast given them blood to drink. It is their due!" And I heard the altar cry, "Yea, Lord God the Almighty, true and just are thy judgments!" Rev 16:4-7

We can apply the work of the third angel to the sphere of the human astral force. To get a picture of this region of our being it is helpful to think about the many differences between plants and animals. It is in our plant-like being that the second angel is active; the etheric region. An important difference between our plant-like being and our animal-like being is our red blood.

In our astral being we experience our desires flowing like rivers and rising up like fountains of water. We must guide them in the most dignified possible way. In this sense, blood is the vehicle of our earthly desires. It is also the vehicle for the fourth member of our being, our 'I', so then it is a question of which one has the greater influence.

When considering this third sphere we could take it to mean not just the astral part of our being but our whole soul. For human beings form their soul out of their astral substance. As we ennoble feeling, thinking and will they become differentiated from our general astral being to form the specific regions of our soul's activity. The more automatic and less conscious our feeling, thinking and will are, the more they are associated with our untamed astral. Here instincts are more strongly at work driven by desires that rise up from the depths of our physical body.

Since this area of our being is akin to the animal kingdom we can say that human beings can act like animals at times. Although it might be more accurate to refer to instinctive human behaviour as sub-human for animal behaviour can often be more dignified than a human being driven by base instinct.

Since the vehicle for our desires is our blood then it is our task to purify our blood. We can do this in a twofold way; by giving dignity to our desires and at the same time working to incorporate our 'I' into our soul. When we are able to achieve this we join the fraternity of saints and prophets.

The blood of the saints and the prophets has been poured out (not shed by men) and those who have been found worthy can drink it. This is the grail cup from which we can drink so that our blood may contain the blood of Christ. What a wonderful notion that those who do the work of purifying their basic astral nature contribute to the 'supply' of Christed blood.

So we might wonder how we can be part of this redemptive work. John gives us the clue in his use of the word judgment. Our judgments need to be true and right yet today we could say that many judgments are based on unconscious instincts. These judgments usually arise from what pleases us and what doesn't please us. This is the kind of oscillation that takes place in our unconscious soul levels. It is neither true nor right (just).

There is an alarming trend in the media today to give people the option of voting on current issues. They ask people whether they agree or disagree with various controversies. This is the work of the beast that empowers people by enabling them to judge without any knowledge of the background to the issue nor knowing the people involved. Only when our blood is alive with the activity of our 'I' and the presence of Christ can we fully see into an issue in a true and right way. Then we will understand the motive behind people's actions and our inclination to judge will disappear.

True, *alethes,* means 'overcoming forgetting', then things are no longer hidden, they no longer escape our notice. Just, *dikaios,* means righteous or as it was earlier used: rightwise, in a straight way. Whenever we are drawn to make judgments we can ask ourselves if there could be something we have forgotten and whether we are taking the straight way.

In the actions of the third angel we can see all the elements of the Last Supper and the deed of Christ. Our challenge is to shake off all our religious notions and its association with today's church and realise that we are now the altar and the consecration takes place within us. Our blood becomes Christ's blood; we ingest his blood which he poured out into this world at the crucifixion. We each have to find a way to make this a reality in the daily moments of our life. Perhaps if we think of ourselves as a sacred altar and see the sacred altar in others, we will hear the inner voice "Yea, Lord God the Almighty (I AM), true and just are thy judgments!" Then we will reach the point where judgment loses the power it has previously had for us. Now it is filled with understanding and the love that is the very substance of the I AM. Then we see the love not the illusory wrath of God.

The fourth angel poured his bowl on the sun, and it was allowed to scorch men with fire; men were scorched by the fierce heat, and they cursed the name of God who had power over these plagues, and they did not repent and give him glory. Rev 16:8-9

The sun is the home of the Cosmic Christ, the one who descended from the heights of heaven into the body of the man Jesus. This is the mighty deed that made it possible for us to connect with our I-being. In this sphere we find the fourth angel at work.

The sun is also the domain of the Exousia, the powers who we can assume are indicated by the words "God who had power over these plagues". These Exousia work through heat and the Greek word for scorched is *kaumatiza* from *kauma* which means heat. It is through the work of the Exousia that we receive into ourselves this fourth member of our being, our 'I'. It is up to us to make it welcome and the only way to welcome it is for our astral / soul being to embrace it.

This is not an easy mission for our 'I' is bigger than our experience of ourselves. Our 'I' encompasses eternity, incarnation after incarnation; we only experience the present. Our 'I' is "thou who art and wast, O Holy One" and while it experiences our life we have to come to experience it.

We could say that for as long as it cannot enter our being and our consciousness, as long as it rays into us from outside, we will be scorched. As long as the untamed desires of our astral rule in our being we will be scorched. So how do we facilitate its approach? One way is to be more aware of what works against it. One particular area is the human expression of egotism. At its extreme our egotism is displayed as an exaggerated sense of self-importance and a feeling of superiority. Not that we should swing to the other pole and become self-effacing, far from it! We should endeavour to allow others to experience who we are rather than engage in self-promotion. Or on the other hand hide who we are through fear that others will intrude – this is also egotism.

At the same time we must give egotism its rightful place. It has an important role in our development, among other things it gives us the courage to stand on our own feet and achieve our potential through the expression of our 'I' given talents. However, we often allow it too much influence thereby placing it at the disposal of the beast. This is especially the case when today we hear human beings say that they have all the answers. Why is it so hard for people to say that they don't fully know and would like to engage in dialogue with others in the hope of coming to a greater understanding together?

What isn't fully grasped is that there are limits to the rational mind which prevent us from fully understanding a thing. We need our spiritual faculties of Imagination, Inspiration and Intuition to know truth. These faculties can only become active through our 'I', then we are willing to set our ideas aside, the ideas that we formed with our rational mind. This too is like allowing the sun to shine within us instead of it beating down on us and scorching us. Indeed, our own ideas can result in some very heated discussions.

In our contemplation of the work of the fourth angel it is helpful to consider what John recorded in chapter 7.

...the sun shall not strike them, nor any scorching heat. For the Lamb in the midst of the throne will be their shepherd, and he will guide them to springs of living water; and God will wipe away every tear from their eyes." Rev 7:16-17

The presence within us of the Lamb, the risen Christ, means that the sun and the heat are within us, so of course they "shall not strike us" from outside. We must become aware of this Lamb/shepherd – notice that the Lamb has become self-shepherding, no longer needing the external shepherd. Awareness of the presence of the Lamb is absolutely necessary if our 'I' is to dock safely. There are many examples in the world today of those who have discovered the power of their 'I' at the exclusion of the Lamb.

For the most part we do not really understand the intensity of our I AM. In chapter 1 we explored the word tribulation which means that something presses upon us. Our I AM, the fullness of our I-being is pressing upon us and we must try not to resist. In our soul we feel threatened, as if an alien is taking us over. We try to defend ourselves by clinging to our astral levels and we become polarised between love and hate – this is the base mood of the unconscious soul. When we hate we curse. We could even go so far as to say that we like to hate, it empowers us. It is as if we need the resistance of the "other side" to feel good about ourselves. Isn't this the mood at sporting events? It is also the mood of our soul in many of our interactions in life. When we become conscious of the self-shepherding Lamb we stand in the middle of any polarity. We can see both sides but we don't stand in one or the other.

Then we can repent, *metanoeo*, which literally means to perceive afterwards. We can see the results of our actions before we act. We can also bear the results of our past actions and every tear will be wiped from our eyes.

> **The fifth angel poured his bowl on the throne of the beast, and its kingdom was in darkness; men gnawed their tongues in anguish and cursed the God of heaven for their pain and sores, and did not repent of their deeds. Rev 16:10-11**

We can apply the work of the next three angels to the development of the three spiritual faculties; Imagination, Inspiration and Intuition. These three faculties are elevated thinking, feeling and will (in that order). It is with these faculties that we live into the higher worlds and begin to grasp spiritual truth. It is when we are able to engage our 'I' consciously in our lives that these faculties begin to stir and we resist them at our peril.

Imagination is higher thinking, a thinking that does not rely on the outer stimulation that comes from whatever we perceive. Nor is this Imagination a fuzzy vision. Imagination arises when we are able to concentrate sufficiently that our mental images come alive. Mostly this does not happen because we are lazy in our thinking. These living mental images can arise when we focus on an idea, perhaps to solve a problem, and in our concentrated effort the idea seems to take on a life of its own. This does not happen in the abstract, logical, linear thinking that we use throughout the day. The ideas that come to us each day are based on what we know – which can have its limits.

In spiritual Imagination it is as if our thought life frees itself from our body and then becomes active. It is through such active ideas that inventions arise or new understandings are reached. While we remain engaged with the logical thoughts that arise 'below' in our soul, we are more likely to reject new ideas. It is when we can step over the boundaries of our soul and participate in mobile Imaginations, into which the spiritual worlds play, that we can be open to new ideas. This then means that we have developed the courage to explore options that never occurred to us previously. In our soul we can be limited; in our spirit we don't experience the same boundaries.

John's description of the fifth angel could be describing what a frightening experience it would be if our faculty of Imagination became active without being prepared for it – it could be like a waking dream. All the levels of human thinking, feeling and will require a delicate balance between body, soul and spirit. When there is a lack of balance mental aberrations arise which we are seeing today in the rise of mental problems.

We could say that the throne of the beast is our thinking. In our being we provide this throne for the beast when we do not rule over our own thinking. Ruling over our thinking means that we allow our ideas to come to life. As long as they have no life, which is the case while we focus on a materialistic view of the world, then we live in an illusion. While we do not seek to understand human spiritual life we dwell in the dark kingdom of the beast and we provide him with a throne in our soul.

Furthermore, as long as we do not strive to develop our faculty of Imagination we will experience anguish. We could liken it to a pregnant woman refusing to release her baby from her womb. As pregnancy must lead to the birth of a child, so our thinking must lead to Imagination. John seems to be suggesting that it could be as painful.

One way we can train our thinking to make the transition to Imagination is to use our will to create an image in our mind, and then to erase it. The more we can do this the more flexible and unlimited our soul will be. So we could create an image of this pregnant woman and then dismiss it from our mind. What usually happens is that it comes back immediately. Our ability to dismiss the idea from our mind indicates the strength of our will.

There are echoes of the prologue of the John's Gospel in John's description of the work of the fifth angel.

In the beginning was the Word, ... all things were made through him (the Word) ... In him was life, and the life was the light of men. The light shines in the darkness, and the darkness has not overcome it. Jn 1:1-5

Could this creative Word, which makes all things, come from the ideas that we express? If this is so then what kind of a world are we creating with the words that we speak, as well as the words that express the ideas that we form in our mind? Obviously more light will shine from Imaginative ideas. Imagination is connected with beauty in contrast to the sense of ugliness in this description of the work of the fifth angel. It is our choice to give the beast a throne in our being or to allow the light of our Imagination to create a world of beauty.

When John says that "men (us) gnawed their tongues in anguish and cursed the God of heaven for their pain and sores, and did not repent of their deeds" he is indicating that if we remain focussed on our own sores and pain we will never see the effects of our deeds. This means that we don't have the courage to face our karma so why would we repent? The faculty of Imagination releases us from the bonds of karma and gives us the opportunity to move forward into the light.

The sixth angel poured his bowl on the great river Euphra'tes, and its water was dried up, to prepare the way for the kings from the east. And I saw, issuing from the mouth of the dragon and from the mouth of the beast and from the mouth of the false prophet, three foul spirits like frogs; for they are demonic spirits, performing signs, who go abroad to the kings of the whole world, to assemble them for battle on the great day of God the Almighty. ("Lo, I am coming like a thief! Blessed is he who is awake, keeping his garments that he may not go naked and be seen exposed!") And they assembled them at the place which is called in Hebrew Armaged'don. Rev 16:12-16

The sixth phase of our development has to do with Inspiration; the inspiring or in breathing of spiritual truth. We become aware of this Inspiration when it 'speaks' within us, when we hear our inner voice. Of course, we can only hear this voice if we are still and quiet within. This could be what is meant by the drying up of the Euphrates. This river is the longest and most important river in South West Asia and its name means to break forth. We could say that the most prominent part of our being is our emotions, our feeling levels, and as we know they often break forth.

Our task is to purify the feeling levels and prevent them from dominating our soul. The inner voice can only rise up on the wings of our purified feelings freed from their lower expression. These feelings then assume their highest role in our being which is to confirm the truth of what we hear. Then we are not misled by the dragon, the beast and the false prophet who constantly try to drown out our inner voice.

John's description of the activity of the sixth angel echoes some facets of the story of Moses as he tries to free his people from Egypt – which is also the story of the human journey. Moses removed water to make a way for people to pass and Moses and Aaron used frogs to plague the Pharaoh who at that time was one of the kings of the world.

At the same time there are references to the life of Jesus; kings of the rising sun (literal Greek) suggest the three magi who attended the birth of Jesus. The issuing from the mouth of foul demonic spirits is suggestive of the power Jesus had to heal. Luke describes this.

And they were all amazed and said to one another, "What is this word? For with authority and power he commands the unclean spirits, and they come out. Luke 4:36

And then the reference to the thief which describes what to expect when we connect up with our I-being. Peter spoke of this in his Letter, "But the day of the Lord (the 'I') will come like a thief," 2Peter3:10. John also spoke of it in chapter three.

If you will not awake, I will come like a thief, and you will not know at what hour I will come upon you. Rev 3:3

Of course the story of the Israelites led by Moses is one of preparation and purification to produce a human being so pure as to be able to withstand the power of the Cosmic Christ. We should never underestimate just what this involved. In so doing Jesus opened up the possibility for all human beings to have access to their individual I-being, before that we were only soul beings who had to be led by external rulers like pharaohs and kings. This ability for self-guidance should also not be underestimated. Whenever we seek guidance it is not to others that we should go, but rather to enter into the silence of our inner being and listen to our own spiritual Inspiration.

This is not always easy because we have to deal with the plagues within our consciousness, the slimy frogs that leap and croak in every corner of our being. They can represent our lower astral nature that jumps from one thing to the next looking for nourishment instead of being nourished by the spiritual gift received from the deed of Christ Jesus, the gift of accessing our 'I'.

We will only fully experience what this means if we assemble "at the place which is called in Hebrew Armaged'don." In Greek, Armageddon is *Har Magedon* which means mountain of Megiddo or mountain rendezvous or meeting place. A mountain indicates higher consciousness and this is where all the forces within us must meet. We will take our garments to this meeting; all the layers of our being clothed in the pure light of all our striving. Our journey, which is our biography, has taught us how to bear the shame of nakedness so that we no longer see ourselves as naked and exposed, we only see the garments that we are creating.

The seventh angel poured his bowl into the air, and a loud voice came out of the temple, from the throne, saying, "It is done!" And there were flashes of lightning, voices, peals of thunder, and a great earthquake such as had never been since men were on the earth, so great was that earthquake. The great city was split into three parts, and the cities of the nations fell, and God remembered great Babylon, to make her drain the cup of the fury of his wrath. And every island fled away, and no mountains were to be found; and great hailstones, heavy as a hundred-weight, dropped on men from heaven, till men cursed God for the plague of the hail, so fearful was that plague. Rev 16:17-21

We have been exploring how each of the seven angels reveals details about the seven stages of the developing human consciousness. This development depends entirely on our ability to deal with our karma. The whole point of karma is for us to become more and more conscious and in this way we redeem ourselves. When it comes to karma we have two choices; drown in the pain of it or find its secret key to freedom. Only when we are able to become the interested observer of our lives, only when we can observe the events in our lives –good or bad - as if they were happening to someone else, will we be able to understand the work of the seven angels.

The seventh angel's work has to do with the faculty of spiritual Intuition which can only become active through our purified will. It is only through pure will that we can maintain equanimity in the face of difficulty. We see this ability in Jesus when he passed through the crucifixion. The loud voice coming from the throne in our temple speaks to us of the one who rules their will. The words "It is done" are parallel to the words of Jesus from the cross when he accomplished his deed.

When Jesus had received the vinegar, he said, "It is finished"; and he bowed his head and gave up his spirit. Jn 19:30

The spiritual insight that comes to us when our spiritual Intuition is active requires that we die to the materialistic view of the world that by its nature excludes spiritual knowledge. Spiritual knowledge is not just about reading spiritual books and acknowledging that there is such a thing as spiritual knowledge. To have spiritual knowledge means to live by the principles of the spiritual world which are often opposite to the principles in society today. When we live by spiritual principles all our actions, all our deeds, which proceed from our will, are done with love. This spiritual love, *agape*, loves everyone equally without fear or favour. It is never motivated by the greed of what will advantage us. This love also recognises the creative work of all spiritual beings both good and bad.

This love is strong, it has to be, because the experience spiritual Intuition means that we enter into things and understand them from within **them**. Imagine entering into an angel, or a crocodile or a violent criminal to fully understand their role in creation? Strength of will is mandatory so that we don't feel overwhelmed. We also need strength to let go of ourselves, of our possessive nature which often wants to cling to pain, anger, opinion, and so on; and in this surrender we experience true selflessness. We don't lose our sense of self, we experience a deep inner sharing – we know and we are known.

John's whole vision of the work of the seventh angel speaks of strength and of the will. "flashes of lightning, voices, peals of thunder" are indications that our 'I' is flashing into our being causing interference. Our habitual method of operating is split into three, all the habitual ways we think, feel and act now work separately, disturbed by this wild weather, and it is up to us to combine them appropriately. This is like having to remember how to drive a car each time we get behind the wheel. Nothing happens automatically anymore, each thought must purposefully be accompanied by the right amount of feeling, each action with the right amount of thought and so on.

One way to strengthen our ability to do this is to focus on some situation, perhaps some story we hear in the news or hear from a friend, and to intensify our feelings about it, then to let our feelings drop back and thoroughly think through all the aspects of the situation. While we do this we can experience the shift in our will as we change direction. By coming to know how our thoughts form, the flow of our feelings, and the force of our will, we can deal with the karmic situations of life differently. Instinctual responses are replaced with considered responses and we become self-informed.

Essentially, with our strength of will we are able to raise our Imaginations and Inspirations to conscious awareness – this is true Intuition. We look at each of these stages individually but we should always be mindful of how they stream together in our consciousness. Of course, the development of our consciousness is a work in progress for in evolutionary terms we are not at the point where we can have this kind of consciousness consistently. However, we do experience it sometimes, in those flashes of knowing that come to us during the day. The only way we can withstand the wild weather that is coming our way, as John reveals, is to prepare now.

The seventh angel poured his bowl into the air, and a loud voice came out of the temple, from the throne, saying, "It is done!" And there were flashes of lightning, voices, peals of thunder, and a great earthquake such as had never been since men were on the earth, so great was that earthquake. The great city was split into three parts, and the cities of the nations fell, and God remembered great Babylon, to make her drain the cup of the fury of his wrath. And every island fled away, and no mountains were to be found; and great hailstones, heavy as a hundred-weight, dropped on men from heaven, till men cursed God for the plague of the hail, so fearful was that plague. Rev 16:17-21

If God remembers great Babylon doesn't this suggest the possibility that God could forget? How would it be possible for God, who is meant to be omniscient (all knowing), to forget?

Perhaps another God is meant here, perhaps the creator Gods from Genesis, the Elohim or *Exousia* as they are called in Greek. It is good to contemplate creativity in the universe and also to realise that we human beings also have a role to play in it. In fact, it is becoming critical that human beings take responsibility for what they can, and do, create.

One way to get a sense of cosmic creativity is to consider how we undertake a creative task, for example, if we were to create a garden. In our imagination we see the garden then, from this image, we work out what materials will be needed and what effort is required from us. We will decide on the focal point and choose plants to complement it. As we begin our work it will become clear that we will need to wait until the plants grow before our garden matches our image. We will also realise that the garden may differ from the image; we may have difficulty with the soil in some parts, some plants may not be suited to the position, and the prevailing weather will affect the growth of the plants. Years later, as we enjoy our garden, we will remember how we started, by preparing its focal point. This is like God remembering great Babylon, the centrepiece of his creation.

Babylon represents that point in evolution when human beings gained their independence and became self-reliant. We explored this in Revelation 14:8. To enable us to make our way God placed something special in the centre of our being. This focal point is our ego represented by Babylon. This ego is like a two-edged sword which can be used for good or it can work against us. Not that we should always be concerned with its good side, we must become familiar with its full spectrum. It is only when we fully experience the power of our ego that we are in a position to make helpful rather than harmful choices. Nor is it about outcomes, it is about actually making the choices. If we are never placed in the position to exercise choice we will not be able to be consciously aware and realise our full potential.

The purpose of the ego is to give us a sense of self. From it we experience ourselves as separate beings in the world. A core function of our ego is self-preservation which means that we put ourselves first. This stands at the polar opposite of the highest expression of our ego, which we call our I AM, when we experience ourselves as an individual among fellow individuals. The primary experience of our ego is that it is polarised by love and hate, like and dislike, which by its very nature creates division. On the other hand, our I AM is inclusive and seeks unity regardless of tastes, opinions and biases. Ego will want to impose ideas on others, or stick to its own ideas; I AM will embrace all ideas. From the I AM perspective we have the ability to see all ideas as part of the mosaic of human life, and for that matter cosmic creativity. When we do this the inner voice in our temple will say, "It is done!"

Increasingly in the news today we hear about how the bad things people do can be excused by all the good things they do, or worse, they are excused because they are deemed to be important people in our social structure. It doesn't work like that. To excuse bad behaviour in this way condones it. How does this happen? Basically it arises out of the unconscious experience of the I AM and it highlights the urgent call to consciously connect up with it.

When people are accomplished, when they express their talent, they are working out of their I AM and they are judged to be good people. Bad behaviour and lack of conscience arises out of the ego. This is because we are meant to have moved beyond the basic expressions of our ego by now. If we haven't then the ego can carry human beings into sub-human areas which are an abuse of God's gift. What is happening so often in the world today is that fleeting experiences of the higher ego can give a person a sense of being invincible. These unconscious experiences are then carried into normal life where previous boundaries disappear which means that Babylon then must "drain the cup of the fury of his wrath".

The consequences of this can be understood from John's words when he says, "The great city was split into three parts, and the cities of the nations fell, and God remembered great Babylon," John could be seeing that our being breaks into three disconnected parts; physical, etheric and astral no longer woven together and working towards the higher consciousness of the I AM. This means that physical urges are no longer moderated by the etheric; etheric drives are disconnected from astral desires so that they cannot be satisfied; and astral desires are let loose because the overarching consciousness, represented by the nations, has fallen. The focal point of creation has been abused and instead of taking responsibility for our own development God is cursed and we live in fear. While we can identify this in the lives of some prominent people each day in the news, we should also be able to identify when it occurs it in our own consciousness.

CHAPTER SEVENTEEN

The Judgment of Babylon

Then one of the seven angels who had the seven bowls came and said to me, "Come, I will show you the judgment of the great harlot who is seated upon many waters, with whom the kings of the earth have committed fornication, and with the wine of whose fornication the dwellers on earth have become drunk." Rev 17:1-2

Judgment is a crucial human activity which we use constantly throughout each day to sustain life in our physical body. Judgement is also a faculty of our soul and spirit. We could say that the activity of judging leads to the decisions that we make after we have weighed everything up. Often, however, we make these decisions prematurely. It would be very easy to make premature decisions about the whole of chapter 17 of The Revelation, or any part of the Bible for that matter.

Judgment is often seen as a condemnation and when we condemn something it usually indicates that we are dismissing it. We dismiss so many things far too quickly that should be contemplated deeply to uncover their mystery. Goethe spoke of judgment as a thinking-beholding. He would have meant that aspect of beholding that the Greek refers to as *idou*, seeing beneath the surface, seeing more than the first thing that meets our gaze.

The human activity of judging is a fundamental activity in our soul directly tied to our level of interest in something. What interests us directly depends on what we love or hate. Society avoids using this word 'hate' - it is judged to be a bad word - and in so doing they deny themselves the opportunity of getting in touch with their inner soul nature. By getting in touch with the force of hate in our soul we allow the pendulum to swing fully the other way giving us a deeper experience of love. In this way we can resist the polarisation or duality of love and hate more easily and be more open to the process of thinking-beholding.

In Greek there are four different words for judgment. The word used here is *krima* which means the result of the process of judgement; the process itself is called *krisis*. So in the *krisis* process we separate out all the things to be considered, we weigh them all up, and then, when we feel satisfied, we reach the point of *krima*. *Krisis* is more about the activity of judging, *krima* is about the position we are in following the activity.

So how does this relate to "the judgment of the great harlot"? Babylon is called the great harlot, the whore, the fornicator, which means that our ego got into bed with the wrong forces. If she is seated on many waters this would indicate that she is resting on many emotions and feelings. This happens when our ego refuses to marry the higher faculties in our being and prefers to sleep around with whatever comes easily and naturally. We must never underestimate our ego, it has given us great pleasure, and great independence, but at the same time we mustn't mistake it for *krima* when it is only *krisis;* it is only a step in the process of experiencing our I AM.

We must also admit that we are fornicating with the earth for as long as we do not fully understand the marriage that has taken place in our soul – St John wrote about this in his Gospel when he described the marriage at Cana when the water was turned into wine. Like any marriage, the ceremony is a new beginning in a relationship. All relationships depend on the deepest possible understanding of the parties in the relationship. So we could ask ourselves how deeply we understand our soul. Are our judgments a process or a series of premature opinions? The kings of the earth are opinions, they are everywhere. If you haven't got an opinion, and it doesn't matter if it doesn't agree with other opinions, you are nobody. Scan the press to see how many conflicting opinions there are about the global financial crisis, for instance. We could ask what they have been drinking to make such wildly divergent statements, and what they are doing is definitely fornication.

Only those who work diligently to acquaint themselves with the activity of their soul, and to understand how it is now married to their I AM, will see that the role of Babylon, the ego, was like an engagement prior to marriage. Who would go back to being engaged after they were married? This marriage in our soul means that now we must satisfy our desires differently.

We become aware of these desires through our feelings. They flow towards us from the future on the promise of satisfaction. They are one side of a spiral which meets the other spiral from our past experiences of what it is like to experience satisfaction. When these two spirals meet we have the opportunity to become conscious of desires in the present. The question is; how conscious are we of them? Only when we spend the time to adequately judge our desires will we satisfy them in the right way. Otherwise they will be the many waters on which we are seated. All our desires which have never been fully satisfied will gnaw at us as wishes and longings. We cannot experience the satisfaction we yearn for while we remain entangled in this earth and in our ego without fully thinking-beholding our spiritual being and our consciousness.

And he carried me away in the Spirit into a wilderness, and I saw a woman sitting on a scarlet beast which was full of blasphemous names, and it had seven heads and ten horns. The woman was arrayed in purple and scarlet, and bedecked with gold and jewels and pearls, holding in her hand a golden cup full of abominations and the impurities of her fornication; and on her forehead was written a name of mystery: "Babylon the great, mother of harlots and of earth's abominations." And I saw the woman, drunk with the blood of the saints and the blood of the martyrs of Jesus. When I saw her I marveled greatly. Rev 17:3-6

There are parallels here with the woman we met in chapter 12.

And a great portent appeared in heaven, a woman clothed

with the sun, with the moon under her feet, and on her head a crown of twelve stars; she was with child and she cried out in her pangs of birth, in anguish for delivery. And another portent appeared in heaven; behold, a great red dragon, with seven heads and ten horns, and seven diadems upon his heads. Rev 12:1-3

Like two pillars we could place these women at each end of creation. One adorned by the cosmos, the other adorned with the gifts of the earth; one producing a child, the other producing a cup of abominations and impurities; one crying out in pain, the other drunk.

The word abomination is interesting; *bdelugma*. It is used in Titus 1:16 about those who profess to know God (or spiritual truth) but deny him by their deeds. In the spiritual economy our commitment to our spiritual development must be accompanied by deliberate actions based on what we learn until they become an integral part of us. Otherwise it is like a gardener describing what he has planted in his garden but nothing ever grows there.

Babylon, representing the great gift of human ego, can also stand for the egotistical human trait of the know-all. When spiritual truth begins to be revealed to those who pursue it, perhaps accompanied by a sense of the existence of God, the immediate experience is the realisation of how little we actually know. Confirmation that we have begun to grasp spiritual truth comes when we are able to handle this sense of knowing little but being patiently determined to know more. For some people this sense of not knowing defeats them.

This woman has reached a certain level in her spiritual development, she has received her rewards; she has gold and jewels and she also has pearls which indicate that she has overcome difficulties coating them with her dedication to her Higher Self. Her achievement stands as a reminder to us that we can drink from the cup, which is meant to contain the blood of Christ, but if this experience is wrongly motivated then we will become drunk. The drunk is the one who is unconscious. Alcohol causes our astral body to separate from our etheric body leaving us with a plant-like dreamy consciousness. We make unwise decisions using this hazy consciousness and we stagger about because we no longer have access to that part of our being which regulates our mobility.

There is so much to contemplate in these verses of The Revelation. Just like the woman in chapter 12 who "fled into the wilderness, where she has a place prepared by God," John is "taken away in Spirit into a wilderness" to be shown this image. A wilderness is a place undisturbed by human activity which means that the human will has not interfered with it. Now, the greatest gift that accompanies the human ego is the freedom to use our will. Each time we use our will we must have thought it through thoroughly. The beast with seven heads and ten horns points to a lack of balance; heads represent thinking and horns represent the will.

And doesn't it seem strange for John to say, "And seeing her I wondered *thauma* a great wonder"? True wonder is felt by those whose soul has been awakened from its dreamy automation. The experience of wonder is accompanied by an experience of spiritual truth. The wonder rings within us to confirm that we see again something we already knew deep within our being. John sees the panorama of all creation; he sees how it all works together for a purpose. He understands the true meaning of judgment, to see the potential in everything.

The harlot is not the subject of moral judgment; she is the one who does what she likes regardless of the spiritual principles she knows. There is a sense that she is too lazy to continue with her spiritual development. She had a taste of it, some successes, and that was enough.

The vast majority of humanity fall into three categories, they get drunk on the taste of spiritual truth, or they are too lazy to investigate and apply it in their lives, or they lack the courage to explore it in the first place. Understanding spiritual principles requires diligence, it requires an open mind and a trust that the unexplained can be revealed to us if we truly long for it. Our challenge is to enter into a wilderness untouched by our egotistical will.

But the angel said to me, "Why marvel? I will tell you the mystery of the woman, and of the beast with seven heads and ten horns that carries her. The beast that you saw was, and is not, and is to ascend from the bottomless pit and go to perdition; and the dwellers on earth whose names have not been written in the book of life from the foundation of the

world, will marvel to behold the beast, because it was and is not and is to come. This calls for a mind with wisdom: the seven heads are seven mountains on which the woman is seated; they are also seven kings, five of whom have fallen, one is, the other has not yet come, and when he comes he must remain only a little while. As for the beast that was and is not, it is an eighth but it belongs to the seven, and it goes to perdition. Rev 17:7-11

How interesting to read that the seven heads are both mountains and kings. It shows that we cannot be definitive when interpreting the meaning of sacred words. It also suggests that we probably should always be open to new ways of looking at things. If we have the courage to be open, and it takes courage because we have to step off the solid foundation of our own ideas, the new ideas that we receive can be surprising.

So then we must ask: why seven heads, mountains and kings? These mountains could be phases of development that we must conquer; they could also represent our will. The heads suggest that the conquering would be done in the area of our thinking. Then each phase has a king, a ruler – which could be good or bad - and when we reach the top we find Babylon already there. We will always find Babylon, our ego, in all our endeavours. Without our ego we would not have the strength to conquer a thing. The role that Babylon plays is entirely up to us and since our emotions and feelings lie at the core of our ego this is no easy task.

The angel is going to great lengths to reveal the full nature of Babylon. Perhaps the message is that we must also go to great lengths to know our own ego. This is not a comfortable thing to do however. It means that we must face our less attractive characteristics. It is our ego that wants to win, and winning can make it necessary to tread on it in order to be victorious. We are always dealing with our karma when we feel the urge to prevail over others. By becoming acquainted with our ego we begin to see that we needn't always win and that we are not always right. Admitting that we are wrong and admitting defeat are some of the hardest things to do in life. Unless we are able to admit that we are wrong and experience defeat we are also admitting that we do not know our own ego.

So scaling the mountain will bring out all our weaknesses, the more we try to hide them the more we will lose our footing. The bottomless pit, as it suggests, is a never ending fall and the beast is there in its 'is-not' state before it returns and is destroyed. So the beast is a temporary thing unlike the lamb "who is and who was and who is to come" meaning that he is eternal.

We give too much value to what is temporary in life. Like the phases of a growing plant we must see that each step is only a temporary stage in the scheme of things. This sense of the timing of stages that arises out of the angels words is like the words in Ecclesiastes.

For everything there is a season, and a time for every matter under heaven: a time to be born, and a time to die; a time to plant, and a time to pluck up what is planted; a time to kill, and a time to heal; a time to break down, and a time to build up; Ec 3:1-3

The one who recognises their ego for what it is will be willing to let it die so that their I AM can be born in their being. This is not just one death; it is a continual series of little deaths in every area of life and in all areas of our consciousness. Our goal is be able to see the spiritual content of the cosmos which, we are told, is obscured by the woman reclining on the seven mountains. We must continue to climb each mountain, five have fallen - have been conquered. If we don't keep moving on we will contribute to the eighth false phase created by the beast. From the peak of the fifth would we want to go back to the third or fourth mountain? Yet this is how many people think. They experience so much discomfort from the effort of coming to know their ego that they want to preserve the past. They "marvel to behold the beast, because it was and is not and is to come" like a magicians trick which brings back a past condition.

Only from the mountain top, where we can be the observer of our life, the interested onlooker who doesn't get caught up in the minor details, will we walk with the Lamb and claim our name that is written in the book of life.

And the ten horns that you saw are ten kings who have not yet received a kingdom, but they are to receive authority as kings for one hour, together with the beast. These are united in yielding their power and authority to the beast; they will make war on the Lamb, and the Lamb will conquer them, for he is Lord of lords and King of kings, and those with him are called and chosen and faithful." And he said to me, "The waters that you saw, where the whore is seated, are peoples and multitudes and nations and languages. And the ten horns that you saw, they and the beast will hate the whore; they will make her desolate and naked; they will devour her flesh and burn her up with fire. For God has put it into their hearts to carry out his purpose by agreeing to give their kingdom to the beast, until the words of God will be fulfilled. The woman you saw is the great city that rules over the kings of the earth." Rev 17:12-18

The angel continues to interpret the mystery and seems to know a lot about the situation that John sees. Rudolf Steiner suggests that this angel is actually Lucifer who feels vindicated because he didn't want human beings to enter into the earth in the first place. He wanted us to stand still in the past and stay in the spiritual worlds which meant that we wouldn't progress and would never experience freedom. It is this freedom that actually causes all the trouble as Lucifer well knows. This state that Babylon is in is evidence of unrestrained freedom but inherently it is an opportunity to move forward.

If we take the horn-kings to represent human will and its potential to be ruled we get a hint of what is in store. Perhaps we could find 10 different expressions of the will, or 10 major tests for the proper development of our will. The angel says that our experience of our will is like a king without a kingdom which suggests that we have yet to earn the right to rule it. If Babylon is anything to go by then things may hang in the balance. What John describes carries a great warning. However, we shouldn't worry about anything being inflicted on us, our greatest concern is about our own ability to spiritualise our whole being. In a nutshell, this story suggests that we must not allow our emotions and feelings to dominate our thinking and our will. Yet they do in so many ways, particularly when we speak before we think blurting out what unconsciously rises up within us. Our Babylon-emotions will pave the way for a mighty war within our being.

Receiving authority as kings for an hour should not be taken literally. The Greek word for hour is *hora* and indicates a period of time, or a season. During this period of time we will have to endure the primary test for the will which means working with the beast. The Greek doesn't say united, it says they are of one mind. So the kings and the beast agree that they face an endurance test.

Since horns are on the head then we can assume that the battle of the will happens in our thinking and it is to do with the whore, our unrefined emotions. As we wrestle with our will and try to rule over our thoughts and refine our emotions we confront the Lamb. It is as if the Lamb is our sparring partner as we fine tune our skills. This brings to mind the statement of Jesus, "Not my will but thine." Lu 22:42 This is not a diminutive statement about handing ourselves over to a higher power, this is a statement of supremacy over the ego that can be inclined to abuse the gift of freedom. This is about aligning our will with the highest purpose. In fact the whole text from Luke says, "Father, if thou art willing, remove this cup from me; nevertheless not my will, but thine, be done." We have to drink the cup of the conqueror.

In this passage the mention of authority, *exousia*, and power, *dunamis*, alerts us that very high beings are involved in this panorama. Then we read that God himself has enlisted the assistance of the kingdom-less kings and the beast to do his work. The whore is to be hated as she sits on the emotions of the general population of the world. These are the ones who have a group consciousness developed mainly through mindlessly believing the media and the subsequent misinformed opinions of friends and family.

These mysterious statements about how the whore or harlot is treated can make some sense if we allocate them to areas in our being.

One: "they will make her desolate and naked;" Desolate *eremoo* means to become like a desert and a desert is a place where things have difficulty growing. This would indicate that our life-force, our etheric, is depleted. Being naked can mean that we are no longer spiritually attired.

Two: "they will devour her flesh and burn her up with fire." Flesh is *sarkas* and means our astral body where our anger can burn like fire unless we use our will to transform it into love. In this way we raise our emotions up and refine our feelings.

If we do not find the Lamb within us, the conquering Lamb, and face the battles set by God with courage and strength then these are the difficulties that we will experience. It is not up to someone to tell us that we are called, chosen and faithful, we must realise this within ourselves. Nor can we just say to ourselves, "I am called, chosen and faithful"; we have to show that we are, through the love and grace that we express in our lives regardless of the circumstances.

Then one of the seven angels who had the seven bowls came and said to me, "Come, I will show you the judgment of the great harlot who is seated upon many waters, with whom the kings of the earth have committed fornication, and with the wine of whose fornication the dwellers on earth have become drunk." .... And I saw the woman, drunk with the blood of the saints and the blood of the martyrs of Jesus. When I saw her I marveled greatly. .... The woman you saw is the great city that rules over the kings of the earth."Rev 17:1-2, 6 & 18

Before we leave chapter 17 there are a few more things to consider about the chapter as a whole in the light of the modern culture in which we live. What the angel shows John has a lot to say about the present human condition. It speaks loudly about how we are being challenged to develop awareness of our will and the consequences of not doing so.

The first step in this process is to have an understanding of how our own will functions. This is very difficult because we are mostly unaware of the activity of our will. Our will is at work, for instance, when we walk; it lies behind every little movement that makes it possible for one foot to be placed in front of the other. We cannot become aware of this level of the will which is buried deep within our being. It must do its work without our interference. Discussions about neurones, ligaments, muscles, etc. only scratch the surface of what is at work here. All we can do is accept that the physical component of our being dwelling in this physical world has these abilities. This is the domain of the kings of the earth.

Our will also underpins all our intentions, all that motivates us to act, to speak, to think etc.. Or at least it should, yet so often it is our emotions that are the driving force behind what we do or what we say. It is easy to confuse actions based on will with those based on emotions. To be able to discern the source of our motives we must become aware of whether our motives arise from our lower ego or our I AM, from Babylon or from the conquering Lamb. Our lower ego carries our emotions and instincts, our I AM carries our pure love-filled will. This is the domain of the conquering Lamb.

So there are two types of will, one which is at work in the hidden processes of our body which we cannot become conscious of and one which operates in our soul and spirit which we must strive to become conscious of. Then there is a third, the pseudo will when our emotions masquerade as will. We could also say that the first type of will, which we also find in the natural world, is destructive. We experience this when we walk some distance - we get tired, depleted of our energy. The second kind of will, its spiritual counterpart, is constructive. This is the will that aligns itself with the will of others in community, for instance.

The great city, Babylon, rules today. The emotions which masquerade as will dominate the consciousness of our global civilisation. We have urgent work to do in terms of being able to use our soul and spiritual will with awareness.

The reason for the urgency is revealed by John when he says, "And I saw the woman drunk with the blood of the saints and the blood of the martyrs of Jesus." The saints and the martyrs of Jesus are those whose whole activity comes from their purified will. Those who are able to act in this way create a rich future for the whole of humanity. The way they use their will is a resource as valuable as "gold and jewels and pearls". But Babylon adorns herself with them instead of using these resources to contribute to the evolution of consciousness for the benefit of all.

This inner work is the reason we are presently incarnated on earth, it is our purpose. Not working with this purpose contributes to the level of war and conflict in the world today. War and conflict arises when human beings externalise their inner work. This dark side of the will can be identified everywhere. Unconsciously many people are experiencing the power of their will which is occurring naturally at this stage in human evolution. So without due preparation people are discovering this inner power which gives them a sense of freedom. It is like giving a child a loaded gun. Hence everywhere we look we see the misuse of the will.

What is the solution to this disastrous situation? Trying to control people with rules and regulations is not the answer. Each person must do the inner work themselves. The only way forward is, by example, for each one of us to work towards the pure expression of the will. This need not be an overwhelming task; it can be as simple as resolving to become conscious of everything we say. For instance, we might avoid habitually saying, "Have a nice day" or "How are you?" unless we are really interested in the wellbeing of the person we address. Or when someone asks us how we are, especially when we are not so well, we can give them an honest answer. If we say, "I am not so well today, thank you for asking", invariably the response will be, "Good." This unconscious response is Babylon the great city, the great group consciousness ruled by pseudo-will which is riddled with the lies of the Ahrimanic beings that pervade all our unconscious actions. It is a lie to ask someone how they are without giving a damn. We have the freedom of choice to stand with the conquering Lamb committed to striving to become aware of our will in our soul and in our spirit. In this way we experience the true community we all yearn for.

CHAPTER EIGHTEEN

The Fall of Babylon continued

After this I saw another angel coming down from heaven, having great authority; and the earth was made bright with his splendor. And he called out with a mighty voice, "Fallen, fallen is Babylon the great! It has become a dwelling place of demons, a haunt of every foul spirit, a haunt of every foul and hateful bird; for all nations have drunk the wine of her impure passion, and the kings of the earth have committed fornication with her, and the merchants of the earth have grown rich with the wealth of her wantonness." Rev 18:1-3

Another way to put these opening words would be: After this I saw another messenger coming down out of heaven, a great *exousia* and the earth was enlightened with his glory, his *doxa*. As previously discussed the Exousia are spiritual beings who work creatively with form. (see Ch 13) In the Hebrew language they are the Elohim, the creator gods in Genesis. It is through their work that human beings are able to connect up with their I AM. Part of this work was, of course, to give us the experience of Babylon as part of the process. We should never underestimate the greatness of Babylon in our development. However at a certain point Babylon must fall to make way for the future.

If such a mighty being reveals itself to John at this stage it would seem that a major milestone has been reached in the development of human consciousness. Glory, *doxa* or illumination, shines in the darkness and reveals the new life that we create by allowing our lower ego to fall. John's description seems to indicate that cosmic purpose is being fulfilled, that a certain stage has been reached by at least some human beings. The presence of the demons, foul spirits and hateful birds seem to be revealed by the light shed by this Exousia. We can be quite certain that they were there all the time, but unseen.

This too is a warning to us that as we are able to develop our spiritual consciousness, our own illumination uncovers all lurks in our being. Hopefully we are strong enough to handle what we see. When it says, "a haunt of every foul spirit", the word translated as 'haunt' is *phulake* which actually means a prison. How often do we forget that these negative forces actually have a purpose in the scheme of things? Until we use them for the purpose for which they have been created, which is to be the force of resistance that propels us forward, they are imprisoned. For as long as we do not do the work created for us by the Exousia we imprison these forces within us.

One powerful way we do this is through anger. When the text says, "for all nations have drunk the wine of her impure passion" - impure passion is *thuma*, erupting anger, which can cause us to lose consciousness just as we do when we have drunk too much wine. Why do we allow this angry agitation to build within us until it explodes? Is it because we want to be less conscious? Is it easier to experience this agitation than to do the work necessary to transmute our anger to love? For that is exactly the purpose of anger at this stage in evolution; to be an agitating force that inwardly strengthens us and makes us alert to a situation that we can only understand fully through the power of purest love. If we express this force as anger we are weakened, if we express it as love the power of our I AM floods into our soul.

Often our anger is usually with ourselves anyway because we wanted things to go differently. Then, especially in our relationships with others, the imprisoned demons, spirits and birds within us are exposed. When faced with the reality of this imprisonment it becomes obvious that we have not freed them and we must immediately face the progress of our own development.

There is also another possibility here. Could it be that we are actually addicted to anger? Like an alcoholic, we want more of Babylon's wine so that we don't have to be so conscious of the work that we must do. All the while our lower ego provides an endless supply of anger to give us the greatest opportunity to experience the purest love. The level of anger, and the freedom to express it, seems to be escalating in every nation of the world. When will be the tipping point? Perhaps it rests with each one of us to use the force of anger for the purpose for which it was created. In all our relationships we have the choice to suppress annoyance and to have loving thoughts.

Is it so hard to love in place of expressing anger? The target of our anger feels it whether we express it directly to them or not. Isn't it fornication to speak lovingly to a person while in our private thoughts we are furious with them? Also, in our relationships, how often do we trade like merchants, wanting to get a better deal for ourselves, at the expense of others. This is abuse of the gift of ego from the creator gods and we will only be able to move on when we are able to identify how we do these things in our lives, privately and publically. One way to bear this truth about ourselves is to share the experience with the conquering Lamb, he is always available (till the end of this age). This Lamb is the pioneer, he knows how much strength and love is needed to become a conqueror.

Then I heard another voice from heaven saying, "Come out of her, my people, lest you take part in her sins, lest you share in her plagues; for her sins are heaped high as heaven, and God has remembered her iniquities. Render to her as she herself has rendered, and repay her double for her deeds; mix a double draught for her in the cup she mixed. As she glorified herself and played the wanton, so give her a like measure of torment and mourning. Since in her heart she says, 'A queen I sit, I am no widow, mourning I shall never see,' so shall her plagues come in a single day, pestilence and mourning and famine, and she shall be burned with fire; for mighty is the Lord God who judges her." Rev 18:4-8

Is this a conversation between our I AM and our ego, our higher and lower selves? If it is, it would make sense of the strange words "repay her double for her deeds" which seems to go against the idea of forgiveness.

Could it be that we misunderstand this idea of forgiveness? Forgiveness is really judgment-free observation. It is about forgetting how our ego was hurt and trying to bring the events in our life into harmony from a higher perspective. The voice is also telling us that when we die, when our being is no longer confined to this physical body then our sins are not "heaped high as heaven" but are joined or glued together, *ekollethesan,* with our I AM which does not fully incarnate.

This also speaks about the notion that when we die we experience any pain we inflicted on others twice as strongly as they experienced it. This is not, as religious leaders so often say, punishment for sins. Sin, *hamartia,* means missing the mark, it means that we haven't achieved our goal.

There is a clear indication here that the voice speaks about reincarnation and the level of consciousness we need to be able to see that our experiences originate in our own actions in previous lives. It could also be that this remembering God is our I AM as well.

One of the greatest issues faced by humanity at present is the inability to see this life in sequence with all the lives we have ever lived. The consequence of which means that we are not aware of our I AM either. We might wonder why this is. If we are not sufficiently developed we could use the knowledge of reincarnation deleteriously. If we live in our lower ego, without awareness of our I AM, an inherent laziness will say, "What I don't achieve in this life I will achieve in the next". However, each incarnation gives us particular opportunities to do certain work. It is like catching a train, we have to arrive at the station on time and take the specific train that will take us to our destination. If we decide to wait around on the platform for a while and miss the train then we have missed the opportunity. This is sin.

The greatest sin of all is not applying ourselves to meet the challenges we face. There is so much impotence in the world today when issues have to be dealt with. The natural inclination is not to upset the equilibrium because we don't want to expend the energy required to resolve it. This is sin. Not doing the work that our I AM placed before us prior to our incarnation is sin. Then, next time, we have to work twice as hard.

How often during the day do we factor in the role of our I AM? Do we think of our I AM watching over our every move, our every thought, our every desire? Why would John mention that God remembers our iniquities? Does God have anthropomorphic tendencies which remember and forget? Or is he pointing out that we must become conscious of our I AM re-membering, linking together, all the lives we have ever lived; every thought, feeling and action.

Iniquities, *adikema*, refer to a lack of conscience. Conscience is simply being able to stand in the other person's shoes; then we treat everyone as we would treat Christ. Not to do this is sin. If we can do this then we bear the plagues, *pléges* which means stripes or wounds, as Jesus bore them when he was crucified. When we cannot bear the pain of situations in our lives it is because the wantonness of Babylon consumes us. The words "pestilence and mourning and famine" should read death, sorrow and famine and tell us that when we egotistically sit like a queen we have no life, no joy, and no sustenance. It is our I AM that judges us for it is our I AM that set the course of our life before we incarnated. So really this is self-judgment. If there is anything in our life that we do not like, then that is a signal that we have work to do. This work is less of a burden if we do it with awareness of our I AM and of the purpose of the Lamb.

And the kings of the earth, who committed fornication and were wanton with her, will weep and wail over her when they see the smoke of her burning; they will stand far off, in fear of her torment, and say, "Alas! alas! thou great city, thou mighty city, Babylon! In one hour has thy judgment come." Rev 18:6-10

There are three types of characters to consider in the next 14 verses; the kings, the merchants and the seamen. What John describes about them will give us some clues about what we are facing as a large proportion of humanity experiences the spiritualisation of their consciousness. What lies at the heart of this matter is how aware we are of what is changing within us. How do we deal with the destruction of a consciousness that obscures the spiritual reality of the cosmos?

We would do well to consider whether we accurately estimate the effect that this will have in our soul. If we are to see the spiritual realities all around us then our soul has to be wrenched out of its familiar patterns. We may even think that because we have a certain amount of spiritual knowledge that we will be okay. In fact those with some spiritual knowledge may be worse off.

If we read up to verse 19 we see that there are similarities in the response of the three types of characters; they all weep and mourn and they all stand far off. This standing far off indicates a separation which is exactly what happens in our soul when our spiritual consciousness awakens; thinking, feeling and will separate and operate independently and it is up to us to combine them in the right way. Of course, we inherently wail whenever something ends, and we are in fear until we can see what will replace what we had. While it's happening we don't have a very clear view, we must wait till we can look back on events, but we do have John's guidance if we contemplate his words.

These kings can represent our will, now separated, standing far off, from thinking and feeling in our soul. When our will is not restrained by thinking and feeling it becomes a very powerful agent. This lack of restraint (wantonness) is mistaken for freedom, the sense that, as a king, we can do anything we want to. This unrestrained behaviour is seen everywhere, it is blatant wantonness which pushes boundaries further and further. Of course, this is the absolute opposite of freedom; freedom is the assurance that we can act appropriately to any given situation. We can only experience true freedom through our spiritual faculties when we are acting out of our I AM. We fornicate, *porneo,* when we are unfaithful to our spiritual nature and follow the instincts of our ego. This choice is always with us.

The problem is that we find the pleasures of the ego very gratifying, and we find connecting with our I AM very arduous. In fact, we seek earthly pleasure to relieve the pressure, the tribulation, of our I AM. These wilful pleasures come in many forms; it could be the forming of simple opinions about others in our minds to expressing these opinions about others violently. We also experience these pleasures when we wilfully impose our ideas on others, when we think that our way is the only way, and especially when we see ourselves as more advanced than others. These kings always tend towards ruling that which is outside them rather than that which is within.

So when the signal comes for our will to be spiritualised, through the destruction of Babylon, there is deep mourning. Weeping *klaio* is a loud expression of grief, and wailing, *kopsontai*, means to cut, to beat. This happens when the "smoke of her burning" appears - this word for burning is really fire *puroseos*, pur meaning fever which suggests raising the temperature to remove impurities.

Fear of torment, *basanismou*, probably comes from *basanos* which is a touchstone used in testing metals. This process, of course, is a testing of our mettle. The consciousness that is Babylon must be judged, *krisis,* it must reach a crisis point. It is this crisis that we must endure so that we can use our will spiritually and experience true freedom.

If we keenly observe current affairs, which we must if we are to be in tune with the development of human consciousness, we will see that now, more than ever, ideas that were relevant yesterday are no longer relevant today. The life of many ideas is incredibly short, even good ideas, but we are being called to move on. Through the right use of our will we can resist being consumed by our own mourning for what is lost and find ways to identify with the future that streams towards us.

The atmosphere of this globe is thick with fear and suffering. We instinctively stand back from suffering when we are cut off from our feelings. Of course, we must, for we can only bear the suffering of strangers when we experience it through our I AM. This is the crisis, this is the judgment that comes in one hour, *hora*, one time period or season. If we remain in Babylon it is unbearable, if we move forward we can bear all things through Christ, the Lamb, who strengthens us.

And the merchants of the earth weep and mourn for her, since no one buys their cargo anymore, cargo of gold, silver, jewels and pearls, fine linen, purple, silk and scarlet, all kinds of scented wood, all articles of ivory, all articles of costly

wood, bronze, iron, and marble, cinnamon, spice, incense, myrrh, frankincense, wine, olive oil, choice flour and wheat, cattle and sheep, horses and chariots, slaves—and human lives. "The fruit for which your soul longed has gone from you, and all your dainties and your splendor are lost to you, never to be found again!" The merchants of these wares, who gained wealth from her, will stand far off, in fear of her torment, weeping and mourning aloud, "Alas, alas, the great city, clothed in fine linen, in purple and scarlet, adorned with gold, with jewels, and with pearls! For in one hour all this wealth has been laid waste!" Rev 18:11-17

Let us say that the merchants represent our thinking, the most conscious activity of our soul. We are much more conscious of our thinking than we are of our feeling and our will. We put great store on our thinking and use it to show how civilised we are, how much more advanced we are than the so-called caveman. The person with the university degree is held in much higher esteem than the one without.

With our thinking we decide what is valuable and what is not valuable. For instance, we live in a society that honours the wealthy person and places little value on those who have nothing. Even when the wealthy misbehave they are forgiven because the values of our culture are so misplaced. Without a full understanding of true human nature, and the development of consciousness, human beings hardly know what to think anymore. Thinking often goes round in circles and becomes a great burden – which is what the word *gomos*, cargo, actually means. The thinkers are overburdened with thoughts that have lost their value.

What was valuable for our developing ego is no longer of value to our Higher Self, our I AM. We have reached the threshold of the human spiritual condition, our previous foundation no longer supports us, Babylon has fallen, and now we need to know how to think differently. The merchants, our thoughts, now "stand far off" indicating that thinking separates out and no longer follows its usual patterns. These are the patterns which have developed since childhood, under the influence of our parents, carers, teachers and leaders, which are not necessarily based on spiritual reality. This thinking usually doesn't recognise how the wealthy person and the poor person can be equal spiritually.

The translators have not really understood what John is telling us here and so they have mistranslated some of the words. The words, "slaves—and human lives" *somaton kai psuchas anthropon* really says "the bodies and soul of humans". We could say that when we operate as dual beings of body and soul, ignoring our spirit, then our values are misplaced and become burdensome. We mourn and weep because our thinking no longer serves our purpose and we cannot yet see its new purpose.

Then John puts it even more plainly in his report: "The fruit for which your soul longed has gone from you," all that we have known up till now is lost, never to be found again. These words *Tes psuches sou apelthen* actually say 'the soul of you passed away'. We cannot comprehend this with today's consciousness but in spiritual terms it is speaking about the death of the soul. The soul as we have known it dies and we have the choice to think, feel and will in a higher way, using our human spirit, or to live on with a dead soul. A resurrection must take place within our being and we must take full responsibility for it. Through close observation of the way we think, feel and act will we come to understand how these soul activities are starting to stand apart and how we must combine them purposefully and differently. This is impossible to do without becoming conscious of our I AM.

We can observe some of the effects of this transition within us and in the world. When thinking works alone, when it is not supported by feeling for what is right and what is wrong, it can conclude that anything is right. When thinking is not guided by our will then our thoughts can go in any direction, often at someone else's suggestion. Up till now these forces of consciousness in our soul worked together so that we could function in the world in harmony with our fellow human beings. Now that these forces "stand far off" it is up to us to combine them consciously in the spiritual regions of our consciousness. This will also mean that we think differently from many of our fellow human beings which can make us unpopular. This is not an easy time for the development of human consciousness. Those who are able to develop their higher consciousness need to have courage. They also need strength to consciously combine their thoughts, feelings and intentions which previously worked together in an unconscious way.

We should take heed of John's warning, "For in one hour all this wealth has been laid waste!" In one season, one period of time, *hora,* our values will no longer have value. Can we even imagine what that will be like? John is calling us to prepare for a shift that is beyond our comprehension, when the pain of the burden becomes too much to bear we must know that we have the unlimited resources of our I AM.

And all shipmasters and seafaring men, sailors and all whose trade is on the sea, stood far off and cried out as they saw the smoke of her burning, "What city was like the great city?" And they threw dust on their heads, as they wept and mourned, crying out, "Alas, alas, for the great city where all who had ships at sea grew rich by her wealth! In one hour she has been laid waste. Rev 18:17-19

What John now describes gives us a sense of what it is like when our feelings stand alone. When they lose their instinctive, habitual moderators; thinking and will. These feelings are like a great ocean in our being, ebbing and flowing.

Feelings gave human beings the first experience of themselves long, long ago. When, for the first time, human beings experienced inner feelings they had their first taste of independence and freedom. At this stage the ability to think and act out of our own will was yet to be experienced. Instead, these faculties were gifted to us from the spiritual worlds, and then from the tribal elder, the pharaoh and the kings. Of course, now the government tries to take on this role just at a time when we no longer need external leadership.

Our first experience of inner feelings began through feelings of sympathy and antipathy. These polar opposites lie at the core of our soul and have such a close association to Babylon. Now, when we allow feelings of sympathy and antipathy, like and dislike, to rule in our soul it is out of that ancient memory of first becoming aware of ourselves. We often experience this when we are tired or anxious, and we see it in the behaviour of babies and small children.

If we are to navigate the collapse of Babylon within our consciousness and allow our Higher Self to direct our thoughts, feelings and intentions, then we must come to terms with our instinct of liking some things and hating others. What is required now is a purity in our feelings that is self-directed according to each new situation we face. It is no longer appropriate to dislike something out of habit. Society is reminding us of this anyway. Now we are asked to be tolerant of the disadvantaged, of other cultures, and of all that is different from us.

One of the first things we can experience when our feelings "stood far off" is a sense of drowning in feelings. When we are left alone with our feelings they can overwhelm us. This is because now our thoughts will only guide our feelings if we combine them ourselves purposefully.

As our I AM has more influence in our soul we feel things differently. For instance, we can feel other people's tragedies intensely. When this happens our first response is to want to assist. Often this is not possible because of the distance that separates us from people experiencing the tragedy, for instance, if we are in America and deeply feel for the children starving in Africa. In that moment of realising that we can do nothing we experience the full force of our will in its powerlessness to do something in the moment.

The fact is that our feelings are assisting us to become much more aware of our will than ever before. Our good intentions direct us to do something but we realise that we can do nothing in that moment. However, like the flap of a butterfly wing on one side of the world, the good work we are doing within our own consciousness, our feelings awakening an awareness of our will and the ensuing powerlessness, we contribute to the evolution of human consciousness. Each human being who changes their inner attitudes, expressing themselves differently in their daily activities they will influence the people they associate with and so on. In this way we direct our will to our own being and don't impose it on others.

Our feelings, our ancient heritage must be guided differently now, no longer the habitual feelings that have always arisen in our soul, now they become pure compassion for all humanity as it mourns the loss of the great city, the great consciousness that has served us so well. As the grief intensifies we want to throw dust on our heads as if to bury what has died.

While part of humanity strives to adjust to the independent functioning of thinking, feeling and will, another part will not understand what is happening. This will call for great compassion from those who are managing the change. Nothing can be done; the time to do things to others or for others has long gone. All those who manage to navigate the change will be a great example to others, matching the greatness of Babylon in the past.

Rejoice over her, O heaven, O saints and apostles and prophets, for God has given judgment for you against her! "*Then a mighty angel took up a stone like a great millstone and threw it into the sea, saying, "So shall Babylon the great city be thrown down with violence, and shall be found no more; and the sound of harpers and minstrels, of flute players and trumpeters, shall be heard in thee no more; and a craftsman of any craft shall be found in thee no more; and the sound of the millstone shall be heard in thee no more; and the light of a lamp shall shine in thee no more; and the voice of bridegroom and bride shall be heard in thee no more; for thy merchants were the great men of the earth, and all nations were deceived by thy sorcery. And in her was found the blood of prophets and of saints, and of all who have been slain on earth." Rev 18:20-24*

While we may not be happy with the changes in our consciousness, and want to look back to what has been, as people often do, the spiritual worlds rejoice. "O heaven, O saints and apostles and prophets" are all those who have elevated their consciousness in the past. Do they rejoice because we have run a good race, or are they depending on us to raise our consciousness at this point in time? Could it be that we human beings must work on our consciousness at given periods of time for a certain effect in the cosmos? How often do we think about what we can contribute to the cosmos instead of what will benefit ourselves?

Perhaps this explains the next words, "for God has given judgment for you against her!" A more literal translation is, 'God has judged your judgement of Babylon'. God judged, *krino*, your judgement *krima* of her. We are so used to associating judgment with God we hardly give any value to our own ability to judge. If God judges our ability to judge then our judgment becomes a very important issue. So how seriously do we take our responsibility to judge?

Mostly we are so quick to judge based on what we like or dislike. Our likes and dislikes are associated with our instincts and therefore have an affinity with Babylon. What if we set aside our predispositions for one thing or another, how differently would we judge? This would open us up to the idea that all things are possible. Judging, reaching a conclusion, closes off a process; remaining open to possibilities continues a process. Here lies the difference between our ego (our lower self) and our 'I' (our Higher Self).

Furthermore, each judgment we make forms the society in which we live. This means that we have a responsibility to contribute to society through the way we judge. We know that if enough people say that something is good, then regardless of whether it is good or not, it is deemed to be so. There are so many examples, one area in particular being what we should eat or not eat which, if taken seriously, could leave nothing safe for us to eat.

Then we are told that six things will either not be found, or not be heard, in us anymore: Babylon, musicians, craftsman, the sound of the mill (not millstone), the light of a lamp, and the sound (not voice) of bridegroom and bride. Could it be that the opportunity to develop our consciousness is taken away from human beings? Or, will we develop our consciousness in an outer way from now on? Perhaps both are possibilities. We hide so much from each other, we keep so much private, which makes it impossible to have strong community with others. Until we stop judging each other – and that can only start with our inner thoughts – we cannot have the openness that is necessary for the next steps. Can we be this transparent in our dealings with others?

One way to test this is to ask ourselves what motivates us to do what we do. As a musician do we play to be appreciated, or do we play to give pleasure to others? In all our craft, all that we make, do we dedicate ourselves to the well-being of humanity? Or are we more concerned about our own wellbeing? Do we shine our inner light so that we can be seen, or so that others may see the way?

Using the metaphor of the millstone to describe what is associated with Babylon makes us realise what a grinding work we have been doing. Now, the millstone is separated from the mill and rushes (not violence) down into the depths of our being so that the sound of a mill *mulou* (not millstone – *mulinon*) "shall be heard in thee no more". When the bride which is our soul, and the bridegroom which is the risen Christ, are no longer heard within us then our being has consummated the precious union - which is our purpose.

CHAPTER NINETEEN

The Song of Triumph in Heaven

After this I heard what seemed to be the loud voice of a great multitude in heaven, crying, "Hallelujah! Salvation and glory and power belong to our God, for his judgments are true and just; he has judged the great harlot who corrupted the earth with her fornication, and he has avenged on her the blood of his servants." Once more they cried, "Hallelujah! The smoke from her goes up for ever and ever." And the twenty-four elders and the four living creatures fell down and worshiped God who is seated on the throne, saying, "Amen. Hallelujah!" And from the throne came a voice crying, "Praise our God, all you his servants, you who fear him, small and great." Rev 19:1-5

What an appropriate part of The Revelation to contemplate at Christmas. Hallelujah! Indeed! for human triumph. Hallelujah! to each of us whenever we resist the influences of Babylon - those inclinations to resist transparency, to resist love – and we are able to put her in her place. While her role in the development of our consciousness was crucial, as with many things, she can encroach into areas where she does not belong. She had a task to do but she can so easily get carried away.

The human journey through Babylon the Great to the New Jerusalem seems so simple, so straightforward, but like all journey's things can happen along the way. The Christmas period is a good time to ponder the human journey and to recognise all the elements within our own consciousness. What takes place in the outer world can be very distracting. We are repeatedly asked to look outside ourselves for gifts, cards, drinks with friends, church services, holidays, and so on, so that we can struggle to look inside ourselves to find the inner gifts, the new relationships between the elements in our soul, and the communion that can take place between our body, soul and spirit.

In all our contemplations, and our resolve to act out of our Higher Self more often, we must clearly understand that our Higher Self cannot be conscious in this physical world. Our Higher Self does not experience time and space, which is why it is eternal. Our Higher Self, over aeons, has created an instrument that could live physically in this universe but, to do this, it had to disconnect itself, or divide into two parts; Higher Self and lower self. The lower self, depicted by Babylon, then had the task of making our conscious awareness grow clearer and clearer. This can only happen up to a certain point under the influence of our lower self. At some point we must connect up with our Higher Self if we are to continue to become consciously aware. In this way the Higher Self becomes consciously aware of this earthly world and can participate, at our invitation, in our daily affairs.

The first human being to be able to do this was Jesus who we meet as the conquering Lamb in The Revelation. When he reached the point of perfection the cosmic Christ could unite with Jesus' consciousness. It wasn't only Babylon who assisted in this process; Jehovah also had a pivotal role. This would be why the so-called multitude cries Hallelujah! – Praise you Jehovah. This word 'hallelujah' appears nowhere in the New Testament except in The Revelation. So Jehovah's work was completed with the birth of Jesus, it was through his guidance that the Hebrew people kept the blood of their race pure so that it could produce a body fit to receive the high spiritual being we call Christ. This is what the story of Christmas is all about.

The cry from what "seemed to be many 'people'" echoes the events in Chapter 5 when the Lamb was praised. Now, those human beings whose inner work has emulated the path of the Lamb are praised. This is not about the few souls in the world that may have achieved perfection; this is about each of us. Even the smallest of our achievements is praiseworthy just as Jesus had to become a baby before he could achieve the ultimate gift of Christening. This is also not about being praised by others, this is about inner recognition for our own achievements. However, if we don't make the right call then Babylon is at work.

We can experience this praise ourselves by creating an Imagination in our minds. We can pause in contemplation and with our thoughts gather all that we have done throughout the past year and offer it up as a gift. This praise for the birth of Christ within our own soul is a continuing process year after year. If we create an Imagination with our thoughts of the heavenly sound *phone*; the tones, melodies and harmonies of all those beings in the spiritual worlds that have experienced our inner work, then this is a picture of true and just judgments. True is *alethes, a-lethes*, which means overcoming forgetting. In creating this Imagination we demonstrate that we do not forget our spiritual home and our real spiritual being. Just judgments mean balanced and harmonised. 'Just' speaks of a continual series of adjustments needed to achieve this balance.

Salvation is not really about being saved, it is about what is preserved, *soteria*, within us that we can now bring to life. The glory, *doxa*, our illumined, light-filled being becomes like a light shining in the cave of our being which is now guided by the powers, the *dunami*, those high spiritual beings responsible for motion and movement. It is the inner movement that brings us the victory over Babylon so that we can stand with the Lamb who reached a pivotal part of his journey at Bethlehem two thousand and ten years ago.

The Marriage of the Lamb

Then I heard what seemed to be the voice of a great multitude, like the sound of many waters and like the sound of mighty thunderpeals, crying, "Hallelujah! For the Lord our God the Almighty reigns. Let us rejoice and exult and give him the glory, for the marriage of the Lamb has come, and his Bride has made herself ready; it was granted her to be clothed with fine linen, bright and pure" --for the fine linen is the righteous deeds of the saints. And the angel said to me, "Write this: Blessed are those who are invited to the marriage supper of the Lamb." And he said to me, "These are true words of God." Rev 19:6-9

Now the sound John hears seems to arise out of natural elements, out of water and thunder. The water could represent our purified feelings and the thunder our pure thinking. It is hard for the modern mind to understand that our feelings and thoughts have a dynamic effect on the universe and all that it contains. If we have a pure thought, a thought that is free of all earthly associations, this thought can rumble in the universe as a truth we have grasped, and the spiritual beings who guide evolution rejoice. Equally, if we are able to guide our feelings to lovingly embrace whatever meets us in the world, regardless of the pain it may cause us, then we have reigned over our own being. Perhaps if we were more aware of the affect we have on the scheme of things we would change our responses to all the events in our lives.

Thunder is a sign of our 'I' being at work in our blood, the waters could even represent our blood. The sound of the thunder in our blood signals the conscious awareness that arises in our thoughts in the presence of our 'I'. This 'I', which, in its highest form, we call the I AM, is the principle which places us above the animal kingdom. The base function of the 'I' is to give the human being the ability to stand upright, to speak and to think. Its highest function is to give us what we could call a cosmic consciousness. In fact, the highest expression of the 'I' is the Lord God in us, *kurios o theo*s which is destined to reign in us.

The story of the burning bush, which burned without being consumed, tells the secret of the God in us. The secret is connected to God saying to Moses, "I AM that I AM" (not I AM who I AM). This I AM is the indestructible part of us that we strive to become aware of.

Then Moses said to God, "If I come to the people of Israel and say to them, 'The God of your fathers has sent me to you,' and they ask me, 'What is his name?' what shall I say to them?" God said to Moses, "I AM WHO I AM." And he said, "Say this to the people of Israel, 'I AM has sent me to you.'" Ex 3:13-14

Moses, of course, was the law giver who received the Ten Commandments when human beings ceased to be guided by the gods and needed some guidelines for their behaviour. Since the coming of Christ we have a new commandment, to love one another (Jn 13:34). The Commandments as external law are no longer relevant to those who are connected to their 'I', now we have the personal responsibility of inner ethical standards guided by love. Those who have the *kurios o theos* reigning in their soul, at least some of the time, always act out of the highest love and it guides the way they think and feel about others. When a level of purity is reached a marriage takes place.

One of the reasons we feel at odds with ourselves at times is because the marriage has not taken place within us. We haven't managed to make the Bride ready. The Bride is our soul preparing herself, purifying herself, to take into herself the risen Christ, the bringer of the I AM. When our soul is veiled in white linen pure and bright it means that we have become fully aware of our feelings, our thoughts and our intentions, they become transparent. Then our deeds become righteous, *dikaiomata,* which means just, straight. We use this word today when we ask someone if they are being straight with us. When our soul forces achieve the perfect harmony it is as if we are covered by a translucent veil. Then we are adorned for the wedding. Then John receives an instruction.

"Write this: Blessed are those who are invited to the marriage supper of the Lamb." And he said to me, "These are true words of God." Rev 19:6

John is again told to write something down. This is a Beatitude, there are seven of them in The Revelation, and this one seems to acknowledge that all the elements within us that have been purified are blessed and have been invited to attend the marriage supper. This would suggest that other parts of us didn't receive this invitation and become part of an ongoing work.

Like the Last Supper, no doubt this is a consecration which takes place because our body and blood have become the body and blood of Christ — which they do when we are able to achieve this level of harmony and purity, which was the purpose of the birth, crucifixion and resurrection of Christ Jesus. In the rarefied atmosphere of this it is tempting to feel defeated thinking that these high mysteries are beyond our reach. It is also tempting to think that these are matters for those committed to the church. This may have been true many years ago when our consciousness was not as developed as it is today. It is no longer true. These things have now entered into the arena of everyday life and have great relevancy for each and every person who strives to the highest expression, to that point when they can say I AM. It is truly humbling if we are able to see the reality of this in our own being – at least sometimes.

And the angel said to me, "Write this: Blessed are those who are invited to the marriage supper of the Lamb." And he said to me, "These are true words of God." Then I fell down at his feet to worship him, but he said to me, "You must not do that! I am a fellow servant with you and your brethren who hold the testimony of Jesus. Worship God." For the testimony of Jesus is the spirit of prophecy. Rev 19:9-10

In the Greek there is no angel speaking, the word *angelos* is not used, it simply says "he", "And **he** said to me, "Write this: ..." It is possible that John is communicating with his own I AM. Our experience of our I AM is a work in progress which we must take step by step. John is revealing to us how he did it and his Revelation shows how Jesus before him did it. We are also shown how they are both doing it now; John here on earth and Jesus in the spiritual worlds. Through his I AM the beings John hears and the images he sees in The Revelation are showing him "what must take place ... for the time is near (ready)." Obviously we should be alert to any sounds and images that may enter our own minds.

There are several statements in chapter 19 that point us back to chapter 1. We could assume therefore that a new stage has been reached. Certainly invitations to the marriage supper of the Lamb would indicate this. A statement that we first met in Rev 1:2 is repeated twice in this text we are considering so it must be significant. The statement is, "the testimony of Jesus", the *marturia* of Jesus.

Witness, *marturia,* is a very specific experience associated with the I AM. This kind of witnessing does not look from a distance; it steps into the event and experiences the full reality of the event as if it were just happening. The witnessing from a distance, as we know, can be very unreliable. The reports of several witnesses to the same event usually vary and sometimes we can even wonder if they were both seeing the same thing. Furthermore, conclusions about what is happening can be very subjective.

So through our I AM we are able to experience exactly what Jesus experienced when he connected with his I AM and was then able to receive the Christ Spirit into his being and become the Lamb. The *marturia* experience reveals every minute detail of the event and a full understanding of why it took place. Such an experience would surely make us fall down and worship, it would be breath-taking. While it may be some time before we can have such an experience, we can begin to have glimpses of it now if we devote ourselves to developing the closest possible connection with our I AM.

As we try to come to terms with our own I AM and what it might be doing in our being, as we try to fit the ideas that we form about it into modern concepts, it is only natural that we should struggle to do this from the perspective of where we stand today in this world. Forming an idea of the magnitude of our I AM which knows every minute detail of every life we have ever lived and every experience we have had between lives is a momentous task. In our limited earthly awareness we can usually only have vague ideas about the totality of our existence in this cosmos – the glimpses we have are our déjà vu experiences.

When we have conscious awareness of our I AM the first thing that we will experience is the marriage of the Lamb because that is the purpose of the Lamb. The Christ deed gave us the possibility of becoming consciously aware of our I AM. Of course, it is understandable that we would be in awe of this mighty I AM that knows us so intimately. We yearn to be known intimately. That yearning in us is the driving force behind our intentions to discover who we really are. It is also the driving force to find a relationship with another person in which we can at least know about the possibilities of this ultimate intimacy.

Naturally we should not worship our I AM (or another person for that matter), that would be egotistical. Our I AM is our fellow servant who works with us to contribute to the development of the conscious awareness of humanity. Our brethren are all those who do this work and who are the pioneers carving the way forward for the rest of humanity. Worship God instead the voice says – *proskuneo* means 'towards-kiss' which supports the idea of yearning for ultimate intimacy.

The words, "witness (not testimony) of Jesus is the spirit of prophecy" make much more sense when we know that as witnesses we will experience the reality of the marriage as if we were there as original participants, then, for Jesus and John, and now, for our own inner development. When we reach this point we will also experience the *pneuma* of *propheteia*, the spirit of prophecy enabling us to scan the full vista, from the past to the future, and recognise our contribution so far, and how best to contribute from now on, for the time is ready.

Then I saw heaven opened, and behold, a white horse! He who sat upon it is called Faithful and True, and in righteousness he judges and makes war. His eyes are like a flame of fire, and on his head are many diadems; and he has a name inscribed which no one knows but himself. He is clad in a robe dipped in blood, and the name by which he is called is The Word of God. And the armies of heaven, arrayed in fine linen, white and pure, followed him on white horses. From his mouth issues a sharp sword with which to smite the nations, and he will rule them with a rod of iron; he will tread the wine press of the fury of the wrath of God the Almighty. On his robe and on his thigh he has a name inscribed, King of kings and Lord of lords. Rev 19:11-16

As our experience of our I AM deepens we begin to see who we really are. We are able to see into the spiritual worlds (heaven opens) to behold the image of our Real Self. This beholding, *idou*, means to enter into, to become one with that which we see and to experience it from the inside. Then we are able to say to ourselves, "That is you!" or as it was put in Exodus 3, "I am that". John says, I am that – a white horse and its rider!

In chapter 6 when we considered the white horse it was suggested that it had a connection to our life-force, the etheric part of our being that gives vitality to our physical body. When our etheric forces are influenced by the Lamb, the risen Christ who shed the physical body and lives now in his etheric body, there is an inner glow and we look young and vital. So even though John describes the horse as white it may have looked like a glowing light. The Greek word for white is *leukos* and comes from *luke* meaning light. Also, white contains within it the seven colours of the rainbow in harmony with each other. Through his inner work John has created this image of who he really is.

Once we behold the image of who we really are we begin to experience true objectivity. We are able to observe ourselves, all that we say, do, think, feel and so on, as if we were observing another person. All bias is set aside and we begin to understand our tendency to lean towards some things and away from others. Then we receive the first of four names which reveal our true nature.

Firstly, we are "Faithful and True", but not a passive faith, this faith is knowledge of the reality of the spiritual world in which our true being exists. Now we can see how this true being participates in our daily life. True freedom is experienced in the moment we can say, "I am that". We are liberated from the tunnel vision that prevents us from seeing the big picture.

Then it says, *"and in righteousness he judges and makes war"* which hardly makes any sense. The literal Greek says, "in justice he is judging and battling" which more accurately describes the processes we will go through. Righteousness, *dikaiosune,* really means justice, and justice really means a series of adjustments. The only way we can have any experience at all of our I AM is if we engage in continual adjustments. The spiritual worlds are in continual movement, they are changed from moment to moment according to all that human beings think, feel and intend. It is awesome to contemplate the cosmic wisdom that can respond to everything each human being thinks, feels and wills.

To get this into perspective we can consider the issue of karma. Each time we address a karmic situation in our lives - or not - an adjustment is required, not only in our own lives but in the life of the person with whom we have the karma. This will then have a ripple effect for our family and friends and so on. When we are disconnected with our I AM we hardly think about who will be affected by the way we respond to life.

Each time we work in concert with our I AM adjustments occur as a matter of course. Nothing can possibly remain the same, even though we may like that to be the case. So each adjustment calls for judging and battling. Judging, *krino*, means to separate, to select, which is usually accompanied by the temptation for bias. Hence there is a battle to maintain the balance as we make our continual adjustments. While we may feel tired just thinking about this work we should realise that the rider on the white horse can assist us as long as "heaven opens".

Of course, our own image may not be a rider on a white horse; it could be a burning bush, so it could be helpful if we tried to discover our own image. Then, when we face life's challenges we can call to mind our own image and know that we are not alone. In this way we will be keeping heaven open and we will be strengthened by our own I AM.

Then I saw heaven opened, and behold, a white horse! He who sat upon it is called Faithful and True, and in righteousness he judges and makes war. His eyes are like a flame of fire, and on his head are many diadems; and he has a name inscribed which no one knows but himself. He is clad in a robe dipped in blood, and the name by which he is called is The Word of God. And the armies of heaven, arrayed in fine linen, white and pure, followed him on white horses. From his mouth issues a sharp sword with which to smite the nations, and he will rule them with a rod of iron; he will tread the wine press of the fury of the wrath of God the Almighty. On his robe and on his thigh he has a name inscribed, King of kings and Lord of lords. Rev 19:11-16

The being that John describes, who is riding the white horse, has many similarities to the Revelation Being we met at the beginning of chapter 1. Then, at the sight of him, John fell at his feet as though dead. John doesn't seem to have the same reaction now. It is as if John has become acquainted with this mighty being through all the images and sounds that have been revealed to him through all the chapters since then.

John knows the secret of the "name no one knows but himself", the name no one else can call us by, which is 'I'. We cannot say, 'I' and mean anyone but ourselves. In fact, today's overuse of this word 'I' has robbed it of its deep significance and mystery. It is a sacred word and we should use it with care and deep reverence for it is the key to The Revelation of who we are as human beings. When we penetrate the mystery of the 'I', as John clearly has, a new nature is given to us. What isn't widely known is that human beings haven't always been able to say 'I' when referring to themselves. In fact, only a few thousand years ago, the use of this word would overwhelm us and we would faint – fall down as though dead -, such is its power.

Now John sees that this name, 'I' is scribed, *gramma,* a word which indicates the one who is qualified (as in Scribe). In chapter 2 this name was scribed on a stone, which presumably was carried around, now it is scribed on the many diadems worn on the head of this rider which is the image of his Real Self. A *diadema*, is a band worn around the head which was used to bind on a turban or tiara, and which Roman Emperors wore as a badge of royalty. It symbolises rulership over our lower nature.

If there were many diadems it would suggest that the process of integrating the power associated with the personal use of our 'I' has many stages as with all things in life. This is our continual battle to use our ego in the highest way possible and thereby discover its secret. It isn't about turning away from our lower self but objectively viewing it from a higher perspective. We can assume that each time we succeed in a certain area we have the letter 'I' inscribed on a band which is part of our being and which will be revealed at some stage in our development.

It isn't just the truth about the human 'I' that we must discover, it is also the truth about Christ who gave us the right to personally use this 'I'. There are many indications in this text that the horse and rider represent John who has discovered the secret of his 'I' as well as fully connecting with the risen Christ. The robe dipped in blood and being called *"the Word of God"* blatantly suggests this. The word 'called' here is *kaleitai* and speaks more about a calling. Similarly, with Faithful and True; whereas the self-known name 'I', and *"King of kings and Lord of lords"* are scribed, earned titles.

The sharp sword speaks to us of steel hardened to withstand stress which indicates the suffering that strengthens the 'I'. This is why Jesus experienced so much suffering on his approach to the cross on Golgotha. If we take John's experiences seriously, which is exactly why he has recorded them, then we can only know our 'I' through suffering; perhaps not physically as Jesus did but perhaps now mentally. Therefore, to deal with the suffering we need the "I am that" experience. By saying, "I am that", we place ourselves in a higher perspective and can then objectively look down on ourselves in this incarnation experiencing painful thoughts and feelings. Perhaps this is why the death of Jesus happened on a cross raised off the ground.

The crux of the matter is that understanding our own human 'I' is not an easy task for there are many forces in this world at work to prevent this. It is our personal responsibility to do this work of our own volition for only we can experience our 'I' just as only we can call ourselves 'I'. Furthermore, this 'I' can only be experienced when we are on this earth and fully engaged with it as we meet the experiences that come our way. This is the only way to become consciously aware, the only way to achieve self-awareness. This is also the reason for, and the proof of, reincarnation; that we must incarnate on this earth, again and again until we have John's experience. This is what must take place as the angel said after John saw the image and "fell at his feet as though dead." "Now write what you see, what is and what is to take place hereafter (soon)" Rev 1:19 to every human being.

Then I saw heaven opened, and behold, a white horse! He who sat upon it is called Faithful and True, and in righteousness he judges and makes war. His eyes are like a flame of fire, and on his head are many diadems; and he has a name inscribed which no one knows but himself. He is clad in a robe dipped in blood, and the name by which he is called is The Word of God. And the armies of heaven, arrayed in fine linen, white and pure, followed him on white horses. From his mouth issues a sharp sword with which to smite the nations, and he will rule them with a rod of iron; he will tread the wine press of the fury of the wrath of God the Almighty. On his robe and on his thigh he has a name inscribed, King of kings and Lord of lords. Rev 19:11-16

Imagine being known as the "Word of God". *Kaleitai* indicates a calling; being called the Word of God would be similar to being called the doctor, the priest or the teacher. The Word, *Logos,* is a deeply mysterious word but for now we could say that it means a spoken word that creates something. John began his Gospel speaking about this L*ogos*.

In the beginning was the Word (Logos), and the Word was with God, and the Word was (a) God. He was in the beginning with God; all things were made through him, and without him was not anything made that was made. In him was life, and the life was the light of men. The light shines in the darkness, and the darkness has not overcome it. John 1:1-4

It is awesome to think about creating something through the words we speak. We would certainly have to be very careful about what we said. While we are a long way from this level of perfection it is always good to keep in mind that we prepare for the future today. Therefore, as part of this preparation we can resolve to be more mindful of the words we speak. Creating a thing through the spoken word belongs to the domain of the Christ-filled I AM, the rider on the luminous horse. It is the task of every human being to work towards this state of being.

Getting in touch with our I AM must start with a conscious experience of our human 'I'. It is so tempting to be drawn outside ourselves into the cosmos with the idea of having a Higher Self that we completely ignore the experience of our human 'I' in daily life. Being able to say 'I' is a sacred gift which we are only just beginning to discover. As more of it is revealed to us we will increasingly use it more wisely, and more sparingly.

If we say to ourselves, for example, "I hate myself for doing that ..." what are we doing with the 'I'-gift, and what are we creating with our speech? First of all, we need to understand why we would feel hate for ourselves. This often comes about when we see the majesty of the human 'I' in another person shining into us and showing up something that we are still working on. What we often don't realise is that the experience of the human 'I' comes first of all from something outside us which we then reflect upon within us. Sometimes, when we catch a glimpse of the purity of the human 'I' in another person it can illuminate what we hate in ourselves. We then want to cast out this disagreeable aspect of ourselves, instead of seeing it as a work in progress, and we can do this by raising a disagreement with the other person. In other words, what we saw in them made us feel small or inferior. Our defence can then be to have a sense of passing the hate that we feel for ourselves over to them.

The reverse of this can happen of course and there is a way of handling it that can dissolve the conflict. When someone raises a disagreement with us, we could begin by accepting what the other person is casting off as a gift and we could say (to ourselves), "Let me carry that for you for a while until you are able to value your human 'I' more." This gives us some of an idea of the power of the creative word.

In this way we unite with the other person instead of distancing ourselves because of the difficulty. This is also true for judging; judging essentially unites things and in this case we are uniting things differently. The armies of heaven, who are look-a-likes for John's image of his Higher Self, speak about the unity that comes from recognising the purity and majesty of the human 'I'. A new community is formed of those who are working to reveal the fullness of the human 'I' and to experience the life-force of Christ in the midst of everyday life. This is in contrast to the old community, the nations, which are now struck (smited) and shepherded with an iron staff. *Poimanei* means shepherding not ruling.

Now John can see that his I AM assists in the pouring out of the wine, which is the blood of Christ. It is as if the crucifixion happens perpetually until the last human being takes up his or her purpose. It is hard for us to understand that outside time and space all things continually happen. The deed of Christ must continue until all human beings take advantage of the purpose for the deed. Such is the love-wrath of God.

When we are successful in this work we earn the title King of kings and Lord of lords. Within, represented by the thigh, and without represented by the cloak, we rule the rulers in our being while at the same time our Lord, our 'I', influences all our thoughts, feelings and actions. Our striving is assisted every step of the way by the Lamb, we just have to see him standing beside us. Perhaps this is why John was the only disciple standing by the cross – he was the only one who saw the power of the risen Christ that was to come.

Then I saw an angel standing in the sun, and with a loud voice he called to all the birds that fly in midheaven, "Come, gather for the great supper of God, to eat the flesh of kings, the flesh of captains, the flesh of mighty men, the flesh of horses

and their riders, and the flesh of all men, both free and slave, both small and great." And I saw the beast and the kings of the earth with their armies gathered to make war against him who sits upon the horse and against his army. And the beast was captured, and with it the false prophet who in its presence had worked the signs by which he deceived those who had received the mark of the beast and those who worshiped its image. These two were thrown alive into the lake of fire that burns with sulphur. And the rest were slain by the sword of him who sits upon the horse, the sword that issues from his mouth; and all the birds were gorged with their flesh. Rev 19:17-21

Then I saw one (not 'an') angel standing in the sun it says in the Greek. This would suggest that this is a significant angelic being. Remember that at the beginning of this chapter John had seen heaven open and he sees this one angel calling to all the birds flying in midheaven. Could this angel be standing above midheaven looking down? Could this sun be the Central Sun, the Galactic Centre at the heart of the Milky Way galaxy that Robert Powell speaks of? (See Christ and the Maya Calender by Robert Powell and Kevin Dann, Appendix 1.) In Robert Powell's understanding this Central Sun, which is beyond our planetary system, is the home of the Trinity. Our sun is its miniature copy. Plato referred to it as the Supra-Celestial sun.

We must agree that these images John presents challenge reality as we know it; an angel calling birds to God's supper to gorge themselves on 'human' flesh, and a war against the rider on the white horse and his companions in which the beast and false prophet are captured and thrown into a lake of fire. It is a lot to happen in a few short verses.

The only way to make some sense of it for our life today – which we must – is to expand our understanding wider and higher. If this angel is standing in the Central Sun beyond our own sun and planetary system, then it must be a very pure angel indeed. Perhaps it is Archangel Michael who works so closely with the cosmic Christ whose home is found in the Central Sun.

So why would this scene suddenly appear to John after he saw the image of his Higher Self? Could all the beings in this image represent the effects of human thinking, feeling and will on the universe? If so, then we can see that these three soul faculties have caused chaos in midheaven. This angel calls all the birds, all the thoughts that human beings think which fill the universe with shapes of energy that can look like birds. Imagine the shapes our thoughts can make; some sharp and jagged like a crow, others soft and fluffy like a duckling, and many more in between. How often do we consider that we create forces with our thoughts? We think our thoughts so privately we can hardly imagine that they might create a force – even though expressions of anger or love are palpable in the air around us!

Flesh is *sarx* which refers to the astral force which human beings have in common with animals but is not found in the plant kingdom (with some exceptions). Our astral force is responsible for motion and emotion, and we could say that the flesh represents human feelings. So these bird-thoughts are feeding on wilful feelings; for kings, captains and mighty men are men of strong will. If we can imagine the human will as a substance which exists spiritually in the cosmos then we can well imagine how much of it there is. Does this God have a great supper to deal with it? Could this supper be like a great waste recycling plant?

If we aspire to connect up with our I AM we are agreeing to take part in a continual battle within our soul. The beast and his assistants will do everything in their power to prevent us from achieving this ultimate human goal. The battlefield is our soul and the elements in the battle are our thoughts, our feelings and our intentions. We could say that with the help of Archangel Michael our will-filled thinking guides our feelings to ever higher expression. When we avoid engaging in the battle the volcanic activity in our soul is alive with the mischief of the beast. When we raise ourselves above this the beast will implode in its own activity, in the lake of fire that burns like sulphur in the human astral that is being refined.

When it says, "the rest were slain by the sword of him who sits upon the horse," we know that when we are connected with our I AM we can start to look after ourselves. These are powerful images for this time in human evolution. There is much to understand about our own consciousness and our own ability to act in a higher way in all the events of life. It is important for us to try to see what transpires and perhaps John is showing that we can do this best by using our spiritual Imagination.

CHAPTER TWENTY

The First Resurrection

Then I saw an angel coming down from heaven, holding in his hand the key of the bottomless pit and a great chain. And he seized the dragon, that ancient serpent, who is the Devil and Satan, and bound him for a thousand years, and threw him into the pit, and shut it and sealed it over him, that he should deceive the nations no more, till the thousand years were ended. After that he must be loosed for a little while. Rev 20:1-3

The beast and the false prophet have been thrown alive into the lake of fire that burns with sulphur. Now the dragon who is the Devil and Satan is sealed in the abyss for a period of time. That seems to have taken care of all the bad guys. We might experience some relief from this idea but if so, wouldn't we be ignoring the purpose of these beings?

It is true that something within us cries out for the good and hopes that all that is bad will keep its distance from us. Rudolf Steiner said that he was often asked why we couldn't just have the good and his reply was that the good is too weak. We need the opposite of good to strengthen it, and this opposition comes from those beings who agreed to sacrifice their progress so that they could stay back and work against evolution enabling human beings to strive for their own freedom. In fact, true good is actually the harmony between opposites and the greatest symbol of this is the three crosses on Golgotha; Christ in the middle with Lucifer and Ahriman on each side of him. Christ, who brought the gift of the 'I' to humanity, is straddled by the beings who work against it.

So if these forces of opposition have been destroyed and detained this would mean that those human beings who have not become free through resisting deception will no longer have the chance of becoming free. "Deceive the nations" suggests that human thinking has been led astray. Deceive, *plané*, means wandering, wandering from the path. If we go bush walking we know that we must be vigilant so that we do not lose our way, so that we keep to the path and arrive home safely. This requires that we put in the effort to be aware of each step that we take. The same is true of life.

Yet how often do we take steps of consciousness without being certain that we are on the right path? Or, take no steps because we are not confident that we know what the right path is? This is the human dilemma. The only way of being confident of not wandering is through our 'I' being. We needn't worry about which path is right, all we need to worry about is our relationship with our 'I'. This relationship is forged through our personal effort, and it is an effort. We must learn to recognise the deception and it is as if the opposing forces are there to show us what it is not. Only in our encounter with them can we know what is not the path. Only by realising how human consciousness can be deceived can we know the truth. We could say that it is like focussing the binoculars until we get the clearest view.

This doesn't mean that we become the supreme critic of world events and human behaviour. It means that we become very aware of every thought that flows through our own minds – which is usually critical of world events and human behaviour! Each time we think negative thoughts about others, and about ourselves, we must strive to restore the balance. This balance is achieved when we are neutral in our observation and simply recognise the forces at play without being judgmental.

There is another aspect to this story too. As long as we do not recognise these beings who sacrificed their progress to stay back and help us claim our freedom, they are held captive. Where are they held captive? This fiery lake and this abyss can be found within us. The fiery lake could be our smouldering anger and the abyss could be the depth of our unconscious will. For as long as we do not utilise the gift of these opposing forces they are bound within us. Whenever we use them to become more consciously aware they are freed to move forward.

So while they are held captive within us - and we shouldn't take "a thousand years" literally, this time span could indicate a complete cycle of time in which certain things are developed, in 2 Peter 3:8 we read "with the Lord one day is as a thousand years, and a thousand years as one day" – we are deceived. We live in an illusion which is continually fed by these beings. Anything that lowers our consciousness; alcohol, drugs, computer games, gambling, even religion, makes us vulnerable to ideas of illusion. We can only avoid deception through our 'I' being. Only when we do the work and experience the balancing and harmonising power of our 'I' as we interact with other people will we be free from illusion.

Then I saw thrones, and seated on them were those to whom judgment was committed. Also I saw the souls of those who had been beheaded for their testimony to Jesus and for the word of God, and who had not worshiped the beast or its image and had not received its mark on their foreheads or their hands. They came to life, and reigned with Christ a thousand years. The rest of the dead did not come to life until the thousand years were ended. This is the first resurrection. Blessed and holy is he who shares in the first resurrection! Over such the second death has no power, but they shall be priests of God and of Christ, and they shall reign with him a thousand years. Rev 20:4-6

Is John seeing thrones on which a king or queen might sit? Or is he seeing members of the third highest spiritual hierarchy called Thrones? If this is the case, then those 'seated' on them, in other words appearing above the Thrones, are the Cherubim who are known as the Spirits of Harmony. This would also make sense when we read that they are the ones to whom judgment was given (not committed). Judgment, *krima*, indicates that a balancing or harmonising has occurred.

These angelic orders, that preside over all the elements of the universe to keep everything running smoothly, are largely unknown to us. Yet our wellbeing depends on them and, according to their various areas of responsibility they keep everything in balance. When in the Bible it mentions 'god' it is often these beings that are meant.

Above them, at the pinnacle, are the Trinity – Father, Son and Holy Spirit – and so it is the nine members of the spiritual hierarchy who connect the Trinity to this earth. When the Christ Spirit descended to this earth, probably from the Galactic Centre or Central Sun as Robert Powell suggests, this Spirit would have had to pass through each of the spheres where the beings of the hierarchy dwell. No wonder the beheaded one is mentioned in the next verse. This sentence should possibly read, "I saw the soul of the one who had been beheaded", in other words, John the Baptist who was beheaded by Herod, and who, by baptising Jesus, witnessed the Christ Spirit entering into Jesus' being "as a dove from heaven". These words indicate that John saw the passage of the Christ Spirit down through the hierarchy and into the body of Jesus as he was baptising him in the river Jordan.

We mustn't be deterred by all this detail that is so divorced from our everyday lives. If we can try to imagine in our own minds these mighty images that John sees they will become more real to us. If we try to imagine how the angelic orders regulate and order everything in the universe then we bring them alive. When we feel the wind blow on our face or see the snow fall or see a strong tree growing, we can acknowledge that all this is possible because of the order created by these beings. Even if we don't know the detail of their tasks we can at least acknowledge that something is regulating our world.

This is actually our task, to develop conscious awareness of the reality of this universe. By being open to possibilities means that these spiritual orders can reveal something of their workings to us. After all it is through their work that we can live on this earth and develop our consciousness. When we start to have ideas about why things happen in a certain way as we observe nature or our fellow human beings, this is the beginning of awareness of a larger reality. Then we become those who do not have the mark of the beast – because we have resisted the work of the beast which is to cloud our consciousness.

These ideas that we might have must always be living ideas; ideas that breathe and develop and never stagnate on a particular point of view. This is what is meant by the words "those who came to life" and "those who did not come to life". The word life *zoe* means to have vitality. When something has vitality it is living and growing and energetic. This vital energy is our life-force, our etheric body which has rejuvenating properties. It is also associated with the resurrection; when Jesus completely received the full force of the Christ Spirit at the crucifixion he no longer needed a physical body, he used his etheric body to appear to the disciples several times which we can read about in the Gospels. This is called the resurrection body. If our own etheric body is vital enough we can share in the first resurrection.

These are the new priests, the ones who have a firsthand experience of the work of the spiritual worlds. These are the ones who see Christ, as St Paul did, and with him can say, "I have been crucified with Christ; it is no longer I who live, but Christ who lives in me;" Gal 2:20 These new priests move silently in the world and touch people in unspoken ways. They are, like John the Baptist, the witness who reunites humanity with its purpose. They are not preachers or converters; they are living examples of truth.

And when the thousand years are ended, Satan will be loosed from his prison and will come out to deceive the nations which are at the four corners of the earth, that is, Gog and Magog, to gather them for battle; their number is like the sand of the sea. And they marched up over the broad earth and surrounded the camp of the saints and the beloved city; but fire came down from heaven and consumed them, and the devil who had deceived them was thrown into the lake of fire and sulphur where the beast and the false prophet were, and they will be tormented day and night for ever and ever. Rev 20:7-10

To take the 'thousand years' literally only serves to disconnect us from our developing consciousness. If we dismiss these stories as a future event that is not relevant in our lives today it is at our peril. John is talking about patterns of things that occur concurrently to one extent or another, within our consciousness and within the universe. We are so enclosed in our skin with our private thoughts that we find it difficult to be inclusive of all that is outside us. This is a strange phenomenon because we only have to do some gardening, for instance, to see how we change the world.

Everything in this universe is interconnected and our every thought, feeling and action has an effect on it. It is up to us to make this experience relevant and real in our lives. Perhaps if we could stand outside the universe (if there is an outside) we would see everything that ever happened within it as if these events were happening at once. In fact, it is our ideas about time that limit us from penetrating the spiritual worlds and therefore limit our understanding of ourselves and our development. So when John speaks about something happening for a thousand years he will be talking about a process that reaches completion. Since it is about the base numbers one and zero or ten, we could well find something significant in that, perhaps to do with the development in ten areas of our being or ten phases in our development, each phase necessary for the next.

It could be that John is pointing to the phases in the development of the forces of resistance who assist human beings to achieve greater awareness. The story goes that the gods could see that human beings would never be more than puppets unless they took responsibility for their own development. This personal responsibility would only arise if human beings had to face obstacles. So members of the various angelic orders offered to remain behind and become the necessary forces of resistance. This idea is almost incomprehensible, yet, if we think about it deeply we can understand why this occurred. The physicists can show us how useful a force of resistance is. Gog of Magog (it seems is the right expression) is a mighty force of resistance if we read about this warrior prince in Ezekiel.

When we consider human nature in all its endeavours, one of the first things we see is that we do not usually expect resistance, we hope that everything will go according to plan, and when this does not happen, which is often the case, we experience a sense of failure and annoyance. Time and again we underestimate the value of the process and look only for results (and pray for removal of obstacles). What matters is the way we engage with what goes wrong. When we read this passage of The Revelation we might experience a feeling of defeat because we thought that Satan was dealt with and then, after a time, he re-emerges and appears to be on the war path.

Couldn't it be possible that he was kept away from us to give us time to strengthen our already won freedom? Then, as if to make sure that we are free, he is back again to test us. When this test is successful "fire came down from heaven and consumed them". The fire beings are the Archangels and this sentence indicates that *satanos*, the Ahrimanic beings, has been reabsorbed into the angelic order to which they belong. Fire is a transformative element; it could be that these beings have done their work and can now be redeemed. Of course this task will not be complete for the whole of the human race for some time because these beings are numbered like the sand of the sea.

"they will be tormented day and night for ever and ever" - this torment, *basanizo* is similar in meaning to the word toil and points to the anti-forces trapped within those human beings who are making no effort to resist illusion and who allow themselves to be unconsciously influenced by *satanos*. The conditions of modern society are such that human freedom is increasingly curtailed by rules and regulations and the toil of the satanic beings is endless; endless because there is no result from their work and no redemption for them. It doesn't mean that we should fight back, we don't have to carry placards down the street, but we can take personal responsibility for what we feel and think, and for our motives, intentions and actions. Each small piece of freedom won by each human being will transform this universe forever.

Then I saw a great white throne and him who sat upon it; from his presence earth and sky fled away, and no place was found for them. And I saw the dead, great and small, standing before the throne, and books were opened. Also another book was opened, which is the book of life. And the dead were judged by what was written in the books, by what they had done. And the sea gave up the dead in it, Death and Hades gave up the dead in them, and all were judged by what they had done. Then Death and Hades were thrown into the lake

of fire. This is the second death, the lake of fire; and if any one's name was not found written in the book of life, he was thrown into the lake of fire. Rev 20:11-15

Again we should ask if this great white throne is an actual seat or whether the angelic order of Thrones is providing a cradle of support to reveal the highest we can know. It must be a mighty being because John says, "from his face earth and heaven fled away, and no region was found for them". This is a similar interaction to Moses' experience in Exodus when he spoke intimately with the Lord who told him, "you cannot see my face; for man shall not see me and live." Ex 33:20 In both of these statements there is the suggestion that another consciousness is needed to make sense of what is being said.

Heaven and earth, life and death, the dead and the living are dualities that are part of time and space in which we live in our earthly condition. We entered into this state of being, as the story of Genesis graphically depicts, to become self-realised individuals and to taste self-won freedom. The only way we can have this experience is through our eternal being, our I AM. This I AM is often referred to in the Bible as The Lord. John, in The Revelation, is sharing with us his own journey to be at one with his I AM and this experience is giving him access to the highest gods who exist outside the duality of heaven and earth. Moses, in Exodus, was talking to his I AM, the face of which he could not see unless he were dead.

When John says that he saw the dead, great and small, could he be looking at all the people he had been over the aeons who, at the end of each incarnation, had died? Wouldn't this be our experience when we see the face of our I AM from which heaven and earth flee? Heaven and earth couldn't be there if we saw, as if standing in a row, all our past personalities.

John must be describing a picture of what we experience when we begin to collaborate with our I AM. This book of life contains our every feeling, thought and deed from every single life we have ever lived on this earth. The word used for life here is *zoe*, the purified etheric forces that underpin this universe. These forces are the scaffolding of our body without which we can have no form, when we die they leave us and our body shrivels. In their purest form they are the forces of resurrection in which we can dwell after death to the extent that we have connected with our I AM and become conscious of the Christ force within us. It is this pure etheric form which Christ Jesus used after his death to appear to the disciples, and in which he can appear to us today to the extent that we have purified our own life-forces.

So we might wonder why this book should be referred to as an etheric book. In our own being it is our etheric vehicle that holds our memory bank, as if in a library. When we remember it, it is as if we open our personal etheric bankbook to see what is stored there. It is interesting to realise that to open the book, we have to take it out of the library and read it in our soul, that region of our being where our feeling, thinking and will operate. We will deal with these memories in the right way to the extent that we are conscious of our feeling, thinking and will. If our consciousness is dim these memories can haunt us or torment us.

This book of life, in terms of the cosmos, contains the memories from every life we (and everyone) have lived on this earth and they are stored in the etheric vehicle of this cosmos and we can only read them when we are connected with our I AM. Mostly this happens in between lives, but only to the extent that we have become consciously aware. Increasingly people are incarnating who are conscious of the contents of the book of life. They can be identified by their purity and their objectivity when dealing with the events in their life. They have a highly developed conscience which expresses itself as love, compassion and respect.

We might wonder about how we might be doing in our striving to become conscious of our I AM and in developing a relationship with the etheric Christ. We might worry about the judgment, the second death and the lake of fiery transformation. We might also wonder what the benchmark might be. But is this the way to see it? Surely we can only deal with our present situation and resolve to be more and more consciously aware of the activity of our soul in our daily lives. By using our spiritual Imagination we can create images of our I AM, of Christ and of all the lives we may have lived, and will live, and realise that underpinning it all is what makes us human; the ability to feel, think and use our will with full awareness. Then we become the interested observer in all that takes place in our lives.

CHAPTER TWENTYONE

A New Heaven and a New Earth

Then I saw a new heaven and a new earth; for the first heaven and the first earth had passed away, and the sea was no more. And I saw the holy city, new Jerusalem, coming down out of heaven from God, prepared as a bride adorned for her husband; and I heard a loud voice from the throne saying, "Behold, the dwelling of God is with men. He will dwell with them, and they shall be his people, and God himself will be with them; he will wipe away every tear from their eyes, and death shall be no more, neither shall there be mourning nor crying nor pain any more, for the former things have passed away." Rev 21:1-4

John now sees the image of the awakened soul prepared for union with the spirit. This Holy City is our higher consciousness made pure by our own striving. The sea is our feelings, our emotions which sweep us this way and that, sometimes irrationally. The only way we can free our soul from its natural inclination towards feeling is to engage with our ability to think. This thinking must be vigorous enough that we might become much more consciously aware than we are now. When our feelings are guided by active thoughts our soul becomes adorned. This word adorned *kosmeo* means to arrange, to put in order. When our feelings, thoughts and intentions are put into the right order they can receive our spirit, but not before.

It is our individual responsibility to create this harmonious order in our soul. We quite possibly underestimate the degree to which our soul needs to be put in order, as well as the effort required to do so. The underlying tenor of our soul is rooted in feeling, for our spirit it is thinking, and our body is underpinned by will. When we can identify the individual quality of these three faculties in our own being we can begin to bring them to harmony and order by balancing our emotions, sharpening our thinking, and allowing a higher conscience to influence our motives. This is our primary task if we are to have any wedding in our being.

When we think about preparing our soul for her wedding the first thing we become aware of is the extent to which our feelings are coloured by all our past experiences and which can be based on some quite unsound ideas. A simple example would be that one person's pain may not be aroused in the same way as another person's pain. Our feelings, especially in this modern world where we can live independently from our family unit, can be quite individual. They can often cause us to be irrational and sometimes it is only when we discuss our situation with someone else that we are able to guide our feelings in another direction. This could be one explanation for the rise of the profession of Psychology over relatively recent decades.

The first heaven and earth must pass away, we must be prepared to leave behind old ideas about heaven being 'up there somewhere' and the earth being our only reality down here. Also, as we cast off the egotistical influences of Babylon our being becomes the Holy City Jerusalem where God can tabernacle. This strange word tabernacle, *skene*, is often translated as dwelling which doesn't give us the idea of a living dwelling created by a purified consciousness which gives as much weight to the spiritual as it does the physical. Tabernacle means a tent, a temporary dwelling which we can pitch here, or there, according to our needs. This dwelling is not fixed, it can move with us as we move to new understandings of who we are and why we are here.

The meaning of the words spoken by the great voice can also be interpreted differently. The translation we are considering says, "Behold, the dwelling of God is with men. He will dwell with them, and they shall be his people, and God himself will be with them;" These last seven words, *kai autos o theos met auton estai*, could easily be translated as 'and self a god within them will be'. In other words, when we achieve conscious awareness through our I AM and through the presence of Christ we will be gods.

It is an astounding thing to contemplate being a god for what would it mean in the scheme of things? For a start it would mean that we are very aware of how we used our feeling, thinking and will. Now, we can cause many ripples through the blind use of these soul faculties and it is probably just as well that we are not aware of the consequences. If we try to align the use of our feeling, thinking and will with the purity of God wouldn't we naturally become like him? Wouldn't we become the creative harmony that he represents in the cosmos? This is what the consummation of the union between our soul and spirit brings. Then there will be no more tears, for our soul would never feel small enough to squeeze them out. When heaven and earth are one, death serves no purpose, and grieving for the past will become a celebration for what the past has created in us.

And he who sat upon the throne said, "Behold, I make all things new." Also he said, "Write this, for these words are trustworthy and true." And he said to me, "It is done! I am the Alpha and the Omega, the beginning and the end. To the thirsty I will give from the fountain of the water of life without payment. He who conquers shall have this heritage, and I will be his God and he shall be my son. But as for the cowardly, the faithless, the polluted, as for murderers, fornicators, sorcerers, idolaters, and all liars, their lot shall be in the lake that burns with fire and sulphur, which is the second death." Rev 21:5-8

This beautiful, hopeful statement, "Behold, I make all things new" doesn't quite express what is meant here. 'All things' is the word *pantos* which means 'entirely' and 'new', *kainos*, means 'something different', something that has never existed before. Therefore the voice is really saying: Behold, I produce something entirely different, something that exists for the first time, which of course is human beings in whom both the I AM and Christ are active.

This is the culmination of a mighty work which must be recorded as the voice directs. "write this" *graphon* which is similar to the word graphic, a vivid image, an engraving, which will create a permanent record. The statement "trustworthy and true" adds weight to this important stage. Trustworthy, faithful, is *pistos* which doesn't speak of blind belief but of knowing, of certainty. True is a*lethes,* which means overcoming forgetting, to reveal what is concealed within us. This recognises that our earthly consciousness conceals so much.

And then he said to me "It is done! I am the Alpha and the Omega, the beginning and the end." This is how it is put in the Greek: *gegonan ego[eimi] to alpha kai to omega* which really says," I have become (not it is done) I AM, the first and the last, the beginning and the end."

Even though it doesn't say, "It is done!" there are still echoes here of the crucifixion, the purpose of which was to combine the I AM of Jesus with the Cosmic Christ here on earth for the first time. This deed paved the way for each human being to follow suit and to become an entirely new being in the cosmos. Entirely new because of the freedom we are given to do it - or not. Those who don't do it are listed and perhaps we can use this list as a guide.

Cowardly, *deilois*, fearful. We now need to become fearless. The purpose of fear was to unite us with the earth. Fear causes our life-force, our etheric force, to contract and disconnect us from the spiritual worlds. Fear has done its job and now we must do everything we can to expand our etheric body so that it unites with the etheric presence of Christ.

Faithless, *apistois*. We can have faith now; we can know the truth, not blindly but with certainty. "You will know the truth and the truth will make you free," said Jesus.

Polluted, *ebdelugmenois* which indicates deception. We no longer need to hide behind all the various deceptions of modern life. Those who express themselves through their I AM, who have a relationship with Christ, are different. The light within us shines and we need to find a way to be with that, and live in this modern world that is so polluted with so many other forces. If we try to hide our light we are the deceivers, neither should we impose it on others for it is up to each person to create their own inner light.

Murderers, *phoneusin* gives a sense of slaughter, to kill something for our own use. Through our I AM we become life givers, not life takers. There are many subtle ways that we can take the life of others; when we dismiss them, criticise them or ignore them, for instance.

Fornicators, *pornois*. Once we connect with our I AM and our relationship with Christ begins to develop we must remain faithful and true. We fornicate, *porneo*, when we are unfaithful to our spiritual nature and follow the instincts of our ego. We are also unfaithful to spiritual truth when we apply earthly concepts to spiritual ideas; earthly concepts are usually the opposite of spiritual truth.

Sorcerers, *pharmakois* points to the magical use of the will which prevails in every area of modern life. The sorcerer uses potions, spells, enchantments and drugs to magically alter things. St Paul tells us that in the twinkling of an eye we will be changed, we don't need to use any tricks.

Idolaters, *eidōlolatrais, eidos* means appearance or likeness, phantom. Our I AM is the real thing, we don't need any pretence and if we apply all of the above we will have the courage to be who we are, as we are. We won't want to conform to the expectation of others. This won't mean that we become protesters, it will just mean that we are comfortable as we are (in our constantly changing and developing state).

Liars *pseudesin*, means false. In all honesty we must realise that much of us is false, we are, after all, a work in progress. We are still learning the free-making truth and, in that, we must try to be more courageous. In fact the more we know, the more we realise what we don't know.

Through the death and resurrection of Jesus Christ we have been given the opportunity to die to this earth and to revive spiritually. If we do not take this opportunity we will die a second death and remain tied to this earth and its deadly concepts. This is a very real possibility for many people today which is deeply sad. Each one of us who can light up within by understanding some spiritual truth can create light by which others can see. When we work with the etheric Christ, even slightly, his light increases and his etheric presence can awaken others who are still asleep. Then it is done because we have become!

Then came one of the seven angels who had the seven bowls full of the seven last plagues, and spoke to me, saying, "Come, I will show you the Bride, the wife of the Lamb." And in the Spirit he carried me away to a great, high mountain, and showed me the holy city Jerusalem coming down out of heaven from God, having the glory of God, its radiance like a most rare jewel, like a jasper, clear as crystal. It had a great, high wall, with twelve gates, and at the gates twelve angels, and on the gates the names of the twelve tribes of the sons of Israel were inscribed; on the east three gates, on the north three gates, on the south three gates, and on the west three gates. And the wall of the city had twelve foundations, and on them the twelve names of the twelve apostles of the Lamb. And he who talked to me had a measuring rod of gold to measure the city and its gates and walls. The city lies foursquare, its length the same as its breadth; and he measured the city with his rod, twelve thousand stadia; its length and breadth and height are equal. He also measured its wall, a hundred and forty-four cubits by a man's measure, that is, an angel's. The wall was built of jasper, while the city was pure gold, clear as glass. The foundations of the wall of the city were adorned with every jewel; the first was jasper, the second sapphire, the third agate, the fourth emerald, the fifth onyx, the sixth carnelian, the seventh chrysolite, the eighth beryl, the ninth topaz, the tenth chrysoprase, the eleventh jacinth, the twelfth amethyst. And the twelve gates were twelve pearls, each of the gates made of a single pearl, and the street of the city was pure gold, transparent as glass. And I saw no temple in the city, for its temple is the Lord God the Almighty and the Lamb. And the city has no need of sun or moon to shine upon it, for the glory of God is its light, and its lamp is the Lamb. By its light shall the nations walk; and the kings of the earth shall bring their glory into it, and its gates shall never be shut by day--and there shall be no night there; they shall bring into it the glory and the honor of the nations. But nothing unclean shall enter it, nor any one who practices abomination or falsehood, but only those who are written in the Lamb's book of life. Rev 21:9-27

What John now sees is what takes place when all things are made new. This is the transformation and perfection that has taken place so that the Bride, the wife of the Lamb, is visible. This perfection lies within each of us as potential and we have the freedom to realise that. If we can penetrate to the truth of this, even in brief moments, a tiny flame deep within us flickers and begins the process of radiant transparency that John describes in this text.

It is awe inspiring to think that our soul could be Christ's bride; that our soul can achieve such perfect harmony so as to be married to the risen Christ. In this marriage they are united through self-achieved purity and harmony and John's description gives us a sense of patterned regularity, each element in its proper place. We could take each element one by one to examine what it means and there would probably be different levels of meaning to be found. One of the key things in this description is the perspective from which it is seen. John says that, "in the spirit he (the angel) carried me away to a great high mountain."

We can gain quite a different understanding of ourselves and our daily activity if we look down on our lives from the highest perspective possible. Spiritual teachers down the ages have urged their pupils to do certain exercises to enhance their conscious awareness, one of which is to view each day in reverse before going to sleep. If we do this as if we were standing on a mountain looking down on the activity of a person way below, moving here and there throughout the day, we can be much more objective than if we relive each moment from within our body. From this higher perspective we may even be able to have a panoramic view of the past and the future, even past and future lives – if only in our imagination.

What is important to realise is that we are building this holy city, the New Jerusalem, now, today. This city is the consciousness that we construct every moment of each day. It is a long and arduous work as we well know, but it is the work not the eventual city that is the point and purpose of it all.

The more we can look down on the construction from the

height of the mountain the greater will be our understanding of our purpose. We will get a greater sense of the fact that we are beings of soul and spirit using our body as a vehicle. This will assist us to stop identifying too strongly with our body and to start to experience our soul and spirit in greater reality. It will also give us a greater respect for our body without which we would not be able to achieve our purpose.

It is helpful to create imaginations of our entry into this earth. We can imagine ourselves as spirit beings condensing into the body created by our mother in her womb. We can review the way we grew up and developed our soul, and in what ways we become conscious of our spirit through our connection with our 'I' being. As we age, after a certain point, we experience our physical body becoming weaker and we get a sense of our spirit preparing to expand back into the universe from whence it came. From this mountain-top perspective we can then see how it is possible that we repeat this process life after life and in this way build this holy city.

The Bible tells this story from the beginning in Genesis to the end in Revelation. It begins with the story of how humanity left the mountain and entered the garden. It ends with humanity returning to the mountain having created the holy city. On this journey we are led by the Lamb, the one who showed us the secret of creating the resurrection body, that body of pure life-force that no longer needs physicality which is the Lamb. When John says, "And the city has no need of sun or moon to shine upon it, for the glory of God is its light, and its lamp is the Lamb," he means that our being has expanded to encompass the sun and moon, we are united with the universe and the density of our being no longer hides the Lamb.

It is our conscious awareness that can reveal to us the secrets that John sees. We can approach these mysteries by thinking about them deeply and vigorously, and even when we think we have reached a conclusion to then continue the thinking process so that we can harvest even more truth. Then, if we are given a deeper understanding to hold it in our hearts as a special gift until we have confirmed it from twelve sides, in this way our beings become the holy city.

CHAPTER TWENTYTWO

Christ's Coming

Then he showed me the river of the water of life, bright as crystal, flowing from the throne of God and of the Lamb through the middle of the street of the city; also, on either side of the river, the tree of life with its twelve kinds of fruit, yielding its fruit each month; and the leaves of the tree were for the healing of the nations. There shall no more be anything accursed, but the throne of God and of the Lamb shall be in it, and his servants shall worship him; they shall see his face, and his name shall be on their foreheads. And night shall be no more; they need no light of lamp or sun, for the Lord God will be their light, and they shall reign for ever and ever. Rev 22:1-5

This image that John is shown seems a bit odd; the river is flowing through the middle of the street – perhaps it is a town square rather than a street, and in the square is a garden. This garden within the holy city reminds us of the Garden of Eden.

And out of the ground the LORD God made to grow every tree that is pleasant to the sight and good for food, the tree of

life also in the midst of the garden, and the tree of the knowledge of good and evil. Gen 2:9
Then, we looked outside ourselves at the garden, now the garden is within us. It is as if we have ingested the garden, using it for our sustenance as we travelled the long and arduous road from Eden to the New Jerusalem. The life of the water and the tree is *zoe*, the life-force that gives all physical things form. Within us this life is our etheric body, also called the body of formative forces, and is therefore a matrix of energy supporting all living things. Whenever anything withers it is because this life-force is departing. Whenever anything dies this life-force is disconnected. This force holds the secret of life on earth, it is the elixir of life, it is the secret anti-aging ingredient and it is also the stuff of the resurrection body of Christ.

The word for tree used here is *xulon* which actually means wood. The Greek word for a living tree is *dendron*. We might wonder why *xulon* was chosen here instead of *dendron*. Could it be suggestive of the wood used to construct the cross on which Jesus was crucified? It isn't hard to imagine the wood coming back to life (*zoe*) and growing leaves after participating in such a mighty deed as the crucifixion.

The globe of this earth has this life element, this etheric element, which is an airy, water-filled garment giving all earthly things their life. The health of the garment depends on the activity of humanity; if we do not strive to develop our own conscious awareness out of our own free will then our etheric forces will dry up, they will become woody which in turn contributes to the woodiness of the earthly etheric garment.

One of the most important factors of the crucifixion was to give new life to the etheric of this earth as well as to each member of humanity. When our etheric force is completely filled with new life we no longer depend on our physical body for our existence. What isn't made very clear in the accounts of the crucifixion in the New Testament is that Jesus' physical body was completely purified by the time that Christ could enter it on the cross, and this meant that it completely disappeared, its material substance dissolved, and Christ was then visible to certain people in his etheric form.

This is the real meaning of the last words in the Gospel of Matthew, "I am with you always, to the close of the age." Mt 28:20

Matthew is actually telling us that Christ is with us in his etheric form now! Regardless of our race, colour or creed Christ is with us in his resurrection body, this is the Easter story. He is waiting for us to become the holy city in which we can dwell with him for ever and ever. If we take the work of the risen Christ seriously the 'wood' within us will grow leaves.

If our etheric forces remain wooden they undermine our will. If our will is weakened, and our capacity to think, which has its seat in our etheric body, is diminished, then we are only left with our instinctual emotions. This is what is happening now, and at a time when more and more people are becoming conscious of their past lives, however dimly, which means that they could encounter people who have killed them in a past life, for instance, hence, increasingly we are hearing about senseless and unfathomable murders. There are many examples of similarly unexplainable events in the daily news.

There is a very urgent need for more and more people to experience the presence of Christ. We can do this simply by imagining what this presence looks like for us. Whatever images we create, if rightly motivated, Christ will fill them. We will see his face, we won't need to tell anyone that we can see his face because it will be obvious by the vitality of our etheric body, we will shine. In Exodus Moses was told, "you cannot see my face; for man shall not see me and live." Ex 33:20 Now, when we become aware of the etheric presence of Christ, "the Lord God - our I AM - will be our light, and we shall reign for ever and ever." Our consciousness becomes the New Jerusalem where no crucifixion is necessary.

And he said to me, "These words are trustworthy and true. And the Lord, the God of the spirits of the prophets, has sent his angel to show his servants what must soon take place. And behold, I am coming soon." Blessed is he who keeps the words of the prophecy of this book. I John am he who heard and saw these things. And when I heard and saw them, I fell down to worship at the feet of the angel who showed them to me; but he said to me, "You must not do that! I am a fellow servant with you and your brethren the prophets, and with those who keep the words of this book. Worship God." Rev 22:6-9

It is helpful to be reminded that Jesus is speaking these words through this angel (see verse 16). Jesus is the human being who was so perfect he could withstand the presence of Christ in his being. We must never underestimate what this entailed. Can we imagine the purity required to enable part of the mighty Trinity to enter into a human body without destroying it? If we can imagine this, even in part, we can certainly understand why it would take many incarnations (as it took Jesus) to gradually raise our conscious awareness to that point where we can experience our I-being and activate the presence of Christ within us – which is our sole purpose.

This being, "the Lord the God (a God could be a better translation) of the spirits of the prophets" could easily be designated as the highest expression of our I-being, our I AM. When our I AM functions in our soul we become the prophet, the seer, and our three spiritual faculties, Imagination, Inspiration and Intuition function in a consciously aware manner. At this level, our I AM is of the same 'substance' as Christ – this is the mystical wedding.

This wedding needs to be experienced in our daily life and this is why we exist on this earth, and have existed at various points throughout human history. In this way we could develop all the various characteristics that we have today. The driving force behind this is our search for the words which are trustworthy and true. The words, the *logoi*, are the mysterious beings which John speaks of at the beginning of his gospel, "In the beginning was the word, and the word was with God and the word was (a) God ..." These primal creative *logoi* are indeed trustworthy and true. This word trustworthy is really faithful, *pistos*, which means knowing for sure, without a doubt; true is *alethes*, a state of overcoming forgetting, which is more than remembering because this is a stage when memory is no longer necessary.

The angel has been sent, *apostello*, which is a commissioning, and a very important commissioning for this angel may have to deal with more than it bargains for. Take note that this word 'soon' which is *tachu*, actually means quickly. Our I AM "has commissioned his messenger to show his (the I AM's) servants (its earthly incarnations) what must quickly take place. And behold, I am coming quickly."

We can take this to mean that at a certain point in our

development things are going to happen, perhaps without warning. St Paul knows all about this, he was knocked to the ground and blinded by a great light without notice. In his first Letter to the Corinthians he was highly qualified to give this warning because it happened to him.

Lo! I tell you a mystery. We shall not all sleep, but we shall all be changed, in a moment, in the twinkling of an eye, at the last trumpet. For the trumpet will sound, and the dead will be raised imperishable, and we shall be changed. For this perishable nature must put on the imperishable, and this mortal nature must put on immortality. 1 Cor15:51-53

Each time we become more aware of spiritual truth, and each time we start to experience the truth of our own being, we take another step towards the imperishable and immortal. It is always hard to notice this while it is actually happening, but if we look back a year ago or more and if we could really experience the comparison of how we were then to how we are now, we will know the degree to which our consciousness has changed. We can do this quite simply by monitoring our responses to life through our feeling, thinking and intentions. If we are committed to work towards a greater experience of our I AM while at the same time finding ways to make the presence of Christ real in this modern world, we will be changed, and John is reporting that it could happen quickly. The church does not assist us in this work. It isn't about the church, it is about what we personally strive to do. Religion seems to have become a noun when really it is a verb. It is something that each of us can personally do to reunite us with what is faithful and true.

And he said to me, "Do not seal up the words of the prophecy of this book, for the time is near. Let the evildoer still do evil, and the filthy still be filthy, and the righteous still do right, and the holy still be holy." "Behold, I am coming soon, bringing my recompense, to repay every one for what he has done. I am the Alpha and the Omega, the first and the last, the beginning and the end." Blessed are those who wash their robes, that they may have the right to the tree of life and that they may enter the city by the gates. Outside are the dogs and sorcerers and fornicators and murderers and idolaters, and every one who loves and practices falsehood. "I Jesus have sent my angel to you with this testimony for the churches. I am the root and the offspring of David, the bright morning star." Rev 22:10-16

The Revelation that John received has shown us a way to understand the development of our conscious awareness and to discover our true nature as human beings. We can only know the true nature of the human being if we know about the human 'I'. We cannot have this knowledge unless we accept the responsibility that accompanies it for this human 'I' is very powerful. That is why the words were sealed up until we could prove that we could handle the freedom necessary to control our own consciousness. By contemplating the words of The Revelation we can unseal the words and experience the prophecy, the unveiling; once unsealed we cannot and must not seal them up again. This is a mighty work for us to do and we need courage and trust to carry out the task set before us.

The task of becoming consciously aware of who we are as beings of soul and spirit is necessarily difficult in order to strengthen us to bear what we will see. The message is clear, let the evildoer and the filthy be. The word evildoer is *adikon*, which really means the one who is unrighteous or unjust. They are the ones who do not make the series of adjustments - which is what justice means - to maintain a balance in their whole being. The process of becoming more consciously aware means that we have to make continual adjustments to the way we feel, think and behave.

It goes without saying that if we have to work so hard to know truth then to know it unprepared would have risks. One difficulty about knowing truth is that we will see the true nature of all those around us and hence their motives. If we don't make adjustments in our mind we could go crazy when we see what really motivates the unjust and the unclean. The unclean are those who reject the purification necessary to see truth. We can do nothing to change them, this is work each of us must personally do.

Again 'quickly' is emphasised, our I AM, *ego eimi*, is not going to give us any warning when it connects up with our being. This connection will happen in our soul and disrupt our thinking and our intentions first. Perhaps it needs to come quickly so that we have no time to resist. Also, perhaps we need to experience a certain amount of alarm to trigger its coming. It is natural for us to reject the feeling of powerlessness, especially when we are bombarded with ideas about positive thinking, but alarm and powerlessness could be the very things which call our I AM to come quickly.

Then the translation seems to suggest that all those that have done the wrong thing will get their punishment. A better rendering of this verse might be, "I am bringing the reward for each human according to his work." The promise of a reward is encouragement to keep going - a hard thing in this world of instant rewards. It might also suggest that if we haven't fully done the necessary work that we will be given a chance to complete it. There is certainly an assurance here that we will be rewarded when our I AM comes into our being. Even though we might not know what to expect, the level of trust that we have in the process could signal our readiness.

"Blessed are those who wash their robes" – what are our robes? Surely they are the layers of our being which we must continually purify. Our etheric and astral bodies become contaminated each day in our encounter with others, especially with those who are neglectful of their own preparation to receive the I AM. This could even include our best friend or partner. We must let them be and concentrate on the daily task of keeping ourselves clean.

Then we are reminded that Jesus is speaking to us. By identifying himself as the offspring of David he could be suggesting that he is the Matthew Jesus rather than the Luke Jesus, the one who had the most highly developed connection with his I AM as part of the preparation for the entrance of the Cosmic Christ into human form. Maybe the morning star that we see at sunrise is to remind us of our connection to the spiritual worlds and all that has been prepared over aeons so that each one of us can make ourselves ready, in freedom, to receive our own I AM.

The Spirit and the Bride say, "Come." And let him who hears say, "Come." And let him who is thirsty come, let him who desires take the water of life without price. I warn every one who hears the words of the prophecy of this book: if any one adds to them, God will add to him the plagues described in this book, and if any one takes away from the words of the book of this prophecy, God will take away his share in the tree of life and in the holy city, which are described in this book. He who testifies to these things says, "Surely I am coming soon." Amen. Come, Lord Jesus! The grace of the Lord Jesus be with all the saints. Amen. Rev 22:17-21

The last breath of The Revelation seems to beckon us so sweetly, "Come." We are called to action, *erchou*. The spirit and the bride call us to action by saying that if we can hear them say "Come" then we must also say, "Come." Who are we saying "Come" to? Certainly not to other people, it is a personal responsibility for each human being to work on their own level of awareness. We would be imposing our will on others if we were to tell them to come. No, this interchange is taking place within us. We could assume that since John has written down The Revelation, now printed in a book for us to read with our present earthly consciousness that we are being called to a higher consciousness. The symbols and images in The Revelation speak silently to our higher consciousness and hardly speak at all to our earthly intellect.

If we have understood any of the messages of this Revelation this could only happen through our spirit and our soul, the bride. To hear, *akouo*, is the inner hearing and understanding that comes to us from our spiritual Inspiration – as the word suggests, we have breathed in something of the truth that lies at the heart of the universe.

This inspiring of truth happens tentatively at first and we must become aware of how our earthly intellect tries to interpret what we hear by using concepts from our modern life. As we have seen throughout all the contemplations of The Revelation, our modern concepts often oppose the spiritual meaning. *Akouo* is a good example for a deaf person can hear what comes to them through their spiritual faculty of Inspiration.

When we are able to refer to our soul as the bride it indicates a purification of our soul; we have dressed her in white and prepared her for the marriage that must take place within us. This preparation takes place when we become aware of the activity of our feeling, thinking and intentions. So each time we are able to guide our feelings in different directions so that feelings of anger, for instance, are turned to love; and each time we control our thinking so that we think things through to the end without bias; and each time we are fully aware of our intentions and motives, we dress the bride so to speak. Even if we do this in a small way we release ourselves from the intensity of how we usually feel, think and behave thereby making a space for our higher feeling, thinking and will to contribute to our developing conscious awareness. They then become the three spiritual faculties; Imagination, Inspiration and Intuition.

Also, we must be on alert because it comes quickly. If, for instance, we are working on our ability to acutely feel the fear another person experiences, then we must be ready to do something with that fear otherwise we will be of no use to them. When we are able to experience their fear in this way they know it for it goes back to them as love – which is the purpose of fear. If, having done this once, we were to go back to dealing with someone else's fear by not feeling it at all, then we will be plagued. If we have experienced our higher faculties of Imagination, Inspiration and Intuition once, and then reject them, we will be plagued. Of course it won't be one or the other; we must find a way for our earthly consciousness and our spiritual consciousness to work together.

It is helpful to think of spiritual knowledge as having a life of its own; if we prepare our soul properly it will reveal itself to us. If we hear its voice, perhaps when we are meditating, and then do not apply that which we heard in our daily life, it will withdraw. Furthermore, we may then be tricked into thinking that we can still have these spiritual experiences but they will not have the purity of the bride.

Then we hear the voice say, "let him who is thirsty come, let him who desires take the water of life freely." These two principles, thirsting and desiring, are fundamental to human life. Without them we would not survive physically on this earth. Once we are fully acquainted with their power we can then apply them to our spiritual life. When we thirst for truth and desire it above all things we will be able to participate in the vital energy that keeps this earth alive, *zoe*, the life-force associated with the resurrection and the ever-present risen Christ. Then it is as if our intellect is freed from our body and we experience a new kind of thinking, a living thinking that we inspire from a higher place in our being. When we become aware of this then we won't add or take away with our earthly intellect, the truth speaks into us and we know it. This is

how John was able to write down The Revelation.
The End – for now.

AFTERWORD

I was introduced to The Book of Revelation, and for that matter the Bible, in 1983 by my spiritual mentor Rev Mario Schoenmaker whom I first met in October 1982. His love for the Bible and his experience of the living Christ flowed from his heart to mine for fourteen years until his death in 1997. I was so astounded by this man and his knowledge that in 1984 I put forward a question for the New Year guidance he gave each year:

"Can we present the teachings differently so that they reach more people?"

I asked this question because the esoteric (hidden under the surface) interpretation of the Bible can use terms that are not easily understood by someone who encounters them for the first time. This was certainly my experience. So I asked the question and this was the response:

"In terms of those who will receive and teach, yes. Thus each one takes [the teachings I give] within oneself, transforms it, adjusts [their] consciousness accordingly and teaches, in accordance, again, with the consciousness around about [them], to the levels that must be reached. But [I] your brother cannot do that, understand that."

In writing these reflections 23 years later I have a sense that I am doing what Rev Mario suggested. Many people all over the world receive them each week and some email me saying that they are so grateful that I have unveiled the Bible for them. I know how they feel because I had the same experience with Rev Mario all those years ago. For me, now, it is as if his words go out all over the world through my consciousness as he predicted in 1984.

What I write is not intended to interpret The Revelation; that has already been done by many people in many different ways. This writing is certainly not intended to be definitive. Nor is it an academic treatise, there are very few references because I have drawn on my own knowledge and understanding always referring to the original Greek words used at the time of Christ. As I explore the meaning of the Greek words I am often surprised to see what is revealed in the meaning of these ancient words. Sometimes it feels like thoughts were thinking themselves in me and when this happens I have to remain open, but also testing these ideas alongside what I know from my own study. I have tried to open up The Revelation as a map of the developing human consciousness. This is just one way of looking into this last book of the Bible. I hope the ideas put forward will be a catalyst for your own insights and inspiration.

Kristina Kaine.

These Reflections were written weekly between April 30, 2007 and April 27, 2010

ADDENDA

Explanation of terms

In this work there are references to some esoteric principles that are not commonly accepted in our culture today, at least not in full. In particular, the human being is recognised as having different levels of functioning as follows.

Physical body: the vehicle which connects each of us to the world through our senses.

Life body: a force that gives life and shape to the physical body, also known as the ether or etheric body. This force is the drive to live. This is the driving force in the human body which tells us to eat and to sleep. The body stays alive and does not die because it has the vital processes that are necessary for life which are breathing, warming, nourishing, secreting, maintaining, growing and reproducing. When we sleep these processes are reduced, when they shut down, we die. This is where our memory images are stored and our thinking processes originate. This can be referred to as the etheric body. Here we have much in common with plant life.

Body of motion and emotion: or astral body. This is where our drives become desires and keep us in their grip until they are fulfilled. Here are the feelings and emotions which urge us to take action to keep warm or cool, to eat or drink and so on. This area, in some respects, can be compared with animal life. In its higher expression this body forms our soul life. Our soul life has three specific fields of operation.

Feeling soul where sense impressions enter.

Thinking soul where we combine images to make sense of the impressions we receive using logic and reasoning.

Willing soul where we become aware of the higher meanings of images we process.

Our spirit also has three areas of operation. They are only activated when our 'I' connects with our soul. They are:

Spiritual Imagination where images take on a life

Spiritual Inspiration when we hear an inner voice giving us new understanding.

Spiritual Intuition is experienced when we can enter into our new understandings and experience them first hand.

Then we have the human 'I' which is the governor by which we stand upright, speak and think. The 'I', from its highest expression in the Real Self or I AM, to its lowest expression in the selfish ego is a continuum of consciousness covering the spectrum from the so-called super-conscious to the unconscious. Our purpose is to express ourselves as consciously as possible through our 'I' rather than unconsciously, habitually, through our unawakened soul and egoistic instincts. This is an evolving process for humanity in general, as well as individually for each of us.

Because the earthly expression of the human 'I' is the mirrored reflection of our Real Self it cannot enter fully into our lives. As our reflection in a mirror is not us, so our earthly consciousness is not our true identity. One way to experience the truth of this is when we get a sense of how our 'I' works in us in various degrees of connection. There are moments in our lives, especially when we are expressing our talents, that this 'I' is very connected to our consciousness but for most of us, most of the time, it stands back and influences us from afar. When it is connected, we experience it within us as a radiating energy that can encompass everything in the environment. One thing to be aware of is that we cannot experience this 'I' theoretically, it makes no sense to us. We have to work out how to experience it in reality; only then can we know it.

The only way to experience it is to first of all become more aware of the activity of our soul. Again, from my book I Connecting: The Soul's Quest (Kindle edition "I AM The Mystery"), this description of the soul may be helpful.

"Aristotle was among the first to write about the human soul. Prior to this, knowledge of the soul (as far as it was developed) was instinctual. Several hundred years before the time of Christ, Aristotle described the soul as having three qualities and he called these three soul qualities: Orektikon, Kinetikon, and Dianoetikon.

Orektikon refers to desires, appetites, sensations, impulses: These things occur in the first soul region where drives and desires are given dignity. Drives (example, the urge to eat) and desires (example, longings and passions) originate in our physical body. As they rise up into our soul regions they are moderated so that they can be satisfied in a dignified way. We can reach a good understanding of this process by comparing the drives of an animal and a human. For example, an animal's drive to eat may be ennobled by a human desire to create aesthetically pleasing food. This region is the gateway to the soul; in this region we receive the impulses, sensations and impressions from the body and from the outside world through the senses. The soul activity of feeling is associated with this region.

Kinetikon means to set in motion, to try every way, reasoning: In this region we think about what came to us through the senses. Our thinking is set in motion and it tries to recreate a harmony of relationship between the new things that enter our soul with what is already in our soul. This is a process similar to the resolving of musical chords or progressive mathematical patterns. We say that, "something doesn't add up" or that we "can't make sense of something" when our thinking is in motion but remains unresolved. This soul region is concerned with reasoning and logic – thinking has its base in this region.

Dianoetikon is about intentions, our will, to be minded or purpose to do: After we have used our reasoning ability, we can come to a point of awareness, of wisdom. It is in this soul region that we develop our intentions, our volition and we reach a resolution that we can act on. It is from this point that we can act from the wise freedom of our own being rather than from the influence of others. This is the highest region of our soul which we are currently developing. All intentions arise out of the force of our will.

Aristotle actually spoke of five members of the soul. In addition to the impulse soul (orektikon), the reasoning soul (kinetikon), and the awareness soul (dianoetikon), he included two lower regions; the plant-like soul and the animal-like soul. The plant-like soul is the area where our drives arise; the urge to eat or drink for the well-being of our physical body. From the animal-like soul arise the desires that motivate us to seek satisfaction of our drives and passions. The higher regions of our soul, according to how they are developed, give human dignity to how these drives and desires are satisfied.

Our main driving forces are found in the forces of growth, reproduction and metabolism – the forces of survival. It is when these drives unite with our desires that they enter the region of our soul. Our soul begins to engage in the process at this point. If we are able to loosen the grip of desires in our soul then they become wishes and longings which, given the opportunity, the 'I' can fulfil through the forces of our will. The more the 'I' is involved the more nobly we will express ourselves." Pages 24-25

These are the principles that I apply to a thoughtful observation of the Koine Greek words chosen by St John when he wrote The Revelation. I unfold The Revelation in terms of the development of modern consciousness. For four years, starting in 2003, I did this in various ways using the Gospel of St John. While the Gospel according to John has a special power to reveal to us our Higher Self, our I AM as St John calls it, I think that John's Revelation, The Apocalypse, can awaken us to the power of Christ that is available within us, as it is within this physical world and ever-present in the nearby spiritual worlds – increasingly, now. To make sense of this we must strive to understand that a mighty cosmic being called Christ, who represents the cosmic I AM, entered into a man called Jesus making him the first human being to connect with his own I AM which then made it possible for the Christ spirit to become active within him. This Christ-ening of humanity is the work that we are currently undertaking, and we take up this work as a personal responsibility.

The Revelation, according to Rudolf Steiner, is a book for training. In 1909 he made this significant statement. Significant because the past is so often dragged into the future when it comes to spiritual knowledge – thereby ignoring this continual development of consciousness.

"What we teach today as Theosophy (and Anthroposophy) will not change in its essence but in its form. When the souls of the present age are born again in future times, they will be mature enough to take up other, higher, future forms of the spiritual life. Our explanation of the Apocalypse will age; future ages will go beyond it. But the Apocalypse itself will not, therefore, age. It is much greater than our explanations and will find even higher, even loftier explanations." May 9, 1909 Reading the Pictures of the Apocalypse

In "The Book of Revelation and the Work of the Priest" Rudolf Steiner referred to his 1909 lectures on the Apocalypse saying:

"My foremost intention at that time was to interpret Anthroposophy itself on the basis of the Book of Revelation."

This confirms that The Revelation to John can be viewed in various ways but we should always be mindful of human development. At this time in our evolution we are called to stand at the interface of our 'I' being with awareness. In its fullness this 'I' being becomes our I AM. It is my hope that my writing assists each one to do this work. It is work that must be done individually, for we are each individuals. This work accentuates this individuality, which can create difficulties in itself, however by standing in our differences, and respecting the differences of others assists us to integrate our 'I' being even more.

REVIEWS

Standing upright and free and in full consciousness of the true purpose of being human in today's world is often hidden from us. "The Soul's Secret" is Kristina Kaine's exploration of The Revelation to St. John. In it she opens up to clear understanding many of the end of time images which are so hard for a modern mind to take seriously. Her voice is calm, her explanations candid. For her, the evolution of the human soul is a work of deep and abiding significance and each one of us is involved in this work.

Reading her reflections week by week has been the source of much purposeful thinking for me but having it gathered together in a book is quite another experience. This visionary text, written by St. John about 2000 years ago, still has much to say to people of our time if a modern translation can make it truthfully available to us. It is my belief that Kristina has achieved this most satisfactorily.

Eve Adams - deep gratitude for proof reading.

In Kristina Kaine's, The Soul's Secret Unveiled in the Book of Revelation, the title of the book immediately alludes to the primary focus of her study of Saint John's Book of Revelation. There are many possible perspectives and levels of understanding that are available to us when reading and studying the Book of Revelation.

This is the genius behind John's work. Kristina has chosen to study John's work from a perspective of asking how does this book address the evolution of the human soul from its deep past and on into its long distant future. There is a macro-perspective that is contained within the Book of Revelation and there is a micro-perspective as well.

It is the micro-perspective which Kristina Kaine has chosen as her overall theme and discourse. The continuous question throughout Kristina's study is: How does each line in the Book of Revelation relate to the human soul as well as the human Ego; the human I AM. Kristina also presents the Greek lexicon in its most esoteric fashion which helps to unlock the mysteries of the Book of Revelation even further than would be normally available to us when only reading standard English translations. This book is highly recommended for any serious student of the Book of Revelation.

Richard Distasi

What a blessing to have Kristina Kaine's sensitive, provocative reflections upon this most mysterious of texts! Blending linguistic and historical scholarship with keen psychological and social insight, The Soul's Secret offers a thoroughly modern, I AM-infused approach to John's Revelation.

Kevin Dann

Deeply insightful and sensitively written this book is a true manual of self discovery. Ms Kaine takes your hand and guides you safely into the depths of your soul in search of your true self. My guess is you will be reading and re-reading this book for years because every time you open it there is the potential for learning something new. This book is for all those who have ever asked themselves this question - Who am I? - and isn't that all of us?

I highly recommend it!

RogerR

Kristina Kaine's biblical reflections bring together scholarship and esoteric traditions, focused through Kristina's meditations on the text. These contemplations on the Revelation to St John are a transforming initiatory experience disguised as a book. Don't miss it!

John Plummer

Kristina Kaine has finally bowed to her fans' request and put her collected weekly contributions in book form. No one has ever claimed that the Book of Revelation - or Apocalypse is easy to understand. Ms Kaine not only explains and clarifies, but also puts a new slant on the hidden meaning of the original Greek idiom. By doing so, she also speaks to us in a new, intuitive language. Kristina Kaine has been kind enough to give us permission to occasionally publish her pieces, which have always been received with great interest by our readers. Thanks, Kristina.

Frank Thomas Smith, Southern Cross Review

http://southerncrossreview.org/

I have studied Kristina Kaine's work for years and am thrilled she is finally publishing this amazing series of re-translations from the original Greek of The Book of Revelation. Any Christian will enjoy reading these essays and contemplating them. I can't praise this work enough. Primarily for transforming consciousness. Wonderful seeds for meditation, too.

Carolyn Jourdan

RESOURCES

Other works by Kristina Kaine

1. I AM The Soul's Heartbeat. Volume 1
The Seven I AM Sayings in St John's Gospel: 2003
2. I AM The Soul's Heartbeat. Volume 2
Christian Initiation in St John's Gospel: 2003 – 2004
3. I AM The Soul's Heartbeat. Volume 3
Finding the Eightfold Path of Buddha in St John's Gospel: 2004
4. I AM The Soul's Heartbeat. Volume 4
Twelve Disciples in St John's Gospel: 2005
5. I AM The Soul's Heartbeat. Volume 5
Seven Signs in St John's Gospel: January to July 2006
6. I AM The Soul's Heartbeat. Volume 6
The Beatitudes in St John's Gospel: August 2006 – March 2007
7. The Soul's Secret Unveiled in the Book of Revelation: April 2007 – April 2010
2 Volumes ebook, 1 volume print
7a. The Virgin and the Harlot, Secret Guide to the Apocalypse retitled and in 1 volume.
8. Who is Jesus : What is Christ Volumes 1-5 May 2010 – September 2016
9. I Connecting 2007 and 2017
10. I Connecting Exercises 2013
11. I Connecting - our true purpose 2018
12. Meditations on The Twelve Holy Nights Vol 1 2011 - 2016, Vol 2 2016-2020
13. To Journey Back October 2016 - 2019
14. Bible Unlocked May 2019
15. The Seven Letters Vol 1-2 June 2019 - June 2021
16. Secrets of the Christian Festivals July 2020

https://www.amazon.com/Kristina-Kaine/e/B00AEW92B2/

References and Resources

The Apocalypse of St John : Rudolf Steiner
The Apocalypse of Saint John : Emil Bock
The Apocalypse : Valentin Tomberg
The Bible, Revised Standard Version
The Book of Revelation : Alfred Heidenreich
The Book of Revelation and the Work of the Priest: Rudolf Steiner
The Burning Bush : Ed Reaugh Smith
Expository Dictionary of New Testament Words : W. E Vine
Reading the Pictures of the Apocalypse : Rudolf Steiner
The Revelation of Saint John : Zachary F. Landsdowne
The Ultimate Vision : Rev Mario Schoenmaker
http://www.osl.cc/believe/revhome.htm Study Guide

Kristina writes regularly about her understanding of the human soul and spirit. She is an associate director of Spiritual Science Bible Studies which distributes her weekly Reflections.

You can read more about her at the following websites.
http://www.spiritualsciencebiblestudies.org/
http://www.facebook.com/EsotericConnection
http://www.soulquesting.wordpress.com/
http://www.kristinakaine.posterous.com/
http://www.bibleunlocked.blogspot.com.au/
http://www.esotericconnection.com/
http://www.i-connecting.com/

Contact email: kristina@esotericconnection.com

ABOUT THE AUTHOR

Kristina Kaine has worked with people all her life: during her early career in medical sales and staff recruitment, and for the last 20 years in her own business which matches people in business partnerships, as well as for home sharing and home minding. Through this rich interaction with people, Kristina has observed the struggle for self identity from many angles. She was awakened to the ideas of Rudolf Steiner by Rev Mario Schoenmaker, attending all of Schoenmaker's lectures for 14 years. After Schoenmaker's death in 1997, Kristina realised the need to explain the knowledge of the threefold human being in simple terms that could be applied easily in daily life. As well as her weekly reflections that are read worldwide, she has set this out in her book, 'I Connecting : the Soul's Quest', which was published in 2007 by Robert Sardello. It is not unusual for her to receive comments about her book like this: "It seems like a very lucid treatment, like looking through a clear glass window through which one can discover and recognize the landscape of the soul."

www.ingramcontent.com/pod-product-compliance
Lightning Source LLC
Chambersburg PA
CBHW071647160426
43195CB00012B/1383